Teaching Academic L2 Writing

The new edition of this comprehensive text fills an important gap in teacher professional preparation by focusing on the grammar and vocabulary that are essential for all L2 writing teachers and student-writers to know. Before L2 writers can begin to successfully produce academic prose, they must understand the foundations of language and master the language tools that they need to build reasonable quality text. Targeting specific problem areas of students' writing, this text offers a compendium of techniques for teaching writing, grammar, and vocabulary to second-language learners.

Updated with current research and recent corpus analysis findings, the second edition features a wealth of new materials, including new teaching activities; student exercises and assignments; and substantially revised appendices with supplementary word and phrase lists and sentence components. Designed for preservice ESL/ELT/TESOL courses as well as Academic Writing and Applied Linguistics courses, this book includes new, contextualized examples in a more accessible and easy-to-digest format.

Eli Hinkel is Professor of Linguistics and MA-TESL Programs at Seattle Pacific University, USA.

Teaching Academic L2 Writing

Practical Techniques in Vocabulary and Grammar

ELI HINKEL

Routledge
Taylor & Francis Group

NEW YORK AND LONDON

Second edition published 2020
by Routledge
52 Vanderbilt Avenue, New York, NY 10017

and by Routledge
2 Park Square, Milton Park, Abingdon, Oxon, OX14 4RN

Routledge is an imprint of the Taylor & Francis Group, an informa business

© 2020 Taylor & Francis

First edition published by Routledge 2004

Library of Congress Cataloging-in-Publication Data
Names: Hinkel, Eli, author.
Title: Teaching academic L2 writing : practical techniques in vocabulary
    and grammar / Eli Hinkel.
Other titles: Teaching academic ESL writing
Description: Second edition. | New York, NY : Routledge, 2019. |
    Includes bibliographical references and index.
Identifiers: LCCN 2019031440 (print) | LCCN 2019031441 (ebook) |
    ISBN 9781138345331 (hardback) | ISBN 9781138345348 (paperback) |
    ISBN 9780429437946 (ebook)
Subjects: LCSH: English language—Rhetoric—Study and teaching. |
    English language—Study and teaching—Foreign speakers. |
    English language—Composition and exercises—Study and teaching.
Classification: LCC PE1404 .H57 2019 (print) | LCC PE1404 (ebook) |
    DDC 808/.042071—dc23
LC record available at https://lccn.loc.gov/2019031440
LC ebook record available at https://lccn.loc.gov/2019031441

ISBN: 978-1-138-34533-1 (hbk)
ISBN: 978-1-138-34534-8 (pbk)
ISBN: 978-0-429-43794-6 (ebk)

Typeset in Dante and Avenir
by Apex CoVantage, LLC

Contents

Preface

Since the late 1970s and the early 1980s, a great deal of time, energy, and other resources have been devoted to teaching L2 writers to construct academic discourse and text; that is, to generate and organize ideas into coherent college and university prose. There is little doubt that L2 writers need to work with many rhetorical and discourse features of written English, and that the teaching of college- or university-level writing cannot do without them. In teaching L2 writing, what has become less important, however, is the overarching concern about the language tools necessary to construct discourse and text – that is, academic vocabulary and grammar. To put it plainly, no matter how brilliant the writer's ideas and insights may be, it is hard to understand them if the language is opaque.

This book has the goal of bridging a fundamental gap that exists in the teaching of second language academic writing and teacher education. The teaching of second language vocabulary and grammar is essential for any writing teacher because for student-writers anywhere learning and using the foundational components of academic prose is not a matter of choice. These are vital academic necessities. The ultimate objective of this book, however, is to benefit language learners who aspire to success in academic degree programs beyond their language courses.

The material and teaching techniques discussed in this book specifically target the areas of L2 text that require substantial improvement, and that improvement is only possible with intensive, extensive, and deliberate attention – and persistence. Language teachers are usually keenly aware of how short course and class times are, and how limited resources can be. In pre-academic courses, the critical preparation for L2 writers seeks to be as efficient and strategic as possible. The teaching techniques addressed here are based on the highly practical principle of maximizing learners' language gains and focusing on a few shortcuts. Vocabulary and grammar instruction works with several sets of simple rules that collectively can make a noticeable and important difference in the quality of students' writing.

Organization of the Book

The philosophical goal of this book is to highlight the fact that without clear, reasonably accurate, and coherent text, there can be no academic writing in a second language. The practical and immediate purpose, however, is to provide a compendium of teaching techniques for the lexical and grammatical basics of academic language that "every teacher (and student) must know."

Several key differences between this book and many other books on teaching L2 writing should be highlighted:

- The decision about what L2 writing instruction has to address and what L2 writers must know is based on the findings of research into academic text and the text produced by L2 writers. Therefore, the material sets out to deal with the gaps in many current curricula for teaching L2 writing. Language components that are traditionally included in L2 teaching but hardly ever found in academic text are also identified throughout.
- Because academic vocabulary, the grammar of formal written English, and specific features of academic prose represent integral aspects of L2 academic writing, curriculum and teaching techniques presented in this book work with these concurrently.
- The curriculum and its elements discussed in the volume are not based on an incremental progression of material, such as, for example, "first, the course covers the present tense, then the present perfect tense, and then the past tense." Although the curriculum is organized in a particular order, instruction on academic language has to include all of its component parts.
- For this reason, the material and teaching techniques discussed here can have a variety of logical organizational structures, all of which could be more or less appropriate for a specific course or a particular group of students in a particular context. It is a widely known fact that few language teachers follow the order of a curriculum developed by someone else, and this book does not expect to be an exception.

This book is oriented towards teachers of high intermediate and advanced academic student writers. One of its fundamental assumptions is that learning to write academic text in a second language takes a lot of hard work and that for L2 academic writers, the foundations of language must be in place before they can begin to produce passable academic prose.

To this end, the teaching materials, teaching activities, and suggestions for teaching are based on a singular objective: to improve the quality of language teaching and student language learning so that L2 writers can succeed in their academic careers.

The volume is divided into three parts. **Part I** begins with an introduction that explains the importance of text in academic writing. It further provides a detailed overview of the essential language skills that every student must have at the college and university level. Chapter 2 delves into the specifics of student writing tasks in the disciplines. Chapter 3 presents guidelines for a course curriculum that targets academic vocabulary, grammar, frequent errors, teaching editing skills, and other writing fundamentals.

The chapters in **Part II** plow into the nitty-gritty of the classroom teaching of language. This section begins in chapter 4 with a core and expanded analysis of the English sentence structure and academic phrases to help writers to construct reasonably complete sentences and edit their own text. The chapters on the essential sentence elements largely follow the order of the sentence. Essential academic nouns and the structure of the noun phrase are dealt with in chapter 5, followed by the place and the types of pronouns in academic prose in chapter 6. Chapter 7 works with the teaching of a limited range of English verb tenses and the ever-important uses of the passive voice. Lexical types of foundational academic verbs and their textual functions are the focus of chapter 8. The construction of adjective and adverb phrases, as well as the essential adjective and adverb vocabulary, follows in chapter 9.

The teaching of academic text building beyond the simple sentence is the focus of **Part III**. Chapter 10 outlines instruction in the functions adverb, adjective, and noun clauses. In chapter 11, the classroom teaching of elements of cohesion and coherence (a famously neglected aspect of L2 writing instruction) is specifically addressed. Chapter 12 concludes with the teaching of hedges and their crucial functions in academic text.

Acknowledgements

For their hard work and long-suffering assistance, my sincere appreciation goes to Bruce Rogers, the Ohio State University, and Rodney Hill. Thank you for your generosity and friendship through the years.

Rodney Hill has created the perceptive, humorous, and spot-on illustrations for the book. Nothing like these anywhere – one of a kind. My infinite and undying gratitude for your creativity and talent, not even to mention having to endure the countless versions of chapters, papers, blurbs, excerpts, tables, pieces, parts, and portions. Thank you more than I can ever say.

Karen Adler, Commissioning Editor at Taylor & Francis, has been open-minded, thoughtful, insightful, and enthusiastic in her role as the leading head-honcho publisher. Thank you and thank you.

My thanks to my many students of all sorts for giving me a chance to work with them and for trying out various strategies, techniques, materials, assignments, activities, exercises, short-cuts, tasks, and topics.

Part I

Academic Text and Teaching Second Language Writing

Chapters 1, 2, and 3 establish the research-based foundations and some of the groundwork for the book. Chapter 1 presents the main principles for teaching second language (L2) writing. These may seem fairly obvious, but they are often overlooked in instruction.

- Learning to write in a L2 is different from learning to write in a first language (L1).
- Teaching L2 writing the way L1 writing is taught is not effective.
- The knowledge-transforming type of writing expected in academic disciplines is different from personal experience narratives or conversational discourse.
- Academic language, that is, vocabulary, grammar, and discourse, cannot be developed through conversational or interactional activities – whether written or spoken. Academic language does not occur in conversations.
- Extensive, thorough, and focused instruction in L2 academic vocabulary, grammar, and discourse is essential for developing L2 written proficiency.

More groundwork is covered in chapter 2.

- Writing requirements in a university.
- Characteristics of academic writing and academic text.
- Common writing tasks students will need to perform in their college and university studies in particular disciplines.

Chapter 3 examines the importance of language accuracy in academic writing, and how to approach the teaching of L2 writing so that accuracy can be achieved.

The Importance of Text in Academic Writing   1

Ongoing Goals in Teaching L2 Skills

Overview

- L2 writers and academic writing skills in English.
- Principles and foundations for learning to write L2 academic prose.
- Academic writing.
- Academic vocabulary and grammar.

Student Enrollments

In the past several decades or so, the proliferation of college- and university-level courses, textbooks, and all manner of learning aids for second language (L2)[1] academic writers has become a fact of life that most language and writing teachers have had no choice but to notice. The rapid rise in the number of L2 teacher-education courses, workshops, and MA-level programs in TESOL has also become commonplace in North American, European, Asian, Australian, and New Zealand education.

The steady rise of L2 writing courses, teacher-education programs, and textbooks is not particularly surprising given college and university enrollment statistics. For instance, at present, approximately 1.3 million international students are enrolled in degree programs in US colleges and universities, that is, slightly over 5% of the entire student population (Institute of International Education, 2018). In the UK, international students represent 6% of those enrolled in colleges and universities. US intensive and preparatory programs also teach L2 and English for Academic Purposes (EAP) skills, including writing, to another several hundred thousand learners, some of whom will return to their home countries, but many of whom will seek admission to institutions of higher learning.

According to the Migration Policy Institute calculations, US colleges enroll more than 2.5 million immigrants in full-time and part-time academic programs. These students represent more than 20% of all university students and 24% of community college students in the country (Zong & Batalova, 2017; Community College Consortium for Immigrant Education, www.cccie.org/resources/fast-facts/).

- Taken together, international and immigrant students represent about 25% to 30% of college and university enrollments in the US.
- Furthermore, although these figures fluctuate widely by location, 24% of the current students in public schools are immigrants and children of recent immigrants, and most plan to continue their education in US colleges and universities (Camarota, Griffith, & Zeigler, 2017).

Academic Writing Skills in English

In the past several decades, a large number of publications have emerged to point out that, despite having studied English, as well as academic writing in their native and English-speaking countries, L2 students experience a great deal of difficulty in their schooling and college/university studies (Durrant, 2014, 2017; Hinkel, 2002, 2015; Leedham, 2016; Schleppegrell, 2002, 2004; Zhang & Mi, 2010). Based on a large body of research, several reasons have been identified for the continuing – predominantly language-related – challenges facing even highly advanced L2 students in their academic writing.

For example, graduate and undergraduate students, after years of language learning, often fail to recognize and appropriately use the conventions of formal written academic discourse and text, such as introductions, topic nominations, conclusions, discourse flow markers, or sentence transitions. Dozens of empirical studies have demonstrated that L2 writers' academic text often lacks sentence-level features typically considered to be basic, for instance, the forms of irregular verbs, appropriate uses of hedging,[2] modal verbs, pronouns, the active and passive voice in humanities and sciences texts, balanced generalizations, and exemplification.

The effectiveness of preparatory language and EAP writing courses in preparing students for actual academic writing in universities has also been discussed extensively (e.g. Ferris, 2009, 2016; Hinkel, 2002, 2015; ICAS, 2002;

Leki, 2007). According to the published surveys of students who matriculate from pre-academic language programs, many find themselves underprepared for the demands of academic work and especially formal speaking and writing. For example, Leedham (2016) investigated specific discourse and sentence-level writing skills of highly advanced L2 university students. Her findings demonstrate that even substantial amounts of reading and writing do not ensure L2 writers' awareness of discourse and language features in academic prose, not to mention the skills to produce it.

> Based on numerous research reports, the conclusion seems clear that explicit instruction in advanced academic writing and text is needed.
>
> A large number of detailed studies have demonstrated that extensive and intensive instruction in academic vocabulary, grammar, and discourse is required for most – if not all – L2 writers.

Since the early 1980s, the predominant method of instruction in L2 writing has remained focused on the writing process, similar to the pedagogy adopted in first language (L1) writing instruction for L1 writers of English (e.g. Caplan & Stevens, 2017; Dudley-Evans & St. John, 1998; Horowitz, 1986; Jordan, 1997).

- The process-centered instructional methodology for teaching writing focuses on invention, creating ideas, and discovering the purpose of writing.
- Within the process-centered paradigm for teaching L2 writing, student writing is evaluated on the quality of pre-writing, writing, and revision.
- Because the product of writing is seen as secondary to the writing process, and even inhibitory in the early stages of writing, issues of L2 grammar, vocabulary, and errors, are to be addressed only as needed in particular contexts.
- In process-centered instruction, there is a generally held belief that L2 writers with proficiency levels higher than beginner learn from being exposed to L2 text and discourse – while reading and writing – and thus acquire L2 grammar and vocabulary naturally.
- Outside L2 writing and English composition courses, evaluations of L2 writing skills in the disciplines and general education courses has continued to focus on the product, rather than the process, of writing.

- In academic courses such as history, sociology, business, or the natural sciences at both the undergraduate and graduate levels, evaluations of L2 students' academic skills are determined by their performance on traditional product-oriented language tasks, most frequently reading and writing.

Outside language and English department writing programs, the faculty in the disciplines are not particularly concerned about the writing process that affects (or does not affect) the quality of the writing product, that is, students' assignments and papers that the professors read, evaluate, and grade.

> The expectations of L2 text required for success in mainstream general education courses, as well as those in the disciplines, have remained largely unchanged, despite the shift in writing instruction methodology.

Similarly, the assessment of L2 writing skills by language teaching professionals on standardized and institutional placement testing has largely remained focused on the writing product, without regard of the writing process (Bridgeman, Cho, & DiPietro, 2016; Knoch, Macqueen, & O'Hagan, 2014).

The disparity between the teaching methods adopted in L2 writing instruction and evaluation criteria of the quality of writing has produced outcomes that are damaging and costly for most L2 students who are taught brainstorming techniques and invention, pre-writing, drafting, and essay "shaping," while their essential linguistic skills, such as academic vocabulary and formal features of grammar and text, are only sparsely and inconsistently addressed. In courses in academic disciplines, brainstorming and idea "invention" are rarely needed because written assignments and tasks are usually specific to the subject matter and course contents.

Principles and Foundations

In this book, teaching techniques and approaches to teaching L2 writing to academically bound students are based on five foundational principles about learning to write in a L2.

The Essential Principles for Teaching L2 Writing

Principle #1. Learning to write in a L2 is fundamentally different from learning to write in a L1. L1 writers already have highly developed, that is, native, language proficiency in English, while most L2 students must dedicate years to learning it as a second language, in many cases as adults.

Principle #2. To date, research has not determined whether a majority of L2 students in colleges and universities can succeed in attaining native-like English proficiency even after years of intensive study that includes exposure to English-language interaction, text, and discourse.

Principle #3. Research has established that applying the writing and composition pedagogy developed for L1 writers to teaching L2 writing – even over the course of several years – does not lead to sufficient improvements in L2 writing to enable learners to produce academic-level text required at college- or university-level.

Principle #4. The knowledge-telling and knowledge-transforming model of the writing process (Bereiter & Scardamalia, 1985, 1987, 1989) stipulates that exposure to conversational language experiences and access to written text applies to practically all language users. However, proficiency in L2 conversational language features, familiarity with L2 writing, and "telling" what one already knows in written form do not lead to producing complex academic writing that relies on obtaining and "transforming" knowledge, that is, logically organizing information and employing language features and style that attend to audience expectations of the academic prose.

Principle #5. Extensive, thorough, and focused instruction in L2 academic vocabulary, grammar, and discourse is *essential* for developing the L2 written proficiency expected in general education courses and studies in the disciplines.

These principles are based on a large body of research, and a great deal of such work is referred to throughout this book.

The Foundations: A Long View

In the past half century, studies of L2 learning have shown that although the rate of L2 acquisition depends on many complex factors, adult learners' ultimate attainment of L2 proficiency does not become native-like even after many years of exposure to L2 in the medium of instruction (Ferris, 2011; Hinkel, 2002, 2003a, b, 2005, 2011, 2015; ICAS, 2002; Leedham, 2016; Leki, 2007; Leki, Cumming, & Silva, 2008; Lillis, 2001; Schleppegrell, 2002, 2004; Schleppegrell & Colombi, 2002).

➢ Unlike learning to write in a L1, learning to write in a L2 requires an attainment of sufficient language proficiency first.

- Fundamental distinctions have been investigated, determined, and specified between advanced academic language proficiency and basic conversational and communicative proficiency necessary to engage in daily interactions.
- Conversational fluency does not carry with it the skills necessary for the production of academic text.

➢ A substantial and advanced L2 proficiency in vocabulary and grammar may not be possible to achieve without explicit, focused, and consistent instruction.

- A large number of studies have established that learning to write in a L2, and in particular, learning to write the formal L2 academic prose crucial in L2 writers' academic and professional careers, requires the development of an advanced linguistic foundation. Without this foundation, learners simply do not have the range of vocabulary and grammar skills necessary for academic writing.
- To date, research has clearly and unambiguously demonstrated that L2 writers' proficiency levels in vocabulary and grammar disadvantage the quality of their formal prose. Numerous investigations report that, even after several years of language learning, L2 writers' text continues to differ significantly from that of novice L1 writers in regard to a broad range of vocabulary and grammar properties.
- The results of dozens of analyses indicate that even advanced and highly educated L2 writers, such as doctoral students enrolled in

universities in English-speaking countries and professionals, have a severely limited lexical and syntactic repertoire compared to their L1 peers.

- In the cases of many undergraduate L2 writers, a restricted access to advanced language features results in simple texts that rely on the most frequent language features that occur predominantly in conversational discourse (e.g. Carson, 2001; Durrant, 2014, 2017; Hinkel, 2002, 2011, 2015; Leedham, 2016).

➤ Writing instruction and teaching strategies designed for L1 writers with highly developed – that is, native – language proficiency, which L2 writers by definition do not have, is not readily applicable to – or even useful for – L2 writing instruction.

- In addition to learning conversational English, L2 academic writers have to learn entirely new ranges of grammar and vocabulary that do not occur in casual speech.
- On the other hand, many L1 writers develop an ability to distinguish between spoken and formal written text types between 4th and 6th grades, and sometimes earlier (Brinchmann, et al., 2015; Kress, 1994, 1996; McCutchen, 2011; Uccelli, et al., 2015).
- Colloquial and conversational vocabulary and grammar are prevalent in L2 academic prose because many L2 writers have far more exposure to conversational discourse than they do to formal writing in English.
- A vocabulary size of approximately 5,000 word families (e.g. *book, bookish, booking, bookstore, bookshelf*) is requisite for relatively fluent L2 reading, even though a dictionary is still necessary at this level (e.g. Hirsh & Nation, 1992; Hu & Nation, 2000; Nation, 2013; Nation & Waring, 1997).

A Historical Note and a Long Perspective

In the late 1970s and early 1980s, some specialists in the teaching of L1 basic writing observed that a number of similarities exist among the strategies used by basic L1 and L2 writers. Therefore, they concluded that if the writing behaviors of both types of writers exhibit similarities, the approaches to teaching L1 writing could be applied to the teaching of L2 students. Although the research on the applicability of L1 writing pedagogy to learning to write in L2 consisted at that time of only a small number of case studies and student self-reports, the methodology for teaching basic L1 writers took hold in L2 teaching.

Following the methodological shift in L1 writing pedagogy, the process-centered paradigm was similarly adopted as the preeminent methodology in teaching L2 writing with a focus on the process of writing, pre-writing, drafting, and revising. The process methodology further presupposes that issues of L2 grammar and vocabulary are to be addressed only as needed in the context of writing. That is, when L2 writers with proficiency levels higher than beginner are exposed to text and discourse to learn from, they will eventually acquire L2 grammar and vocabulary in the course of their education.

In the context of schooling, two different types of curricula that seek to combine instruction in both language and school subjects are prevalent in various world regions. **Content-based** language and subject-matter instruction is commonly adopted in US and Canadian school curricula, while **genre-based** language teaching predominates in the UK, Australia, and New Zealand. A less prevalent curricular model that corresponds to North American content-based instruction has emerged more recently under the umbrella term of Content and Language Integrated Learning.

Content-based teaching in the form of sheltered instruction observation protocol (SIOP) has been widely adopted in US schools with large numbers of ELLs. The SIOP model represents a framework for teaching school subjects and language in mainstream classes. To this end, SIOP also addresses various classroom strategies and teaching techniques for ELLs. Under the auspices of the US Department of Education, the What Works Clearinghouse (WWC) has examined 32 studies of SIOP effectiveness that were published or released between 1983 and 2012.

According to this review (What Works Clearinghouse, 2013, p. 1), seven of the empirical studies of SIOP effectiveness do not meet "evidence standards," 22 do not have "an eligible study design" because they "do not use a comparison group" or present only meta-analyses and literature reviews, and the remaining three include student samples with "less than 50%" ELLs. Thus, "the lack of studies meeting WWC evidence standards means that" no conclusions can be made "based on research about the effectiveness or ineffectiveness of SIOP on English language learners" (p. 1). As with the content-based curricular design, the effectiveness of genre-based curricula and teaching methods has not been established empirically.

Theoretically, the teaching of the writing process allowed language teachers and curriculum designers to accomplish their instructional goals based on solid research findings and pedagogical frameworks (Raimes & Miller-Cochran, 2017; Reid, 2000). However, these were developed for a different type of learners who were L1 writers. In addition, because many writing teachers are trained in methodologies for teaching the writing process, employing these approaches, techniques, and classroom activities entailed working with known and familiar ways of teaching.

> A key reason for the enormous popularity of L2 process instruction lies in the fact that the teaching of L1 writing relied on the research and experience of the full-fledged and mature discipline of rhetoric and composition.

The teaching of the writing process fundamentally overlooks the fact that L2 writers may simply lack the necessary language skills, e.g. vocabulary and grammar, to benefit from writing process instruction.

Differences between L1 and L2 Writing

The differences between L1 and L2 writing are so extensive that they can be identified in practically all aspects of written text and discourse. Based on the findings of hundreds of studies, compared to the discourse structuring and idea development in L1 writing, the distinctive characteristics of L2 writing seem to be unmistakable and highly prominent.

According to numerous studies of L1 and L2 written discourse and text, the most important differences between them extend to just a few of the following examples (all excerpts from students' academic assignments).

- Discourse moves and rhetorical organization, e.g. the norms of rhetorical idea structuring or explanatory information often do not conform to those in comparable written genres in English,[3] e.g. *First, it is a great idea. *Myself is a good example, and now is very common.*
- The structure, mis-placements, or omissions of thesis statements, e.g. *My paper will support the point about prevention. *I don't agree with the opinion about great inventions in my essay.*

- Logical and conceptual rhetorical development, argumentation, persuasion, and exposition/narration.
- Omissions of counterarguments and potentially divergent readers' reactions, e.g. *I will discuss the positive side of Bachelor' degree. *I am standing on the opposite side of standard of learning.*
- Insufficient or absent argument support or relying on direct claims and statements of personal opinions and beliefs in lieu of more substantive information, e.g. *If people recycle, we will save the environment, and so recycling is the solution.*
- Shorter and less elaborated texts.
- Assumptions about the reader's knowledge and expectations, e.g. references to assumed common knowledge and familiarity with certain classical works, *everyone knows, as the famous philosopher said.*
- Usage of language and rhetorical features of formal written text, such as fewer/less complex sentences, descriptive adjectives and adverbs, passives, nominalizations, conversational amplifiers and emphatics, e.g. *In summary is very important always follow the professional goals. *Everyone goes to school, and the highest necessity is self-achievement.*
- Restricted vocabulary that often lacks variety, specificity, and sophistication, fewer idiomatic and collocational expressions, frequently repeated words, such as nouns, verbs, adjectives, and adverbs, e.g. *Based on my own experience, many people experience the same one, as the investment advisor and me. *Teachers should take into account that teaching is very important in providing students for better learning and the teachers' quality of teaching.*
- High frequencies of incomplete or inaccurate sentences, such as missing sentence subjects or verbs, incomplete verb phrases, sentence fragments, e.g. *The notion of progress that everything in the world will improve through technology has destroyed environments and human beings, and human beings can ruin themselves, because the global warming in the world show that humans have damaged nature.*
- Inconsistent uses of verb tenses, significantly higher rates of personal pronouns, e.g. *I, we, he,* and lower rates of impersonal and referential pronouns, e.g. *it is clear, it seems, for this reason,* and fewer academic hedges, e.g. *typically, perhaps, in particular.*

At present, research has clearly and unambiguously demonstrated that L2 writers' skill levels in vocabulary and grammar disadvantage the quality of their formal prose.

> Even after several years of language learning, the properties of L2 writers' text continues to differ significantly from that of novice L1 writers in regard to a broad range of language features. Even advanced and highly educated L2 writers, such as doctoral students in universities in English-speaking countries and professionals, have a severely limited lexical and syntactic repertoire compared to their L1 peers.

For example, Silva's (1993, p. 668) survey of L2 writing research includes 72 empirical studies published between 1980 and 1991. His conclusions are that "in general, compared to L1 basic writing, L2 writers' texts were less fluent (fewer words), less accurate (more errors), and less effective (lower holistic scores)" and "exhibited less lexical control, variety, and sophistication overall." Silva summarizes his research overview by stating that "the research comparing L1 and L2 writing . . . strongly suggests that . . . they are different in numerous and important ways. This difference needs to be acknowledged and addressed by those who deal with L2 writers if these writers are to be treated fairly, taught effectively, and thus, given an equal chance to succeed in their writing-related personal and academic endeavors."

Talking Shop

Empirical studies of students' essays set out to investigate whether TOEFL writing approximated writing required in university courses, that is, what the Educational Testing Service (ETS) refers to as an aspect of test and task authenticity. To achieve this goal, the uses of vocabulary and grammar in three types of texts produced by the same students were compared in language corpora of over 300 essays, or more than 700,000 words, including:

(a) Actual academic course assignments, e.g. lab reports, case studies, and literature surveys.
(b) Integrated TOEFL essays, that is, written responses to readings (also called writing-from-reading).

(c)   Independent TOEFL opinion essays that are written to test prompts without readings (an example below).

The findings of two studies demonstrate that the language of the TOEFL content-based essays include both similarities and differences compared to university written assignments at least in some respects. On the other hand, TOEFL opinion essays written to independent prompts differ linguistically from almost all types of university writing tasks (Biber, Reppen, & Staples, 2017; Staples, Biber, & Reppen, 2018).

An Example of an Independent TOEFL Writing Prompt

A teacher's ability to relate well with students is more important than excellent knowledge of the subject being taught. Use specific reasons and examples to support your answer.
(ETS Corpus of Non-Native Written English,
https://catalog.ldc.upenn.edu/LDC2014T06.
Retrieved on March 30, 2019)

Additional comparative corpus analyses have also found that opinion essays written to prototypical testing and assessment prompts show little resemblance to students' university course writing (Moore & Morton, 2005; Weigle & Friginal, 2015).

Academic Writing

In their examination of the writing process, Bereiter & Scardamalia (1985, 1987, 1989) distinguish two types of writing: knowledge-telling and knowledge-transforming. They explain that "telling" about personal experiences or opinions represents the easiest form of writing production that is accessible to practically all language users, who often perform such tasks in conversations. Such writing assignments as, for example, *My first day in the United States, My most embarrassing/happiest day*, or *My views on teenage gaming/animal research* do not require writers to do much beyond telling what they already know and simply writing down their memories or opinions in response to the prompt.

> Writing personal narratives/opinions ("telling" what one already knows) is not similar to producing academic writing that requires obtaining and transforming knowledge.

To produce an essay, writers need to organize the information, often in chronological order, according to a structure appropriate within the composition and in accordance with a few prescribed conventions for discourse organization, e.g. overt topic markers and/or lists of reasons (*my first reason, the second reason, the third reason, . . . in conclusion . . .*) that are also retrieved from memory.

> In the case of L2 students, personal opinion writing tasks can be produced even within the constraints of limited vocabulary and grammar because the extent of the textual simplicity or complexity in the writing is determined by the writer.

- Opinion essays (Bereiter & Scardamalia, 1987, p. 8) include only two main elements: the "statement of belief and reason."
- Opinion writing also necessitates knowledge-telling because stating one's views requires little information beyond the writer's personal beliefs or thoughts.
- In this type of essay, writers can produce text on practically any topic within their available knowledge without external information or support.

> Opinion-based written assignments or essays report personal thoughts in the form of a simple discourse organization that usually meets the expectations of the genre.

In many cases, the teaching of L2 writing focuses predominantly on topics purposely designed to be accessible for L2 learners. Writing prompts in many L2 writing classes are often highly predictable and may actually require students to produce personal narratives and experiences, e.g.:

- *Why I want to go college.*
- *Holidays in my country.*

- *The person who influenced me most.*
- *My family/best friend.*
- *My favorite sport/pet/book/ movie/class/teacher/relative.*

Opinion essays are also ubiquitous at high-intermediate and advanced levels of pre-university language or EAP instruction because they appear to be pseudo-academic and are based on short readings, e.g. ***Read the article/text and give your reaction/response to (its content on) online privacy/gender roles/ pollution/social media/TV and online advertising/teenage smoking/choosing a career/immigration/women in the military***. However, a counter-productive outcome of topic accessibility is that L2 learners have few opportunities to engage in the disciplinary and academic writing expected of them in their university courses.

In addition to knowledge-telling in writing, the Bereiter and Scardamalia model of writing also addresses a far more psychologically complex type of writing that they call knowledge-transforming. Knowledge-transforming is considerably more cognitively complex than knowledge-telling because writers do not merely retrieve information already available to them in memory, but derive it from reading and integrate it with that already available to become obtained knowledge.

> Knowledge-transforming necessitates thinking about an issue, obtaining the information needed for analysis, and modifying one's thinking. This type of writing leads writers to expand their knowledge and develop new knowledge by means of processing new information obtained for the purpose of writing on a topic.

Knowledge telling and knowledge-transforming require different rhetorical and text-generating skills for producing writing. Such important considerations as content integration, expectations of the audience, conventions and form of the genre, the use of language (e.g. vocabulary and grammar), the logic of the information structuring, and rhetorical organization are all intertwined in knowledge-transforming, e.g. defining terms, explaining ideas, and clarifying.

> In general terms, the classical academic model of writing is expected in the disciplines where students are required to obtain, synthesize, integrate, and analyze information from various sources, such as published materials, textbooks, or laboratory experiments.

Advanced cognitive and information-processing tasks entailed in transforming knowledge and demonstrating knowledge in writing place great demands on L2 writers' language skills.

Academic Vocabulary and Grammar

> Intensive and consistent instruction in L2 vocabulary and grammar, as well as discourse organization, is paramount for academic L2 writers.

Instruction in L2 vocabulary and grammar improves learners' receptive and productive skills and provides important means of expanding learners' vocabulary and grammar ranges necessary in L2 reading, writing, listening, and other fundamental functions in education. Persistent instruction increases learners' vocabulary range in writing to include the foundational university vocabulary and progress beyond it.

> In vocabulary instruction, the productive knowledge of vocabulary for speaking and writing requires more learning and work, as well as greater motivation, than receptive knowledge for listening and reading, in which effective and measurable gains can be made within a matter of days.

The fact that consistent grammar instruction is important to develop learner language awareness and improvement in the quality of L2 production has long been established. Grammar is an essential tool for constructing at minimum comprehensible sentences that can become a part of coherent text.

> A fundamental basic fact is that "without grammar very little can be conveyed" (Wilkins, 1972, p. 111). Grammar is the tool without which phrases, sentences, and text – spoken or written – cannot be produced.

Talking Shop

Frequent words, e.g. *time, person, world, nation, increase, company, problem*, are easy to learn because they occur in many everyday contexts. On the other hand, **academic vocabulary** is less frequent, and it occurs predominantly in more formal – but not necessarily strictly academic – speech and writing, e.g. *area, authority, benefit, concept, environment, factor, function*.

Domain-specific vocabulary is words and phrases that are used in specialized texts, such as math, e.g. *decimal, divisible, rectangle*, the sciences, e.g. *mineral, fossil, combustion*, or history, e.g. *monarchy, nobility, hierarchy*.

In teaching, identifying the differences between the three types of vocabulary is important. List examples of the three types of vocabulary are presented below.

Frequent Words

feel, seem, how, high, too, place, little, world, very, still, nation, hand, old, life, tell, write, become, here, show, house, both, between, need, mean, call, develop, under, last, right, move, thing, general, never, same, another, begin, while, number, part, turn, real, leave, might, want, point (West, 1953, A General Service List, word frequencies 105–150)

General Academic Words

alternative, analyze, approach, arbitrary, assess, assign, assume, compensate, complex, comply, component, concept, conclude, consist, constant, construct, consult, contact, context, criterion, data, define, definite, denote, derive, devise, dimension, distinct, element, environment, equate, equivalent, establish, evaluate, evident, formulate, guarantee, hypothesis, identify, ignore, illustrate, impact, implicit, imply, indicate (Xue & Nation, 1984, A University Word List, 45 words, Level 1)

Domain-specific Words: Science, 8th Grade

acceleration, atmosphere, calories, carbon, chemical weathering, circuit, climate, comet, conduction, convection, crust, dependent variable, deposition, electron, erosion, experimental control, fossil fuel, frequency, gravitational force, heat transfer, hypothesis, independent variable, inertia, law, magnetic force, mantle, mass, neutron, pressure, proton, planet, plate tectonics, scientific method, speed, seismic wave, theory, thermal energy, star, velocity, variable, volume, weather, weight (Beck, McKeown, & Kucan, 2013, Tier 3 Lists in Content Domains; Marzano, 2004, Core Content Vocabulary Lists, 48 items, 55 words total)

The purpose of this book is **not** to help students attain the skills necessary to become sophisticated writers of fiction or journalistic prose. The narrow and instrumental goal of instruction presented here deals with helping L2 writers to become better equipped for their academic careers.

Furthermore, outside of a brief nod in chapter 11, the contents of the book do not include the teaching of the discourse features of academic writing, such as introductions, thesis statements, body paragraphs, and conclusions. Dozens of other books on the market, both for teachers and for students, address the organization of information in academic and student essays according to the norms and conventions of academic writing in English.

While both discourse and language play a crucial role in teaching L2 writing, the curriculum and teaching techniques discussed in this book focus primarily on vocabulary, grammar, and the rhetorical characteristics of academic text. Whenever possible, variations in language uses across different disciplines such as business, economics, psychology, or sociology are discussed throughout the volume.

This book presents a compendium of many practical teaching techniques, strategies, and tactics that a teacher can use in writing instruction to help students improve the quality of their academic text. These include the following components of academic prose that need to be intensively and extensively taught and practiced:

- Phrase and sentence patterns frequent and necessary in academic writing.
- Academic phrases and sentence stems.
- Academic nouns and verbs essential for developing and using more advanced vocabulary than can be attained by means of spoken interactions and conversations.
- The textual and discourse functions of the essential verb tenses and the passive voice.
- The textual functions of main and subordinate clauses.
- Formal written adjectives, adverbs, hedges, and pronouns.

Endnotes

1 In this chapter and the rest of the book, the term second language (L2) refers to a language that a person learns in addition to his or her first language (even when it is his or her third or fourth language), as well as a foreign and/or an additional language.

2 Hedging refers to the uses of particles, words, phrases, or clauses to reduce the writer's responsibility for the extent and truth value of statements, to show hesitation or uncertainty, and display politeness and indirectness. Hedging in academic writing is discussed in detail in chapter 12.

3 According to the linguistic convention of data designation, * (an asterisk) marks intentionally incorrect examples. A question mark (?) designates intentionally questionable – but not necessarily incorrect – data.

Further Reading

Silva, T. (1993). Toward an understanding of the distinct nature of L2 writing: The ESL research and its implications. *TESOL Quarterly*, *27*(4), 657–676.

A seminal publication that shines a great deal of light on the fundamental distinctions between L1 and L2 writers, and the key difference in how these two types of novice academic writers can and should be taught.

Webb, S., & Nation, I.S.P. (2017). *How vocabulary is learned*. Oxford: Oxford University Press.

Arguably, one of the best, clearly written, and well-rounded books on how to teach and learn L2 vocabulary for listening, speaking, reading, and writing, for almost any level of proficiency, from beginning to advanced.

Ur, P. (2012). *Vocabulary activities*. Cambridge: Cambridge University Press.

A practical, down-to-earth, and hands-on compendium of vocabulary teaching strategies and techniques, with a broad perspective on the role of vocabulary in language teaching and uses (including corpus data and searches).

References

Beck, I., McKeown, M., & Kucan, L. (2013). *Bringing words to life: Robust vocabulary instruction* (2nd edn). New York, NY: Guilford Press.

Bereiter, C. & Scardamalia, M. (1985). Cognitive coping strategies and the problem of "inert knowledge." In S. Chipman, J. Segal, & R. Glaser (Eds.), *Thinking and learning skills: Research and open questions, Volume 2* (pp. 65–80). New York, NY: Routledge.

Bereiter, C. & Scardamalia, M. (1987). *The psychology of written composition*. New York, NY: Routledge.

Bereiter, C. & Scardamalia, M. (1989). Intentional learning as a goal of instruction. In L. Resnick (Ed.), *Knowing, learning, and instruction* (pp. 361–391). New York, NY: Routledge.

Biber, D., Reppen, R., & Staples, S. (2017). Exploring the relationship between TOEFL iBT scores and disciplinary writing performance. *TESOL Quarterly, 51*(4), 948–960.

Bridgeman, B., Cho, Y., & DiPietro, S. (2016). Predicting grades from an English language assessment: The importance of peeling the onion. *Language Testing, 33*(3), 307–318.

Brinchmann, E., Hjetland, H., & Lyster, S. (2015). Lexical quality matters: Effects of word knowledge instruction on the language and literacy skills of third- and fourth-grade poor readers. *Reading Research Quarterly, 51*, 165–180.

Camarota, S., Griffith, B., & Zeigler, K. (2017). *Mapping the impact of immigration on public schools*. Washington, DC: Center for Immigration Studies.

Caplan, N. & Stevens, S. (2017). "Step out of the cycle": Needs, challenges, and successes of international undergraduates at a US university. *English for Specific Purposes, 46*, 15–28.

Carson, J. (2001). Second language writing and second language acquisition. In T. Silva & P. Matsuda (Eds.), *On second language writing* (pp. 191–199). New York, NY: Routledge.

Dudley-Evans, T. & St. John, M. (1998). *Developments in English for specific purposes*. Cambridge: Cambridge University Press.

Durrant, P. (2014). Discipline- and level-specificity in university students' written vocabulary. *Applied Linguistics, 35*(3), 328–356.

Durrant, P. (2017). Lexical bundles and disciplinary variation in university students' writing: Mapping the territories. *Applied Linguistics, 38*(2), 165–193.

Ferris, D. (2009). *Teaching college writing to diverse student populations*. Ann Arbor, MI: University of Michigan Press.

Ferris, D. (2011). *Treatment of error in second language student writing* (2nd edn). Ann Arbor, MI: University of Michigan Press.

Ferris, D. (2016). Promoting grammar and language development in the writing class: Why, what, how, and when. In E. Hinkel (Ed.), *Teaching English grammar to speakers of other languages* (pp. 222–239). New York, NY: Routledge.

Hinkel, E. (2002). *Second language writers' text*. New York, NY: Routledge.

Hinkel, E. (2003a). Simplicity without elegance: Features of sentences in L2 and L1 academic texts. *TESOL Quarterly, 37*, 275–301.

Hinkel, E. (2003b). Adverbial markers and tone in L1 and L2 students' writing. *Journal of Pragmatics, 35*, 1049–1068.

Hinkel, E. (2005). Analyses of L2 text and what can be learned from them. In E. Hinkel (Ed.), *Handbook of research in second language teaching and learning* (pp. 615–628). New York, NY: Routledge.

Hinkel, E. (2011). What research on second language writing tells us and what it doesn't. In E. Hinkel (Ed.), *Handbook of research in second language teaching and learning, Volume 2* (pp. 523–538). New York, NY: Routledge.

Hinkel, E. (2015). *Effective curriculum for teaching L2 writing: Principles and techniques.* New York, NY: Routledge.

Hirsh, D., & Nation, I.S.P. (1992). What vocabulary size is needed to read unsimplified texts for pleasure? *Reading in a Foreign Language, 8,* 689–696.

Horowitz, D. (1986). Process, not product: Less than meets the eye. *TESOL Quarterly, 20*(1), 141–144.

Hu, M. & Nation, P. (2000). Unknown vocabulary density and reading comprehension. *Reading in a Foreign Language, 13*(1), 403–430.

ICAS (2002). *Academic literacy: A statement of competencies expected of students entering California's public colleges and universities.* Sacramento, CA: Intersegmental Committee of the Academic Senates of California Colleges and Universities.

Institute of International Education (2018). *Open doors.* New York, NY: Institute of International Education.

Jordan, R. (1997). *English for academic purposes.* Cambridge: Cambridge University Press.

Knoch, U., Macqueen, S., & O'Hagan, S. (2014). *An investigation of the effect of task type on the discourse produced by students at various score levels in the TOEFL iBT writing test.* Princeton, NJ: Educational Testing Service.

Kress, G. (1994). *Learning to write.* London: Routledge.

Kress, G. (1996). *Before writing: Rethinking paths to literacy.* London: Routledge.

Leedham, M. (2016). *Chinese students' writing in English: Implications from a corpus-driven study.* London: Routledge.

Leki, I. (2007). *Undergraduates in a second language: Challenges and complexities of academic literacy development.* New York, NY: Routledge.

Leki, I., Cumming, A., & Silva, T. (2008). *A synthesis of research on second language writing in English.* New York, NY: Routledge.

Lillis, T. (2001). *Student writing: Access, regulation, desire.* London: Routledge.

Marzano, R. (2004). *Building background knowledge for academic achievement.* Alexandria, VA: Association for Supervision and Curriculum Development.

McCutchen, D. (2011). From novice to expert: Implications of language skills and writing-relevant knowledge for memory during the development of writing skill. *Journal of Writing Research, 3*(1), 51–68.

Moore, T. & Morton, J. (2005). Dimensions of difference: A comparison of university writing and IELTS writing. *Journal of English for Academic Purposes, 4,* 44–66.

Nation, I.S.P. (2013). *Learning vocabulary in another language* (2nd edn). Cambridge: Cambridge University Press.

Nation, P. & Waring, R. (1997). Vocabulary size, text coverage, and word lists. In N. Schmitt and M. McCarthy (Eds.), *Vocabulary: Description, acquisition and pedagogy* (pp. 6–19). Cambridge: Cambridge University Press.

Raimes, A. & Miller-Cochran, S. (2017). *Keys for writers* (8th edn). Boston, MA: Cengage.

Reid, J. (2000). *The process of composition* (3rd edn). New York, NY: Pearson.

Schleppegrell, M. (2002). Challenges of the science register for ESL students: Errors and meaning-making. In M. Schleppegrell & M. Colombi (Eds.), *Developing advanced literacy in first and second languages* (pp. 119–142). New York, NY: Routledge.

Schleppegrell, M. (2004). *The language of schooling.* New York, NY: Routledge.

Schleppegrell, M. & Colombi, M. (2002). *Developing advanced literacy in first and second languages: Meaning with power*. New York, NY: Routledge.

Silva, T. (1993). Toward an understanding of the distinct nature of L2 writing: The ESL research and its implications. *TESOL Quarterly, 27*(4), 657–676.

Staples, S., Biber, D., & Reppen, R. (2018). Using corpus-based register analysis to explore the validity of high stakes language exams: A register comparison of TOEFL iBT and disciplinary writing tasks. *Modern Language Journal, 102*(2), 310–332.

Uccelli, P., Galloway, E., Barr, C., Meneses, A., & Dobbs, C. (2015). Beyond vocabulary: Exploring cross-disciplinary academic-language proficiency and its association with reading comprehension. *Reading Research Quarterly, 50*, 337–356.

Weigle, S. & Friginal, E. (2015) Linguistic dimensions of impromptu test essays compared with successful student disciplinary writing: Effects of language background, topic, and L2 proficiency. *Journal of English for Academic Purposes, 18*, 25–39.

West, M. (1953). *A general service list of English words*. London: Longman.

What Works Clearinghouse (2013). *WWC intervention report: Sheltered instruction observation protocol (SIOP)*. Washington, DC: Institute of Education Sciences, US Department of Education.

Wilkins, D. (1972). *Linguistics in language teaching*. London: Edward Arnold.

Xue, G. & Nation, I.S.P. (1984). A university word list. *Language Learning and Communication, 3*, 215–229.

Zhang, Y. & Mi, Y. (2010). Another look at the language difficulties of international students. *Journal of Studies in International Education, 14*, 371–388.

Zong, J. & Batalova, J. (2017). *College-educated immigrants in the United States*. Washington, DC: Migration Policy Institute.

Student Writing in Colleges and Universities

2

Overview

- Writing tasks in colleges and universities.
- The most important characteristics of academic writing.
- The most common written academic assignments and tasks.
- The need for explicit language instruction.
- Vocabulary ranges.
- L2 vocabulary and reading.
- L2 vocabulary and writing.

Although L2 instruction takes place in various domains of language skills, such as reading, speaking, and listening, learners who undertake becoming proficient L2 writers are usually academically bound. Most students who prepare to enter degree programs dedicate vast amounts of time and resources to learning to produce written academic discourse and text. The teaching of academic English must include a writing component. It is an established fact that L2 students need to develop academic writing skills, but it is not always clear what types of writing and written discourse requires instruction to prepare for degree studies, e.g. assignments in academic disciplines rarely require proficient personal narratives or autobiographies.

By and large, what L2 writers need is to become relatively good at demonstrating academic knowledge within the formats expected in academic discourse and text. More importantly, L2 students' academic achievements often depend on their ability to construct written prose of at least passable quality. This chapter presents an overview of the written discourse genres and tasks common in colleges and universities in English language contexts, as well as students' learning needs.

Writing Tasks

Undergraduate students in US colleges and universities are required to take general education courses in such disciplines as the sciences, history, philosophy, psychology, and sociology prior to their studies in their chosen majors. One implication of this structure is that the greatest demand on students' language skills occurs during the first two years of their academic careers, when they are expected to read large amounts of diverse types of academic text, write short and long assignments, and take tests and exams.

At the college and university level, the purpose of written assignments, examinations, and tests is to assess students' familiarity with the course material. Examinations and assignments vary in types and formats that can range from multiple choice tests to lengthy term papers, as well as essay tests and short responses to questions. Standardized and widely administered multiple choice tests, such as the TOEFL, IELTS, ACT, or SAT, also incorporate essay components designed to measure writing proficiencies according to specific and well-publicized scoring criteria.

Beginning in the early 1980s, numerous studies have investigated the types of writing assignments and tasks required of undergraduate and graduate students in academic courses in various disciplines, such as the natural sciences – e.g. biology, chemistry, and physics – engineering, business, and the humanities, including English. More recently, examinations of large collections of university assignments have been reported and published, some based on rhetorical classifications, e.g. essay or poem, and others analyzed as computerized and tagged language corpora. The summary below presents an overview of book-length investigations and research reports with collections of over 500 student tasks.

Large-Scale Research Reports on Academic Assignments: A Summary

- Melzer (2014) looked at 2,101 assignments from 100 colleges and universities, over 400 courses, upper and lower divisions. He classified the assignments as:

  o Transactional – 83%
  o Exploratory – 13%

- o Expressive – 3%
- o Poetic – <1%

- Gardner and Nesi (2013) and Nesi and Gardner (2012) identified a number of genre families in a study that collected a corpus of 1039 assignments, with 268 Arts and Humanities, 233 in Life Sciences, 225 in Physical Sciences, and 313 in Social Sciences. Their categorization of first-year assignments includes the following for a total of 840:

  - o Essays – 416
  - o Methodology recounts – 120
  - o Explanations – 81
  - o Critiques – 78
  - o Exercises – 28
  - o Case studies – 26
  - o Design specifications – 24
  - o Narrative recounts – 18
  - o Problem questions – 12
  - o Proposals, empathy writing, and literature surveys – 10 each
  - o Research reports – 7

- Garbati, et al. (2015) present an overview of 544 academic assignments in five public Ontario universities, with 323 in humanities, 117 in business, and 104 in science. Their report provides the assignment classification as:

  - o Tutorial, website, written, or personal assignments – 20%
  - o Essays – 11%
  - o Papers – 9%
  - o The remainder – 80%, lab reports, online discussions, annotated bibliographies, peer reviews, and unmarked drafts

---

Regrettably, few, if any, of these classifications of assignments have a great deal of instructional or pedagogical utility. For instance, the fact that an assignment is classified as an "essay" does not shed a great deal of light on the actual student writing task, whether it involves course or literature syntheses, reviews or evaluations, descriptions of facts or events, or any number of other requirements.

In addition, practically all writing assignments involve more than one writing task, such as exposition in the introduction, followed by, for instance, cause/effect or comparison/contrast discourse structure, and then possibly a brief synopsis in the conclusion. For instance, most types of course assignments can include summaries of published works or syntheses of multiple sources. In this case, the writing tasks would call for an information synthesis, paraphrasing, or restatement skills.

Close to 2 million US high school graduates took the ACT in 2018, around 55% of the entire graduating class. The percentage of those who met ACT college-readiness benchmarks:

English – 60%, Reading – 46%, Math – 40%, Science – 36%
All four subjects – 27%

The Most Important Characteristics of Student Academic Writing

The value and importance of the essential L2 writing skills have been well researched and clearly established in college and university faculty surveys carried out by the Educational Testing Service (ETS), ACT, and the College Board that designs SAT tests. The College Board is also the creator of Accuplacer, an online testing battery in school arithmetic, college-level math, reading, and writing. The writing test consists of an essay that is scored according to specified criteria. The WritePlacer and WritePlacer-ESL (2018), a computerized placement test used to assess the students' writing proficiencies, is used by 1,300 colleges and universities in North America and close to 20 other countries.

Three sets of rankings below present an encompassing view of academic writing requirements in US and Canadian colleges and universities. The writing tasks are evaluated based on widely applicable study findings and scoring guides.

(1) The first report (column 1 in the table below) tabulates the results of faculty surveys on the characteristics of academic literacy and writing abilities necessary for students in California post-secondary education systems. It is the only study of its kind with 142 institutions (ICAS, 2002).

(2) The second study (column 2) was commissioned by ETS and focuses on the rhetorical modes and academic task types typical of students' written assignments in 33 US universities (Rosenfeld, Courtney, & Fowles, 2004).

(3) The third (column 3) specifies the College Board WritePlacer-ESL scoring criteria for L2 writers specifically (College Board, 2016, 2017a, 2018). The scoring guide was tested and normed in 21 two- and four-year colleges.

Academic Writing Tasks and Skills in Colleges and Universities		
California Universities (33) & Community Colleges (109) (ICAS, 2002)	33 US Universities (Rosenfeld, Courtney, & Fowles, 2004)	WritePlacer-ESL (College Board, 2016, 2017b, 2018)[1]
Most Frequent Writing Tasks (in declining order)		
Analysis 60% Synthesis from several sources 58% Factual description/short answer 50% Brief summaries 38%	Analysis/synthesis, from multiple sources (3.8 of 5) Extraction/summary of essential info (3.8 of 5) Observations (e.g. events, behaviors, experiments) (3.8 of 5)	A response to a statement essay of 300 to 600 words A developed point of view, clearly and effectively supported position, insightful and engaging ideas
Top-rated Discourse Skills		
Effective thesis Logical reasoning Well-chosen examples	Organized and coherent ideas/ information (4.1 of 5) Clear writing with smooth idea transitions (3.8 of 5)	Strong focus, organization, supporting details, audience awareness
Structure ideas in a sustained way Support main points with precise facts/ examples	Focused, supported discussion with relevant examples/ reasoning (3.8 of 5) Logical reasoning (3.8 of 5)	Appropriate reasoning and examples
Most Important Language Skills (in declining order)		
Appropriate academic vocabulary 88% of faculty Varied sentence structure, correct grammar, and punctuation 86% of faculty	Grammar and rules of standard written English (4.1 of 5) Accurate spelling/ punctuation (4.0 of 5) Writing edited for clarity, coherence, and correctness (3.9 of 5)	Wide-ranging and complex vocabulary, infrequent errors in word choice, word forms, and spelling

Most Important Language Skills (in declining order)		
Accurate spelling 75% of faculty Writing that is edited and relatively free of error 66% of faculty	Precise vocabulary without empty/vague phrases (3.9 of 5) Effective word choice (3.8 of 5)	Sophisticated and varied sentence structure and grammar forms, few errors word order, punctuation, etc.
Not Typically Found	Least Important Skill	
Personal info/essay 10% (Comp & Writing courses)	Persuasive writing, appeals to readers' experiences, or values (2.2 of 5) Evaluations of rhetorical techniques (2.2 of 5)	

The surveys of written assignments at the post-secondary level show that papers of around 5–10 pages are relatively frequent in humanities and social sciences courses, assigned 1–3 times per term. Extensive lab and experiment reports are required in the sciences (Garbati, et al., 2015; Hale, et al., 1996; ICAS, 2002). In many short assignments of 1–3 pages, students are asked to summarize and synthesize information from multiple sources, carry out interviews, and refer to published works, e.g. articles or book chapters.

> Only 20% of the faculty who teach courses other than composition indicate that they provide assistance with assignments and instruction in research (ICAS, 2002).

In a separate subset of ETS survey items, teaching faculty also rank the specific L2 writing skills that, in their experience, contribute to the students' academic success in their courses (Rosenfeld, Courtney, & Fowles, 2004; Rosenfeld, Leung, & Oltman, 2001). The two ETS studies demonstrate unambiguously that L2 grammar and vocabulary skills play a crucial role in student writing.

Three Most Important L2 Academic Writing Skills (in Declining Order)

(1) Discourse and information organization.
(2) Standard written English, that is, grammar, phrasing, and sentence structure.
(3) Academic vocabulary.

The College Board (2018) WritePlacer-ESL is a widely used automatic scoring software that is designed to provide "a direct measure of the writing skills of students who identify as English language learners" (p. 1). The task is to write a 300 to 600 word essay in response to short prompts "by drawing on a broad range of experiences, learning, and ideas." In their essays, L2 writers need to "develop [their] points of view and support [their] position with appropriate reasoning and examples."

Talking Shop

Traditional views and expectations hold that college and university students are required to do a great deal of writing. However, the trends in colleges and universities have changed with the times and are continuing to change.

A study of academic assignments across disciplines in one university finds that only 31% include written papers, essays, or final research projects, and 10% consist of other tasks, such as online postings or business letters. In fact, 24% of the courses surveyed in the study require no writing at all (Graves, Hyland, & Samuels, 2010). According to another investigation by Caplan & Stevens (2017), overall, 98–99% of the university faculty rank critical thinking and understanding lectures as the most important student skills, while writing short test answers, essays, and research papers are a priority for 62–75%.

A proprietary marketing research firm surveyed 1,140 students in US universities in 2018 (Whitford, 2018). Based on the findings, around 30% of the respondents have never written an assignment longer than 10 double-spaced pages, and 46% believe that they do not need any additional writing instruction at all. Specifically, in such disciplines as English, philosophy, and history, only 9% say that they need any more spelling or grammar instruction, compared to 16% in business.

WritePlacer-ESL writing tasks appear to strongly resemble those originally designed by ETS for the Test of Written English (TWE) in the mid-1980s. The TWE prompts and scoring criteria were subsequently adopted for the later versions of the TOEFL, including the current internet-based TOEFL iBT. The TOEFL iBT writing tasks consist of two versions: integrated writing and independent writing. In integrated tasks, test takers are required "to write a response to material they have heard and read," and independent writing requires composing "an essay in support of an opinion" (ETS, 2010, p. 6).

The independent test of writing is unchanged from the traditional task that has been administered on TWE for the past many decades: "This is the same type of task on the TOEFL and the Test of Written English" (p. 20). More specifically, the purpose of TWE and the writing section of the TOEFL iBT is to assess idea development, essay organization, and the uses of language to express ideas. A few brief definitions are also provided: "development is the amount and kinds of support (examples, details, reasons)" for the ideas that are presented in the essay "using clearly appropriate explanations, exemplifications, and/or details."

The WritePlacer-ESL writing prompts and TOEFL independent writing tasks originally developed for TWE seem remarkably – unmistakably – similar, as the examples below demonstrate (College Board, 2016, 2017b; ETS, 2004, 2010, 2012).

Examples of Prompts on TOEFL Independent Writing and WritePlacer-ESL*

TOEFL Writing Prompts	WritePlacer-ESL Prompts
People attend college or university for many different reasons (for example, new experiences, career preparation, increased knowledge). Why do you think people attend college or university? Use specific reasons and examples to support your answer.	Is an education a requirement for a successful career? Explain the topic and either agree or disagree with the statement, offering support for your position.
Do you agree or disagree with the following statement? Always telling the truth is the most important consideration in any relationship. Use specific reasons and examples to support your answer.	Do you agree or disagree with the following statement? Trust is an important component of any healthy relationship.

TOEFL Writing Prompts	WritePlacer-ESL Prompts
Supporters of technology say that it solves problems and makes life better. Opponents argue that technology creates new problems that may threaten or damage quality of life. Using one or two examples, discuss these two positions. Which view of technology do you support? Why?	Scientists and politicians argue over whether global warming and climate control present a real threat to human welfare. Take a position on this issue and explain whether or not you believe this to be a serious problem for humanity.
How do movies or television influence people's behavior? Use reasons and specific examples to support your answer.	Do works of art have the power to change people's lives? Some people say a book or a movie has the power to do just that. Are they exaggerating, or can art have such a large impact on individuals?

*Released by ETS and the College Board between 2004 and 2016.

In addition to the similarity of the writing prompts, the scoring criteria for writing also seem to be very similar.

Scoring criteria for TOEFL Independent Writing and WritePlacer-ESL

TOEFL iBT Independent WritingTop Score of 6	WritePlacer-ESLTop Score of 6
An essay at this level largely accomplishes all of the following: • Effectively addresses the topic and task. • Is well organized and well developed, using clearly appropriate explanations, exemplifications, and/or details.	An essay in this category demonstrates strong control of the elements of on-demand essay writing in English. • The writing sample exhibits strong control of focus, organization, and supporting details, with a sense of audience awareness. The writing sample exhibits an insightful and engaging expression of ideas. • The writing sample exhibits strong control of a wide and complex range of vocabulary, with infrequent errors in word selection, word forms, and spelling.

TOEFL iBT Independent WritingTop Score of 6 *(cont'd)*	WritePlacer-ESLTop Score of 6 *(cont'd)*
• Displays unity, progression, and coherence. • Displays consistent facility in the use of language, demonstrating syntactic variety, appropriate word choice, and idiomaticity, though it may have minor lexical or grammatical errors.	• The writing sample generally exhibits strong control of sophisticated and varied sentence structure, with few errors. • The writing sample exhibits strong control of grammatical forms. Some errors in word order, punctuation, and other aspects of grammar do not interfere with comprehension.
TOEFL iBT Writing Guide for Students	**WritePlacer-ESL Writing Guide for Students**

The Writing section is scored by:
• Rating the independent writing essay on overall writing quality, including:
  o Development and organization.
  o Grammar.
  o Vocabulary.
	The following four characteristics of writing will be considered.
	• Word Use – The extent to which you are able to use a wide range of words and phrases accurately.
	• Sentence Use – The extent to which you are able to use a variety of sentence patterns with both independent and dependent clauses.
	• Grammar – The extent to which you are able to express ideas using grammatically correct English.
	• Organization and Development – The extent to which you are able to focus on the assigned topic and to develop ideas clearly.

The scoring criteria for both writing tests, TOEFL independent writing and WritePlacer-ESL, can be summarized as follows:

- A relatively rigid discourse organization that follows a classical form with an overtly stated central idea or focus with supporting details and examples.
- Developed language skills, that is, vocabulary and grammar.

- Complex sentence structure.
- To the extent possible, error-free text, including punctuation and word forms.

A Summary: University Writing Skills and Tasks

On the whole, a great deal of agreement has been identified among the disciplinary faculty across many dozens of institutions, as well as ETS and College Board tests. The following discourse, organization, and language characteristics are essential in students' written work (College Board, 2016, 2018; ETS, 2004, 2010, 2012; ICAS, 2002; Rosenfeld, Courtney, & Fowles, 2004):

- An effective thesis.
- Well-chosen and detailed examples.
- Extensive and broad vocabulary.
- Complex, varied, and accurate grammar.

The typical university writing tasks expected of students have remained very similar and consistent. Numerous researchers into types of academic writing and criteria for the evaluations of writing in the academy have actually commented that these have largely remained unchanged since at least the early 2000s (e.g. Coffin, et al., 2003; Curry & Lillis, 2004; Hinkel, 2002, 2011, 2015; ICAS, 2002).

Frequent Writing Tasks in Colleges and Universities

- **Analytical writing** predominates in the academy. Around 60% of the faculty assign analytical and synthesis papers (ICAS, 2002; Rosenfeld, Courtney, & Fowles, 2004). A majority of teaching faculty in the US see analytical/synthesis writing as the most frequent in their undergraduate classes (ranked 3.8 of 5, "very important").
- **Extracting information and summarizing important points** is also common when students work with texts (e.g. textbooks, supplemental articles, or additional readings). In the ICAS survey, 38% of the faculty required brief summaries regularly. Many disciplinary faculty ranked extracting information from several sources as "very important" (Rosenfeld, Courtney, & Fowles, 2004).

- **Factual reports and observations**, e.g. of lab experiments, behaviors, or events, occupy a prominent place in academic student writing. These are noted in both university studies and are as prevalent as analysis/synthesis or summative writing.

Another prominent finding, however, pertains to the types of writing that are hardly ever found outside composition classes. In fact, the ICAS (2002, p. 23) report points to "a mismatch between students' preparation and the abilities needed to complete typical college writing tasks."

Writing Tasks NOT Common in University Assignments

- **Personal essay and example** assignments are encountered predominantly in composition and English department courses, English for Academic Purposes (EAP) programs, and standardized assessments.
- **Argumentation essays**, probably the most popular in EAP classes, rarely show up outside these and other composition assignments. The ICAS (2002, p. 23) report also specifically notes the prevalence of argumentation essays exclusively in composition classes, while "only about one-third of the students are sufficiently prepared" to write on analysis and synthesis tasks.
- **Persuasive writing**, likely taught in every L1 or L2 composition program in North America, is not considered to be important to students' success outside these courses.

The Need for Explicit Instruction

In a major study that surveyed 77 published research reports on the effectiveness of explicit grammar instruction, Norris and Ortega (2000, 2001) normed the results of investigations in an attempt to achieve consistency across various investigative and analytical methodologies. Their systematic review shows that in grammar learning, focused instruction of any sort is far more effective than any type of teaching methodology based on exposure to L2 without explicit teaching.

> The findings of dozens of studies clearly establish that focused and explicit instruction results in large language gains over the course of the instructional term and that the effects of the instruction seem to be durable over time.

Furthermore, Norris and Ortega explain that explicit instruction based on inductive teaching – when the learner discovers the rule – or deductive approaches – when the teacher explains the rule – leads to greater L2 gains than implicit instruction of any sort without explanations. Thus, given that academically bound L2 learners need to make substantial L2 gains to begin their studies, it is unmistakably evident that L2 grammar and vocabulary should be taught thoroughly and intensively (Frodesen, 2014; Hinkel, 2002, 2003, 2011, 2015; Nation, 2013; Nation & Webb, 2011; Schleppegrell, 2004; Waring & Nation, 2004).

- When students matriculate from language programs, the quality of their writing and text is evaluated by specialists who have little language background, that is, faculty in the disciplines.
- Later on, when students' academic studies are completed, the quality and accuracy of their text is continually appraised by subsequent non-specialists in on-the-job writing whenever college-educated learners write email, notes, reports, and old-fashioned memos.
- Considerate, understanding, and compassionate language teachers who seek to benefit their students have to teach the skills and language components that students must have to achieve their desired professional and career goals.
- If instruction in the essential language skills is not provided, students are largely left to their own devices when attempting to attain the L2 proficiency needed for their academic and professional endeavors.

For example, the most frequently encountered nouns in course materials across all disciplines in college and university general education courses are words such as *aesthetic, ambiguity, anomaly, apparatus, aristocrat,* and *attribute*. In all likelihood, few practicing language teachers have undertaken to teach the meanings of these words, unless they fortuitously occur in student reading texts.

Fluency-development activities in writing that require students to keep personal journals or free writing are not designed to increase learners' academic vocabulary or grammar range, with its almost requisite use of the passive voice, impersonal constructions (*it seems, it is possible/necessary/apparent*), and complex hedging (*according to, it may well be, based on the data*).

> In fact, typical fluency-based activities encourage the use of immediately accessible vocabulary and grammar structures without a means of language gains.
>
> Activities with little language learning can – and often do – lead to misrepresentations of the high degree of accuracy expected in formal academic prose.

A teacher of academic writing would do a disservice to academic L2 writers by not preparing them for academic writing assignments, particularly those in the more common forms the students are certain to encounter in their disciplinary studies. In writing tasks, college and university students must produce text that is academically sophisticated enough to demonstrate their understanding of and familiarity with the course material.

Vocabulary Ranges

In regard to the vocabulary range required to produce competent written prose, a great deal of disagreement accompanies the amount of vocabulary necessary for or known by university-educated native and non-native speakers. One of the key issues in the debate is whether the amount of vocabulary should be measured in terms of individual words or word families. The difference between the two types of measurements is substantial. Counting words is crucially different than counting word families, which consist of base words and their derived forms, e.g. *child, children, childhood, childish*.

Although the vocabulary counts undertaken by researchers in the 1970s and 1980s relied on individual words, in the past three decades, practically all measurements of vocabulary have largely dealt with word families. Nonetheless, since much of the research into L2 reading and writing deals with the counts of words and word families, both types of studies are briefly referred to here.

A large number of investigations carried out on the essential skills needed to produce school and academic writing have been based on large and small data sets. By and large, these consist of studies with foci on the vocabulary found in practically all types of academic prose and thus typically also expected in student writing, as well.

Many analyses of school and academic writing at various levels have demonstrated that student prose is expected to adhere to fairly regular conventions in vocabulary and multiword phrases, also called **collocations**, that is, **words that often co-occur together in discourse** (*in sum* or *in conclusion*, but not ***for a conclusion/*from my paper**) (Hinkel, 2017, 2019; Laufer & Waldman, 2011).

> A vast body of studies has clearly and unambiguously demonstrated that L2 writers' vocabulary levels and grammar skills disadvantage the quality of their formal prose.

Even after several years of language learning, L2 writers' text continues to differ significantly from that of novice L1 writers in regard to a broad range of vocabulary and grammar properties. The results of dozens of analyses indicate that even advanced and highly educated L2 writers, such as doctoral students in universities in English-speaking countries and professionals, have severely limited lexical and grammar ranges compared to their L1 peers of similar backgrounds and education.

The findings of the research on the amount of vocabulary accessible to native and non-native speakers are presented below as a point of reference. The importance of a solid base in academic vocabulary in production of L2 writing is also discussed in numerous publications.

Vocabulary Sizes*

Native Speakers of English	Number of Word Families
Average native speaker	17,000
First-year college students	16,679
Older adults	21,252
Educated native speakers	30,000 (approximately)
Junior high school students	9,684
An average novel for teenager	5,000 words (not word families) (approximately)
Non-native Speakers of English	
Graduate/post-doctoral non-native students (receptive vocabulary only)	8,000–9,000 (approximately)

*Based on the data provided in the following publications: D'Anna, Zechmeister, & Hall (1991), Nation (2006), Nation (2013), Goulden, Nation, & Read (1990), Zechmeister, D'Anna, Hall, Paus, & Smith (1993), and Zechmeister, Chronis, Cull, D'Anna, & Healy (1995).

The data demonstrate unambiguously that academic L2 vocabulary has to be taught and learned, and there is not a moment to lose. That is, the vocabulary range of junior high school students may be similar to that of highly educated non-native speakers of English, such as post-doctoral students in English-speaking countries (Nation & Waring, 1997; Waring & Nation, 2004). It seems clear, however, that the types of accessible word families of school-age learners is not likely to be the same as that of post-doctoral L2 students. In general terms, the vocabulary needed for teaching adults – and particularly so for teaching academic L2 writing – is not similar to that suited for teaching school age learners.

L2 Vocabulary and Reading

Practically all researchers of L2 reading and vocabulary agree that high frequency words are easy to learn, and they allow learners to do a great deal in a second language. These are required in all forms of language usage: speaking, listening, reading, and writing. High frequency lists consist mostly of function words, e.g. articles, prepositions, pronouns, and common content words, such as *make, more, state, what, when,* or *work.* West's (1953) General Service List includes 2,000 words, and 80% of these are function words.[2] These essential and most common words are easy to learn simply because they are so common.

On the other hand, even frequent academic words, e.g. *authority, democracy,* or *random,* do not occur nearly as often, and these need to be actively taught – and learned (Nation, 2005, 2011, 2013; Webb & Nation, 2017).

> Early vocabulary learning is easy because early learning includes highly frequent words, but less frequent words, such as those in basic academic vocabulary, are harder to learn, and they need to be taught.

Given that the most common 500 high frequency words on – as one example – West's (1953) list consist of *a, the, and, by, but, in, out, we, you, I, do, this,* and the like, the vocabulary scale below seems to be readily understandable.

Reading Skill Levels and L2 Vocabulary Size

0–500 word families

- Pictures and illustrations are required for comprehension.
- Only a few content words recognized in unsimplified L2 text.
- Only extremely simplified texts (such as those for very young children) can be understood.
- Identifying letters or letter strings (words and phrases) immediately can be difficult.
- Reading takes place letter-by-letter or word-by-word.
- The beginnings of sentences are often forgotten when the end is reached.

500–1,000 word families

- Native speaker texts can be completely incomprehensible.
- Dictionary use represents the main reading strategy.
- Word-by-word reading, followed by re-reading, when meaning continuity is lost.
- Making text-based inferences is not possible.
- The meaning of the message is difficult to retain, and the content of reading is soon forgotten.
- Slow and predictable plots in graded readers can be comprehensible.
- Overall, reading is slow, laborious, and exhausting.

1,000–2,000 word families

- Dictionary usage is the main reading strategy, with the exception of highly predictable texts.
- Unsimplified texts remain so complex that they are soon abandoned.
- Content words can be occasionally identified in stretches of text.
- Humor and textual irony are inaccessible.
- Most texts are processed at the sentence level, and complex story plots can be difficult to follow.

2,000–5,000 word families

- Most words in text are understood but not immediately.
- Dictionary use is frequently required.
- Text structure can become accessible at the discourse level.

5,000+

- Most L2 text at the level of general interest can be understood, but not when the topic is specialized.
- Introductory academic texts may require occasional use of a dictionary.

(Adapted from www.robwaring.org/vocab/principles/early.htm, retrieved on May 3, 2019)

Researchers use a variety of tests to measure students' vocabulary sizes. Some of these are rough and approximate instruments, but some are normed and standardized with a relatively high degree of accuracy (e.g. Nation, 2006, 2011; Nation, 2013). Scanning a newspaper page and deriving bits of basic news reports can be possible with a vocabulary range of 1,000 to 2,000 words, even though the details of news stories will not be understood. To read a newspaper and be able to understand at least some of the news stories, learners would require familiarity with 2,000 to 3,000 or 4,000 words, and attaining this much vocabulary takes a bit of work. Along these lines, most L2 students who aspire to academic studies in a country where another language represents the medium of instruction – and is required for all academic writing tasks – need to have a vocabulary of over 5,000 words, which includes academic words that have to be systematically and persistently learned.

> A vocabulary size of approximately 5,000 word families is required for relatively fluent L2 reading, even though a dictionary is still necessary at this level (e.g. Hirsh & Nation, 1992; Hu & Nation, 2000).

According to Hu and Nation (2000), with text coverage of 80% (20 out of every 100 words unknown to the reader), that is, a vocabulary range of slightly over 1,000 words, reading and comprehending text may be difficult. Typical non-academic or general interest L2 texts, say a newspaper article, cannot be understood adequately enough for learners to correctly answer comprehension questions.

In general, 98% text coverage (1 unknown word in 50) is needed for most L2 learners to understand what they are reading. Based on the results of several experiments, Hu and Nation (2000) conclude that it is possible for some learners in the 90% and a few more in the 95% group to have adequate or close to adequate comprehension, but for a majority of learners this amount of accessible vocabulary is too small to understand the text well enough to account for its contents.

L2 Vocabulary and Writing

The data below highlight the types of written text that non-native speakers can produce, depending on their accessible vocabulary range. Knowing 500 or 1,000 of the most frequent English words does not allow L2 learners to produce writing, however simple, because these mostly consist of articles, prepositions, pronouns, and basic nouns and adjectives (e.g. *say, much, think, feel, people, world, show, house*). As is apparent from the outline of the writing skills at various vocabulary levels, clearly L2 learners with vocabulary sizes of 500 or 1,000 words cannot be expected to produce much text.

L2 Vocabulary Size and Writing Skill Levels

0–500 words

- Only very basic sentences with extremely poor choice of words.
- Series of correct or incorrect phrases without sentences.
- Translated phrases and sentences.

500–1,000 word families

- A small number of compound sentences (e.g. **Mary read, and Peter sang.**)
- The use of only basic phrase and sentence conjunctions (e.g. **and, but, then**).
- Translated sentences that consist of largely translated phrases.

1,000–2,000 word families

- Complete dependence on a bilingual dictionary when writing longer texts.
- Poor word choice.
- Occasional collocations (words that often co-occur together in discourse, e.g. **do work** or **save time**, but not ***make an accident***), but many awkward and strange phrases.
- Disjointed ideas/incoherent in spots.

2,000–5,000 word families

- Highly pre-patterned and predictable texts can be produced without a dictionary (e.g. **Students study hard at school**).
- Spontaneous writing and writing on new topics are almost completely dependent on bilingual dictionary use.

5,000+

- A bilingual dictionary is used only rarely in routine types of writing, mostly for the purpose of identifying subtle differences in word meanings or looking up specific terms.
- Extensive reliance on a bilingual dictionary in writing specialized texts, such as homework assignments.
- Consistent and repeated errors and misused words (e.g. **Bob come yesterday*).
- Un-idiomatic text, short on collocations.

(Adapted from www.robwaring.org/vocab/principles/early.htm, retrieved on May 3, 2019)

In fact, basic written prose can begin to emerge only when the learner's vocabulary range exceeds 2,000 words. The descriptions of student writing found at the level of over 5,000 words seem to be typical of what is considered to be relatively advanced in advanced L2 writing classes or many community colleges. At this juncture, it is important to note that the text produced by L2 writers with such a high level of vocabulary – that is, around 5,000 words – seems to be far from impressive, as many L2 teachers know from experience.

> Academic vocabulary must be taught simply because it does not occur in routine interactions and conversational exchanges.

Hu and Nation (2000, p. 406) point out that "the relationship between text coverage and vocabulary size is strongly affected by the kind of text that is looked at." That is, knowing high frequency English words does not enable the readers to understand academic text well. Conversational vocabulary and grammar provide poor coverage for academic text, and having a large conversational range does not necessarily enable L2 learners to read and write academic prose.

Chapter Summary

Undergraduate students are required to take general education courses in such disciplines as the sciences, history, philosophy, psychology, and sociology prior to their studies in their chosen majors.

- The value and importance of the essential L2 writing skills have been well researched and clearly established in college and university faculty surveys carried out by the Educational Testing Service (ETS), ACT, and the College Board that designs college placement and SAT tests.
- The writing tasks are evaluated based on widely applicable study findings and scoring guides. The three most important L2 academic writing skills are:
  - o Discourse and information organization.
  - o Standard written English, that is, grammar, phrasing, and sentence structure.
  - o Academic vocabulary.

- Focused and explicit instruction results in large language gains over the course of the instructional term, and the effects of the instruction seem to be durable over time.
- In fluency-based activities, the use of immediately accessible vocabulary and grammar structures provide little opportunity for language gains.
- Early vocabulary learning is easy because early learning includes highly frequent words, but less frequent words, such as those in basic academic vocabulary, are harder to learn, and they need to be taught.
- A vocabulary size of approximately 5,000 word families is necessary for relatively fluent L2 reading, even though a dictionary is still necessary.
- Basic written prose can begin to emerge only when the learner's vocabulary range exceeds 2,000 words.
- Conversational vocabulary and grammar provide poor coverage for academic text, and having a large conversational range does not necessarily enable L2 learners to read and write academic prose.
- For L2 writers to produce academic prose, intensive vocabulary work is required. Academic L2 writers need to attain proficiency in academic language simply because without it they are considerably disadvantaged in their academic work.

Endnotes

1 Although the Accuplacer test was redesigned, and the new version has been administered since early 2019, the WritePlacer-ESL scoring guidelines have remained largely unchanged.
2 Full versions of Michael West's (1953) General Service List that consists of about 2,000 most frequent words are easily available online.

Further Reading

Birch, B. (2021). *English L2 reading: Getting to the bottom* (4th edn). New York, NY: Routledge.

A thorough and comprehensive book in its 4th edition that explains clearly how L1 orthography, phonology, and word structure can influence English L2 reading at the "bottom" of the – very basic – reading process. It provides a thorough but very accessible linguistic examination of the lowest levels of the reading process. The text clearly explains the strategies that readers of other languages develop in response to their own writing systems, e.g. Chinese, Japanese, Arabic, Hebrew, other alphabets, or transparent Roman alphabetic systems, contrasted with an explanation of the English L1 reading.

Corson, D. (1985). *The lexical bar*. Oxford: Pergamon Press.

Three measuring instruments are used in this study of 12- and 15-year-old children's passive vocabulary, active vocabulary, and lexical diversity among two social class backgrounds in North London and South Yorkshire. Highly significant differences are found in lexical access, by age, to word meanings in the school curriculum. Because Greco-Latin words dominate in learning and schooling, a "lexical bar" is at work among socio-economic classes where English is the principal language of communication. This bar hinders the language users from a ready access to the vocabulary essential for success in education.

Hu, M. & Nation, P. (2000). Unknown vocabulary density and reading comprehension. *Reading in a Foreign Language, 13*(1), 403–430.

A well-known study examines the relationship between text coverage and L2 reading comprehension. Reading comprehension was measured in two ways: by a multiple-choice reading comprehension test, and by a written cued recall of the text. The results show that with a text coverage of 80%, that is, 20 out of every 100 words (1 in 5) were unknown, no one gained adequate comprehension. With a text coverage of 90%, a small minority gained adequate comprehension. With a text coverage of 95% (1 unknown word in 20), a few more gained adequate comprehension, but they were still a small minority.

References

ACT (2018). *The condition of college and career readiness: National 2018*. Retrieved from www.act.org/content/dam/act/unsecured/documents/cccr2018/National-CCCR-2018.pdf

Caplan, N. & Stevens, S. (2017). "Step out of the cycle": Needs, challenges, and successes of international undergraduates at a US university. *English for Specific Purposes, 46*(1), 15–28.

Coffin, C., Curry, M., Goodman, S., Hewings, A., Lillis, T., & Swann, J. (2003). *Teaching academic writing: A toolkit for higher education*. London: Routledge.

College Board (2016). *Accuplacer program manual*. New York, NY: College Board. Retrieved from https://secure-media.collegeboard.org/digitalServices/pdf/accuplacer/accuplacer-program-manual.pdf

College Board (2017a). *Next-generation Accuplacer test specifications*. New York, NY: College Board. Retrieved from https://accuplacer.collegeboard.org/sites/default/files/next-generation-test-specifications-manual.pdf

College Board (2017b). *Next-generation writing sample questions.* New York, NY: College Board. Retrieved from https://accuplacer.collegeboard.org/sites/default/files/next-generation-sample-questions-writing.pdf

College Board. (2018). *WritePlacer guide with writing samples.* New York, NY: College Board. Retrieved from https://accuplacer.collegeboard.org/sites/default/files/accu placer-writeplacer-sample-essays.pdf

Curry, M. & Lillis, T. (2004). Multilingual scholars and the imperative to publish in English: Negotiating interests, demands, and rewards. *TESOL Quarterly, 38*(4), 663–688.

D'Anna, C., Zechmeister, E., & Hall, J. (1991). Toward a meaningful definition of vocabulary size. *Journal of Reading Behavior, 23*(1), 109–122.

Educational Testing Service (2004). *Test of written English guide* (5th edn). Princeton, NJ: Educational Testing Service.

Educational Testing Service (2010). *Test and score data summary for TOEFL internet-based and paper-based tests.* Princeton, NJ: Educational Testing Service.

Educational Testing Service (2012). *The official guide to the TOEFL test* (4th edn). New York, NY: Educational Testing Service.

Frodesen, J. (2014). Grammar in second language writing. In M. Celce-Murcia, D. Brinton, & M. Snow (Eds.), *Teaching English as a second or foreign language* (4th edn) (pp. 238–253). Boston, MA: Cengage.

Garbati, J., McDonald, K., Meaning, L., Samuels, B., & Scurr, C. (2015). *Writing assignments and instruction at Ontario's publicly funded universities: A view from three disciplines.* Toronto: Higher Education Quality Council of Ontario.

Gardner, S. & Nesi, H. (2013). A classification of genre families in university student writing. *Applied Linguistics, 34*(1), 25–52.

Goulden, R., Nation, P., & Read, J. (1990). How large can a receptive vocabulary be? *Applied Linguistics, 11*(2), 341–363.

Graves, R., Hyland, T., & Samuels, B. (2010). Undergraduate writing assignments: An analysis of syllabi at one Canadian college. *Written Communication, 27*(3), 293–317.

Hale, G., Taylor, C., Bridgeman, B., Carson, J., Kroll, B., & Kantor, R. (1996). *A study of writing tasks assigned in academic degree programs.* Princeton, NJ: Educational Testing Service.

Hinkel, E. (2002). *Second language writers' text.* New York, NY: Routledge.

Hinkel, E. (2003). Simplicity without elegance: Features of sentences in L2 and L1 academic texts. *TESOL Quarterly, 37*(2), 275–301.

Hinkel, E. (2011). What research on second language writing tells us and what it doesn't. In E. Hinkel (Ed.), *Handbook of research in second language teaching and learning, Volume 2* (pp. 523–538). New York, NY: Routledge.

Hinkel, E. (2015). *Effective curriculum for teaching L2 writing: Principles and techniques.* New York, NY: Routledge.

Hinkel, E. (2017). Prioritizing grammar to teach or not to teach: A research perspective. In E. Hinkel (Ed.), *Handbook of research in second language teaching and learning* (pp. 369–383). New York, NY: Routledge.

Hinkel, E. (2019). Teaching strategies and techniques: Collocations and multiword units. In E. Hinkel (Ed.), *Teaching essential units of language: Beyond single-word vocabulary* (pp. 107–133). New York, NY: Routledge.

Hirsh, D. & Nation, P. (1992). What vocabulary size is needed to read unsimplified texts for pleasure? *Reading in a Foreign Language, 8*(2), 689–696.

Hu, M. & Nation, P. (2000). Unknown vocabulary density and reading comprehension. *Reading in a Foreign Language, 13*(1), 403–430.

ICAS (2002). *Academic literacy: A statement of competencies expected of students entering California's public colleges and universities*. Sacramento, CA: Intersegmental Committee of the Academic Senates of California Colleges and Universities.

Laufer, B. & Waldman, T. (2011). Verb-noun collocations in second language writing: A corpus analysis of learners' English. *Language Learning, 61*(2), 647–672.

Melzer, D. (2014). *Assignments across the curriculum: A national study of college writing*. Logan, UT: Utah State University Press.

Nation, I.S.P. (2005). Teaching and learning vocabulary. In E. Hinkel (Ed.), *Handbook of research in second language teaching and learning* (pp. 581–595). New York, NY: Routledge.

Nation, I.S.P. (2006). How large a vocabulary is needed for reading and listening? *The Canadian Modern Language Review, 63*(1), 59–82.

Nation, I.S.P. (2011). Research into practice: Vocabulary. *Language Teaching, 44*, 529–539.

Nation, I.S.P. & Webb, S. (2011). Content-based instruction and vocabulary learning. In E. Hinkel (Ed.), *Handbook of research in second language teaching and learning, Volume 2* (pp. 631–644). New York, NY: Routledge.

Nation, P. (2013). *Learning vocabulary in another language* (2nd edn). Cambridge: Cambridge University Press.

Nation, P. & Waring, R. (1997). Vocabulary size, text coverage, and word lists. In N. Schmitt & M. McCarthy (Eds.), *Vocabulary: Description, acquisition, and pedagogy* (pp. 6–20). Cambridge: Cambridge University Press.

Nesi, H. & Gardner, S. (2012). *Genres across the disciplines: Student writing in higher education*. Cambridge: Cambridge University Press.

Norris, J. & Ortega, L. (2000). Effectiveness of L2 instruction: A research synthesis and quantitative meta-analysis. *Language Learning, 50*(3), 417–528.

Norris, J. & Ortega, L. (2001). Does type of instruction make a difference: Substantive findings from a meta-analytic review. In R. Ellis (Ed.), *Form-focused instruction and second language learning* (pp. 157–213). Ann Arbor, MI: University of Michigan/ Wiley-Blackwell.

Rosenfeld, M., Courtney, R., & Fowles, M. (2004). *Identifying the writing tasks important for academic success at the undergraduate and graduate level*. Princeton, NJ: Educational Testing Service.

Rosenfeld, M., Leung, S., & Oltman, P. (2001). *The reading, writing, speaking, and listening tasks important for academic success at undergraduate and graduate levels*. Princeton, NJ: Educational Testing Service.

Schleppegrell, M. (2004). *The language of schooling*. New York, NY: Routledge.

Waring, R., & Nation, P. (2004). Second language reading and incidental vocabulary learning. *Angles on the English Speaking World, 4*(1), 11–23.

Webb, S. & Nation, P. (2017). *How vocabulary is learned*. Oxford: Oxford University Press.

West, M. (1953). *A general service list of English words*. London: Longman.

Whitford, E. (2018). Minimal writing? No problem. *Inside Higher Ed*, July 31. Retrieved from www.insidehighered.com/news/2018/07/31/new-study-shows-few-students-see-need-more-writing-instruction

Zechmeister, E., Chronis, A., Cull, W., D'Anna, C., & Healy, N. (1995). Growth of a functionally important lexicon. *Journal of Reading Behavior, 27*(2), 201–212.

Zechmeister, E., D'Anna, C., Hall, J., Paus, C., & Smith, J. (1993). Metacognitive and other knowledge about the mental lexicon: Do we know how many words we know? *Applied Linguistics, 14*(1), 188–206.

Designing a Course of Study

3

Overview

- Accuracy in academic writing.
- Instructed L2 grammar and noticing.
- Incidental learning of grammar and vocabulary.
- The benefits of written academic discourse conventions.
- Lexical phrases and sentence stems.
- Teaching self-editing skills.
- Unimportant features of academic text.

The purpose of this chapter is to establish a research-based framework for teaching academic writing courses that focus on just the core, the most essential academic skills for students' college and university work. The L2 writing course curriculum needs to be designed around the key areas that deal with the following areas of instruction:

- Accuracy in grammar and vocabulary.
- Intensive academic vocabulary teaching and learning.
- The fundamental editing of one's own text.

> The essential elements of the course that must be addressed can be designed to be flexible within the course structure. The amount of effort and time devoted to each can be adjusted for a particular group of students.

This chapter presents an overview of research to show why certain core components of language are critical in teaching L2 academic writing. It lays the groundwork for the teaching approach developed in the subsequent chapters on sentence and phrase structure, nouns, pronouns, verb tenses, verb lexical classes, and rhetorical features of text, such as cohesion and hedging. Also discussed are the benefits and shortfalls of incidental vocabulary learning and the grammar and vocabulary that are usually taught in language classes but that may be relatively unimportant.

The course of study outlined in this chapter centers on current research findings about what it takes to attain viable academic L2 writing skills and presents dozens of techniques for teaching them. The teacher's work load and the student's "**learning burden,**" that is, "the amount of effort required" to learn L2 grammar and vocabulary are expected to be realistic but certainly not very light (Nation, 2013; Peters, 2016; Webb & Nation, 2017).

> The learning burden differs from word to word depending on the word's meaning, form, and uses in speaking and writing, as well as other words that frequently occur with it, e.g. **account (for)**, **civic**, **commodity**, **contingent (on)**, **method**. Teaching and learning academic words takes a substantial amount of work.

Accuracy, Academic Text, and Practical Goals

As the teaching of English was becoming increasingly important during and after World War II, Charles Fries developed one of the first US textbooks for training English language teachers. In 1945, his definition of syntactic and lexical accuracy in L2 use was very flexible and pragmatic:

> The "accuracy" which is advocated here does not mean the so-called "correctness" of the common handbooks. . . . The accuracy here stressed refers to an accuracy based upon a realistic description of the actual language as used by native speakers in carrying on their affairs. . . . It is fruitless to argue in the abstract concerning the relative merits of the various types of English. . . .
>
> In learning English as a foreign language it is necessary to decide upon a particular type to be mastered, for there is no single kind that is used throughout all the English speaking world. The practical approach

is to decide for the kind of English that will be used by the particular group with which one wishes to associate. . . .

(Fries, 1945, pp. 3–4)

The important point made by Fries many decades ago is that language learners need to identify their goals for learning and the groups of people with which they wish to "associate." In the case of academically bound learners, these people consist of the college and university faculty, advisors, tutors, and administrative staff. Outside colleges and universities, this group includes employers and colleagues whose opinions also matter.

It goes without saying that the native speakers of any language are exposed to their L1 throughout their entire lives in their families, schools, and communities. On the other hand, most L2 writers study English as a Foreign Language (EFL) in their native countries or learn English as new arrivals in an English-speaking setting. A large majority of L2 college students begin their academic studies as adults.

It is a fact that L2 writers' vocabulary and grammar ranges are usually limited compared to those of college and university L1 students. For L2 writers, producing academic prose is not a trivial task. Without direct and intensive instruction in how to construct academic text, L2 students often find themselves at a great disadvantage in their academic and professional careers (Darling-Hammond, 2015; Gibbons, 2014; Hinkel, 2011, 2014, 2015; Schleppegrell, 2004).

- Research has demonstrated that English-language academic writing is governed by several rigid conventions in its discourse structure and language features.
- Based on the findings of numerous studies, and to put it simply, discourse teaching techniques and strategies can aim for maximum gain for minimal work by capitalizing on the rigidity and conventionalization of written academic prose in English.

Instructed Vocabulary and Grammar

Grammar teaching can be made productive for learners if it is cumulative, that is, when the curriculum builds on the structures that learners already know or from the linguistically simple to more complex constructions (R. Ellis, 2005, 2015; Ferris, 2009, 2014; Larsen-Freeman, 2015; Larsen-Freeman & Celce-Murcia, 2016). To this end, grammar curricula even at the intermediate levels of student proficiency can begin with an examination and analysis of structures in formal writing. Initially, the goal of instruction is to develop learners' awareness and **noticing** of frequent and specific constructions, and then building on this foundation, grammar regularities can be explicitly addressed and practiced in writing (Batstone & R. Ellis, 2009; James, 1998; Ur, 2011, 2013).

Frequent grammar constructions are found in abundance in practically all academic prose, and they readily lend themselves to ongoing instruction:

- At the high intermediate and advanced levels, grammar teaching can focus on constructions typically found in language textbooks and introductory academic materials, e.g.
    - o History texts heavily rely on the past tense.
    - o Psychology, economics, and social sciences books are practical in instruction on the present tense and the passive voice.
- At higher proficiency levels, teaching can highlight the effects of grammar on discourse and text, e.g.
    - o Tense uses in generalizations and thesis statements.
    - o The key formality differences between *lots/tons* and *a large number/ amount, totally* and *a great deal*, or *no way* and *not likely*.
- The discourse functions of grammar components can be *noticed, analyzed, and practiced* (these are parallel verbs), such as
    - o Referential and impersonal pronouns, e.g. *it may be, it appears*.
    - o The hedging (softening) functions of modal verbs, e.g. *can, could, may, might*.
    - o Parallel phrases, e.g. *in books and articles*, or *listening, speaking, and reading*.

> The goal of grammar practice (practice, and practice) is to help learners develop **productive** fluency in academic writing and a degree of automaticity in generating academic prose.

Practice activities can include brief restatements of chapter and section contents, summaries, paraphrases, explanations, or using sources in short pieces of writing at lower proficiency levels and longer essays for advanced learners.

Raising learners' awareness of the structure of complete sentences in academic prose (as opposed to **sentence fragments**), as well as important distinctions between conversational and formal written language, should represent ongoing instructional objectives at all levels of proficiency. Because in

English-speaking countries most learners are exposed to a great deal more conversational discourse than formal writing, they usually employ conversational grammar and vocabulary in their academic essays (Hammerly, 1991; Hinkel, 2016, 2017, 2019; Shaw & Liu, 1998).

While working with written academic discourse at any level of learner proficiency, it is paramount to take opportunities to bring learners' attention to academic discourse organization and discourse moves, contextualized vocabulary, and definitions of frequent discipline-specific terms usually provided in almost all introductory academic texts for first- or second-year students.

Incidental Learning and Noticing

In general terms, two types of vocabulary and grammar learning have been identified in research:

(1) **Intentional or explicit learning** that takes place through focused study.
(2) **Incidental learning**, when new vocabulary and grammar structures are "picked up" from exposure to and experience with language.

> A large number of research reports have established that typically, learners need at least ten or twelve repeated exposures (also called **spaced repetition**) to a word over time to learn it well and retain it.

To further complicate matters, several studies of adult L2 learners concluded that the long-term retention of words learned incidentally and through exposure in extensive reading can be particularly low (Brown, Waring, & Donkaewbua, 2008; Huang, Willson, & Eslami, 2012; Hulstijn, 2001; Laufer & Hulstijn, 2001; Pellicer-Sánchez & Schmitt, 2006; Webb, 2008).

On the whole, because L2 learning is determined by a number of complex factors, such as L1 literacy and culture, personal motivation and goals, as well as L1 and L2 similarities, the processes of L2 vocabulary and grammar learning have not been clearly understood (Schmitt, 2000; Webb & Nation, 2017). In all likelihood, an effective curriculum for L2 teaching relies on both explicit and implicit learning and incorporates a balanced amount of focused study and opportunities for exposure to academic language and text (Nation, 2013).

> There is little doubt that for incidental learning of academic vocabulary and grammar to occur, students have to have extensive exposure to academic reading with repeated uses of structures and words.

For instance, extensive reading can be carried out in class and out of class. But an important fact is that students need to be interested in the subject-matter to sustain the effort that reading the material often requires. Learning language through extensive reading requires students to work hard, concentrate, and memorize the new vocabulary. In the days when most forms of entertainment rely on visual media, such as social media, videos, and the Internet, the number of learners who read for pleasure has declined. As a result, a majority of readers, especially when they are reading in a L2, read for information.

To increase learners' motivation in extensive reading, the teacher may need to find out what types of subject-matter can be of particular use or interest to a specific group of students. For example, learners who plan to enroll as undergraduates in colleges and universities in English-speaking countries are required to take courses in disciplines that range from humanities to the sciences, and their exposure to useful vocabulary can be flexible. On the other hand, matriculated or graduate students may be more motivated if they read texts that deal with their chosen specialties rather than general education courses.[1]

One of the crucial features of effective learning is noticing words and grammar structures, their uses and meanings, and contexts in which they occur (R. Ellis, 2015, 2016; Laufer & Hulstijn, 2001; Pellicer-Sánchez, 2015). To learn different meanings that words and constructions may have in different contexts, learners need to pay attention to textual features as they read or write. For example, in written academic text, the modal verb *may* rarely has the meaning of permission as is described in most grammar books but usually has the function of a hedging device, as in **rain <u>may</u> occur in the evening**.

> The two greatest issues with noticing words and features that learners need to know are:
>
> - What specific language elements they should notice.
> - What about these elements requires attention.

- The teacher's job is to guide learners' attention and point out the important and necessary vocabulary and grammar constructions and then to discuss their uses and meanings in the academic text.
- The discussion of vocabulary items, subsequent to noticing, represents a highly productive activity for learning new words in reading.

Noticing forms of words and structures can take place while students listen and read, participate in activities, or look up words in a dictionary.

A Few Caveats

- To notice uses, meanings, and functions of words and grammar constructions, learners need to be aware of language as a complex system. For example, to be productive in the long run, working in context requires:
  - o Identifying nouns, verbs, prepositions, and adverbs.
  - o Noticing that sometimes, words or parts of words can have different syntactic properties and, therefore, play different roles in sentences.
- Noticing and identifying the functions of words and structures is a slow and laborious process.
- Deliberate attention to language affects a student's reading or listening speed.
- It takes away some of the enjoyment of reading because it removes attention from the context and information to focus it on the linguistic component parts.

In many cases, pre-teaching texts at the appropriate level of difficulty and providing word definitions as they occur in the text, as well as explaining the text's purpose, can simplify the learning tasks, particularly when the pre-reading (or pre-listening) activities are followed by a discussion or another focused activity.

For example, R. Ellis (2008) found that simple and short definitions that include only a few important characteristics of a word or structure lead to significant increases in vocabulary gains. Similarly, vocabulary learning from cards with L1 approximations is also effective when accompanied by a contextualized reading/activity in L2. In general, explicit vocabulary and grammar teaching can contribute directly to learners' development of implicit L2 knowledge (R. Ellis, 2002, 2015).

In grammar learning, becoming aware of how structures are used, combined with explicit teaching, can provide an additional benefit because learners can notice structures that they might otherwise simply miss. According to R. Ellis (2005, 2008), noticing and awareness play a particularly prominent role in developing accuracy in uses of structures and noticing errors.

- If learners notice correct uses of structures, they can then compare them to those they themselves produce and self-correct.
- Self-correction or editing are activities that undertake an analysis of errors that begin with noticing (James, 1998).
- Explanations of structure forms and their regularities further aid language learning, e.g. in English, subject–verb agreement is based on a system of regularities that is so complex that it requires teaching even to L1 writers. It may be unreasonable to expect that L2 learners be able to figure out the systematic intricacies that govern subject–verb agreement on their own.
- However, noticing combined with an explanation may help L2 writers improve their skills.

> When, guided by the teacher, learners are engaged in conscious noticing and learning, explicit teaching of vocabulary and grammar plays a crucial role.

For instance, carefully selected thematic writing tasks that require learners to employ specific vocabulary and grammar structures can lead to increased opportunities to revisit and practice what was learned or noticed earlier. Learners can be engaged in varied tasks to promote vocabulary gains and retention, and teachers can employ diverse attention-focusing techniques when designing classroom teaching activities.

Teaching Academic Discourse Structure

To some extent, the uses of specific linguistic features may depend on the discipline for which an assignment is written. Predictably, an essay in history, business case studies, or descriptions of experiments in psychology may contain a greater number of past tense verbs than a paper that discusses generally applicable observations and interpretations of research data. For example, most introductory textbooks in philosophy, sociology, economics, or biology include high numbers of present tense verbs.

Since the 1960s, an ever expanding body of work has come to elucidate a broad range of properties of L2 discourse and text, as well as regularities in the structure of L2 written prose. For instance, since the 1980s and 1990s, much has been learned about the structuring of ideas in written prose and the smaller, essential components of discourse, also called discourse moves. Numerous cross-cultural investigations in structuring discourse have also compared how ideas are organized and presented in various rhetorical traditions and learner writing (e.g. Grabe & Kaplan, 1996; Hinds, 1987; Hinkel, 2005, 2011, 2013; Leki, Cumming, & Silva, 2008; Scollon, Scollon, & Jones, 2012; Swales, 1990).

Virtually all studies to date have identified fundamental and pronounced differences between all facets of writing in L1 and L2 discourse and text. A large body of research has addressed a broad range of abstract rhetorical concepts:

- Discourse organization and information structuring.
- Topic appropriateness, development, and continuity.
- Types and arrangement of evidence.
- Text cohesion, coherence, clarity, and style.

These rhetorical properties of academic prose appear to be greatly influenced by discourse and text construction norms that can differ substantially across languages and cultures.

Many researchers have concluded that L2 written discourse paradigms are principally and strategically different from those found in L1 writing. In light of these crucial and profound differences, it stands to reason that instruction in constructing L2 written discourse cannot be derived from that developed for L1 writing pedagogy, that is, learning to write in a L2 is a process foundationally and substantively distinct from learning to write in a L1.

A large body of work has determined that English-language academic writing is governed by a number of rigid conventions in its discourse structure (Hinkel, 2011; Swales, 1990, 2004). These conventions are observed and marked by certain prescribed uses of language components, such as sentence constructions, phrases, and vocabulary.

Typically, instruction focuses on such central characteristics of formal academic writing as the discourse organization (e.g. introduction, body, conclusion, and other discourse moves), the presence and the placement of the thesis statement, the structure of the paragraph (e.g. the topic sentence), the rhetorical support for the thesis included in every paragraph, and an avoidance of needless digressions, repetition, and redundancy, among many other factors (Ferris, 2011; Scollon, Scollon, & Jones, 2012, van Dijk, 2010). A curriculum for teaching L2 writing has to focus learners' attention on these throughout the course of instruction (see chapter 12).

The reason that the discourse properties of academic writing can be difficult for most L2 students to learn is that they represent for the most part culturally bound and abstract characteristics of academic prose that are frequently absent in written discourse in rhetorical traditions other than the Anglo-American (Hinkel, 2014; Silva, 1997; Swales & Feak, 2012).

> What is appropriate and inappropriate in structuring academic written discourse in English is highly conventionalized and formulaic.

The summary of thousands of publications on discourse organization and text structuring skills is presented below. The greatest advantage of written discourse conventions and formulaic structure is that with the groundwork in place and with consistent practice, L2 writers can become relatively adept at the task.

Teaching Priorities in Discourse Organization Skills

Ongoing: Writing fluency, the development of ideas, examples, and illustrations.

➤ Introduction + The Thesis/Position Statement ~~

     o   To signal the structure, order, and flow of information/ideas.

➤ Conventionalized Discourse Organization ~~

     o   The structure, order, and flow of information/ ideas.

➤ Connectedness of Ideas and Cohesion ~~

     o   To the thesis and within paragraphs to the main points.

➤ Supporting Information, Ideas, and Facts ~~

     o   Related to the thesis and within each paragraph to the main point.

     o   Explicitly marked and stated.

- ➤ Major supporting points/arguments.
  - ○ Paragraphing: Division (coherence) and connectedness (cohesion).
  - ○ Cohesion and cohesive ties: Lexical – rephrased ideas, phrases, and words (two or three close synonyms); pronoun reference.
- ➤ Avoiding: digressions and repetitions.

- ➤ Conclusion/Closing statement(s).

Ongoing: Discourse-based Academic Vocabulary and Grammar ~~

- ➤ Conventionalized discourse-markers and phrases, e.g. **the purpose of this paper is to, this essay will discuss, the main point, to conclude.**
- ➤ Academic hedges, e.g. **often, usually, possibly, perhaps, may, seem, appear.**
- ➤ Grammar accuracy – sentence construction and word forms.
- ➤ Complex sentences with subordinate clauses.
- ➤ Editing and identifying errors.

Recurrent Lexical Phrases and Sentences Stems

Language instruction that has the goal of preparing students for academic studies in English-speaking countries needs to be designed to develop learners' practical and useful skills, directly relevant to producing academic text. For learners, becoming fluent and proficient in using vocabulary and grammar takes a great deal of time and work simply because the English grammar system is complex, and the number of words to be learned, retained, and practiced is enormous.

Teaching grammar for writing cannot take place in isolation from the lexical discourse properties of text, e.g. the verb tenses in academic prose are determined by the type of context in which they are used: the present tense is useful in citations of sources but not descriptions of case studies (Grabe & Kaplan, 1996; Ferris, 2011; Swales, 2004; Swales & Feak, 2012).

Most importantly, grammar instruction has to take place in tandem with instruction on vocabulary and recurrent academic phrases.

- In language uses of any kind, many words are combined in various patterns to create new meanings that cannot be predicted from the meaning of their component parts.
- Lexical phrases can be rigid and inflexible in their forms, or flexible with variable components.

Examples of Frequent Recurrent Phrases

a recent/new development	a wide/broad range	all in all/on the whole
based on/on the basis of	give a priority	give an example
give credit	give rise to	in general
in sum	make a decision	make a point
on the one hand	on the other hand	take into account

In language analyses, combinations of words that frequently occur and re-occur together are called **multiword units, lexical phrases, collocations, chunks, formulaic sequences, formulaic language, prefabricated constructions, lexical bundles**, and the like. These can be laborious to learn and use correctly because they consist of two or more component parts.

> To be sure, in any language, there are probably different ways to say something or convey a thought, but quite often even when the meanings of phrases can be transparent, "the problem is that native speakers do not say it in that way" (Shin & Nation, 2008, p. 340).

A great deal of research carried out on the effectiveness of learning grammar in contextual recurrent phrases and **sentence stems**, that is, whole sentences and phrases, and pre-patterned expressions, has shown that these are indispensable in both L1 and L2 learning and use (Cowie, 1992; N. Ellis, 1997; Hinkel, 2015, 2019; Nattinger & DeCarrico, 1992; Pawley & Syder, 1983; Shin & Nation, 2008; Simpson-Vlach & Ellis, 2010).

> In general, all writers of prose in any genre have stock expressions that are used repeatedly and that are not their own invention (Graff, Birkenstein, & Durst, 2018). Many formulaic markers of discourse moves are encountered so frequently that they usually go unnoticed.

Stock lexical phrases can become an efficient means of expanding L2 writers' language range, particularly when learners are also taught how to substitute discrete elements in practical ways.[2] For example, the fact that the function of noun clauses is similar to that of simple nouns can be addressed by means of substitutions in patterned expressions common in academic prose:

The experiment/data/study shows that ~~~
    ~~~ xxx increases(with yyy)/an increase of xxx/the growth/rise of xxx.

> As Wilkins (1972, p. 102) comments, learning a L2 in lexical and grammatical units (chunks), instead of discrete words or word elements, can often "cover in half the time what is . . . expected from a whole year language learning."

According to N. Ellis (1997, pp. 129–130), language chunks can consist of entire memorized sentences or phrases that include from four to ten words. Pre-patterned phrases can allow learners to create new constructions to add to their stock of academic language. For learners, commonly occurring sentences, clauses, and phrases can be "viewed as big words" and memorized as lexicalized stems. Preconstructed phrases and sentences can be called "institutionalized" because they occur more frequently in certain types of discourse than in others (Pawley & Syder, 1983).

Many adults can recite L1 or L2 poems or texts that they learned several decades earlier, and there is little reason to doubt that L2 learners are quite capable of similar feats in their L2 writing.

Key Advantages

Language instruction almost always takes place under great time constraints for many teachers and learners, and it is important to maximize language gains and make learning as efficient as possible. There are five key advantages:

(1) Using recurrent phrases in instruction and learning to write is likely to be one of the few available expedient routes to relative L2 accuracy and fluency that leads to production and subsequent automatization.

(2) For language learners, a tremendous advantage of working with constructions lies in expedited learning and reduced work load in the long run. For example, high-frequency and recurrent word combinations, phrases, and expressions can be learned as whole units, instead of just their elements that have to be further assembled during the process of language production.

(3) Differences and similarities between phrases allow learners to create new constructions in various combinations or to modify those that are already learned and accessible.

(4) For L2 learners and academic writers, common or frequently repeated problem areas, say, with articles and prepositional phrases, or sentence fragments (incomplete sentences), can also be relatively easily avoided, if these are dealt with as whole units, instead of being incrementally assembled.

(5) In language teaching, a very efficient perspective is to look at grammar and vocabulary as a continuum of constructions, from the highly systematic and regular (e.g. 3rd person singular verbs) to the much more fixed, such as collocations, or idioms, e.g. *change direction, a new direction, a big/ extensive/dramatic change, a shift from/to, innovative/product/method/ process, this evidence sheds a great deal of light on.*

In language teaching, recurrent phrases can be used with language elements of all shapes and sizes, from single words (*few/a few*, *little/a little*) to phrases to whole sentences or even sets of sentences, including the perennial areas of difficulty, such as idioms and metaphors, e.g.:

- *find ~~ out/a way/success/value/interesting/hard/time/a minute/ words/solution.*
- *In this paper, I/we report on/discuss xxx.*
- *In the past two decades, xxx has been studied by many researchers/ economists.*
- *The main points of xxx are . . .*
- *The author states that . . .*
- *The articles also explains that . . .*

To some extent, the uses of specific language features may depend on the discipline and context in which spoken or written text is produced. Predictably, for example, business case studies, reports in biology or chemistry, or descriptions of experiments in psychology may contain a higher number of past tense verbs than a paper that discusses generally applicable observations. Moreover, most introductory textbooks in philosophy, the social sciences, economics, or communications include high numbers of present tense verbs (Nation, 2013; Swales, 1990, 2004).

However, despite some amount of variation that can be noted in texts across disciplines, recurrent attributes of L2 and academic prose have been well researched and established (Martinez & Schmitt, 2012; Nation, 2011; Nation & Webb, 2011). Other studies of L2 and academic text have identified a range of vocabulary and grammar components that require focused instruction and concerted effort from both teachers and learners (Nation, 2009, 2013).

Among the most urgent language features that require persistent and intensive instruction, the following are a top priority. All these can be taught and learned in conjunction with the lexicalized phrases and sentence stems.

Top Priorities: Teaching Language, Lexical Phrases, and Sentence Stems

- The sentence and phrase structure, and sentence constructing skills (chapter 4).
- Subordinate clauses for background information, e.g. **Although xxx, yyy,** or **The article explains that . . .**
- Functions and uses of verb tenses in context and discourse, e.g. the citational or historical present, as in **Smith (2025) stateS/findS/noteS/The study reportS.**
- Functions and uses of passive phrases in academic prose, e.g. **this issue has been examined/the problem/cause of xxx is discussed/presented/ addressed.**
- Functions of adverbs to mark discourse organization, e.g. **in addition, as a result, for this reason, as well (as), at the same time, to begin, at the outset.**
- Functions and uses of hedging devices in academic prose, e.g. **usually/ typically/by and large, occasionally/periodically/in some cases.**

Although at first glance teaching the features of academic discourse and text may seem somewhat overwhelming, the fact that academic prose is highly formulaic and conventionalized provides a considerable benefit. When the stock pre-patterned phrases and sentence components are in place – with practice – producing solid academic prose in both speech and writing becomes a learned skill. This is true about both L2 and L1 writers who learn formal speaking and writing in the course of their schooling and education. (A comprehensive list of recurrent phrases and sentence stems for academic speaking and writing can be found in Appendices A and B to this book.)

Throughout this book, appendices at the end of most chapters include stock lexicalized sentence stems and phrases that can be very effective and efficient in teaching skeletal elements in academic writing.

Talking Shop

Nearly 2 million US high school graduates took the ACT test in 2018, 55% of the entire graduating class. Every year, ACT reports the national scores in the four subject tests: English, Mathematics, Reading, and Science.

In late 2016, a subset of narrower Reporting Categories has been added within each of the four reported broad subject-area scores to provide for rubric-centered and more detailed breakdowns of the major scores. The purpose of the detailed within-score Reporting Categories is to identify the rubric components used to score the subject area tests in accordance with the ACT College Readiness Standards. The ACT statement explains that the Reporting Categories are designed to measure test takers' abilities in applying their knowledge and skills in the specific skill sub-area.

The ACT Three Reporting Categories: English

(1) Production of writing: Topic development, organization, unity, and cohesion.
(2) Knowledge of language.
(3) Conventions of Standard English.

In the 2019 report, the ACT National Profile, Graduating Class 2018, the English reporting categories presented the following scores:

The ACT 2018 Scores in English Reporting Categories

- Production of writing – 57%.
- Knowledge of language – 61%.
- Conventions of Standard English – 58%.

(www.act.org/content/dam/act/unsecured/documents/cccr2018/P_99_999999_N_S_N00_ACT-GCPR_National.pdf)

Teaching L2 Writers to Edit Their Text

Editing one's own text and learning to identify mistakes is notoriously difficult even for advanced L2 academic writers. Causes of errors can be numerous and may be an outcome of first-language transfer, incomplete understanding of word meanings or syntactic rules, or casual mistakes. In addition, in different grammar and vocabulary contexts, seemingly similar types of errors can have a variety of causes, e.g. a lack of subject and verb agreement can be an outcome of mis-identifying the subject noun phrase, confusing count and non-count nouns (see chapter 5), or simply omitting the inflection marker *-s* with either a noun or a verb. For instance, James (1998, p. 97) refers to "dictionaries of errors," and then there is a 350-page volume published by Cambridge University Press that is devoted to descriptions, analyses, and corrections of errors made by speakers of about 20 languages.

Figuring out the causes of errors may not be particularly useful because they can be highly numerous. However, for academic writers, learning to identify and correct their own errors is essential. In composition and writing instruction, **peer editing** is often employed with the stated learning goal of providing student writers a more realistic audience than only the instructor, developing learners' editing skills, and establishing a social context for writing. However, peer editing (also called **peer response**), as a technique for teaching writing, was originally created for L1 college writers who are probably more socially and culturally open to the idea of reading and responding to their classmates' writing.

Although some researchers of L2 writing believe that the benefits of peer editing outweigh the disadvantages and that peer response to writing can be made effective when used with care, others have voiced concerns about the effectiveness of this technique among various cultural groups (Grabe & Kaplan, 1996; Ferris, 2009; Tsui & Ng, 2000).

In L2 writing instruction, teacher feedback on errors, however, does seem to be effective. In fact, a scholarly *Journal of Response to Writing* publishes two issues annually, in addition to numerous books, handbooks, articles, guidelines, and professional materials in research. The areas of study include written feedback to student writers, teacher education, teaching methods and techniques, types of effective or less effective written error correction, guided self-assessment, self-editing, learning analyses, and writing feedback in academic disciplines for both undergraduate and graduate writers. In short, working with written errors, corrective feedback, responding to writing, and response contexts have a prolific research agenda.

> Teaching L2 writers to become independent self-editors represents a crucial component of writing instruction.

Some approaches to teaching L2 writing advocate text-level editing only at the final stage of writing, after discourse organization and content are attended to. On the other hand, because the ultimate objective of editing instruction is to teach essential self-editing skills, these can be useful for the duration of L2 writers' academic careers. Working on vocabulary and grammar errors can take place at any point of essay development.

- Self-editing instruction can proceed in stages and be selective.
- The initial objective is to raise students' awareness of ubiquitous and manageable errors, as well as promote noticing skills.
- Editing exercises can begin with texts that are not students' own and that contain limited and controlled types of errors.
- Both research and experience have shown that explanations of how particular structures can be used in context and typical errors that occur with these structures may need to be persistent to be effective.

> At the outset, it is reasonable and manageable to begin self-editing work on four to six types of errors, depending on their complexity, e.g. countable and uncountable nouns, singular and plural noun choices, repetitive uses of frequent nouns, present and past tenses, unmarked tense shifts, irregular verbs.

Error exercises of the first group of errors can be assigned as homework and followed up by an explicit in-class analysis and discussion, either in small groups or as a whole class. Explanations of erroneous structures and their correct uses contribute to overall instructional input in L2 learning (R. Ellis, 2005, 2015; James, 1998). Editing exercises assigned as homework or for in-class practice can be expanded to errors in contexts that are immediately applicable to students' own errors in writing. Most teachers usually note the specific structures or discourse features that require additional attention when they read and mark students' writing.

> One of the most important aspects of effective and productive error correction is that it has to be directly relevant, timely, and applicable to students' own writing.

Editing students' own errors can begin in tandem with editing exercises. Ideally, the types of errors in exercises should match those addressed in the teacher's marking and correction.

- At the beginning of instruction, writing assignments can be based on two drafts.
- Then later, as the students' skills improve, only one draft of writing assignments should be evaluated, similar to the assignments in college and university courses.
- A gradual increase in students' responsibility for the quality of their writing throughout the course usually leads to considerable learning benefits when students are required to pay close attention to language and editing.

Steps in Teaching Self-Editing Skills

The First Writing Task

- In the first draft of the first assignment, the teacher should correct all errors of the selected types practiced in the exercises.
- In the second – and final – draft, the teacher highlights all remaining errors of these types and corrects many.

The Second Task

- In next assignment, the teacher should correct only some errors of these types in the first draft and underline other errors of these same types, with explicit instructions that the student needs to correct the underlined structures.
- In the second – and final – draft, the teacher should correct only the most complex occurrences of these types of errors, and the responsibility for the rest needs to be shifted from the teacher to the student.

> It is vital that the first group of error types not be abandoned when editing practice on the second group of errors begins. The work on error correction is typically cumulative.

- When practice exercises on the second group of errors begin, the teacher should not correct the errors from the first group, except in rare cases of complex constructions, but underline or highlight them in student writing, as they occur. Teacher corrections should be limited to the second group of error types, as in Step 1.

The Third Task

- When working on the third assignment, the first group of errors should become fully a student's responsibility. The types of errors in editing exercises can be expanded to the next group of four to six types.
- Again, in the first piece of writing that takes place during the work on the second group of errors, the teacher should correct all occurrences, and highlight them in subsequent student writing (see Step 2), and the cycle is repeated.

Throughout instruction, it is very important that the teacher be consistent in correcting, underlining, or highlighting, and shifting the responsibility for editing errors to students (Ellis, 2015; Hinkel, 2015). By the end of the course, it is reasonable to expect students to notice and correct 20 to 40 common types of errors in their own writing.

Some examples of the grouped error types can include, beginning with the most accessible:

The Essentials and the Basics

- Non-count academic nouns, e.g. **education, equipment, information, knowledge**.
- Frequent quantifiers, e.g. **few/a few, little/a little**. Academic quantifiers with non-count nouns, e.g. **a great deal of/much knowledge/traffic**.
- Subject–verb agreement – with or without quantifiers, e.g. **some/many books** + plural verb or **some/much information** + singular verb.
- Subject noun + prepositional phrase and verb agreement, e.g.

    - *The researcher <u>with</u> two assistants investigate<u>S</u> . . .*
    - *The researcher <u>and</u> two assistants investigate<u>Ø</u> . . .*

- Compound noun phrases, e.g.

    - *taxØ rate(s), courseØ schedule(s), groupØ type(s), populationØ increase(s), researchØ plan(s)*
    - *A five-credit-hourØ university composition course(s).*
    - *A twenty-five-yearØ old **student(s)**, but the student is twenty-five **years** old.*

Beyond the Basics

- Word order in noun and adjective clauses, e.g.

    - *The authors state <u>that they know which way the wind is blowing</u>.*
    - *It is not clear <u>whether the price will rise</u>.*
    - *The lab <u>where the research takes place</u> is located in Pennsylvania.*

- Word order in **how-** noun clauses, e.g.

    - *The scientists described <u>how they identified the virus</u>.*
    - *The scale was used to measure <u>how much the minerals weighed</u>.*

- Word order with adverbs of manner, time, and indefinite frequency, e.g.

    - *Stock market buyers need to (<u>carefully</u>) consider the prices <u>carefully</u>.*
    - *<u>Usually</u>, car mileage (<u>usually</u>) depends on the size of its engine.*

- The placement **also** and **even**, e.g.

    - *(<u>Also</u>) Pizza consumption has (<u>also/even</u>) shown a steady growth.*
    - *(<u>Also</u>) Pizzeria owners and managers can (<u>also/even</u>) participate in pizza skills competitions (also).*

- The placement and uses of **enough**, e.g.

    - *Based on the consumption numbers, Americans cannot get their pizzas fast <u>enough</u>.*
    - *The project was not funded well <u>enough</u> to complete the experiment.*
    - *high <u>enough</u>, <u>enough</u> time/funds, <u>enough</u> of that/them*

- Optional: the placement and uses of **almost, almost + enough**, e.g.

    - *almost + enough time/funds, almost never, almost the same, almost finished*
    - *almost + every (+ noun)*

- Quantifiers with prepositional phrases, e.g.

  - *some/many/most managers*
  - *Some/Many/Most of the managers in the accounting department.*
  - *most* as an adverb, e.g. *The stock price of tech companies grew the most in 2020.*

L2 writers may not be able to identify and correct all errors addressed in instruction no matter how much effort and time during one or two L2 writing courses is devoted to the task. Teaching learners to edit their writing independently does not have the goal of making their writing error-free, nor could it. It is crucial for both teachers and students to set realistic expectations of noticeable improvement in grammatical accuracy.

> The purpose of self-editing instruction and error correction is not the elimination of errors, but error reduction and improvement.

What Not to Teach, or What to "Un"-Teach

Research has established that colloquial and conversational vocabulary and grammar constructions are prevalent in L2 academic prose because many L2 writers have far more exposure to conversational discourse than they do to standard and formal writing. Frequently, however, L2 writers may not be aware, for example, that such vocabulary as **huge, dude, stuff, guy, thing**, or **cool**, or constructions such as **this paper doesn't prove anything**, are inappropriate in academic writing.

Numerous studies have demonstrated that the distinctions between academic and conversational language need to be emphasized throughout the teaching of formal writing at any level (e.g. Chang & Swales, 1999; Hinkel, 2002, 2011, 2015; Horowitz, 1986; Leedham, 2016; Leki, Cumming, & Silva, 2008; Schleppegrell, 2004). However, an additional reason that colloquialisms are typically found in L2 academic prose is that L2 writers simply lack the vocabulary and grammar essential for producing written academic text.

Vocabulary and grammar constructions outlined below rarely occur in academic writing and need to be "un-taught." That is, students need to be taught specifically not to use these features in their academic writing. Alternative and more academic vocabulary grammar have to be taught.

Conversational Vocabulary and Grammar Constructions That Need NOT Be Taught

Top Priorities

Vocabulary

- Indeterminate and vague nouns, e.g. *human(s)*, *human being(s)*, *people*, *society*, *stuff*, *thing(y)*, *world*, *-ever* nouns, as in *whoever*, *whatever*.
- Tentative verbs, e.g. *like*, *plan*, *try*, *want*.
- Mental process verbs that rarely occur in formal and informational texts, e.g. *believe*, *feel*, *forget*, *guess*, *hear*, *know*, *learn*, *love*, *prove*, *remember*, *see*, *think*.
- Phrase conjunctions, *and*, *or*, *but*.
- Repeated and simplistic sentence transitions, e.g. *first(-ly)*, *second(-ly)*, *third(-ly)*, *mainly*, *basically*, *finally*.

Grammar

- First and second person pronouns and contexts that require their uses, e.g. personal narratives/examples/experiences, in lieu of rhetorical support.

Second Priorities

Vocabulary

- Intensifiers and emphatics of any type, e.g. *absolutely*, *a lot*, *complete(-ly)*, *deeply*, *for sure*, *hugely*, *total(-ly)* or *I do agree that this method is better*.
- Indefinite nouns and pronouns, e.g. *everyone*, *no one*, *nothing*, *anyone*, *some*, *something*.

Grammar

- *Be* as a main verb with predicative adjectives, e.g. *Students are diligent, and they are always busy*.
- Modals of obligation, *must*, *have to*.
- Contractions, *don't*, *can't*, *won't*.

Third Priorities

Grammar

- Future tense verb uses, e.g. *the income of these people is going to/will rise if they get education.*
- Progressive verb uses, e.g. *I am explaining my point of view clearly.*
- Rhetorical questions, e.g. *Do you know what the purpose of life is? Why doesn't he help the people that he is researching?*
- Cause constructions, very rare in academic prose, e.g. *because, because of.*
- *by*-phrase passives, e.g. *the depth is determined by the technician during the experiment.*

Needs Analysis

To date, a vast body of research has identified the prevalent properties of L2 academic writing and text. However, students are different in each class, and so are their language learning needs. For this reason, identifying the linguistic and discourse features that need to be taught to a particular group of students represents an important starting point when developing L2 academic writing courses.

A teacher may choose to analyze diagnostic essays that can be very useful in at least the initial course planning. Although the writing of different students may include a broad range of issues that can benefit from instruction, it is usually not difficult to identify commonalities.

Realistic Teaching Goals

- Not every issue in student writing needs to be addressed in teaching, just the important ones.
- Problems in student writing can be broadly similar but not necessarily identical.
- If the writing of most (or even several) students exhibits a specific problem (e.g. sentence fragments, countable/uncountable nouns, or conversational language), then it should be explicitly addressed.
- A flexible course plan can be amended when the teacher concludes that (further) instruction is not needed.

Generally, the following aspects of L2 academic writing need at least some degree of polishing and additional work in practically all instruction:

- Academic vocabulary and, specifically, nouns and verbs.
- Sentence boundaries and phrase construction.
- Verb tenses and conventions in academic discourse.
- The forms and functions of the passive voice.
- Noun clauses.
- Hedging broad generalizations and strong claims.
- Cohesion devices – other than sentence transitions.

A Final Note

One of the crucial issues in L2 learning is that most of it cannot take place in the classroom because learning the language well enough to be able to write academic papers requires a great deal more work than can be done in class. Hence, if learners are seriously motivated, the greatest portion of the work that, in fact, represents language learning has to be done out of class. The learning of many L2 academic skills, such as writing, reading, vocabulary, and essay editing, is largely a solitary activity.

On the other hand, if students approach L2 learning as being engaged in interactive and social classroom activities, their conversational listening and speaking skills may improve dramatically, but attaining L2 proficiency sufficient to write academic papers may continue to be a remote objective.

> Unfortunately, to date, a method of L2 learning well at school or in college that is more effective than memorizing and practicing vocabulary, practicing grammar structures in writing, producing large amounts of academic writing, and improving one's self-editing skills, has not been invented.

Students' motivation to study and learn usually increases markedly if the teacher explains that L2 learning takes a great deal of hard work and persistence, and there are few ways known to humanity of how to make it either easier or quicker.

When a teacher develops a course of study, it is very helpful to explain it because if learners understand the direction of the course and the incremental means of attaining its objectives, they are able to take the responsibility for their own learning.

- It is important for students to be informed of weekly and daily learning objectives, as the course moves along its path.
- These explanations do not need to be detailed or justified by research, but they need to be grounded in students' own learning and academic goals.

Chapter Summary

A great deal of research on L2 vocabulary learning carried out in the past several decades points to a direct connection between an improvement in learners' vocabulary base and range and the quality of their academic writing. While much vocabulary instruction focuses on reading as a means of helping learners to expand their vocabulary range, numerous studies have shown L2 vocabulary learning is different from the acquisition of L1 vocabulary from reading. Teaching reading in order to encounter essential academic vocabulary can be inefficient and sometimes ineffective because the vocabulary that students must know simply does not occur frequently enough to be learned from mere exposure to L2 text.

- Explicit teaching and extensive grammar practice lead to marked improvements in L2 productive skills, that is, speaking and writing.
- One of the most practical and efficient approaches to teaching formal grammar entails learning frequent recurrent academic phrases and sentence stems with suitable replacements of their component parts.
- For the vast majority of L2 academic writers, intensive and concerted effort in learning essential academic vocabulary is key to successful academic writing.
- Incidental learning of vocabulary and grammar can supplement – but does not replace – intensive and focused vocabulary learning by means of vocabulary and sentence-stem memorization and practice.
- Independent self-editing skills require much training and practice (and practice and practice).
- In addition to determining what should be taught in L2 writing, research has also identified vocabulary and grammar that represent a low return on investment of teachers' and students' effort and time.
- A course curriculum that is rooted in L2 proficiency goals can increase motivation, when the goals are explicitly articulated in terms of learners' own language learning needs for success in their academic studies.

Endnotes

1 It is important to keep in mind that what is of interest to the teacher may not be to the students. Most experienced instructors know that political events, elections, controversies, or issues of the moment, hotly debated in the location where students study, can actually be of little relevance to a majority of L2 students, who can be new to their geographical region or community.

2 In addition to many other vocabulary researchers, Peters (1983, p. 109) points out that despite the linguistic and psycholinguistic evidence that memorizing language chunks represents an effective and unrestrictive means of expanding learners' lexical and grammatical ranges, a cultural and "pedagogical bias" exists against the idea of memorization of long chunks of text.

Further Reading

Cowie, A. (1998). *Phraseology: Theory, analysis, and applications.* Oxford: Oxford University Press.

An established and acclaimed collection of articles on the foundational phraseology in language usage and comprehension. The authoritative contributions examine the crucial role played by ready-made word combinations in language acquisition and adult language use. This is the first comprehensive account of the subject to be published following decades of study. Following an introductory overview, the chapters provide a guide to phraseology for linguists and language teachers.

Hinkel, E. (2015). *Effective curriculum for teaching L2 writing: Principles and techniques.* New York, NY: Routledge.

The book outlines a big picture for curricular thinking about teaching L2 writing and designing courses as efficiently as possible. The material connects curriculum, writing instruction, and language building, and offers a step-by-step guide to curriculum design for teaching second language writing, with practical examples and illustrations. The central premise is that writing and language instruction need to be integrated, based on a clear understanding of the writing needs of academic writers, and that principled and language-focused curricula are necessary to guide this endeavor.

Nattinger, J. & DeCarrico, J. (1992). *Lexical phrases and language teaching.* Oxford: Oxford University Press.

A well-known and an award-winning book on teaching, learning, and using lexical phrases in a range of discourse types. Research and discourse analyses show that units of language serve as an effective basis for both second and foreign language learning. In speaking and writing, important and common lexical phrases are a must for language users – they are essential in text coherence.

References

Batstone, R. & Ellis, R. (2009). Principled grammar teaching. *System, 37*, 194–204.

Brown, R., Waring, R., & Donkaewbua, S. (2008). Incidental vocabulary acquisition from reading, reading-while-listening, and listening to stories. *Reading in a Foreign Language, 20*(2), 136–163.

Chang, Y. & Swales, J. (1999). Informal elements in English academic writing: Threats or opportunities for advanced non-native speakers. In C. Candlin & K. Hyland (Eds.), *Writing texts, processes and practices* (pp. 145–167). London: Longman.

Cowie, A. (1992). Multiword lexical units and communicative language teaching. In P. Arnaud & H. Bejoint (Eds.), *Vocabulary and applied linguistics* (pp. 1–12). London: Macmillan.

Darling-Hammond, L. (2015). *The flat world and education: How America's commitment to equity will determine our future.* New York, NY: Teachers College Press.

Ellis, N. (1997). Vocabulary acquisition: word structure, collocation, word-class, and meaning. In N. Schmitt & M. McCarthy (Eds.), *Vocabulary: Description, acquisition, and pedagogy* (pp. 122–139). Cambridge: Cambridge University Press.

Ellis, R. (2002). The place of grammar instruction in the second/foreign language curriculum. In E. Hinkel & S. Fotos (Eds.), *New perspectives on grammar teaching in second language classrooms* (pp. 17–35). New York, NY: Routledge.

Ellis, R. (2005). Measuring implicit and explicit knowledge of a second language: A psychometric study. *Studies in Second Language Acquisition, 27*, 141–172.

Ellis, R. (2008). *The study of second language acquisition* (2nd edn). Oxford: Oxford University Press.

Ellis, R. (2015). *Understanding second language acquisition* (2nd edn). Oxford: Oxford University Press.

Ellis, R. (2016). Grammar teaching as consciousness raising. In E. Hinkel (Ed.), *Teaching English grammar to speakers of other languages* (pp. 128–148). New York, NY: Routledge.

Ferris, D. (2009). *Teaching college writing to diverse student populations.* Ann Arbor, MI: University of Michigan Press.

Ferris, D. (2011). Written discourse analysis and second language teaching. In E. Hinkel (Ed.), *Handbook of research in second language teaching and learning* (pp. 645–662). New York, NY: Routledge.

Ferris, D. (2014). Responding to student writing: Teachers' philosophies and practices. *Assessing Writing, 19*(1), 6–23.

Fries, C. (1945). *Teaching & learning English as a foreign language.* Ann Arbor, MI: University of Michigan Press.

Gibbons, P. (2014). *Scaffolding language, scaffolding learning: Teaching English language learners in the mainstream classroom* (2nd edn). Portsmouth: Heinemann.

Grabe, W. & Kaplan, R. B. (1996). *Theory and practice of writing.* London: Longman.

Graff, G., Birkenstein, C, & Durst, R. (2018). *They say/I Say: The moves that matter in academic writing* (4th edn). New York, NY: Norton.

Hammerly, H. (1991). *Fluency and accuracy*. Clevedon: Multilingual Matters.

Hinds, J. (1987). Reader versus writer responsibility: A new typology. In U. Connor & R.B. Kaplan (Eds.), *Writing across languages: Analysis of L2 text* (pp. 141–152). Reading, MA: Addison-Wesley.

Hinkel, E. (2002). *Second language writers' text*. New York, NY: Routledge.

Hinkel, E. (2005). Analyses of L2 text and what can be learned from them. In E. Hinkel (Ed.), *Handbook of research in second language teaching and learning* (pp. 615–628). New York, NY: Routledge.

Hinkel, E. (2011). What research on second language writing tells us and what it doesn't. In E. Hinkel (Ed.), *Handbook of research in second language teaching and learning* (pp. 523–538). New York, NY: Routledge.

Hinkel, E. (2013). Research findings on teaching grammar for academic writing. *English Teaching, 68*(4), 3–21.

Hinkel, E. (2014). Cultures of learning and writing in the US academy. In M. Cortazzi & L. Jin (Eds.), *Researching intercultural learning: Investigations in language and education* (pp. 21–35). London: Palgrave Macmillan.

Hinkel, E. (2015). *Effective curriculum for teaching L2 writing: Principles and techniques*. New York, NY: Routledge.

Hinkel, E. (2016). Practical grammar teaching: Grammar constructions and their relatives. In E. Hinkel, (Ed.), *Teaching English grammar to speakers of other languages* (pp. 171–191). New York, NY: Routledge.

Hinkel, E. (2017). Prioritizing grammar to teach or not to teach: A research perspective. In E. Hinkel (Ed.), *Handbook of research in second language teaching and learning* (pp. 369–383). New York, NY: Routledge.

Hinkel, E. (2019). Teaching strategies and techniques: Collocations and multiword units. In E. Hinkel (Ed.), *Teaching essential units of language: Beyond single-word vocabulary* (pp. 107–133). New York, NY: Routledge.

Horowitz, D. (1986). What professors actually require: Academic tasks for the ESL classroom. *TESOL Quarterly, 20*, 445–462.

Huang, S., Willson, V., & Eslami, Z. (2012). The effects of task involvement load on L2 incidental vocabulary learning: A meta-analytic study. *Modern Language Journal, 96*(4), 544–557.

Hulstijn, J. (2001). Intentional and incidental second language vocabulary learning: A reappraisal of elaboration, rehearsal and automaticity. In P. Robinson (Ed.), *Cognition and second language instruction* (pp. 258–286). Cambridge: Cambridge University Press.

James, C. (1998). *Errors in language learning and use*. London: Longman.

Larsen-Freeman, D. (2015). Research into practice: Grammar learning and teaching. *Language Teaching, 48*, 363–380.

Larsen-Freeman, D. & Celce-Murcia, M. (2016). *The grammar book: An ESL/EFL teacher's course* (3rd edn). Boston, MA: National Geographic/Cengage.

Laufer, B. & Hulstijn, J. (2001). Incidental vocabulary acquisition in a second language: The construct of task-induced involvement. *Applied Linguistics, 22*(1), 1–26.

Leedham, M. (2016). *Chinese students' writing in English: Implications from a corpus-driven study*. London: Routledge.

Leki, I., Cumming, A. & Silva, T. (2008). *A synthesis of research on second language writing in English*. New York, NY: Routledge.

Martinez, R. & Schmitt, N. (2012). A phrasal expressions list. *Applied Linguistics, 33*(3), 299–320.

Nation, I.S.P. (2009). *Teaching ESL/EFL reading and writing*. New York, NY: Routledge.

Nation, P. (2011). Research into practice: Vocabulary. *Language Teaching, 44*, 529–539.

Nation, P. (2013). *Learning vocabulary in another language* (2nd edn). Cambridge: Cambridge University Press.

Nation, P. & Webb, S. (2011). Content-based instruction and vocabulary learning. In E. Hinkel (Ed.), *Handbook of research in second language teaching and learning, Volume 2* (pp. 631–644). New York, NY: Routledge.

Nattinger, J. & DeCarrico, J. (1992). *Lexical phrases and language teaching*. Oxford: Oxford University Press.

Pawley, A. & Syder, F. (1983). Two puzzles for linguistic theory: Nativelike selection and nativelike fluency. In J. Richards and R. Schmidt (Ed.), *Language and communication* (pp. 191–225). London: Longman.

Pellicer-Sánchez, A. (2015). Incidental L2 vocabulary acquisition form and while reading. *Studies in Second Language Acquisition, 31*(1), 1–34.

Pellicer-Sánchez, A. & Schmitt, N. (2006). Incidental vocabulary acquisition from an authentic novel: Do things fall apart? *Reading in a Foreign Language, 22*(1), 31–55.

Peters, E. (2016) The learning burden of collocations: The role of interlexical and intralexical factors. *Language Teaching Research, 20*(1), 113–138.

Schleppegrell, M. (2004). *The language of schooling*. New York, NY: Routledge.

Schmitt, N. (2000). *Vocabulary in language teaching*. Cambridge: Cambridge University Press.

Scollon, R., Scollon, S., & Jones, R. (2012). *Intercultural communication* (3rd edn). London: Blackwell.

Shin, D. & Nation, P. (2008). Beyond single words: The most frequent collocations in spoken English. *English Language Teaching Journal, 62*(4), 339–348.

Shaw, P. & Liu, E. (1998). What develops in the development of second language writing? *Applied Linguistics, 19*(2), 225–254.

Silva, T. (1997). On the ethical treatment of ESL writers. *TESOL Quarterly, 31*(2), 359–363.

Simpson-Vlach, R. & Ellis, N. (2010). An academic formulas list: New methods in phraseology research. *Applied Linguistics, 31*(4), 487–512.

Swales, J. (1990). *Genre analysis*. Cambridge: Cambridge University Press.

Swales, J. (2004). *Research genres: Explorations and applications*. Cambridge: Cambridge University Press.

Swales, J. & Feak, C. (2012). *Academic writing for graduate students* (3rd edn). Ann Arbor, MI: University of Michigan Press.

Tsui, A. & Ng, M. (2000). Do secondary L2 writers benefit from peer comments? *Journal of Second Language Writing, 9*(2), 147–170.

Ur, P. (2011). Grammar teaching: Research, theory, and practice. In: E. Hinkel (Ed.), *Handbook of research in second language teaching and learning* (pp. 507–522). New York, NY: Routledge.

Ur, P. (2013). Language-teaching method revisited. *ELT Journal, 67*(4), 468–474.

van Dijk, T. (2010). *Discourse and context*. Cambridge: Cambridge University Press.

Webb, S. (2008). The effects of context on incidental vocabulary learning. *Reading in a Foreign Language, 20*(2), 232–245.

Webb, S. & Nation, P. (2017). *How vocabulary is learned*. Oxford: Oxford University Press.

Wilkins, D. (1972). *Linguistics in language teaching*. London: Edward Arnold.

Part II

Sentences and Their Parts
Vocabulary and Grammar

The chapters in Part II cover the core information for teaching English sentence and text construction.

- The useful and practical sentence slot technique for teaching the regularities of English sentences and their elements is introduced in chapter 4. Sentence slots are highly helpful for L2 writers to efficiently improve their writing.
- The major components that fill the slots in sentences, how they are used, and how they can be effectively taught are discussed in chapters 5–9.
- Nouns, noun phrases, and pronouns are covered in chapters 5 and 6.
- Verb tenses and voice, and lexical classes and functions of verbs, are addressed in chapters 7 and 8.
- The types and functions of adjectives and adverbs, as well as adjective and adverb phrases, in academic writing are presented in chapter 9.

Sentences, Phrases, and Text Construction

4

Overview

- Rigid and mobile sentence elements.
- The order of elements in the noun phrase.
- The order of elements in the verb phrase.
- Transitive and intransitive verbs.
- Compound sentences.
- Common errors in sentence construction.

The structure of a basic English sentence is relatively easy to teach because English has rigid word order, e.g. the subject is followed by a verb, which is followed by an object. Although many variations of this skeletal structure are possible, the additions also adhere to somewhat inflexible patterns. For example, a prepositional phrase cannot be a sentence subject: only noun phrases can, and a verb must be present in every sentence for it to be grammatical. In this case, the structure *For most students go to the US to study* is incorrect because a prepositional phrase occupies the subject position.

The simplest approach to teaching basic sentence structure can take advantage of the relative rigidity of English sentence structure. An example of a basic sentence structure can consist of the following:

(1) An optional adverb/prepositional phrase.
(2) A subject noun or noun phrase.
(3) A verb.
(4) An object if the main verb is transitive, that is, it requires a direct object.

The essential sentence elements and their positions relative to one another are sometimes called <u>slots</u>, and in many sentences, some slots can be empty, e.g. the object slot is not filled if the verb is intransitive (does not require an object).

> In English sentences, **the verb phrase is required for all sentences to be grammatical**. The subject slot can be empty only in the case of imperatives (commands), e.g. *Ø close the door.*

The approach to teaching sentence- and phrase-structure systems of English described below does not place a great deal of emphasis on conveying a particular meaning. Rather, students can be taught to use the regularities and the rigid order of sentence and phrase elements to increase their grammatical accuracy. For academic L2 learners, a reasonable degree of grammatical accuracy represents a crucial factor in their academic, professional, and social opportunities (Celce-Murcia, 1993; Fries, 1945; Hammerly, 1991; Hinkel, 2015, 2016).

Rigid and Mobile Sentence Elements

In general, the breakdown of a sentence into ordered and sequential slots is based on three fundamental principles.

The Fundamental Principles of Sentence Structure

Basic English sentences are not very complicated.

> **Principle #1**. Sentence elements are ordered and can be identified relative to other sentence elements, e.g. in most sentences, other than questions, the subject noun phrase precedes the verb.

Minimal Sentence Slots

Subject	Verb/Predicate
Particles	*expand.*
Flowers	*bloom.*
Computer technology	*evolves.*
The temperature	*rises.*

> **Principle #2.** The contexts in which sentence elements occur determine the grammar variations among them, e.g. singular subject nouns require singular verbs, or (transitive) verbs that require an object (e.g. **construct**, **develop**, **make**) have to be followed by an object.

On the other hand, prepositional phrases are slippery elements, and they can occur in various slots – at the beginnings or ends of sentences and/or following a subject or an object noun phrase.

> Sentence structures are always dynamic, but variations among them follow predictable patterns, and these have to be explicitly (and persistently) taught.

- _Subject or object slots_ can be filled by all sorts of words or phrases that can be nouns or pronouns, e.g.
  - Proper and common nouns, e.g. *John, Smith, desk*.
  - Countable and uncountable nouns, e.g. *pens, equipment*.
  - Abstract and concrete nouns, e.g. *happiness, a cloud*, or gerunds (a gerund is a noun that is derived from **a verb + ing**), e.g. *reading, writing*.
  - Compound noun phrases, e.g. *vegetable soup, a grammar book*.
  - Pronouns, e.g. *I, we, they, one*.
  - Sets of parallel nouns, e.g. *pens, pencils, and papers; flowers and trees*.

> Noun phrases include all their attendant elements, e.g. articles, possessives, quantifiers, and numerals, e.g. **a book**, [**Ø** article] **information, their book, most of the book(s), three books**.

In fact, subject and object slots are usually filled by a **noun phrase** rather than a single-word noun because in real language use, <u>**single-word nouns are relatively rare**</u>. Proper (**Mary**), uncountable (**wood, dust**), and abstract (**knowledge**) nouns represent a majority of all such cases.

The simplest way to explain the noun phrase is to practice identifying the "main" noun and all its "pieces", e.g.

- **vegetable soup/the blue book** – does the word **vegetable** describe the **soup**? Does the word **blue** describe the **book**? Do these two words go together?
- **most of the book** – do the words **most**, **of**, and **the** refer to the **book**? Do all these words go together?

Similar techniques for identifying elements and their order in the verb phrase and the prepositional phrase are discussed later in this chapter.

A practical and simple technique for identifying entire noun phrases, their elements, and the singular vs. plural subjects is to replace phrases with pronouns.

Locating the Subjects and their Elements

Sherlock Holmes	**_was_** _a famous private detective._
_He_	**_was_** _a famous private detective._
Mary Peters and John Smith	**_are_** _planning to attend the conference._
[1 + 1] They	**_are_** _planning to attend the conference._
The seminar and the technology presentation	**_start_** _at 9 am on Saturdays._
They	**_start_** _at 9 am on Saturdays._
The idea to develop a new type of packaging	**_appealed_** _to store managers._
_It_	**_appealed_** _to store managers._

> Once the noun phrase is replaced with a pronoun, subject–verb agreement is relatively easy to check.
>
> An important step in locating the subject noun phrase in a statement is to (1) find the verb, then (2) go to the left to begin looking for the subject noun.

The Basic Sentence (optional sentence elements are shaded)

Sentence Slots			
(Adverb/ Prepositional Phrase – Optional)	**Subject Noun Phrase**	**Predicate Verb Phrase**	Object Noun Phrase
↓ (In the evening/ Every day)	*They/* *Students/* *Group members*	***study.*** (intransitive verb – optional object)	
		review (transitive, object required)	*class materials.*

Building on this core structure, it is possible to construct more complicated sentences that adhere largely to the same order of elements.

> This approach to sentence structure analysis is highly flexible because it accounts for practically any number of grammatical and contextual variations, even though the core sentence elements remain rigid in their order relative to one another.

> **Principle #3.** Sentence elements are organized according to a hierarchy of their importance for a sentence to be grammatical:
>
> Each English sentence must have **the subject and the verb**, and in most cases an object or a subject complement that describes the subject (e.g. *Bob is* **tall/at home**).

Other elements, such as adverbs or prepositional phrases are mobile and can occur in a few highly predictable locations.

Two Sentences with Prepositional Phrases

Subject Noun Phrase	Two Prepositional Phrases that Describe the Subject	Predicate Verb Phrase	Object Noun Phrase	Adverb/ Prepositional phrase
Interaction		develops	social patterns	
	↓ among people from different organizations			↓ among those organizations.
A player	↓ from the visiting team in the match	kicked	the ball	↓ into the goal.

The previous sentences include several units (prepositional phrases) that are added to the core structure.

In practical terms, explanations of English sentence structure that are based on the core elements with other elements added can greatly simplify instruction in learning to identify the subject, the predicate verb phrase, and the importance of subject-and-verb agreement (see further discussion later in this chapter). For instance, in the case of a compound noun phrase and/or a compound verb phrase, a similar approach can be very useful.

A Sentence with a Compound Subject Noun Phrase and a Transitive Verb

Subject Noun Phrase (Parallel Nouns)	Predicate Verb Phrase	Object Noun Phrase	A Prepositional Phrase that Describes the Object	Adverb/ Prepositional Phrase
Talent, training, and effort	affect	placement	↓ of the individual	↓ in professional organizations.

In teaching, analyzing sentences as sequences of units that are relative to one another in their order and importance can provide a practical and useful tool for dealing with large and small features of sentences, from subordinate clauses to the role of nouns as subjects or objects, parallel structures, or the effects of verb transitivity on the presence of objects.

> The slot organization of sentence elements accounts for fluidity in sentence construction and stylistic variation.
>
> This analysis is sufficiently clear-cut for L2 writers to understand how to use it to their advantage in both constructing new sentences and editing their text.

Speaking broadly, noun phrases have a limited number of functions:

- A sentence subject.
- An object.
- A complement.

The type of the main verb largely determines the structure of a sentence.

The Order of Elements in the Noun Phrase

Rigidity in the order of sentence slots can be very profitable for teaching elements of the noun phrase structure and the verb phrase structure. For example:

- Articles *a, an, the* mark noun phrases and the article is always the first element in the noun phrase, e.g. *the book, a lunch.*
- Articles occur in the same slot as proper noun possessives, e.g. *John's book/lunch*, possessive pronouns, e.g. *his/her/their book*, or indefinites, e.g. *some/any/every book.*

> Articles cannot be used together in the same position as proper nouns (e.g. names), possessives, or indefinites (e.g. **some, any, each**) – once the pronoun or article is in the slot, the slot is full.

Articles and possessives can be followed by quantifiers, e.g. *the five books, John's five books*, and quantifiers by adjectives, e.g. *the ten blue books, Mary's/ her ten blue books.*

Indefinite Articles Cannot Be Used with Two Types of Nouns

(1) General/non-specific **plural** nouns, e.g. **_Researchers_ investigate _processes_ in language learning.**

(2) Non-count nouns, e.g. **_Health/honesty_ is more important than _wealth._**

On the other hand, definite articles are possible in specifically marked contexts, such as ***The researchers* from the Famous University** . . . or ***The health* of the patient/*The honesty* of the accountant.** . . . Articles, plural, count, and non-count nouns of all sorts are discussed in detail in chapter 5.

> In general, noun phrases are not very complex.
>
> - In noun phrases with plural main (head) nouns, all elements are optional, except, of course, the main noun.
> - In noun phrases with singular head nouns, the article or the possessive also represents a required element.

The Basic Noun Phrase

Article or Possessive Noun/Pronoun	Quantifiers	Adverbs to Describe Adjectives	Adjectives	Main (Head) Noun
The/Ø	ten	really/most	important	books
Their/ Mary's	two	very	good	grades
A		highly	qualified	teacher

The Order of Elements in the Verb Phrase

The type of the main verb determines the sentence pattern and its optional and required slots. Main verbs belong to several classes that vary in their prevalence in academic texts.

- Analyses of large language corpora demonstrate clearly that action verbs, e.g. **walk, sing, talk** are far less common in academic prose than **be**-verbs in all their forms.
- Other verb types common in academic texts are linking verbs that connect the subject to the complement, e.g. **appear, become, seem**, intransitive verbs that do not require an object, and transitive verbs that do require direct objects, e.g. **read a book, write a paper**.

The discussion of the main verb types below is organized based on their prevalence in academic prose, as identified in various analyses of academic English language corpora (Biber, et al., 1999; Carter & McCarthy, 2006; Leech & Svartvik, 2003; Quirk, et al., 1985).

Be-verbs

Copula **be** main verbs can be followed by:

- Nouns and noun phrases.
- Adjectives and adjective phrases.
- Adverbs of time and place (**when** and **where** words and phrases).

Main **be**-verbs are often considered to be a subset of linking verbs (see the next section).

Be-verb Patterns

Be-verbs	Nouns, Adjectives, OR Adverbs of Time/Place
is	*a book* (noun)
are	*the most important books* (noun phrase)
was	*important* (adjective)
were	*highly important* (adjective phrase)
is/are	*yesterday/in January* (words and phrases of time)
was/were/been	*here/in the text/on the top* (words and phrases of place)
can/will/may be	*the case* (noun phrase) *true/necessary* (adjective) *on time/at the right place* (adverb phrases)

Because sentences with **be**-verbs are easy to construct, many L2 writers overuse them in their academic writing (Hinkel, 2002, 2003, 2016).

(1)   The most common structure that follows **be** is the prepositional phrase (a preposition and a noun/noun phrase, e.g. **in the lab, at the start**.

(2)   The second most prevalent pattern is **be**-verbs with adjectives (also called predicative adjectives because they are a part of the sentence predicate).

(3)   In some texts, predicative adjectives that follow **be**-verbs and linking verbs are also called subject complements because they describe (complete) the subject noun. (The function of adjectives is to describe nouns, no matter whether adjectives precede nouns or occur behind **be**- and linking verbs.)

*A **good** [attributive adjective] book [noun]*	*is*	*a joy.*
A book	*is*	***good*** [predicative adjective].
The student	*is*	***very intelligent*** [predicative adjective phrase].

Linking Verbs

The most common linking verb, **become**, can be followed by nouns and adjectives, but not adverbs. However, most other types of linking verbs, such as **seem/appear, get, prove, remain, sound, smell, turn**, rarely occur with nouns. (**Get** is common only in conversations and informal spoken discourse.)

- By far, the most prevalent structures with linking verbs include adjectives, e.g. *become old/cold, **seems small/large, proved boring/exciting***.
- Another prevalent <u>conversational</u> pattern includes an insertion of the preposition *like*:

  — *He seemed like a nice man.*
  — *That seemed like a boring movie.*

Linking Verb Patterns

Linking Verbs (**become, seem**)	Nouns and Adjectives **only**
becomes	*a task/a consideration*
became	*a difficult task/an important consideration*
seems	*a good plan* (a noun phrase – relatively rare)
seemed/remained	*ridiculous/wonderful/cute*

The adjectives and nouns that occur after linking verbs, similar to those with *be*-verbs, are a part of the sentence predicate that complement the subject noun.

> Because **be**-verbs and linking verbs (**appear, become, seem**) are **the only two types** that can be followed by adjectives, identifying linking verbs can be based on the presence or absence of the predicative adjective. That is, *if a = b, then b = a*.

If an adjective follows the verb, it is probably a *be*- or linking verb.

> The presence of a predicate adjective can be used for catching missing **be**-verbs, in structures such as ***it possible** or *****average temperature high***.

Intransitive Verbs (object not required)

Intransitive verbs (those that do not require an object or an adjective for a sentence to be grammatical) are actually somewhat infrequent.

- Altogether, intransitives number fewer than 25.
- In fact, most verbs in English can be both transitive and intransitive, e.g. *John reads/writes; Mary reads/writes a book.*

Because intransitive verbs make for short sentences, they are usually followed by optional adverb phrases (some exceptions, such as *reside* and *glance* require an adverb, e.g. *Bob resides on/glanced at Market Street*).

Intransitive verbs are relatively tricky because they are often found in two-word verbs – and are therefore idiomatic, e.g. **turn in, turn up, turn around**.

The majority of intransitive two-word verbs occur with adverbs.

---

in – out   *John jumped <u>in</u>/slept <u>in</u>, and a fight broke <u>out</u>.*
up – down   *Mary cannot come <u>down</u> because something came <u>up</u>.*
over   *However, Peter can take <u>over</u>/move <u>over</u>/run <u>over</u>.*

- **Two- or three-word verbs are highly infrequent in academic prose** and may not be worth the effort expended on teaching them, unless the goal is to work on L2 conversations.
- These verbs are hardly ever used in academic prose (Biber, et al., 1999).
- The most common are *to be set out in* or *to be set up in* used at the rate of 0.002% (20 occurrences per million words).

Common Intransitive Verb and Adverbial Combinations

Intransitive Verb	Adverbial
remain	on the job/at rest
occurred	regularly/in the library
look	carefully/everywhere/up
gave	in/out/up

In general terms, intransitive verbs are simple to use, but they are important inasmuch as they have to be distinguished from transitive verbs that are far more numerous and complex.

Transitive Verbs (Object or Adjective Required)

Transitive verbs require direct objects (monotransitive verbs with one object, e.g. *cause an accident*), direct and indirect objects (ditransitive verbs with two objects, e.g. *give John a sandwich*), or direct objects and additional noun or adjective complements (e.g. *elect Mary president, consider Jane smart*).

The important thing about transitive verbs is that all of them require a direct object (always used without a preposition), similar to the noun complement following **be**- or linking verbs. Here are some examples.

John	reads	a novel.
This book	is	a novel.
His memoirs	became	a novel.

The tricky aspect of object constructions is to distinguish between direct and indirect objects (this distinction will become very important in chapter 7 in the discussion of passive verbs).

All verbs that require two types of objects entail an element of meaning associated with giving and can be called giving verbs, and these are highly frequent.

Frequent "Giving" Verbs

announce	give	owe	recommend	show	tell
bring	hand	pass	remember	speak	write
deny	lend	pay	report	suggest	
describe	mention	prove	sell	take	
explain	offer	read	send	teach	

Two Effective Techniques to Tell Direct and Indirect Objects Apart

(1)   To determine which object is direct and which is indirect, a "giving" preposition **to** or **for** may be inserted, e.g.

The professor sent me <u>an email message</u>.
*The professor sent <u>an email message</u>   **to**   me.*

If you can put the preposition in front of the noun or pronoun, it is the indirect object, because direct objects never occur with prepositions. For instance, all verbs listed above take the preposition **to**, and a few others take **for**.

answer	catch	design	find	order
build	change	do	hire	prepare
buy	close	draw	leave	save
call	correct	fill	make	

(2)   The second technique for distinguishing direct and indirect pronouns is to ask a **what** (or **whom**) question:

- <u>Option 1</u>: *The professor sent me **(what?)** [an email message]*
- <u>Option 2</u>: ***What** did the professor send? [an email message]*

Overnight delivery companies fill <u>the market demand</u>.

- <u>Option 1</u>: *Overnight delivery companies fill **(what?)** [the market demand]*
- <u>Option 2</u>: ***What** do overnight delivery companies fill? [the market demand]*

The noun that answers the **what** question is the direct object.

Direct objects are important to identify when the voice is changed from the active to the passive: direct objects become subjects of passive verbs, and indirect objects are not affected. For example,

Advertising	*brings*	*new information*	*to consumers.* [active] →
New information	*is brought*		*to consumers.* [passive]

On the other hand, transitive verbs that require object complements (adjectives or nouns) are relatively easy to figure out.

- Noun complements, e.g. ***consider the book a problem***, the first noun is the direct object, and the second noun is the object complement, e.g. ***the book [is] a problem***.
- Adjective complements, e.g. ***consider the book difficult***, the only noun that follows the verb is the direct object, e.g. ***consider <u>the book</u>***. . . .

A very useful technique can be used to decide whether an adjective or adverb should be used after a verb.

> *Mary considers her job hard/easy.*
> **John finds his course hardly.*

The insertion of **to be** can clarify the ambiguity, e.g.

> *Mary considers her job **[to be]** hard/easy.*
> **John considers his job **[to be]** hardly.*

One of the common learner errors entails inserting ***as*** in the wrong place and with the wrong verbs, such as ***consider***, e.g.

> **We consider our changes in the program design **<u>as</u>** important.*
> **Locke considered this human talent **<u>as</u>** a gift.*

With object complements, **<u>as</u>** is required with only three frequent verbs that learners need to remember – <u>but not with **consider**</u> (a very frequent L2 error), <u>which takes **to be**</u>.

> **refer (to) as, know as, and think (of) as**
> *We refer to Locke as the greatest philosopher of our time.*

The Order of Elements in the Main Verb Slot

Several verbs, such as *be*, *have*, or *do*, have a variety of grammar and vocabulary functions: they can be **main or auxiliary** verbs.

*John **is** a student, and he **does** his homework daily.*
~~~ [*be* and *do* are main lexical verbs]

*Bob has been **work**ing on his term paper.*
~~~ [**work** is the main lexical verb; **has** and **been** are auxiliary]

The order in which main verb elements occur is also rigid and can be illustrated by means of slots, similar to the elements of the noun phrase.

A Top-most Rule that Applies at All Times in Formal Writing
No Exceptions
Every English sentence must have a verb to be grammatical.
However, only the main verb is absolutely essential, and all other slots inside the verb phrase system are optional.

Here are a few examples.

Peter		cooks/cooked.	[The essential main verb]
Peter	should	cook.	[Optional **should** + the main verb]
Peter	should have	cooked.	[Optional **should** and **have**, + the main verb]
Peter	has been	cooking.	[Optional **has**, **been**, and **-ing**, + the main verb]

INSIDE THE VERB SYSTEM

- The optional slot is reserved for modal verbs, e.g. *can*, *may*, *should*, or the future tense marker, *will*.

- If this slot is <u>occupied</u>, then the rest of the slots can contain only the **base form** of the main verb, e.g. *I/he should go, we/she can sing*.
- If the slot is <u>not occupied</u>, then the form of the main verb depends on **the tense and the number** of the subject noun, e.g. *I walk, he walks, they walked*; *I go, he goes, they went*.

The Modal Verb Slot

Subject Noun Phrase	Modal/Future Verbs (Optional)	The Main Verb
Mary/I/They/Students	should/may/will	come and go
I/We/They/You/Students		walk and talk
Mary/He/She/It		walk**S** and talk**S**/walk**ED** and talk**ED**
John/I/We/He/Students		**came and went**

- The verb phrase can include more slots than just those for modals/future markers and the main verb.
- For this reason, the slot system has to allow for more options to account for various tense auxiliaries, such as *was, have/has* or *been*.
- <u>All sentence verbs have some sort of tense.</u>

For example, even in the case of modal verbs (*can, could, may, might*), two options are possible, e.g. *should cook* or *should have cooked*, not to mention such complex constructions as *will be cooking* or *will have finished/sung* (an outdated construction that can still be found in most L2 grammar textbooks).

> The tense of the verb is the first thing that needs to be identified because it determines what happens to the rest of the elements in the verb system.

For example, a couple of leading questions are very useful in teaching:

— *What tense is used in the preceding text – the present or the past?*
— *Are time markers and adverbs found to allow the tense switch?*

> **Identifying the tense/time** to use **verbs in a particular context** is the first step, followed by marking the verb for a particular tense.

The tense can be marked (e.g. *talk**S***, *talk**ED***, *go**ES***, *went*) or unmarked (e.g. *I/we/you/they talk/go*).

> Once the tense of the verb is determined, it creates a domino effect in the rest of the verb phrase elements.

Another important element of the verb system is __aspect__, such as progressive and/or perfect, and both require auxiliaries, e.g.

- o   *is singing* [progressive].
- o   *has sung* [perfect].
- o   *has been singing* [perfect progressive].
- o   *were eating* [progressive].
- o   *had eaten* [perfect].
- o   *had been eating* [perfect progressive].

Progressive Verbs: The Order of the Verb Phrase Elements

	be	**+ the base** form of the main verb	**+ -ing**
present →	*am/is*	*+ sing*	*+ -ing*
	I am/He is	*singing*	

Perfect Verbs: The Order of the Verb Phrase Elements

	have	**+ past participle**
present →	*have/has*	*+ spoken/eaten*

In addition, perfect and progressive aspects can occur together in the present perfect progressive, e.g. ***have/has been speaking***, or the past perfect progressive (***had been singing***).

A Quick Overview
Auxiliary Verbs with a Few Tense and Aspect Combinations

am/is/was		*sing+ing/* *cook+ing*	[**BE** + base verb + *-ing*]
have/had		*talked/* *spoken*	[**HAVE** + past participle]
has/had	*been*	*talking/* *speaking*	[**HAVE** + **BE-en** (past participle) + base verb + *-ing*]

For the various elements of the verb phrase, such as the tense, modals, and other auxiliaries, a slot system can be created specifically tailored toward the regularities in the verb system.

(1)   The **tense** determines the form of verb in the next slot, e.g.

- Present tense   →   *walk/walk**s***.
- Past tense   →   *walk**ed***.

  <u>With additional **aspect** auxiliaries</u>, e.g.

  o   Present progressive   →   *is walk**ing***.
  o   Past progressive   →   *was walk**ing***.
  o   Present/past perfect   →   *has/had eat**en***.

(2)   The **aspect** (including zero marked aspect as in simple tenses) determines the form of verb in the slot that follows it – usually, the main verb (e.g. progressive – the base verb + *-ing*; and perfect – the past participle).

(3)   The combination of the **tense and both progressive and perfect aspects** results in a series of verb elements:

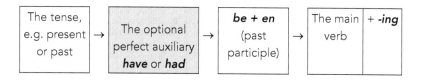

A gigantic English verb phrase system is summarized below, but it is likely too complicated to teach all its component pieces at one time. It is useful, however, because it demonstrates clearly how difficult and problem-prone the verb phrase can be, but fortunately many of the (confusing) combinations are rare in academic writing.

The Verb Phrase Slots

Tense/Aspect	Modal (Optional)	HAVE (Optional)	BE (Optional)	Main Verb
Present Simple				cook(s)/speak(s)
Past Simple				cooked/spoke
Present/Past Progressive			be (present/past) am/is/was/ were	Verb + -ing cook+ing/ speak+ing
Present Perfect		have/has		Verb – past participle cooked/spoken
Past Perfect		had		cooked/spoken
Present Perfect Progressive		have/has	be- past participle been	Verb + -ing cooking/speaking
Modal/Future	will			cook/speak
Modal/Future Progressive	may		be	cooking/speaking
Modal/Future Perfect	will/may	have		cooked/spoken

> The verb phrase has only two essential elements, the tense (+ aspect) and the main verb.

In light of the enormous complexity of the English verb system, it is hardly surprising that many advanced L2 learners often have trouble using verb tenses and aspects appropriately in their academic writing. Techniques for teaching L2 academic writers to get around the complexities of the verb phrase are further discussed in chapter 7.

Subject and Verb Agreement

Based on the system of required and optional sentence slots, in the teaching of subject and verb agreement, two easy techniques can be used. However, both require a successful identification of the main (head) subject noun or noun phrase.

> One of the thorniest issues with subject and verb agreement is that the head subject noun can be difficult to locate and separate from other elements, e.g. prepositional phrases, that sometimes sit between the subject and the verb.

A couple of simple teaching techniques are certainly worth the time and work in the long run, though.

How to Teach It

Trouble Spot

The subject noun phrase is often obscured by the prepositional phrases that follow it, making the use of the appropriate verb form somewhat difficult.

TEACHING TIP #1

An example of a trouble-spot sentence:

> Current **developments** <u>in technology and broadcasting</u> **are** at a crossroads comparable to the early development of television.

The main noun phrase includes the plural noun **developments** that requires the verb **are** also to be plural; however, the prepositional phrase **in technology** *and broadcasting* contains two singular nouns that obscure a connecting relationship between *developments* and *are*.

- The first step is to identify the prepositional phrases and the nouns that are included in the sentence subject.
- Then they can be safely "ignored," for example, and blocked off with a thumb, a piece of paper, or a cap of a pen.
- As the Basic Sentence illustration shows, prepositional phrases always sit at a lower level than the subject and the object phrase.

In academic written text, only six prepositions account for 90% of all prepositional phrases (Biber, et al., 1999; Carter & McCarthy, 2006).

of	in	for	on	to	with

An additional six prepositions each account for approximately 1.00% of all prepositional phrases.

about	at	between	by	from	like

> To identify a sentence subject correctly, all phrases that are located between the subject and verb and that are marked with any of these 12 prepositions simply need to be ignored.

An example for teaching:

> *Some improvement in employees' working conditions*   *come about. . . .*
> *Some improvement*   *come about. . . .*

This technique for identifying head subject nouns can also be effectively applied to blocking off adjectives, adverbs, or whole subordinate clauses (see also chapter 10).

TEACHING TIP #2

This technique for finding sentence subjects can very useful for learners at intermediate and higher levels of proficiency.

- The first step is to convert sentences into yes/no questions and moving the verb to the front of the question.
- Then the subject is the very first element or phrase that occurs after the verb.

Here are couple of examples for teaching.

(1) *One of the most powerful ways of increasing one's levels of education is reading.*

  $\boxed{Is}$ (main verb) <u>one</u> [*of the most powerful ways of increasing one's levels of education reading*]?

(2) *Various personal accounts of the events during World War II help the reader to construct a full picture of the impact of war on families.*

  $\boxed{Do}$ <u>various personal accounts</u> [*of the events during World War II*] $\boxed{help}$ (main verb) *the reader . . .?*

Thus, if the subject noun is singular, then the verb needs to be singular (as in (1)), and if the subject is plural, the verb is also plural (as in (2)).

Other types of elements that locate themselves between the subject and the verb can include adjective phrases and clauses or appositives. All these can be done away with by means of the analysis of slots and **yes/no** questions.

(3) *Someone who is self-confident is less likely to find a given situation stressful.*

  $\boxed{Is}$ [main verb] <u>someone</u> (*who is self-confident*) *less likely to find . . .?*

(4) *Psychologists working from a biological perspective point out that similar experiences can lead to different reactions.*

  $\boxed{Do}$ <u>psychologists</u> (*working from a biological perspective*) $\boxed{point\ out}$ [main verb] *that . . .?*

Compound Sentences

Compound sentences are those that consist of two or more simple sentences. (Similarly, compound nouns and compound verbs consist of two or more parallel nouns or verbs; see chapter 11 for further discussion.) Compound sentences can be pretty easy to teach.

(1)   Comma + Coordinating Conjunction

Sentence #1	, and	Sentence #2
	, or	
	, yet	
	, but	

*Washington is the nation's top cherry producer, **and** farmers in the state grew a record 85,000 tons of cherries last summer.*

Sentence #1,	Sentence #2	, and	Sentence #3
		, or	
		, but	
		, yet	

*People like to eat sweet cherries, bakers put them in their pies, **and** jam-makers cannot get enough of them.*

- In formal academic text in general, compound sentences may be of limited value, and most are found in informal prose.
- Formal written discourse highly prefers the use of comma in compound sentences joined by conjunctions (Leech & Svartvik, 2003; Quirk, et al., 1985).

The use of commas without conjunctions results in one of the **most frequent sentence-boundary errors found in L2 writing**, usually referred to as run-on sentences (or comma splices).

★The new advances in technology in the 21st century are amazing, we now have the Internet to connect people for communication, scientists have invented new AIDS drugs.

Run-ons of this type are relatively easy to fix by simply inserting a coordinating conjunction at the sentence boundary after the comma.

(2) <u>Semicolons (rare in formal writing)</u>

Semicolons may not be worth a whole lot of time and work. They are used without coordinating conjunctions, but they can conjoin **only fairly short sentences**, and this is the main reason that these punctuation marks are rare in academic prose.

| Sentence #1 | ; | Sentence #2 |

Books are sold here ⌐ software and magazines are next door.

Semicolons can also be used with sentence transitions (conjunctive adverbs), such as *however, thus,* or *therefore.*

Sentence #1	*; however,*	Sentence #2
	; thus,	
	; therefore	

When teaching the comma + coordinator and semicolon uses in compound sentences, it is useful to mention that these two patterns largely have the same "power" to conjoin short simple sentences and mark their boundaries. However, their "power" is less than that of a period.

Punctuation

The easiest punctuation rule of all can be obtained from the system of sentence slots:

> No <u>single</u> (lonely) commas can be used between required sentence slots.

Commas are separators of sentence elements, and the essential sentence slots, such as subjects and verbs, verbs and direct objects, and direct objects and indirect objects, cannot be separated. No matter how long the subject or object noun phrases might be, the required sentence slots are never separated by single commas (appositives, *My father, the scientist*, are discussed in chapter 5). These structures actually occur inside the subject slot and are set off by two commas. However, **paired** commas, e.g. *Smith (2003), who researched xxx,* mark modifiers of the head / subject noun phrase. Such modifiers are a part of the noun phrase.

Common Errors: Missing or Too Many Required Sentence Slots

> One of the most common errors in L2 sentences is the missing main verb or its elements, e.g. *Without any doubt, school life a very important period of life for students.*

Other types of sentence-level errors that are frequently found in student writing can be the following:

- More than one subject noun (phrase), e.g. *Freud, he* . . .
- Prepositional phrases used as sentence subjects, e.g. *In my country happens all the time.*
- Missing objects of transitive verbs, e.g. *Science proposes.*
- Missing subject or object complements, e.g. *The Internet has become.*

Although some of these errors cannot be completely avoided, L2 writers can be taught to edit many of them by means of identifying the filled or unfilled required sentence slots.

> In practically all cases, a grammatical sentence must include:
>
> (1) A subject noun phrase.
> (2) A verb.
> (3) Most often, a direct object.

The examples in the following section are from student academic essays and demonstrate how teaching students to identify the required sentence slots can lead to correction of many sentence- and phrase-level errors.

> A good number of various L2 errors can be corrected relatively easily when sentences are parsed (divided or chopped up) into slots.

Counting Sentence Parts

Checking sentences for grammaticality entails locating all required sentence elements and making sure that they occupy their correct slots.

Step #1. Find all verb phrases and go to the left to locate their subject noun phrases.

*With the Google maps, Ø ← [verb] **could be** anywhere in several seconds.*

Step #2. Block off all the prepositional phrases that sit between the subject noun phrase and the verb.

*Medical technology ~~for both patients and doctors~~ [verb] **are** safe after testing.*

Step #3. Go to the right of the verb phrase and locate the direct object, the subject complement, or the object complement.

*Insurance companies **can** still [verb] **access** → to people's health records.*

Step #4. Find the required slots and check to see if they are empty or overfilled.

*Policy-makers [verb 1] **are** [verb 2] **respond** to public opinions.*

Step #5. Fill the required slots, if they are empty, or delete overfillers.

*Who [add **IS**] consider[add **-ED**] successful can be hard to define.*

The following examples illustrate this.

(1)   *There are differences and similarities between the two major theories are easy to notice.*

The Original Sentence							
Subject	Verb	Object/ Complement	Prep. Phrase	Comma + Conjunct. or;	Subject	Verb	Object/ Complement
There	are	differences and similarities	between the two major theories		Ø	are [verb without a subject]	easy to notice.

The Corrected Sentence							
Subject	Verb	Object/ Complement	Prep. Phrase	Comma + Conjunct. or;	Subject	Verb	Object/ Complement
There	*are*	*differences and similarities*	*between the two major theories*	*, and* [comma + conjunct added]	**they** [Subject added]	*are*	*easy to notice.*

(2) *These chemical elements, they combine at a high temperature.*

The Original Sentence		
Subject	**Verb**	**Object/Complement**
1. These chemical elements, 2. they	combine	at a high temperature.

The Corrected Sentence		
These chemical elements	*combine*	*at a high temperature.*

(3) *We are work very hard to reach our dream.*

The Original Sentence				
Subject	**Verb**		**Main Verb**	Object/Complement
	Tense (+Auxiliary)			
		Aux **be**	+**ing**	
We	*(present)*	*are*	*work*	*very hard to reach our dream.*

The Corrected Sentences (Two Possibilities with Slightly Different Meanings)				
We	*(present)*	**Ø**	*work*	*very hard to reach our dream.*
We	*(present progressive)*	*are*	*work +* **ing**	*very hard to reach our dream.*

For additional examples of sentence correction see Strategies and Tactics for Teaching.

Chapter Summary

Rigid and predictable patterns in English syntax provide a framework for teaching sentence structure by means of slots that must or may be filled. Sentence slots are easy to explain, and students can use the slot patterns to more effectively edit their own writing for grammaticality:

- Sentences must have a verb and a subject (except for imperative sentences with an "understood" subject *you*).
- In academic writing, adverbs and prepositional phrases are mobile, but subjects and verbs are not.
- Noun phrases must include a main (or head) noun, which can be preceded with, in this order:

   (a)   An article or possessive.
   (b)   Quantifiers.
   (c)   Adverbs to describe adjectives.
   (d)   Adjectives.

- Main *be*-verbs can be followed by nouns, adjectives, or adverbs / adverbial phrases of time or place.
- Main linking verbs (**become, seem**) are similar to main *be*-verbs and can be followed by nouns or adjectives, **but not adverbials of any kind**.
- Transitive verbs require a direct object (**Bob reads <u>books</u>**), and some transitive verbs (**giving** verbs) can also take an indirect object (**Stuart sends <u>Kevin</u> messages**).
- Inserting the prepositions *to* or *for* or asking a **what** question work like a charm for identifying the direct object.
- The verb phrase has two essential elements: tense (which can be marked or not, e.g. *I go/we go*) and the main verb. Optional verb slots include modals and auxiliary verbs.
- Isolating <u>the Subject</u> and <u>the Verb</u> helps greatly for checking the subject-verb agreement.

Strategies and Tactics for Teaching and Teaching Activities

Teaching Activities

Teaching suggestions are presented here from simpler to more advanced.

The primary instructional objectives are to <u>reduce the frequency of preventable errors</u> and/or fine-tune students' self-editing skills.

The exercises and teaching activities are designed to focus on the following sentence structure skills:

- Identifying missing or incorrectly added sentence elements based on the regular structural patterns in English (focus noted, e.g. find and correct all errors in subject–verb agreement).
- Identifying and correcting incorrectly used sentence and phrase elements (focus unspecified).
- Noticing and correcting fragments and run-ons.
- Editing entire text passages written by someone other than the editor.
- Editing one's own essay-length texts.

The practice with identifying regular sentence patterns is cumulative. When the work with particular focus structures is completed, the structures cannot be simply abandoned on the assumption that students can productively use them in writing and editing.

- All grammar, vocabulary, and editing practice must be designed to build on the structures:

  (a) From the familiar to the unfamiliar.
  (b) From the structurally and functionally simple to more complex constructions.

- Depending on the students' proficiency level, the sentences in this exercise can be extracted from authentic texts of varying degrees of complexity.
- Selecting somewhat lengthy sentences, such as those in authentic texts or academic textbooks, can be essential in the long run.
- The sentences should include prepositional, adjective, and adverb phrases that sit between the subject and the verb.

A realistic degree of sentence complexity represents a key feature of this practice.

Useful sentences can be reasonably easily adapted from those found in the science and health sections of online posts or newspapers, popular print media such as magazines, Internet news, business reports, movie reviews, and introductory college-level textbooks.

All exercises exemplified below can be assigned as individual or group tasks, or homework with a follow-up in-class discussion.

Sentence-level Practice: Dividing and Chopping Up Sentence Slots[1]

- Draw a vertical line to separate subjects and predicates in as many cases as you can identify.
- Also mark various parts of the verb phrase: auxiliary verbs, the main verb, and the object noun or the subject complement.

(1) The experiment proved the point.
(2) Later studies and additional experiments provide additional positive information.
(3) Researchers at Excellent State University report early evidence that berries are actually good for one's health.
(4) Various fruit trees and berry shrubs have been selling quite well in Oregon and neighboring states.
(5) Making phone calls is usually difficult for those individuals who do not speak the language very well.
(6) At this time of year, all over the country, celebrities, politicians, and writers have been asked to give graduation speeches in high schools and colleges.

Dividing and Chopping Up Sentence and Phrase Slots

- Find all subject phrases, all predicate phrases, and all objects / complements in all sentences.
- Circle the entire subject and predicate and include all their elements.
- Do not forget that sentences can be compound and complex, in addition to simple.
- After all subject, predicate, and object phrases are found, underline the main subject noun, the main predicate verb, and the main object noun.

(1)   Vitamin C and minerals, such as iron, can be found in many types of foods.

(2)   Frequently, a shortage of Vitamin D occurs during the winter months.

(3)   Nationwide, the average commute increased 3.1 minutes from 22.4 to 25.5 minutes during the previous year. Among the 25 large cities, Seattle's average commute time ranked 7th in among the top 10 large cities, up slightly from the 9th just a couple of years ago. San Francisco, Atlanta, Chicago, Baltimore, Boston, and Los Angeles were ahead of Seattle on the latest list.

(Adapted from the US Census Community Survey, Transportation Survey, April 30, 2019)

(4)   The basic categories of marketing mix elements are product, place, price, and promotion. The product variable includes design, innovation, the brand name, packaging, labelling, and customer service. The brand name refers to the various methods of communicating the qualities of the product or company. The computation of the price for goods and services includes discounts. For consumers, time, energy, effort, and attention that are required in order to obtain the product are also added to the cost.

(5)   Business research methods of setting prices are in the domain of pricing science. Pricing goods and services involves establishing appropriate price levels. Using discounts, rebates, and other techniques is a way of adjusting prices to make them low in the short term. Cost, competition, and desired profit determine prices. Distribution of products and services deals with the process of delivering goods to the consumer. In management, decisions about transportation and storage are examples of distribution activities.

(6)   The science, art, and technology of enclosing products for distribution, sale, and use are usually known as packaging. Packaging also refers to the technology of designing and producing packages. The entire system of preparing goods for transport, sale, and consumer use depends on the type of product that is packaged. Package containers protect, transport, and sell. Good examples of common types of packaging can be cardboard boxes, paper and plastic bags, bottles, cans, envelopes, wrappers, and trays. Packaging simplifies the use or storage of products and makes them easier to identify.

(Adapted from https://en.wikipedia.org/wiki/Marketing, www.ftc.gov, www.fda.gov, www.gsa.gov)

Text-level Editing Practice with an Explicitly Stated Focus[2]

Identifying specified missing or incorrectly added sentence elements:

- The exercise can consist of typed or scanned (but not photocopied) short text excerpts from one to four sentences.
- Typed or scanned text can allow the flexibility of deleting or adding elements without visible deletions and omissions.
- Missing and added elements are included in the square brackets and they should **not** appear in the student copy of the text.

INSTRUCTIONS FOR STUDENTS

Correct all errors in (1) **the subject–verb agreement** *and (2)* **object/adjective constructions** *that follow the verb phrase.*

For parents, air travel with kids differ[S – deleted] greatly from the days when they could take [object missing – their bags/noun] and head out for a vacation or a fun trip to a distant location. . . . Parents who [ARE – deleted] unfamiliar with airline rules or new to air travel can find [missing object – guidelines/tips/noun] for both adults and children on how to prepare and be safe. Many families across the country believes [added -S] that it [IS – deleted] especially important for parents to pack a bag of toys and snacks to keep a child occupied during the flight. Many experts says [added -S] that the best way to do this [IS – deleted] to select games and activities that can keep children's attention.

(Adapted from www.faa.gov)

Text-level Editing Practice without an Explicitly Stated Focus

- This exercise can be used as individual or small group practice, or assigned as homework to be spot-checked and discussed in class, as needed.

INSTRUCTIONS FOR STUDENTS

Correct all errors that you can find. Be ready to explain each structure that you believe to be incorrect and show how you arrived at your conclusion.

Text #1

Direct mail marketing generate about billions of dollars per year in sales. There is at least two considerations related to direct mail advertising that needs to be taken into account. Direct mail advertisers, or direct marketing companies, as they are sometimes called, develops and maintains customer information data. Data information include name, address, age, education, occupation, family size, and income. They also contain a recent list of products that purchases. Your name is probably on the list, marketers sell to other mailers. Direct mail are more intelligent than ever before. Each of the digital technologies combine email, text, and direct mail and allow businesses to better target consumers with more relevant messaging. Implementing smarter direct mail campaigns help users reach their marketing and sales goals. A combination of marketing campaigns that integrate direct mail and digital media are far more successful than digital campaigns alone.

(Adapted from www.usps.gov)

Text #2

The human family relationship in the 21st century complex. Society is composed of individuals pursue different goals in life and have different interests and personality. The family is the basic form of society we are from the moment we are born.

Text #3

A big problem in this story. Mathilde in the story "The Necklace," she needs to work very hard for 10 year to earn some money to replace the lost necklace. After she done her jobs, which is work for ten years to replace it, she can breathe freely. Do not see is that, a small problem or big problem.

Sentence Building I

Students receive "stripped down" sentences without optional slots and are asked to build them up.

INSTRUCTIONS FOR STUDENTS

Add optional elements to these sentences that consist only of filled required slots. Be ready to explain the differences between the meanings of the original sentences and your own.

For example, here are a few sentence variations.

* ***Sports shoes are popular.***

    - *Many <u>sports shoes are popular</u> among young people/people of all ages.*
    - *Usually/Typically/Generally, <u>sports shoes are popular</u> in many countries/ around the world.*
    - *Various brands/types of <u>sports shoes are popular</u> and fashionable, and they are used/worn every day.*
    - *<u>Sports shoes are popular</u> because they are comfortable and convenient.*
    - *<u>Sports shoes are popular,</u> and they can have many names in different locations.*

(1) People like playing soccer.
(2) Soccer is the most famous game.
(3) The game is played by two teams.
(4) The rules of the game require advancing a round ball.
(5) The equipment for playing soccer is not expensive/is uncomplicated/is affordable.
(6) Important soccer games are broadcast on TV/streamed online.

Sentence Building II

* Lists of academic nouns and verbs have been extracted from the University Word List, developed by Paul Nation (see also chapters 5 and 8).
* Students receive a few of these items singly or in combination and work to build sentences that include them.
* The teaching focus (and a bit of a discussion) is on required and optional sentence slots.
* This activity can be carried out in pairs or be assigned as homework to be discussed in class or small groups.
* The same exercise can be repeated for nouns and adjectives and adverbs (chapter 9).

INSTRUCTIONS FOR STUDENTS

Construct sentences with the following verbs and be particularly careful with required and/optional sentence elements, e.g. some of these verbs require objects and some do not. You can include as many of these verbs as you like in a single sentence.

Academic Verbs for Sentence Building

accumulate	concentrate	contradict	estimate	generate
accelerate	conclude	elaborate	establish	identify
challenge	constitute	eliminate	found	integrate
communicate	cooperate	emphasize	function	

Sentence Building III

- This task can be associated with an assignment on a particular topic or consist of individual sentences.

<u>INSTRUCTIONS FOR STUDENTS</u>

Complete the following sentences and pay special attention to required and optional slots.

(1) The first step in a research project

_____.

(2) The statement of a problem can consist of _____.

(3) _____ gather data, such as facts and information.

(4) _____ can be divided _____.

(5) Each research design _____.

(6) The researcher collects _____.

Endnotes

1 In this chapter and the rest of the book, the practice sentences and texts are excerpted from authentic L2 student writing. The samples and text selections are adapted from freely accessible materials disseminated by the US Census Bureau, USPS, the US Department of State, the US Department of Agriculture, the US Government Publishing Office, the US Department of Health and Human Services, the Federal Aviation Administration, US government pamphlets, research reports, fact sheets, instructional manuals, and handbooks.

2 The benefits of various types of editing/error correction practice (sometimes also called "negative models" or "negative instances") have been noted by many researchers since at least the 1960s, such as Pit Corder, Hector Hammerly, Carl James, and Teresa Pica, to mention just a few.

Further Reading

Hinkel, E. (Ed.). (2016). *Teaching English grammar to speakers of other languages*. New York, NY: Routledge.

A practical introduction to research-based methods of grammar teaching that can be useful and usable in a broad range of instructional settings. The book provides a rounded overview of the principles, strategies, and techniques in L2 grammar teaching for pre-service and in-service teachers to help them develop their professional knowledge and skills.

Larsen-Freeman, D. & Celce-Murcia, M. (2016). *The grammar book: An ESL/EFL teacher's course* (3rd edn). Boston, MA: Cengage.

Insightful and thorough grammatical descriptions of English constructions that are designed for classroom applications. The linguistic system and details of English grammar, as well as their contextual variations and teaching suggestions, are organized into sections based on Form, Meaning, and Use.

Swan, M. (2017). *Practical English usage* (4th edn). Oxford: Oxford University Press.

A reference grammar specifically oriented for language teachers and pedagogy. With the primary model of British English, the book features basic descriptions of grammar and usage, as well as selected vocabulary that can be problematic for language learners. The most recent changes within British English, the stylistic differences between British and American usage, and novel Americanisms are also taken into account.

References

Biber, D., Johansson, S., Leech, G., Conrad, S., & Finegan, E. (1999). *Longman grammar of spoken and written English*. Harlow: Pearson.

Carter, R. & McCarthy, M. (2006). *Cambridge grammar of English: A comprehensive guide*. Cambridge: Cambridge University Press.

Celce-Murcia, M. (1993). Grammar pedagogy in second and foreign language teaching. In S. Silberstein (Ed.), *State of the Art: TESOL essays* (pp. 288–309). Alexandria, VA: TESOL.

Fries, C. (1945). *Teaching and learning English as a foreign language*. Ann Arbor, MI: University of Michigan Press.

Graff, G., Birkenstein, C., & Durst, R. (2018). *They say/I say: The moves that matter in academic writing* (4th edn). New York, NY: Norton.

Hammerly, H. (1991). *Fluency and accuracy*. Clevedon: Multilingual Matters.

Hinkel, E. (2002). *Second language writers' text*. New York, NY: Routledge.

Hinkel, E. (2003). Simplicity without elegance: Features of sentences in L2 and L1 academic texts. *TESOL Quarterly, 37*, 275–301.

Hinkel, E. (2015). *Effective curriculum for teaching L2 writing: Principles and techniques*. New York, NY: Routledge.

Hinkel, E. (2016). Practical grammar teaching: Grammar constructions and their relatives. In E. Hinkel (Ed.), *Teaching English grammar to speakers of other languages* (pp. 171–191). New York, NY: Routledge.

Leech, G. & Svartvik, J. (2003). *A communicative grammar of English* (3rd edn). London: Routledge.

Nattinger, J. & DeCarrico, J. (1992). *Lexical phrases and language teaching.* Oxford: Oxford University Press.

Quirk, R., Greenbaum, S., Leech, G., & Svartvik, J. (1985). *A comprehensive grammar of the English language.* New York, NY: Longman.

Swales, J. & Feak, C. (2012). *Academic writing for graduate students* (3rd edn). Ann Arbor, MI: University of Michigan Press.

Appendix A to Chapter 4

Sentence Stems for Written Academic Discourse

The teaching of sentence and phrase structure needs to co-occur with instruction on vocabulary and common academic collocations.

- Using stock sentence stems in actual writing is probably one of the most efficient ways of expanding L2 writers' vocabulary and grammatical range, particularly when supplemented with substituting discrete elements.
- Grammatical constructions, such as commonly occurring sentences, clauses, and phrases, can be viewed as "big words" and memorized as lexicalized stems.

All sentence stems presented in Appendices A and B can be used for Sentence Building activities (see above in this chapter), as well as activities in slot structure analysis and the replacement of slot elements (see also chapters 5, 8, and 9).

Openings/Introductions

The central issue in xxx is yyy . . .

The development of xxx is a typical/common problem in . . .

Xxx and yyy are of particular interest and complexity . . . .

For a long time xxx, it has been the case that yyy

Most accounts/reports/publications claim/state/maintain that xxx

According to Smith/recent (media) articles/reports/studies, xxx is/seems to be yyy.

One of the most controversial/important/interesting issues/problems/xxxS (recently/in recent literature/media reports) is yyy.

Thesis/Topic Statements

The purpose of this essay/paper/analysis/overview is to xxx e.g. take a look at/examine/discuss yyy.

The main emphasis/focus/goal/purpose of the/this essay/paper/project is to xxx e.g. is to analyze/provide an overview/discussion of xxx

This paper describes and analyzes . . . xxx.

This paper discusses/examines/investigates xxx.

This paper claims/shows that xxx is/is not yyy.

This essay/paper addresses/examines/

*   is designed to*

*   analyze/provide an overview of/take a look at xxx.*

My aim in this paper is to . . .

In this paper, I/we report on/discuss . . .

I intend/will demonstrate/show/explain/ illustrate that xxx

My (basic/main/most important) argument/claim is largely/essentially that xxx

Secondary purpose

The primary aim/purpose of this paper is xxx. In addition, it examines/discusses . . . yyy

Additionally, yyy is discussed/examined.

A secondary aim of this paper is to yyy.

Another reason/point/issue addressed/discussed in this paper is yyy.

Rhetorical Mode/Discourse Organization Statement

This paper (will) compare(s)/describe/illustrate xxx first

*   by analyzing/comparing/demonstrating yyy (that yyy is zzz),*

*   then by yyying zzz, and finally by yyying aaa.*

This paper first analyzes/discusses xxx,

*   followed by an examination/illustration/overview of yyy and zzz.*

Other Types of Sentence Stems for Essay Development

Assertion

It can be claimed/said/assumed that xxx

It seems certain/likely/doubtful that xxx

I/we maintain/claim that xxx

Agreement with the author/source

As XXX perceptively/insightfully states /
  correctly notes /
  rightly observes /
  appropriately points out,   xxx is/seems to be yyy (adjective/noun)

I/we rather/somewhat/strongly agree with/support (the idea that) xxx
XXX provides/lends support to YYY's argument/claim/conclusion that zzz

Disagreement with the author/source

I/we rather/somewhat/strongly disagree with XXX/ that yyy.
As XXX states (somewhat) unclearly/erroneously,
XXX does not support YYY's argument/claim/conclusion about zzz/that zzz
Although XXX contends that yyy, I/we believe that zzz
However, it remains unclear whether . . .
It would (thus) be of interest to learn more about yyy/how . . .

Comparison

Both xxx and yyy are (quite) similar in that zzz
Xxx is like/resembles yyy
Both xxx and yyy are/seem to be zzz (adjective/noun).
Xxx and yyy have/share some aspects of zzz.
Xxx is similar to/not unlike yyy (with respect to zzz).

Contrast

Xxx is (quite) different from yyy (in regard to zzz).
Xxx is not the case with yyy/the same as yyy.
Xxx does not resemble yyy (in regard to zzz).
Xxx contrasts with yyy (with regard to zzz.)
Xxx is unlike yyy in that/with respect to zzz

Recommendations

Let me recommend/suggest that xxx be/have/do yyy
What I want/would like to recommend/suggest is that xxx
One suggestion is/may be that xxx (do yyy)

Citing sources/Supporting arguments, claims, conclusions, and generalizations

As proof/evidence/an example (for this), (let me cite/quote xxx)
According to xxx,
As XXX says/claims,

XXX provides evidence/support for yyy/that yyy
XXX demonstrates that yyy
    shows evidence for yyy/that yyy
Xxx is an illustration/example of yyy.

Citing sources/Referring to external sources of knowledge

It is/has been (often) asserted/believed/noted that xxx   *(YYY, 2023)*
It is believed that xxx   *(YYY, 2025)*
It is often asserted that xxx
It has been noted that xxx

Classification

Xxx can/may be divided/classified into yyy (and zzz.)
Xxx and yyy are categories/divisions of zzz.
There are xxx categories/types/classes of yyy.

Generalization (see also chapter 11)

Overall,
In general,
On the whole,
Generally speaking,
In most cases,
One can generalize that xxx
For the most part,

With the exception of xxx,
With one exception,

Closing statement

In sum/conclusion,
To sum up/conclude,
To tie this (all) together,

(Adapted from Graff, Birkenstein, & Durst (2018);
Nattinger & DeCarrico (1992); and Swales & Feak (2012))

Appendix B to Chapter 4

The Most Frequent Verb/Preposition Combinations in Academic Prose

The Top Most Frequent

be applied to	be known as	depend on	result in
be associated with	be used in	lead to	
be based on	deal with	refer to	

The Second Most Frequent

account for	be included in	come from	look at
allow for	be involved in	consist of	obtain [noun] from
add to	be related to	contribute to	occur in
be composed of	be required for	differ from	think of
be divided into	belong to	look for	

(Adapted from Carter & McCarthy, 2006; Biber, et al., 1999) (see also Appendix to chapter 7)

Nouns and the Noun Phrase

5

Overview

- Nouns: THE only accurate definition ever.
- Nouns and lexical substitutions to expand vocabulary.
- Vocabulary in academic writing.
- 380 essential nouns in academic texts.
- Singular and plural noun forms with different meanings.
- Gerunds and nominalizations in academic text.
- Compound noun phrases.
- Strategies for teaching nouns and teaching activities.

Most L2 students who have learned a second or foreign language and attempted to use it for their daily tasks are painfully aware of how an insufficient noun and verb repertoire can become a severe handicap in practically any interaction, even trying to place an order in a restaurant. In academic texts, when students need to demonstrate their understanding of assignments and readings and in addition explain their ideas, the shortfalls in their vocabulary often turn into great obstacles.

Both in reading and writing, many L2 students are faced with either having to look up numerous words in a dictionary or make do with the lexicon accessible to them. If they elect to look up words, then translating dictionaries often provide "matching" items than can render a student's text incomprehensible. On the other hand, working with English–English dictionaries may take an inordinate amount of time – again due to the simple fact that one needs to have a solid vocabulary foundation in place to be able to understand distinctions between partial synonyms in dictionary entries.

Research has demonstrated that L2 writers whose time is limited and who are dealing with large amounts of reading and writing fall back on the vocabulary immediately accessible to them or found in the reading at hand (Laufer & Ravenhorst-Kalovski, 2010; Nation & Webb, 2011). The laborious processes of vocabulary teaching and learning can be further constrained when teachers and teacher educators believe that mere exposure to and reading eventually results in academic vocabulary acquisition. As a large body of research shows clearly, even advanced L2 students enrolled in their academic programs have a restricted vocabulary range (e.g. Ferris, 2011; Hinkel, 2002, 2011; Jordan, 1997; Leki, 2007; Leki, Cumming, & Silva, 2008).

> A key job for L2 writing teachers is to help students build up vocabulary and develop essential language tools for writing in academic courses.

The following teaching techniques for academic nouns focus on meeting fundamental learning needs:

- Contextualized vocabulary for lexical substitutions, e.g.

    consensus → agreement, accord, unity, common view.

- Essential and foundational vocabulary for academic reading and writing.
- The grammar of nouns and attendant meaning changes (*technology – technologies*).
- Increasing the range of abstract nominalizations (*achievement, addition*), gerunds (nouns that are derived from verbs, as in **verb+ing, read+ing, speak+ing, listen+ing**), and compound noun phrases (**business case studies**).

Experience has shown that explaining to students why something is taught and how the material and teaching techniques can improve their writing usually creates a more interested and receptive audience, who have their self-interest in mind. In addition, such explanations can improve the teacher's credibility and give the impression of efficiency, preparedness, and professional competence (assuming that the teacher wants to make such impressions).

A Noun – The Definition

This is the only accurate definition that is ever needed in language teaching and learning.

A noun is not a person, place, or thing because a place (as in *here, there,* and *everywhere*) is often in fact an adverb or an adverb phrase, e.g. *in the garden, at home.*

A Noun is – a <u>Who</u> or a <u>What</u>

Language learners often confuse nouns and adverbs when they work with the standard description of a noun as a person, place, or thing. Being able to identify nouns is important for pluralization and ensuring subject–verb agreement.

Contextualized Groupings of Nouns to Expand Vocabulary

When they write university assignments, students often have a familiar noun or two that they use repeatedly in similar contexts. Such overuses of nouns result in redundant text constructions that create an impression of poor and awkward vocabulary. Here's an example.

> The _people_ with _higher level of education_ definitely have a better future than the _people_ who have less. Mostly, _people_ also choose _higher education_ because of its _status_. _People_ would rather have an average _status_ than a low _status_. The _reason_ is that the society views these _people_ as underachievers in the community. In the 21st century, one of the _reasons_ that _people_ will try to get _higher education_ is to have a better _status_. The other _reason_ is to earn more money. With _status_ and money, _people_ can afford to have a higher standard of living.
>
> (From a student assignment on the economic impact of education on the life of a local community)

In this excerpt, the noun **people** is repeated seven times, **status** five times, and **higher education** and **reason** three times each. These repetitions clearly demonstrate the shortfalls in the writer's vocabulary.

In studies of particularly problematic areas in L2 writing, misused words and lexical redundancy are among the most egregious shortfalls, on par with errors in verb tenses and subject and verb agreement (Ferris, 2011; Hinkel, 2002, 2003, 2013).

To help learners expand their vocabulary range in the domain **people**, alternatives can be provided and practiced in context:

| **People** – | adults, employees, individuals, population, the public, residents, community, group members, workers |
| **Status** – | social position, professional standing, prestige, prominence |

Higher education –	*college or university education, advanced training, university degree studies, education beyond the high school, professional preparation, professional training*
Reason –	*aim, basis, cause, consideration, expectation, explanation, goal, purpose, thinking, understanding*

- Teaching indispensable academic vocabulary with **a few close, frequent, and carefully selected** synonyms provides an important long-term advantage: L2 writers can immediately see their uses and practicality.
- Expanding students' vocabulary in more than one academic discipline simultaneously is a gradual and painstaking process.
- Making vocabulary substitutions in the context at hand, that is, in students' writing, is easier and more practical than teaching vocabulary out of context.
- Directly relevant and immediately applicable vocabulary teaching meets students' needs for developing sets of interchangeable lexical "plugs" – to be used and re-used in various written assignments.
- Vocabulary alternatives are essential for maintaining text cohesion and lexical substitutions.

Extensive research on L2 academic prose has shown that even advanced L2 writers employ lexical substitutions significantly less frequently than first year L1 students simply because of a severely restricted vocabulary range (e.g. Hinkel, 2002, 2003; Leki, 2007; Plakans & Gebril, 2012; Staples & Reppen, 2016).

To write papers for disciplines, students need to know key terms used in each domain of study, such as economics, sociology, or history.

- Discipline-specific terms are heavily emphasized in courses, lectures, and textbooks, and most students learn them as a part of their course work.
- In discipline-specific papers, increasing the vocabulary associated with nouns can be essential.

The following excerpt below comes from a student's sociology assignment on gaming behaviors.

> *Playing games is a very popular <u>activity</u> in Asia <u>young generation</u>. The <u>activity</u> for <u>young generations</u> make friends and teamwork. <u>Young generation</u> want to reach the top score for many different reasons. Games are major free time <u>activity</u> for <u>young generation</u>, and if you are really good, you can make money. Its not dangerous like climbing a mountain, and <u>young generation</u> want to succeed. Playing games is not so expensive like shopping or traveling, and its a top technology <u>activity</u> that make the <u>young generation</u> smarter because you need thinking quickly.*

The repetition of the word **activity** and the phrase **young generation** can be avoided by means of alternative nouns, pronouns, and a bit of sentence-combining, e.g. the first sentence in this excerpt can be easily combined with the second. The first order of priority, however, is vocabulary work.

Young generation –   *youth, youngsters, young adults, the age groups of xxx and yyy, those who are younger than zzz, teenagers, people in their 20s*

Activity –   *pastime, pursuit, interest, hobby, recreation, entertainment,* diversion

Playing games –   *gaming, gamers*

The teacher's job is to pre-select applicable and contextually appropriate vocabulary substitutions that can meet students' learning and writing needs without pitfalls.

The example below is extracted from an assignment in an economics course:

> *There are at least 2800 <u>companies</u> listed on the New York Stock Exchange, 1000 <u>companies</u> on the American Stock Exchange, 2700 <u>companies</u> traded on the over-the-counter, to name a few. This is only publicly traded <u>companies</u> in the US, not to mention the foreign <u>companies</u>. With so many options, how should we decided which <u>company</u> to be our best shot? . . . A lot of ratios could be used to measure the <u>company's</u> profitability. The combined use of*

these ratios can not only tell us if the <u>company</u> is making money but also give us some information such as the expenses and the number of outstanding shares inside the <u>company</u>. You are rich because others are poorer than you. If every <u>company</u> in the world makes more than two million dollars this year and your <u>company</u> only makes one million dollars. Your <u>company</u> is still profitable but it is not worth investing.

In this example, in addition to other problems, such as fragments, personal pronoun uses, punctuation, and a somewhat informal register, the noun ***company*** is repeated excessively. However, other nouns are readily accessible and practical for students to use in similar courses and contexts:

Company –   *business, firm, enterprise, venture* (if new)

Most experienced teachers have discovered that they cannot just recommend that their students use a thesaurus. As with dictionaries, using a thesaurus without the adequate vocabulary base needed to tell appropriate from inappropriate entries can be difficult. For example, the noun ***company*** has 42 partial synonyms. Of these only a few might be contextually useful, and these are actually not included on the list.

<u>An example from an online Thesaurus:</u>

Top 6 synonyms for the word ***company***, out of 42 total, and none seem to apply in this context.

Company –   *association, club, community, group, party, team*

The distinctions among the meanings of ***company***, ***club***, ***association***, and ***community*** are substantial enough to make the student's excerpt very confusing.

> A strong vocabulary base is needed to consult dictionaries and thesauri and choose a noun appropriate in a particular context.

Talking Shop

In L2 instruction, learning new vocabulary is often referred to as **"the learning burden"** (Nation, 2013; Webb & Nation, 2017). The learning burden of a word entails knowing its form, meaning, and use – including its spoken form, written form, word parts, other words that frequently occur with it, as well as the constraints on its use. Each word has its own learning burden, and it can be pretty heavy, e.g. ***commitment, conception, theory.***

Learning academic vocabulary takes a lot of hard work. Learning hundreds of words with abstract meanings, such as ***analysis, assumption, status***, or ***reason***, requires serious motivation, effort, attention, and persistence. And more persistence.

How to Teach It

(1) Online dictionaries and thesauri are prevalent, but they largely follow the same format as the old-fashioned print English–English dictionaries and thesauri. For many academic learners, these can be too advanced and difficult to navigate. They are typically developed and maintained for L1 users of English.

(2) Considerable language proficiency is required to work through ordinary dictionary entries, and thesauri can supply dozens of words with similar meanings that are not in fact very similar.

(3) Academic L2 writers may not be in great need of 20 partial synonyms of any word.

> **Limiting vocabulary substitutions to only the 3 or 4 most practical, frequent, and useful words, for each word, is of crucial importance. No more than 3 or 4.**
>
> There is a lot of vocabulary to learn, and it is a tedious and time-consuming process.

(4) The easiest and most straightforward dictionaries are those that are found in popular and freely available search engines. Unlike online thesauri, search engine dictionaries provide a limited and manageable number of synonyms that can be expanded by clicking on MORE, but for L2 writers, these are likely to be sufficient.

(5) With the teacher's guidance, a short and flexible list of 3–4 frequently occurring items can be selected for usage in a variety of academic contexts.

An example of how to use a search engine – entering the term "**<u>definition</u>**" or "**<u>synonym</u>**" produces the same results. For example:

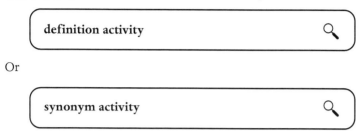

definition activity

Or

synonym activity

ac·tiv·i·ty

noun
1. the condition in which things are happening or being done.
   "there has been a sustained level of activity in the economy"
2. a thing that a person or group does or has done.
   "the firm's marketing activities"
   synonyms: pursuit, occupation, interest, hobby, pastime, recreation, diversion; More

---

USEFUL AND FREQUENT SYNONYMS

To make short lists of **practical and frequent** nouns with similar or contextually suitable meanings, not much research is needed.

Activity: *pursuit, occupation, interest* – and more specialized – *hobby, pastime, recreation*

> For students, it is highly useful to keep vocabulary notebooks – paper or electronic. They are a great time-saving device, essential for vocabulary review and retention.

The efficiency and effectiveness of vocabulary notebooks has been thoroughly researched since at least the 1920s, e.g. the work of Harold Palmer, and Thorndike & Lorge (1944). Here's an example.

Action Point

Frequent and multipurpose vocabulary can be assembled in small synonym sets, around 3 or 4 for each item. A main word is presented to students, and then they have a couple of minutes to make short synonym lists selected from a search engine dictionary:

<u>company</u> – a commercial business
           <u>synonyms</u>: firm, business, corporation, organization

<u>reason</u> – a cause, explanation, or justification for an action or event
           <u>synonyms</u>: cause, basis, purpose, objective, goal

<u>status</u> – the relative social, professional, or other standing
           <u>synonyms</u>: standing, social position, level

Additional teaching activities can include a focus on sentence and phrase examples, as well as word-building with prefixes, suffixes, and derivations, e.g. **give a reason, for this/that reason, reason+ing, reason+ able** (not **too many!**).

Vocabulary in University Writing

In general, the importance of noun usage in academic prose cannot be overestimated.

- Nouns dominate in all types of academic prose: slightly more than 60% of content words in academic prose are nouns.
- Nouns are many times more common than pronouns in academic writing, although pronouns dominate in conversations.
- A foundational academic vocabulary for writing basic academic prose consists of at least 2,000 to 3,000 words (a minimum of 5,000 words are requisite for functional academic reading and writing).
- Research has established that 95% of all academic undergraduate texts can be understood and written within this lexical range.

(Based on Biber, et al., 1999; Nation, 2013; Schmitt, 2000,
2008; Swales & Feak, 2012)

Words commonly found in academic texts are different from those used in casual conversations.

Academic vocabulary and grammar need to be explicitly and persistently taught because they do not occur in conversational discourse.

Productive and Receptive (Passive) Vocabulary

Productive vocabulary refers to the vocabulary items that learners can use in speech or writing.

Receptive (passive) vocabulary represents the words that learners are familiar with and understand in listening and reading.

> In written production, one of the most important instructional goals is to increase L2 writers' **productive** vocabulary range.

Numerous studies of advanced L2 academic prose show that they contain two to three times as many simple nouns, such as *people*, *world*, *human*, *man*, *woman*, *stuff*, *thing*, *way*, than similar prose of L1 high school graduates (Hinkel, 2002, 2003; Leedham, 2016; Leki, 2007).

- Extensive research on large corpora of English words has identified lists of **most common vocabulary** items employed in undergraduate and introductory textbooks across several disciplines (Coxhead, 2000; Nation, 1990, 2013).
- The University Word List and the Academic Word List include, respectively, 800 words and 567 head words of word families in academic texts.
- The list below includes **only 375 words** extracted from the University Word List.

Lists of words, such as the noun list in this chapter, the verb list in chapter 8, or the entire University Word List, can be handed out to students with an explanation of what it is and why they need to have it. When the words from the lists come up in readings, exercises, and activities, it important to point them out to provide learners a sense of purpose in light of the amount of tedious and difficult work they need to do to improve their vocabulary. Many of these are frequently used as nouns but can also appear in noun, verb, or adjective form.

Most Common Nouns in Introductory University Texts

The words in the **bold font** are found most frequently and in highly varied texts across all disciplines (extracted from Nation, 1990, 2013). In many cases, noun and verb forms can be identical (e.g. *access, aid, influence, advocate*). These are included on both the list of common nouns and verbs (see chapter 7).

abstract	access	acid	adjective	adult
aesthetic	**affect**	affluence	aggression	aid
alcohol	ally	**alternative**	ambiguity	analogy
anomaly	anthropology	apparatus	appeal	appendix
approach	area	aristocrat	arithmetic	aspect
aspiration	assent	asset	astronomy	atmosphere
atom	attitude	attribute	auspices	awe
axis	battery	benefit	biology	bomb
bore	breed	bubble	bulk	bureaucracy
calendar	capture	carbon	career	catalog
category	cell	challenge	channel	**chapter**
chemical	circuit	circumstance	classic	client
clinic	code	coefficient	collapse	column
comment	commodity	commune	competence	complement
complex	**component**	compound	compulsion	concentrate
concept	conduct	configuration	conflict	confront
congress	conjunction	consent	console	constant
construct	contact	**context**	contingent	continent
contract	contrast	controversy	**convert**	creditor
crisis	**criterion**	critic	crystal	culture
currency	cycle	cylinder	**data**	debate
decade	decimal	decline	deflect	democracy
denominator	design	detriment	diagram	diameter
digest	**dimension**	discourse	doctrine	domestic
drain	drama	drug	duration	dynamic
economy	electron	**element**	embrace	emotion
energy	**entity**	**environment**	episode	equilibrium
equipment	equivalent	ethics	exhaust	expert
exponent	export	extract	faction	factor
fallacy	fare	fate	feature	finance
fluid	focus	fossil	fraction	fragment

fraud	friction	frontier	fuel	function
fundamental	fund	fuse	geography	geometry
germ	goal	grant	graph	gravity
guarantee	harbor	hero	hemisphere	heredity
hierarchy	horror	**hypothesis**	image	**impact**
implement	import	impulse	incentive	incident
incline	income	index	individual	inflation
innovation	instance	instinct	integer	intellect
interlude	interval	interview	intimacy	issue
item	job	journal	label	laboratory
labor	launch	layer	lecture	leisure
lens	locomotion	logic	luxury	magic
magnitude	major	margin	material	mathematics
matrix	maximum	medium	metabolism	metaphor
method	microscope	military	**minimum**	molecule
momentum	monarch	morphology	motive	muscle
myth	navy	**negative**	nerve	network
niche	norm	notion	novel	null
nutrient	objective	odor	option	orbit
outcome	overlap	oxygen	parenthesis	parliament
peasant	pendulum	**period**	**perspective**	pest
phase	phenomena	philosophy	planet	plot
pole	policy	pollution	port	**portion**
positive	postulate	**potential**	premise	preposition
prestige	principle	priority	process	project
propensity	proportion	proprietor	protest	province
prudence	psychology	quote	radical	radius
range	ratio	rebel	rectangle	reform
region	reign	release	relevance	research
reservoir	resident	residue	resource	**reverse**
rhythm	rigor	**role**	route	saint
sanction	satellite	schedule	scheme	score
section	**segment**	**sequence**	series	sex
shift	sibling	site	skeleton	sketch
sociology	source	species	spectrum	sphere

statistic	**status**	stereotype	strata	stress
structure	style	**sum**	**summary**	supplement
surplus	survey	switch	symbol	symptom
synthetic	tangent	tape	task	team
technique	**technology**	telescope	**tense**	terminology
territory	terror	text	texture	theft
theorem	**theory**	tissue	tone	topic
trace	tractor	**tradition**	traffic	trait
transition	treaty	trend	triangle	**usage**
vein	velocity	version	vertical	vocabulary
volt	volume	x-ray		

The lists of the most common nouns employed in academic texts are accessible to most interested teachers, and for this reason, finding vocabulary alternatives is relatively easy in various contexts, e.g.

alternative –	*option, choice, other possibility*
competence –	*capability, ability, proficiency, skill*
fragment –	*piece, particle, shard, snippet*
sphere –	*(1) domain, field, area, arena, department*
	(2) a round solid figure, globe

The crucial factors in the success of academic vocabulary learning are:

(1)   Contextualization (and thematic organization).
(2)   Repeated exposure to appropriate-level academic texts.
(3)   Deliberate noticing and making written notes of how various words are used.
(4)   Sequencing the learning of easier words before more difficult ones.

For example, nouns such as *triangle, traffic, tradition,* and *topic* can be accessible even to beginners. Similarly, if intermediate learners already know the noun *feeling,* they can be in a good position to learn *affect* and *emotion.*

> Learning academic vocabulary, like many other aspects of learning, can become productive through **repeated exposure** and **contextualized repetition (and more repetition).**

If vocabulary dealing with *planet, policy, pollution, release, research*, and *residue* is worked on in the early phases, these nouns need to be reviewed and practiced in context later in the course.

In vocabulary work, it is important to set realistic but challenging goals. For example, contextualized exposure to 700–1,000 words during one 10–12 week term may be reasonable, assuming that students are assigned homework or projects outside the class (see Strategies and Tactics for Teaching and Teaching Activities below).

Talking Shop

Intensive Vocabulary Learning – Research Pointers

(1) Gaining initial familiarity with the meanings of 30 words per hour is possible when various vocabulary learning techniques are combined, e.g. word lists, vocabulary logs, and key words (Schmitt, 2000).

(2) This rate of learning, however, requires learners to be focused and motivated, but as vocabulary grows, so does the ability to increase the vocabulary range.

(3) The greater the students' vocabulary repertoire, the wider the possible exposure to new vocabulary through reading.

(4) Thus, learners with a vocabulary range of 5,000 general and academic words combined are likely to have an easier time learning new words than those with 1,500.

Articles and Singular/Plural Choices

The English article system is highly irregular, idiomatic, and context-bound. That is, in many cases, it is difficult to tell whether a definite or an indefinite article is appropriate in different contexts, or even if an article is required at all. Comprehension is far easier than production.

To reduce the rate of L2 article problems in writing, using plural nouns instead of singular count nouns can be a practical option. This teaching technique does not do away with all the article errors, but it reduces their frequency.

Here's an example from a student's assignment on investment risk.

> *Taking risks can produce bad __result__. For example, __the investor__ buys stocks from new __company__, and he expects to gain their capital. These people, however, may lose some of their money on __stock__ if their estimation about the stock is false. Stock __price__ declines from $10 to $6 after they bought the stocks at $10 each. Despite the bad __result__ of taking __risk__, people can succeed and accomplish their __goal__ because the stock market can give them __chance__ to become successful.*

This excerpt contains nine errors in article and singular/plural noun uses. Most of these can be avoided (or corrected), if plural nouns are used instead of singular.

> *Taking risks can produce bad __results__. For example, __investors__ buy stocks from new __companies__, and __they__ expect to gain (break even on) their capital (investment). These people, however, may lose some of their money on __stocks__ if their estimations (evaluations/appraisals/expectations of) (~~about~~) the __stocks__ are false (incorrect/inaccurate). [If/When] stock __prices__ decline from $10 to $6 after they bought[buy] the stocks at $10 each, [investors lose money]. Despite bad __results__ of [from] taking __risks__, people can succeed and accomplish their __goals__ because the stock market can give them __the/a chance__ to become successful.*

In general, in L2 teaching, the tendency is to gloss over the frequent and ubiquitous problem areas that students encounter in real language production and that seem to defy instruction, such as articles or singular/plural nouns (more on these below). The reason is that, by and large, rules are not intended to account for specific occurrences of articles but rather serve as overarching guidelines.

> **Learning to cope with difficulties in L2 writing and finding practical work-arounds is a paramount language skill.**
>
> This skill differs substantially from learning general rules that apply to most (or many) article uses in English.

Students usually appreciate a tip that they can easily put into practice, and using plural instead of singular nouns to avoid at least some of the problems associated with article use is a good one.

Non-count and Irregular Nouns

In English, non-count nouns are relatively few. However, they can play an important role in making text appear idiosyncratic because they are very common in academic texts (see the list of frequent nouns above).

> **Count nouns** are nouns that can be counted. They can be singular or plural and can be used with singular or plural verbs.
>
> **Non-count nouns cannot be plural**, and they cannot be used with a plural verb or indefinite articles *a/an*. Some are commonplace in speaking and writing, but others are predominantly academic.

Ubiquitous and Absolutely Essential Non-count Nouns

grammar	hair	help	information
life (existence)	music	news	people
progress	rain	research	slang
sleep	snow	space	vocabulary

Less Frequent Non-count Nouns, but Worthwhile

bread	baggage/luggage	corn	grass
silver	gold	dirt	dust

Academic Non-count Nouns

Academic nouns that have only a singular form are essential for any type of language production. Typically, L2 grammar books provide lists of these nouns divided according to their semantic classes, e.g. groups made of similar items, mass nouns, abstractions, or names of recreational activities (*baseball, basketball, soccer, tennis, camping*).

Based on classical linguistic definitions, the semantic noun classifications seem logical and organized, but on the other hand, to L2 learners they do not always make sense. For instance, why should *baggage, clothing,* and *furniture* items, which one can easily count, be non-count, and what could possibly be the difference between *baggage* and *bags*? Furthermore, it seems that students who do not plan to enroll in veterinarian studies may not need to know that the plural of *calf* is *calves*, and learners who do not play board games should not bother remembering that *chess* does not have a plural form.

> The trouble with non-count nouns is that in English, their singularity or plurality is often simply lexicalized (idiomatic) and cannot be explained logically.

Many lists of non-count nouns are organized based on their semantic categories, e.g. whole groups made up of similar items, Fluids, Solids, Abstractions, Languages, Recreations, Activities, and Natural Phenomena. However, to know that *homework, slang, vocabulary, news, advice, music, laughter,* and *wealth* represent abstract phenomena, one needs to have a relatively good vocabulary range to start with.

- It is a fact that current, popular, and culturally biased methodologies for L2 teaching disdain memorization and frown on attempts to assign lists to be memorized.
- Unfortunately, there may be few means of learning academic vocabulary other than memorization, followed by extensive contextualized practice.
- Attaining L2 proficiency sufficient for success in academic reading and writing in any L2 (particularly one without L1 cognates) may be unlikely without memorization and serious work required for retention. Successful L2 learners are closely familiar with the tedium entailed in learning lists of exceptions to almost all language rules.

> The list of non-count and other irregular nouns that are necessary for producing academic texts is actually small.

The organization of non-count nouns exemplified below is structural, rather than semantic, to be manageable for learners and learning. It is based on explicit and overt noun markers, such as suffixes.

Identifying and Learning Non-count Nouns by Their **Endings**
Plural Forms Cannot be Used

Noun Ending	Examples and Notes
-work nouns	homework, coursework, work, fieldwork, that is, all types of work performed by people (**but not** framework and network)
-age nouns	courage, voltage, postage, luggage, baggage, barrage, garbage (**but not** garage or package)
-edge nouns	knowledge, heritage, pledge
-ice nouns	advice, juice, practice, malice, **including** ice
-ware nouns	freeware, hardware, shareware, software, silverware, flatware, stoneware
-fare nouns	welfare, warfare, fare
-th nouns	breadth, health, warmth, wealth, strength, truth, youth (**but not** myth, depth, width, or length – see also singular and plural meanings of nouns below)
many -a/ence, -ment, -ness, -(s/t)ure, -(i)ty, -ing nouns	derived nouns often have different meanings in singular and plural forms (below); referred to as abstractions in students textbooks
nouns that have the same form as verbs (see any dictionary)	air, fish, fog (up), help, ice, iron, mail, play, oil, rain, slang, snow, smoke, traffic, water, weather, work [some nouns are duplicated in these categories based on the "whatever works" principle]
nouns that exist only in noun form (ditto)	art, business, energy, fun, grammar, music, oxygen, trouble, vocabulary, wisdom (see below on different meanings of singular and plural forms)

Frequent nouns that are always plural are just a handful. These require plural verb forms when used in the subject position, and are never used with indefinite articles *a/an*.

Nouns That Are Always Plural

clothes	glasses	grounds	jeans	odds	pants
people	savings	shorts	stairs	surroundings	tropics

Languages and People Rules

- Noun endings *-n* or *-i* – the plural marker is required.

  American, Korean, Mexican, Chilean, German, Moroccan, Indonesian, Italian, Norwegian, Iraqi, Irani, Emirati, Pakistani, Saudi, Somali

- No plural with any other types of nouns and adjectives that refer to languages and people.

  Arabic [language] – *Arab* [person] have different adjective – noun forms.

- Nouns that refer to both languages and people and do not take plural markers.

  Amharic, Chinese, Danish, Japanese, Vietnamese, Burmese, Dutch, French, Finnish, English, Portuguese, Spanish, Turkish

- Names of languages and people that function as nouns or adjectives

  o   If the name is followed by another noun, then plural markers cannot be used with the first noun (see compound nouns below).

  Indonesian students/people/professors/culture
  American textbooks, Chinese/Japanese speakers

  In this case, **Indonesian/American/ Somali** has the function of an adjective.

  > In English, adjectives never take the plural form, no matter what ending they have.

  o   If a noun does **not** follow immediately, then the plural form is required.

  Indonesians, Americans, Somalis, Jordanians, Qataris

  > A good rule of thumb is to focus on the people/languages nouns and adjectives that are very frequent and show up in students' texts.
  >
  > Addressing these specific items can be more expedient than working with the entire list.

Possessive Nouns

Possessive nouns are relatively rare in academic prose.

Awkward examples from student texts that might be worth a few minutes.

?Indonesia's economy   ?company's management   ?course's assignments

- In L2 writing, these possessive constructions should be replaced with alternatives.
  - o adjective + noun, e.g. ***Indonesian economy***
  - o compound noun phrases, e.g. ***company management, course assignments***
- Possessive constructions are usually limited to nouns that refer to humans.

  John's lunch, teacher's pet

- However, even in the case of nouns that refer to groups of humans, the use of possessives can be obscure:

  *faculty's office, *employee's parking, *government's benefits

In the cases where possessives can be used, the rule to follow is that if the noun is singular (***a boy, a nurse***), then the apostrophe is placed at the end of the singular noun (***a boy's, a nurse's***). However, if the noun in plural (***students, professors***), then the apostrophe is still placed at the end of the noun, but only the original *-s* is needed (***students', professors'***).

Essential Nouns in Academic Texts

The University Words List and the Academic Word List include only a little over 30 essential non-count nouns.

32 Essential Academic Non-Count Nouns

alcohol	atmosphere	awe	biology	consent
equipment	ethics	friction	geography	geometry
gravity	hemisphere	inflation	integrity	intimacy

labor	logic	mathematics	minimum	maximum
navy	philosophy	pollution	prestige	psychology
reluctance	research	sociology	trade	traffic
vocabulary	welfare			

Irregular Plural Forms of Nouns

Other very common nouns from the University Word List and the Academic Word List that have irregular plural forms are Greek and Latin in origins. Nouns such as *overseas*, *series*, and *species* have identical plural and singular forms (*one series – several series, one species – many species*).

Plural Markers of Frequent Greco-Latin Academic Nouns

Singular Endings	Plurals Forms and Examples
-is	**-es** analysis – analyses, axis – axes, basis – bases, crisis – crises, emphasis – emphases, hypothesis – hypotheses, parenthesis – parentheses
-ex/ix	**-ces** index – indices, matrix – matrices
-um	**-a** medium – media, stratum – strata
-on	**-a** criterion – criteria, phenomenon – phenomena

Although teachers may attempt to design activities and exercises to provide students practice with these nouns, it is doubtful that many enjoyable tasks can be constructed with nouns such as *axis*, *crisis*, and **hypothesis**. Nonetheless, it is essential for students to know the meaning, pronunciation, and spelling of these nouns at least to recognize them when they appear in academic reading and lectures. There are few better solutions to the dilemma of learning them beyond simple memorization and practice.

Singular and Plural Nouns with Different Meanings

Many essential countable nouns, such as **business**, **development**, **difficulty**, **failure**, **industry**, **injustice**, **technology**, **truth**, have different meanings in singular and plural forms. The singular form **technology** refers to all types of **technology** as a concept, but the plural **technologies** to various types / subsets of **technology**, such as computer, automotive, or telecommunication.

> In the singular, abstract nouns refer to concepts or whole notions, and in the plural, to specific instances, types, kinds, and occurrences of these notions.

For example,

> *The development of the economy is the most important job of the government in my country.*

In this sentence, the noun **development** refers to the entire collective notion that consists of many components, such as **the development of agriculture, transportation, and commerce**. On the other hand, the plural form **developments** refers to events and occurrences:

> *Many developments in the political arena point to a possibility of early elections.*

The plural form **developments** refers to small and separate events or occasions. In other words, when used in the singular, these nouns refer to overall concepts and constructs, and in the plural, to smaller instances / subdivisions of these constructs.

The same principle of identifying meanings of singular and plural forms can apply to other nouns that may be considered non-count but are employed in both plural and singular forms.

Common Singular and Plural Nouns with Different Meanings

beer – beers	cake – cakes	change – changes	cheese – cheeses
chocolate – chocolates	coffee – coffees	coke – cokes	hair – hairs
glass – glasses	milk – milks	paper – papers	tea – teas
time – times	wine – wines	work – works	youth – youths

All these refer to whole notions, concepts, or mass quantities or one instance of in singular and specific instances in plural.

*Beautiful **hair** [as a total mass/collective] requires much care.*
OR
*If you've found two gray **hairs** [two instances/small occurrences of] on your head, do not panic. We have a solution to grays.*

Most nouns that can have different meanings in singular or plural are usually (and unfortunately) found in the lists of non-count nouns that are ubiquitous in L2 grammar texts. To avoid confusion, some researchers (DeCarrico, 2000, p. 21) have called them "crossover" nouns, and if this label is helpful to learners, there is no reason not to use it.

Gerunds and Abstract Nominalizations

Both gerunds and nominalizations represent nouns and noun-like forms derived from other parts of speech.

- Gerunds are always derived from verbs. A gerund can be derived from practically any verb by means of adding *-ing* to its base form.

  read – reading, learn – learning, sing – singing, listen – listening

- Nominalizations can be derived from verbs, adjectives, and other nouns.

  develop – development, ship – shipment, dark – darkness, warm – warmth

Meanings and Uses

> **Gerunds and nominalizations are very frequent in generalizations.** They refer to concepts, actions, and processes that would be difficult to convey by other lexical means.

Here's an example:

*Social **structure** influences **institutions**, **culture**, and social **interactions** because those at the top of the **structure** gain the greatest benefit by **developing**, **maintaining**, and **protecting** the prevailing **institutions** and **culture**. **Traditions** and **culture** normally affirm the social **institutions** and human **arrangements**. Behavioral and **relationship** patterns have enduring **functions** across an entire* *society. Taken together, social <u>arrangements</u>, <u>culture</u>, and <u>institutions</u> are important to what individuals do.*

(Adapted from https://en.wikipedia.org/wiki/Sociology)

Gerunds, even more than nominalized nouns, refer to processes that are in fact incomplete, and are sometimes called **process nominals**, e.g.

— *developing (ideas)*	— *development*
— *creating (software)*	— *creation*
— *observing (animals)*	— *observation*
— *suggesting (new plans)*	— *suggestion*

<u>A Key Meaning Difference between Gerunds and Nominalizations</u>

- **Gerunds refer to processes.**
- **Nominalizations refer to abstractions, concepts, or actions.** As in the example above, ***instituting*** something is different from ***an institution***, and ***organizing*** from ***an organization***.
- Most academic nouns of either type exist **only in one form**, e.g. *reading, writing, teaching, learning, hoping,* OR *culture, moisture, revolution, possibility, probability.*

An important characteristic shared by gerunds and nominalization is that they are frequently **followed by prepositional phrases.**

- *a chance of obtaining funding/success/data*
- *a discussion about books/classes/equipment*
- *an opportunity for improving one's diet/progress/health*

The Most Frequent Nouns (Singular or Plural) with ***of*** + <u>gerund</u> (verb+***ing***)

advantage of	cost(s) of	effect(s) of	experience of
form(s) of	idea of	importance of	means of
method of	possibility of/for	practice of	problem(s) of/with
process(es) of	purpose(s) of	system(s) of	way(s) of

Analyses of written and academic English corpora have demonstrated that gerunds (**verb + ing**) and abstract nouns dominate in academic and professional texts. One of the reasons may be that academic discourse deals with abstract concepts more frequently than other genres do (Biber et al., 1999; Carter & McCarthy, 2006; Leech & Svartvik, 2003).

- Abstract nominalizations are encountered far more frequently in academic writing than in any other discourse.
- Conversational vocabulary has the lowest rates of nominalization occurrences among all other language genres.

Advanced L2 writers employ significantly fewer gerunds and nominalizations than first-year L1 students without college writing experience (e.g. Hinkel, 2002, 2003; Leki, 2007). In part for this reason, L2 academic prose, both spoken and written, appears to be far less "academic" than may be expected at the college or university level. In addition, L2 writers may simply find it challenging to convey abstract concepts, explain their ideas, and demonstrate their familiarity with readings and material.

Using gerunds and abstract nominalizations can help students' texts appear more "academic." These structures are essential for the development of students' academic language skills.

Gerunds

Traditionally, practically all L2 grammar books provide lists of verbs that are followed by gerunds, infinitives, or both, e.g.

- *enjoy* + *swimming* (but not **to swim*)
- *decide* + *to go* (but not **going*)
- *like to dance/dancing*

Although these lists are essential, in reality, the uses of gerunds are a bit more complicated than this. (For a list of frequent transitive verbs, see chapter 4.)

The point of fact is that when gerunds are derived from transitive verbs, which require a direct object, the process nouns retain this transitivity feature.

For example, this sentence is incorrect because *develop* is a transitive verb, which requires a direct object.

*Developing is expensive.

Thus, the correct sentence requires an object because the noun *software* is in fact the object retained from the old days when *develop* was originally a verb.

Developing software is expensive.

- A good explanation to give students can be a metaphor that when a verb goes to a new job and becomes a noun, it takes its possessions with it.
- When a verb is converted to a nominal by means of adding *-ing* to its basic form (**suggest**+*ing*), it drags the object with it, e.g.

  Suggesting a new plan requires preparation.

In addition, another level of complexity is added with gerund singular and plural distinctions, when **some gerunds can be used in plural, and some cannot**, e.g.

reading – readings, swimming – *swimmings.

As a general rule, gerunds that refer to **concrete objects and events** can take plural, and other gerund forms that refer to processes cannot.

Therefore, gerunds that can be used in a plural form are far less common than those that are non-count, e.g. **beginnings, endings (of books/ movies/stories), markings, paintings** (but not **clothings*).

Abstract Nominalizations

Abstract nominalizations are more complex than gerunds because several different suffixes exist, all of which have the function of converting words, including simple nouns, to abstract nouns.

> Nouns with the suffix **-ness** refer to characterizations and states, while **-ion** nouns are particularly prevalent in the academic genre.

Abstract Nominalizers and Noun Endings

Ending	Examples
-age	acreage, coverage, courage, marriage, mileage, shortage, voyage
-ance/-ence	absence, appearance, assistance, dependence, diligence, resemblance
-cy	accuracy, democracy, fluency, occupancy, privacy, urgency, vacancy
-ity	ability, capacity, complexity, equality, priority, similarity, simplicity
-ment	accomplishment, announcement, development, document, government
-ness	awareness, business, directness, fairness, goodness, greatness, kindness
-ion	action, condition, election, relation, revolution, situation, solution
-ure	creature, culture, departure, exposure, pressure, procedure, signature

Lists of these suffixes are found in most L2 reading and vocabulary books.

> In general, it is **not** possible to predict what types of verbs, adjectives, or nouns can be derived by the suffixes **-ment**, -**ness**, -**ity**, or -**ure**.

The Most Frequent -**tion** Abstract Nouns

action	addition	application	association
communication	concentration	direction	distribution
education	equation	examination	formation
infection	information	instruction	operation
organization	population	production	reaction
relation	situation	variation	

Other types of nominalizers are also highly frequent, but they are semantically simpler than abstract nouns because, in most cases, they refer to people or concrete objects that perform a particular action or are from/in a particular place.

Academic People and Object Noun Nominalizers

-er/-or	-ee	-ent/-ant
doctor, teacher, senator	employee, interviewee	applicant, attendant, student

Compound Noun Phrases

Noun phrases can consist of several nouns where **the first noun or two function as adjectives to describe the main (head) noun.**

- composition _**class**_
- university composition _**class**_
- university-level composition _**class**_

In these phrases, the noun _class_ **is the head noun**, and all other nouns describe the _class_. These structures can come in various forms:

o Two simple nouns (**_book cover_, _vocabulary list_**)
o Gerund/nominalization and another noun (**_listening activities_, _automobile production_**)
o Fused verb + particle constructions (**_setup_, _handout_, _wash-back effect_**)

> Compound noun phrases are extraordinarily frequent in academic texts.

The following research findings apply to most noun compounds (Biber, et al., 1999; Carter & McCarthy, 2006).

(1) Compound nouns are far more common in written than any type of conversational genres.
(2) Noun compounding represents a highly productive structure, that is, new constructions appear, and some disappear from use.
(3) Formal written texts include far more of these constructions than informal discourse.

How to Teach It

> **Trouble Spot**
>
> In L2 texts, one of the typical errors is pluralization of the descriptive nouns in the compounds.

For example:

> *a five-credit**S**-hours course   *a 20-year**S**-old student   *a 5-dollar**S** bill

Avoiding these errors is relatively easy to teach.

> In English, adjectives do not take plural, and the structures are incorrect because only the main (head) noun can be used in plural.

(For an in-depth discussion of adjectives see chapter 9).

> *blue**S** books, *big**S** blue books

With compound nouns, the first job is to **identify the main noun** (usually **the last one in the string of nouns**) that can take the plural:

> a five-credit-hour **course(s)**, a 25-year-old **woman (women)**

> In most compound noun phrases, e.g. **the vegetable garden**, only **the last (head) noun takes the plural marker -s**. Other nouns, which describe it, do not.

Exceptions to this rule are very few, and they almost always include "exclusive plurals" (Carter & McCarthy, 2006; Quirk, et al., 1985), when it is known that the descriptive noun includes more than one entity, e.g. **arts degree, customs officer** (e.g. it is also possible to say **art degree** when one type of art is involved).

> **Trouble Spot**
>
> Another typical problem with compound nouns is that compounding can take place only if an adjective form of a particular noun does not exist.

In compound noun phrases, very common L2 errors can be, for example:

*nation flag   *economy data   *culture norms   *rain weather

These constructions are incorrect because adjectival forms of nouns have to be used if they exist: **national, economic, cultural,** and **rainy.**

On the other hand, there are no adjectives that can be derived from **vegetable, noodle, rice,** or **table,** e.g.:

vegetable soup   noodle dish,   rice bowl   table top   course schedule

A word of caution: When it comes to adjectives derived from nouns, the meaning of the adjectives can be very different from that of the noun:

– *composition teacher* vs. *?compositional teacher*
– *book* vs. *bookish*
– *territory* vs. *territorial*

Chapter Summary

To increase the learner's vocabulary range, several simple and effective teaching techniques can be highly productive:

- Academic vocabulary work at all levels of language learning, from beginning to advanced.
- Contextualized vocabulary substitutions of frequent and useful nouns that are repeated in L2 prose do not require much work beyond small sets of 3 or 4 synonyms.
- Practice, activities, and review of the list of highly common nouns employed in academic texts across various disciplines.
- A reasonable number of words learned during a 10–12 week period can range from 700 to 1,000, and the rate of instructed learning can be as high as 10 words per hour (or more).

Many specific L2 problem areas can be explicitly addressed in effective teaching.

- Count and non-count nouns classified based on their endings. In general, only 32 non-count nouns are frequent in academic texts.
- Abstract plural and singular nouns with different meanings in singular and plural. Most learners are not aware of this distinction that should be addressed in teaching.
- Gerunds and nominalized nouns cannot be learned through exposure to conversational discourse and fluency-building activities.
- A few simple techniques dealing with compound noun phrases to help learners overcome some of the typical problems.

Strategies and Tactics for Teaching and Teaching Activities

Teaching Activities

The learning goals of the teaching suggestions and activities presented below are to promote academic noun learning and retention.

- Noticing the uses and meanings of nouns (see chapter 3).
- Incidental learning of words (see chapter 3).
- Discussing contextualized occurrences of nouns and their lexical substitutions.

It is very important that the teacher follow up on the assigned exercises and vocabulary learning tasks: review, review, review.

Learning 10 new words per hour is not an unreasonable rate (see chapter 3). It is through the discussion and activities that the words are actually learned. In-class discussions and/or follow-up work with nouns and other words provide the most important benefits because they give students additional opportunities for review.

All teaching activities exemplified in this chapter and other chapters have been used for decades with L2 writers at various levels of proficiency, from beginning to advanced. The teaching suggestions presented here are based on using texts easily obtainable online, e.g.

advertisements, book cover descriptions, and news reports. Example texts are also easy to find.

As a general rule, if text simplification is needed, it is best to eliminate rare words rather than those that are common, even if they are lexically and structurally complex.

Prefixes and Suffixes – Dictionary Work and Practice

Words that begin with a specific prefix can allow learners to figure out its meaning and practice vocabulary, or the meaning can be presented in advance in complex vocabulary. For example:

Nouns with **Pro-**
(word element meaning **forward, toward the front, in advance, for**)

procedure	course of action, action plan, series of steps, method, system, technique
profession	career, occupation, job, business, craft
proposal	plan, idea, suggestion, putting forward
profit	financial gain, return(s), earnings, benefit
progress	forward movement, advance, headway
project	assignment, program, enterprise, undertaking
promise	declaration that one will do or not do, assurance, guarantee
promotion	encouragement, advancement, moving to a higher position or rank

- It is important that dictionary-based exercises include dictionaries of appropriate difficulty level. For example, learners' dictionaries can be used for beginners and intermediate-level students, and advanced learners can work with unsimplified dictionaries.
- The work on a particular prefix/suffix can coincide with other practice with prefixes/suffixes with similar meanings (e.g. *for-/fore-*, *pre-*, *head-*) and exercises found in all vocabulary textbooks.
- Together with prefixes and their meanings, some amount of attention to parts of speech and noun suffixes may prove useful in the long run (e.g. noun suffixes *-ion*, *-ure*, *-ment* are different from adjective suffixes *-i/able*, *-a/ent*, *-ive*).

Graded Exposure to Authentic Texts
(Increasing Lexical Complexity)

(1) **Beginning or intermediate levels**. Various advertisements or book cover descriptions with frequent noun uses can provide exposure to contextualized vocabulary learning.

- The useful and practical nouns (verbs, adjectives, or prepositions) can be blocked out to create blanks for a fill-in-the blank practice with authentic language.
- The nouns, words, or phrases from the original are listed below the text to be used as prompts for blank filling. Here's an example.

If you sometimes have problems _____ and adapting to American culture, or have difficulty communicating with _____ of American English, this excellent program is for you.

Each course has two _____ (1) recordings and videos about cross-cultural _____ and important American _____; and (2) extensive examples of cross-cultural communication. Language practice will focus on American English sounds and _____

To help you better understand the material, the program includes conversational _____, comprehension questions, readings, interviews, and one-on-one _____. Guided by our experienced and caring teachers, you can learn to use English for everyday _____.

Omitted Gerunds and Nominalizations

components	traditions	understanding	speakers	pronunciation
expressions	sessions	conversation	interactions	

Vocabulary Expansion Practice

component – part, element, unit	conversation – speaking, talking, discussing
understanding – comprehending	expression – phrase, construction

An activity, as in (1), can be used without the list of original nouns (or other types of words). In this case, students are asked to come up with vocabulary alternatives or various possibilities for appropriate context completion.

For instance, all appropriate vocabulary replacement options can be acceptable, if students supply them.

(2) **Intermediate or high-intermediate levels**. News media posts or articles on various topics of interest, as well as science and market reports, can become good practice for increasing text complexity and lexical variety (see an example below).

- When the original nouns/words are not provided, students can work in groups to complete the text and supply as much contextually appropriate vocabulary as they can.
- Groups can compete for finding as many lexically appropriate and grammatically correct fillers as possible.
- The winner of each "blank" can be awarded a token (for example, a piece of colored paper). The group that accumulates the most tokens wins the competition.

Students usually enjoy this type of competition, and the amount of discussion associated with appropriate lexical and syntactic choices of words can be highly productive.

(3) **High-intermediate levels**. Students can work in groups or complete the assignment as homework, followed by a substantial class discussion of their lexical choices. For example:

- Why is a particular word appropriate/inappropriate in this sentence?
- What better word can be found?
- Why is another choice of word better?
- How many parts does a particular word consist of?
- What are they?
- Is this word a noun, an adjective, a verb, or an adverb, and how do we know?
- What lexical substitutions for this word can we think of?
- Are some better than others and why?

(4) **Advanced levels**. This technique can be used with excerpts from introductory texts in the disciplines or literature on any topic that the teacher considers to be useful and appropriate.

Lexical Substitution Practice

Restatement and paraphrase are often considered to be essential academic tasks. However, many L2 writers lack the necessary lexical and reading skills to be able to restate an idea. Teaching restatement by means of lexical substitutions is simpler than paraphrasing, and lexical restatement can be practiced even with high beginners.

INSTRUCTIONS FOR STUDENTS

> *Replace the underlined nouns with other nouns (or phrases) with similar meanings.*

(1) Education abroad is rapidly expanding due to an increasing number of adventurous students who take advantage of going abroad to explore their ethnic roots.
   [*education – studying, going to school, learning; abroad – in a foreign country; expanding – growing, becoming popular; roots – origins, family history*]
(2) Several factors play an important role in this trend.
   [*facts, points, ideas, components*]
(3) *Colleges and universities in England remain the top* destination *for US students.*
   [*choice, place, location, goal*]

Paraphrase practice is a little more complex and requires examples for students to complete it successfully. However, if the lexical substitution work takes place prior to restatement, students will have little trouble.

INSTRUCTIONS FOR STUDENTS WITH AN EXPLICITLY STATED FOCUS

> *Explain in your own words and in one sentence what these three sentences say together.*

(An alternative: In writing practice, after students produce a paragraph or an essay, the teacher can underline nouns/words in the student texts to be replaced with other words with similar meanings.)

Editing Practice: Noun Forms and Uses

(a) Noticing and drawing attention

The first step in teaching students to edit their own text is to present them with a text written by someone else with several mistakes of the same or similar types. (Someone else's writing is far easier to edit than one's own – trust me on this one!)

Technology can provide various ways for communicate. Most American have a lot of technologies, but in my country, people still don't think that phones are better than vising family. With the technology development, we, people, can get more and more benefit. We use technologies doesn't mean we abandon the traditional way to communicate with other people. I really enjoy to meet with friends and have fun with family. But everybody is so busy today, technology provides a more convenient way for communication. Everybody have different way to communicate, and I believe technology make us having more communicate with other, it also makes our life more beautiful.

(From a student essay on the influence
of technology on communication)

- The text and mistakes can be shown and discussed in class.
- Students can work on several similar texts in small groups and then present their findings to the class with explanations for each error they have identified.

In this way, the entire class may have additional opportunities for noticing and working with problematic nouns.

(b) Teaching L2 writers to edit their own prose

- When proof-reading text for grammar or word form errors, most students begin reading their text from the beginning.
- In doing so, the reader almost immediately gets caught in the flow of the text and stops paying attention to errors in word/noun form.
- Furthermore, when students read their own text silently, they employ only one type of memory – visual.
- For students in ESL/EAP programs in English-speaking countries, aural memory (remembering how the word sounds) can provide an additional boost in mistake-hunting power.

TEACHING EDITING TECHNIQUES

This proof-reading technique can help students locate and correct <u>about one third to half of the word-form errors</u> in their writing.

(1) It is far more effective to start reading one's own text from the **beginning of the last sentence to the end of this sentence**.
(2) Then the reader moves up to the one before last sentence and reads it to the end of this sentence.

(3) Then moves up one sentence higher still (the third sentence from the end) and proof-reads it.

(4) In this way, the reader proofs the text by reading it backwards, sentence by sentence, to avoid getting caught up in the text flow.

(5) The proof-reading of the text should be done **aloud** (but not necessarily loudly), while paying close attention to word forms.

(6) In most cases, students need to be shown this technique only once because it is simple to understand and use.

(7) L2 writers need to be reminded to proof-read their text, read it out loud, and follow what is written (rather than what they think is written).

Reminding writers to proof-read is not a new task for any teacher of writing.

For example:
[**This is the last sentence to be proof-read #6**]
When I was a child, all the technologies in my hometown were still simple.
[**Then read sentence #5 to the end**]
Started from television to computers, all were changed.
[**Then read sentence #4 to the end**]
Basically, all technologies that people discovered in communications were not to make money.
[**Then read sentence #3 to the end of the sentence**]
They were made for improvements.
[**Then continue with sentence #2 to the end of the sentence**]
It is true that until now there are no technologies that can promote person contact.
[**Start reading here to the end of the sentence #1**]
For example, people can only hear voices from phone and people can only see the faces and voices through internet.
(From a student's text on technology and communication)

Gerund Practice

As has been mentioned, gerunds that are derived from transitive verbs often retain their objects even when they are used as sentence subjects.

Identifying the sentence subjects
- Identifying gerunds that are sentence subjects is important in subject–verb agreement editing.
- To raise students' awareness of gerund complexities, many gerund + direct object constructions can also be found.

Students usually learn a great deal from such practice and enjoy it. Here's an example.

> *Please explain* **which verb form is correct** *in this sentence. How many are possible and why?*
> - *Trusting friends becomes / become necessary in a time of trouble.*
> - *Eating fresh vegetables is / are recommended for children and adults of all ages.*
> - *Reading books is / are essential in learning a second language.*
> - *Hiding cookies from children is / are something that many parents do, when they want to control their children's diet.*
> - *Writing exercises help / helps students to improve their vocabulary skills.*
> - *Choosing universities is / are complicated for teenagers without their parents' assistance.*

Gerund + direct object constructions are very common, and many similar sentences can be made for practice.

> - *understanding parents / children / students*
> - *building blocks (of houses)*
> - *buying cars*
> - *answering phones*
> - *winning prizes*

Further Reading

Folse, K. (2004). *Vocabulary myths*. Ann Arbor, MI: University of Michigan Press.

A solid and research-based overview of eight vocabulary teaching myths that seem to be widespread and persistent. The book draws on the author's own personal experience and research to explain the vital importance of L2 vocabulary learning. Solid and well-grounded recommendations of strategies and methods are also highlighted to improve vocabulary instruction and classroom techniques.

Hinkel, E. (2003). Simplicity without elegance: Features of sentences in L2 and L1 academic texts. *TESOL Quarterly, 37*, 275–301.

A quantitative analysis of 1,083 L1 and L2 academic texts shows that advanced non-native English-speaking students in US universities employ excessively simple grammar constructions and vocabulary, such as vague nouns (e.g. *people, things, stuff*), and conversational adjectives (e.g. *good, bad, big, small*) at frequencies significantly higher than those found in basic L1 texts.

Hinkel, E. (2011). What research on second language writing tells us and what it doesn't. In E. Hinkel (Ed.), *Handbook of research in second language teaching and learning, Volume 2* (pp. 523–538). New York, NY: Routledge.

A chapter in a handbook that reviews and summarizes a large number of investigations in the language and discourse features of L2 prose. To a large extent, research on L2 usage patterns has led to a greater understanding of many issues that confound L2 writing and its teaching and learning. This synopsis focuses on what is known and what still requires further investigation

References

Biber, D., Johansson, S., Leech, G., Conrad, S., & Finegan, E. (1999). *Longman grammar of spoken and written English*. Harlow: Pearson.

Carter, R. & McCarthy, M. (2006). *Cambridge grammar of English: A comprehensive guide*. Cambridge: Cambridge University Press.

Coxhead, A. (2000). The new academic word list. *TESOL Quarterly, 34*(2), 213–238.

DeCarrico, J. (2000). *The structure of English: Studies in form and function for language teaching*. Ann Arbor, MI: University of Michigan Press.

Ferris, D. (2011). *Treatment of error in second language student writing* (2nd edn). Ann Arbor, MI: University of Michigan Press.

Hinkel, E. (2002). *Second language writers' text*. New York, NY: Routledge.

Hinkel, E. (2003). Simplicity without elegance: Features of sentences in L2 and L1 academic texts. *TESOL Quarterly, 37*(2), 275–301.

Hinkel, E. (2011). What research on second language writing tells us and what it doesn't. In E. Hinkel (Ed.), *Handbook of research in second language teaching and learning, Volume 2* (pp. 523–538). New York, NY: Routledge.

Hinkel, E. (2013). Cultures of learning and writing in the US academy. In L. Jin & M. Cortazzi (Eds.), *Researching intercultural learning: Investigations in language and education* (pp. 21–35). New York, NY: Palgrave Macmillan.

Jordan, R. (1997). *English for academic purposes*. Cambridge: Cambridge University Press.

Laufer, B. & Ravenhorst-Kalovski, G.C. (2010). Lexical threshold revisited: Lexical text coverage, learners' vocabulary size and reading comprehension. *Reading in a Foreign Language, 22*(1), 15–30.

Leech, G. & Svartvik, J. (2003). *A communicative grammar of English* (3rd edn). London: Routledge.

Leedham, M. (2016). *Chinese students' writing in English: Implications from a corpus-driven study*. London: Routledge.

Leki, I. (2007). *Undergraduates in a second language: Challenges and complexities of academic literacy development*. New York, NY: Routledge.

Leki, I., Cumming, A., & Silva, T. (2008). *A synthesis of research on second language writing in English*. New York, NY: Routledge.

Nation, I.S.P. (1990). *Teaching and learning vocabulary*. Boston, MA: Heinle & Heinle.

Nation, P. (2013). *Learning vocabulary in another language* (2nd edn). Cambridge: Cambridge University Press.

Nation, P. & Webb, S. (2011). *Researching and analyzing vocabulary*. Boston, MA: Cengage.

Plakans, L. & Gebril, A. (2012). A close investigation into source use in integrated second language writing tasks. *Assessing Writing, 17*(1), 18–34.

Quirk, R., Greenbaum, S., Leech, G. & Svartvik, J. (1985). *A comprehensive grammar of the English language.* New York, NY: Longman.

Schmitt, N. (2000). *Vocabulary in language teaching.* Cambridge: Cambridge University Press.

Schmitt, N. (2008). Instructed second language vocabulary learning. *Language Teaching Research, 12*(3), 329–363.

Simpson-Vlach, R. & Ellis, N. (2010). An academic formulas list: New methods in phraseology research. *Applied Linguistics, 31*(4), 487–512.

Staples, S. & Reppen, R. (2016). Understanding first-year L2 writing: A lexico-grammatical analysis across L1s, genres, and language ratings. *Journal of Second Language Writing, 32*(1), 17–35.

Swales, J. & Feak, C. (2012). *Academic writing for graduate students* (3rd edn). Ann Arbor, MI: University of Michigan Press.

Thorndike, E. & Lorge, I. (1944). *The teacher's word book of 30,000 words.* New York, NY: Teachers College Press.

Webb, S. & Nation, P. (2017). *How vocabulary is learned.* Oxford: Oxford University Press.

Appendix to Chapter 5

Lexical Expressions with Various types of Nouns and Noun Phrases

Negative Openings: Uncountable Nouns

(However),

little information	is available about xxx
little attention	has been devoted to yyy

Negative Openings: Countable nouns

few reports	→	have discussed/examined zzz
few discussions	→	have addressed/noted/examined
few articles	→	have focused on/noted
few studies	→	have investigated/dealt with

(Adapted from Swales and Feak, 2012)

Most Common Phrases Found in Academic Prose

on the other hand	due to the fact that	on the other hand the
it should be noted	it is not possible to	a wide range of
there are a number of	in such a way that	take into account the
it is clear that	take into account	can be used to
in this paper we	in the next section	a large number of

(Extracted from Simpson-Vlach & Ellis, 2010)

Most Common <u>Noun</u> Phrases Found in Academic Prose

Nouns with Prepositional Phrases

the relationship between the	the difference between the
an important part in	an important role in
an increase in the	the same way as

Prepositional Phrases Followed by the *Of*-phrase

as a result of the	as in the case of the	at the end of the
at the beginning of the	at the time of the . . .	at the time of writing
from the point of view (of)	in the context of the	in the division of labor
in the course of the	in the early stages of	

Four-Word Units: Noun Phrases Followed by an *Of*-phrase

(and) the development of the	and the number of	both sides of the
different parts of the	one of the main/most	other parts of the
part(s) of the body	parts of the world	point of view of
the ability of the	the base/basis of the	the beginning of the
the case of a/the	the center of the	the composition of the
the context of the	the course of the	the division of labor
the early stages of	the edge of the	the effect(s) of the
the end of the	the existence of a	the first of these
the form of a/the	the formation of the	the importance of the
the length of the	the level of the	the needs of the
the point of view	the purpose of the	the rest of the

Five-Word Units: Noun Phrases Followed by an *Of*-phrase

one of the most important	the aim of this study	the first part of the
the point of view of	the presence or absence of	the rate of change of

(Extracted from Biber, et al., 1999)

More on the Noun Phrase

6

Pronouns

Overview

- Personal pronouns in academic text and other genres.
- Uses of impersonal pronouns.
- Demonstratives, text cohesion, and lexical substitution.
- Indefinite pronouns and learning to do without them.

Although the term "pronouns" suggests that they can be used in place of nouns, in reality pronouns have characteristics and functions that make them different in important ways.

(1) Unlike nouns, pronouns represent a closed class of words (Quirk, et al., 1985). That is, they are limited in number and function, and new words of this type are not coined.

(2) Unlike nouns, pronouns can be used in place of whole phrases or concepts with noun functions, e.g. the phrase *the big blue grammar books* can be replaced by a pronoun *they*, which refers to the entire noun phrase.

(3) In English, pronouns have syntactic properties that nouns do not have: pronoun forms can vary depending on whether they occur in the sentence subject or object position (*I/me, she/her*) or refer to first, second, or third person, or male or female (*his, her, their, our*).

In addition to personal pronouns, various other types of pronouns are very common in English:

- Demonstratives (*this/that, these/those*).

- Indefinites (*somebody, anybody, everything*).
- Slot fillers (*it* and *there*), also called "dummy subjects" or clefts.

In general, pronouns have a referential function, and their uses are to connect discourse elements.

- Pronouns of all kinds are pervasive in academic writing, due to their prominent role in text cohesion.
- Although these language components are highly frequent, they are often slighted in L2 writing instruction because they can appear to be misleadingly simple both syntactically and lexically.
- In large-scale analyses of L2 writing, a range of issues have been identified with pronoun usage in text (Harwood, 2006; Johns, 1997; Leki, Cumming, & Silva, 2008).

> Additional levels of complexity arise when culturally based considerations of appropriateness in pronoun use are transferred from L1 to L2, as is the case, for example, with personal pronouns.

In L2 writing instruction, and especially in the teaching of composition, frequent use of personal pronouns is often perceived to be appropriate and acceptable, particularly so in essays on personal views and ideas. On the other hand, large corpora of formal academic text have found that in many disciplines, the use of personal pronouns is very infrequent (Biber, et al., 1999; Carter & McCarthy, 2006; Leedham, 2016). In regard to L1 and L2 essay texts, prominent and significant distinctions have been identified between L1 basic writers' uses of various types of pronouns and those encountered in L2 academic prose in English (Ädel, 2006; Hinkel, 2002, 2003a; Leedham & Fernandez-Parra, 2017).

This chapter will begin with an examination of personal pronouns in academic texts, followed by slot fillers (*it* and *there*), and then demonstrative and indefinite pronouns and their functions in academic writing.

Personal Pronouns in Academic Texts

The textual purpose of personal pronouns in written discourse is to refer directly to the writer, the audience, and specific things or persons other than the writer or the audience.

> Corpus analyses demonstrate clearly that personal pronouns are orders of magnitude more frequent in conversations than in any other type of discourse, spoken or written.

In addition to conversations, personal pronouns are also encountered in fiction, but only rarely in academic text. As Biber, et al. (1999, p. 333) point out, personal pronouns mostly refer to persons, and "human beings are a more marginal topic" in academic prose.

Talking Shop

Cambridge University and Oxford University English dictionaries are highly regarded authoritative resources that usually include grammar and style guides. Here's the Cambridge Dictionary online excerpt on personal pronouns and noun phrases in formal styles and writing.

Detached Impersonal Style

Formal styles are common in English writing. There are many different kinds of formal style, and choice of grammar and vocabulary is important. Formal styles commonly contain few personal pronouns; noun phrases and the passive voice are commonly used. The more formal the style, the more likely it is that it will appear detached and impersonal.

- Few personal pronouns

Pronouns are replaced by impersonal constructions with *it* and **there**. Compare:

More personal
We suggest that you leave the building after 8 pm.
I should like to note a number of things here.

More detached and impersonal
It is suggested that you leave the building after 8 pm.
There are a number of things to note here.

- Noun phrases

Noun phrases, rather than verb phrases, are common in detached impersonal styles. This process is sometimes called nominalization.
Compare:

More personal
She will retire as company director in May next year.

More detached and impersonal
Her retirement as company director will be in May next year.
(https://dictionary.cambridge.org/us/grammar/british-
grammar/writing/detached-impersonal-style)

First Person Pronouns

In formal academic prose, the uses of first person pronouns usually mark personal narratives and examples, and these are rare (Paltridge, 2014; Paltridge & Starfield, 2011; Swales & Feak, 2012). Many researchers of academic discourse and prose have noted the highly depersonalized and objective character of academic prose that requires "author evacuation" (Johns, 1997, p. 57).

Formal and academic discourse and text strongly discourage personal pronouns, personal tone, and personal references.

In fact, according to Swales' (1990) seminal analysis on the written academic genre, academic texts are often expected to project objectivity and depersonalize text by means of vocabulary and grammar. Swales further argues that the teaching of writing needs to address the text and discourse conventions of the academic community. That is, L2 writing instruction needs to prepare students to write in the disciplines. Academic writing is a socially situated act that extends far beyond the writers' analyses of their inner explorations and thoughts.

Second Person Pronouns

Second person singular and plural pronouns are also very infrequent in academic prose because they are employed to address the reader directly (Swales & Feak, 2012). These pronouns require a specific individual to whom the text is addressed, and marks the conversational discourse (Carter & McCarthy, 2006).

Frequency Rates of First- and Second Person Pronouns in
Formal Academic Prose

Overall		
	I, me, we, us	0.006% (6 per 100,000 words)
	you	0.001% (1 per 100,000 words
Philosophy (the highest L1 corpus rate)		
	I, me, my, we, us, our	0.65% (6.5 per 1,000 words)
Marketing		
	I, me, my, we, us, our	0.62% (6.2 per 1000 words)
Applied Linguistics		
	I, me, my, we, us, our	0.48% (4.8 per 1,000 words)
L2 Academic Writing		
	I, me, my, we, us, our	1.89% in business/economics (1.89 per 100 words) 3.97% in humanities (3.97 per 100 words)
	you, your	0.50% in business/economics (0.5 per 100 words) 1.15% in humanities (1.15 per 100 words)

(Adapted from Biber, et al., 1999; Hyland, 1999, 2000; Hinkel, 2002, 2003a, 2005a)

Based on corpus studies of L1 academic texts, the rates of occurrences of *I, me, we*, and *us*, as well as *you* and *your*, constitute only a fraction of a percent (Biber, et al., 1999). To be sure, some amount of variation of personal pronoun use has been noted across various disciplines from philosophy to applied linguistics.

On the other hand, in L2 academic texts, personal narratives and examples can be common, and rates of first and second pronoun usage are orders of magnitude higher than in any type of L1 formal prose. In an example of a senior-level psychology assignment, included below, the use of personal pronouns may make the text appear to be a personal narrative.

> *Extroversion*
>
> *Is it possible for everyone to change one's behavior and thoughts by different environmental factors? **I** believe the answer is no doubt. One's childhood experience and background constitute his disposition for the first period. During this period, his family or school teachers might influence his development of character. Furthermore, he, as an adult in the second period, could transfer whether from introversion to extroversion or from extroversion to introversion, depending on his religion, culture, and personal experience in society. Perhaps, his personality will be changed again in the future. The best successful example is **my** personal experience to support this approach. **I** was so isolated and shy that **I** was not popular in **my** parents' eyes when **I** was a child. It won't be changed until **I** entering high school. Mr. Lee, one of **my** high school teachers, encouraged **me** and helped **me** to understand **my** own ability in languages that completely decided **my** future. After **I** attending many speech contests in school, **I** have become a self-confidence and talkative girl as a leader. Most friends consider **me** to be an extroverted person. Nevertheless, **I** discover that **my** personality has changing again and again after getting **my** teaching experience.*
>
> (From a senior student assignment in psychology)

In student writing, as in this excerpt, the use of a personal example as supporting information does not in fact demonstrate familiarity with course material and relevant sources. In academic prose, personal examples are typically seen as anecdotal and not particularly generalizable. That is, the writer is expected to provide formal academic evidence, such as studies, findings or data, to support her position that extroversion is a variable trait.

Third Person Pronouns

In addition to first-person narratives, L2 writers also employ third-person recounts and stories to support their positions. In many cases, due to narrative-like academic prose and restricted vocabulary, L2 writing includes high rates of third person pronouns (Hinkel, 1999, 2002, 2011; Leki, Cumming, & Silva, 2008). For example, in an essay on the economic benefits and pitfalls of credit cards, the student writer tells the story of his friend.

> *It is true that credit cards are really popular these days, but it has problems, like debt. For instance, one of **my** friends, who is Dan, had two gold credit*

*cards. But **he** didn't concern the budget of **his** account, while **he** was using the plastic money. So, **he** had heavy debt on **his** account. It took about two and half years to pay off **his** debt. After **he** had big trouble with charge cards, **he** cut **his** two gold credit cards with scissors. Now **he** does not have any kinds of credit cards.*

*Moreover, according to the Federal Reserve statistic, only 33% of the credit card holders pay full pay amount and another 67% pay only minimum amount or less than a full amount. The statistic shows **us** how people are abusing the credit card, and the phenomenon gets worse and worse.*

(From a student assignment in micro-economics)

In this example, the function of personal or third-party recounts is largely the same, that is, to provide validation for the main points expressed in the essay. Another point to make is that despite the fact that in many cases, L2 writers are familiar with employing published sources (e.g. *the Federal Reserve statistic*) as a means of rhetorical support, this technique might not be used consistently or in suitable contexts. In the credit card excerpt, the statistic cited by the student does not support the observation that users abuse credit cards or the claim that *the phenomenon gets worse and worse.*

Thus, instruction on the limited power of personal narratives to support essay points should coincide with the teaching of citing elaborated discussions of data and sources, combined with the fact that the citations must validate all points made in the text, and not just some of them.

In general terms, L2 writers need to be explicitly instructed to **avoid** the uses of:

- Personal examples, narratives, and recounts of personal experiences.
- Addressing the reader directly and, thus, second person pronouns.
- Personal tone and its attendant linguistic features, such as adjectives (**wonderful, great, terrible, horrible, disgusting**), adverbs (**very, much, really, definitely, pretty (good)**), and context-specific nouns (**winner, loser, miracle, magic**).

If these textual features appear in student texts, they can be replaced by common nouns or impersonal/indefinite pronouns (see below).

Action Point

A small list of frequent phrase substitutions to avoid personal pronoun uses can be very handy in academic writing across a range of disciplines. Students also can put together their own minimal phrase lists depending on the topic of writing or for particular writing assignments. Here are a few examples of phrase replacements without personal pronouns and references.

I think / I feel / I believe	– *According to the data/figures/ statistics,*
I will argue/provide/show	– *This paper/essay will argue/provide/ show*
You will see/notice	– *It can be seen/noticed*
You should call your doctor.	– *Patients can call their doctors.*

Personal stories, examples of personal experiences, as well as direct appeals to the audience, e.g. **you** or **your**, are typically considered conversational and are rarely found in formal academic writing. Additional alternatives can include, for example, **in fact, it seems, it appears, based on research/study findings/the fact that**. . . .

Even highly advanced L2 writers overuse first and second person pronouns in assignments in various disciplines, such as business, finance, and management. For example, in the excerpt below from an assignment on profitability, first and second person pronouns are employed in contexts where common nouns may be more appropriate. As has been mentioned (see chapter 3), L2 writers who are pressed for time and are dealing with high demands on their language skills often rely on employing vocabulary immediately accessible to them.

An excerpt from a student's academic assignment on profitability illustrates the use of first person pronouns that do not seem to be necessary.

*Profitability is especially useful for potential investors. Comparing Martin Marietta to its competitors over the profitability ratios, **we** can see that it performed well above the industry. The only concern is its business nature. Any political change will influence its business. If **our** perception toward the world future situation is same as current one, then Martin Marietta is a good buy. If not, then if the money **you** have is for the rest of **your** life then* *try some other industry. Otherwise, in the good time **you** get stable return and in war time, **you** get a lot more back. **My** recommendation is that if Martin Marietta gets new contracts in the new administration, **you** should buy their stock.*

(From a student paper on profitability)

In this excerpt, the uses of first person pronouns can be replaced by impersonal constructions.

we can see	→	– *it is easy to see* – *one can see* – *an analysis can show*
*If **our** perception toward the world future situation*	→	– *in the future, if the situation remains the same/all things being equal* – *if the world does not change much/a great deal* – *if the present situation continues to hold/remain the same*

Similarly, second person pronouns can be replaced by the indefinite pronoun *one* or frequent nouns, such as **buyers/investors.**

*if the money **you** have is for the rest of **your** life*	→	– *if the money one/buyers/investors invest(s) is/represents their entire savings* – *if one invests all his or her money*
*in the good time **you** get stable return and in war time, **you** get a lot more back*	→	– *in peace time one receives a stable return, and war increases the return on investment* – *the investment earns a stable return in peace and a larger one in the event of war*

A Point Worth Making in Teaching

- In conversation, the first person pronoun *I* is repeated 10 times more frequently than **all other personal pronouns combined** (Biber, et al., 1999).
- Thus, the uses of the first person pronoun tend to impart conversational and colloquial style to written academic prose.

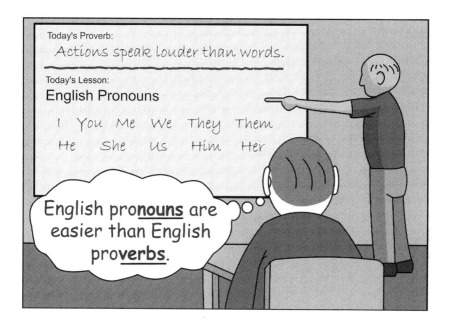

Pronouns as Noun Replacements

In academic prose, the use of third person singular and plural pronouns impart detachment, formality, and objectivity. Although functions of pronouns are far more complex than mere noun replacement, in L2 academic prose, their uses may be necessary when a particular noun is repeated to excess. For example, in the following excerpt from a student's assignment, the noun phrase *employed women* is repeated several times in a relatively short text.

> As the number of **employed women** has increased, marketers and consumer researchers interested in **employed women** who are young and have great consumption power. Women's employment outside of the home has led to changes the lifestyle which affect consumption patterns. As their lifestyle is changed, the **employed women** have been dominated by many factors in selecting clothing. What factors influenced the **employed women** in the selection of apparel? So it is important for marketers to understand the factors that have impact on **employed women's** clothing decision making.

However, merely replacing repeated nouns and noun phrases with corresponding pronouns (e.g. *employed women – they*) can lead to ambiguous and unclear constructions. For example:

> ?Many **stores** accept credit **cards**, but **they** can be expensive.

The reason that simply substituting pronouns for repeated nouns may not work very well in this example is that the sentence *many stores accept credit cards* contains two plural nouns: *stores* and *credit cards*, and both can be referred to by the pronoun *they*, resulting in a confusing structure.

Another problem with replacing nouns with pronouns can be noted if a relatively lengthy amount of text separates the noun and the pronoun replacement:

> Some **scholars** argue that political and economic situations, and ideology affect education. That is, the content and the method of education change not due to the **problems** in education in itself, but due to the political and economic situations, and ideology at the time. The **reasons** for the change are outside of education. **They** interpret history of education of the early republic period, the late eighteenth and early nineteenth century.
>
> (From a student essay on ideology in education)

- In this example, the pronoun **they** in the third sentence refers to **scholars** in the first.
- However, in the context of the excerpt, it may be somewhat difficult to track back the reference and determine that *they* does not refer to, for instance, the nouns *reasons* or *problems*.

> Repeated pronouns as noun replacements can be just as redundant as repeated nouns.

For example:

> With above context, some scholars believe that poor people or poor classes in our society maintain **their** own unique culture. Usually, **they** are dirty and are reluctant to clean their environment. **They** are also lazy and don't like to work hard. **They** depend on the income from **their** daily job or temporary employment or **they** receive welfare benefits. **They** are skeptical about life and aggressive to the current social structure. **They** use alcohol and drugs, and **they** are criminals. These attitudes of the first generation can be transferred to the next generation and be maintained for a long time.
>
> (From a student's assignment on socioeconomic stratification and discrimination)

This and earlier examples illustrate that merely replacing nouns with pronouns can be somewhat tricky and requires detailed familiarity with contextual constraints on pronoun referential uses and functions.

Replacing redundant nouns with other contextually suitable nouns, as well as pronouns, can be a productive way to construct a less repetitious text.

It-cleft and Impersonal *It* Structures

The impersonal pronoun *it* with copula *be* (where *it* is also called a dummy subject because it is empty of meaning) are more common in academic texts than practically any other written or spoken genre (Biber, et al., 1999). In academic prose, <u>*it + be*</u> constructions have several discourse and text functions.

(1) The most frequent – to depersonalize text and create an impression of the writer's distance and objectivity.
(2) To focus the sentence on information provided later in the sentence.
(3) To provide an element of hedging when accompanied by:

   o <u>*it + be*</u> + adjectives, as in *it is clear/useful/important/advantageous.*
   o <u>*it +*</u> linking verbs, as in *it seems*, *appears*, or *looks*.

For example:

> *It seems that every generation elicits new efforts to use different technologies to resolve unanswered or problematic questions.* (American Mysteries, Riddles, and Controversies; www.archives.gov)

It-cleft constructions are syntactically complex, and for this reason, they frequently present an area of difficulty for academic L2 writers. In the practical reality of writing an academic course assignment, many *it*-cleft structures can be avoided and replaced by other simpler constructions with similar functions.

How to Teach It

Trouble Spot

Missing *it + be* constructions when they are necessary.

Example trouble-spot sentences:

> *Companies may be difficult to hire qualified employees when the job market is high.*
> *Students are useful to practice individual notes and scales after they learn the piano keys.*

It-cleft constructions can be confusing. The concept of a dummy subject is not particularly easy to understand for speakers of many languages other than Germanic.

(A similar issue may arise with existential **there** subjects that are often confused with locative adverbials **there** – see below.)

For the teacher, the easiest way to correct the first sentence is simply to re-write it as in **it is difficult for companies to hire qualified employees . . .**

A better long-term solution can be to provide and teach **syntactically simpler options**.

TEACHING TIP #1

    (a) <u>*Hiring/To hire qualified employees*</u> *may be difficult for companies . . .*
    (b) *For companies,* <u>*qualified employees may be difficult to find/hire*</u> *. . .*

In these alternatives, the sentence focal information – that follows the **it + be** construction – is moved from the beginning of the sentence to the position of the sentence subject, with its important informational role.

TEACHING TIP #2

Impersonal **it** constructions can be presented as sentence slots (see chapter 4):

- Some are always filled regardless of context.
- Some are open for optional informational content.

Filled Slot	**+ BE** Slot	Adjective	(Optional Prepositional Slot)	Infinitive Slot
IT	may be/is	hard/easy	for xxx	to study.

A similar system of slots can be used for other structures with the dummy subject *it*:

Filled Slot	+ *seems/appears*	THAT-Clause
IT	*seems*	*that oil reserves should last for another forty years.*

A big advantage of this visual piece-by-piece constructing of sentences with *it* is that students can see that the subject has no referent (and is thus "empty" of meaning) and that it is a "constant" and invariable feature of *it*-cleft constructions.

TEACHING TIP #3

Various analyses of written academic corpora have shown that the non-referential *it* occurs frequently in the following combinations. These most-frequent constructions are useful for academic writers to know:

The Most Frequent *It*-cleft Constructions in Academic Writing

(1) With **Adjectives**.

   it is (not) (im)possible to/that   *it is interesting to*
   it is likely/unlikely that   *it is difficult/easy to*
   it is important to/that   *it is (not) clear that*
   it is necessary to   *it is true that*

(2) With **Modal Verbs** (**may, can, might, could**) – **it may be that . . .**

(3) With **Modal Verbs and Adjectives**.

   it may (not) be (im)possible to/that   *it may be necessary to/that*
   it should be possible to/that   *it is clear that*
   it is important to/that

(4) With **Passive Verbs**.

   it can be seen that   *it has been suggested that*
   it should be noted that   *it has also been ~~*
                                  determined, found,
                                  argued, stated,
                                  implied, shown,
                                  noted, written

Most passive constructions are accompanied by *that*-clauses that contain the focal information.

There Existential Subject

Like the non-referential *it*, the existential *there* has little semantic content. However, the syntactic structure of *there*-constructions is much simpler than *it*-constructions.

> The existential *there* is frequent in L2 writing, but not in formal academic prose.

The discourse function of existential constructions is to introduce new information and/or topics, and most co-occur with place and time adverbs, e.g. *there are few of them in the world today, there are many such teachers in my country.*

- The existential *there* structures are particularly rare in academic writing: they are encountered fewer than 10 times per 1 million words (Biber, et al., 1999).
- The subject *there* is more frequent in conversational than written discourse.
- Because *there*-constructions are relatively syntactically simple, L2 academic writers tend to overuse them in their prose (Hinkel, 2003a).
- For this reason, students may be encouraged to employ them sparingly and judiciously.

In academic writing, *there*-subjects occur only in a handful of constructions, such as:

- *There + seem/appear to be.*
- *There + be + supposed to be.*
- *There + used to be*

in past time and past tense contexts

- *There + exist*

the most common alternative to *be*-verbs found almost exclusively in academic prose

Referring to Earlier Text: Functions of Demonstratives

Demonstrative pronouns (***this, that, these, those***) play an important role in text cohesion because they have indexal (pointing) and referential functions. However, demonstratives can be ambiguous and vague when it is not immediately clear what specific noun or phrase they refer to.

Research into academic text has found that demonstratives are comparatively common precisely due to their lack of specificity and their ability to project objectivity (Swales, 2005).

> - ***This*** occurs far more frequently than ***these, that,*** or ***those***. The combined frequency rate of all demonstrative pronouns stands at 0.45% per million words of academic prose (Biber, et al., 1999).
> - In general, demonstratives are one of the simplest cohesive devices in English (but contextually simple is not the same as easy for L2 writers to use).

In L2 writing, the limited cohesive capacity of demonstratives is often misconstrued, and the occurrences of these pronouns can be highly frequent (Hinkel, 2001a, 2001b, 2002).[1] The example below is extracted from a student's academic assignment on the rising costs of farming.

> *Since cows are housed in areas that cannot be kept clean, there is an increased disease incident and other health problems, which result in high input costs.* ***This*** *is the reason why other farming systems are being considered for lowering* ***this*** *cost of milk production.*

In the example, the first occurrence of ***this*** actually refers to several "reasons" that "other farming methods are being considered," that is, a lack of cleanliness in cow housing, increased incidence of disease, and the high input costs.

> In English, a singular demonstrative pronoun, **this** or **that**, has a limited referential capacity and cannot refer to a number of referential points at one time.

The second ***this*** refers to a plural noun ***costs*** that is not located in the immediate proximity to the pronoun. In both cases, the use of demonstratives makes the text appear confusing.

The use of demonstratives requires adherence to largely rigid noun-pronoun agreement in number.

- Singular pronouns _**this**_ and _**that**_ cannot refer to plural nouns.
- _**This**_ and _**these**_ can "point" to **nouns in their close proximity** (or a close proximity to the speaker as in **This is a great computer**, when one is looking or pointing at a computer).
- _**That**_ and _**those**_ are markers of a more **distant reference**.
- Neither type of demonstratives can refer to a sizeable portion of text, as can often be encountered in L2 texts (Hinkel, 2001a, 2002).

Action Point

"Pointing" to close proximity noun phrases or information (as in summaries, for example) is the main text and discourse function of _**this**_ and _**these**_. However, based on large corpus analyses, Swales (2005) concludes that the uses of _**this**_ in reference to noun phrases strongly dominate in academic prose and calls _**this**_-references without noun phrases "unattended."

In L2 teaching, an expedient technique for locating the unattended _**this**_ and _**that**_ is to identify specifically and explicitly what the pronouns refer to in context (as above). For example, **What does _this is reason_ refer to? What does _this cost_ refer to?** (Swales & Feak, 2012, p. 43).

Here's an introductory excerpt from an L2 undergraduate assignment in organizational behavior, on the topic of balancing individual achievement with group success, "using support from assigned readings." The teaching technique for explicitly identifying attended and unattended pronoun references can be used, e.g. **What does _this_ refer to in "this is a tricky situation"?**

Introduction

*_**This** is a tricky situation because make me think about very important and famous people around. And the problem is out there. Now we don't have the time enought to do **this** kind of "moral judgements." The life is going so fast, and we decide to take **this** option, not thinking about it. The problem with **this**, is that we really needs to take **this** time to think a little bit more. If we compare our ability to get more information about people, we are in an advantaged level. For **this**_

> *reason,* **this** *level of knowledge should open our mind to increase our ability to put many things in the balance at the same time, and then based on readings, in* **this** *case, a person's achievement decide if* **those** *goals are more important than the group.*
>
> For the plentiful uses of **this**, **these**, **that**, and **those**, teaching activities can include similar examples or self-editing practice of students' own texts.

Referring to Earlier and Following Text: Nouns to Enumerate

In addition to demonstratives, various lexical means of establishing text cohesion have been identified and can be used with greater positive effect and sophistication for the text. In English, a number of lexically simple nouns can refer to several textual points or entire classes of nouns at one time. For example:

(1) *Employment participation depends on people's demographic* **characteristics***, such as gender, age, education, marital status, and the presence of young children at home. Economic* **factors** *and government policies also affect labor force participation.* (www.cbo.gov/publication/53452#section2)

(2) *How do health sciences respond to the* **problems** *outlined in the article on air and water pollution?*

Enumerative nouns such as *factor* and *problem* have a cohesive property of "catch-alls" because they usually refer to a few points previously mentioned or those that follow. Although not particularly lexically sophisticated, they appear to be more advanced than, for example, demonstrative pronouns (Hinkel, 2015). These academic nouns are rare in conversations because their functions in text are lexically and semantically complex.

- Many highly useful and flexible enumerative nouns are essential for L2 writers to learn and use.
- The explicit teaching of enumerative "catch-all" nouns has an additional benefit of highlighting the differences between informal conversations and formal writing.

The Most Frequent Enumerative "Catch-all" Nouns

advantage	approach	aspect	attempt
background	behavior	category	challenge
change	characteristic	circumstance	class
consequence	course [of action]	criterion(ia)	deal
difficulty	dilemma	disadvantage	drawback
element	episode	event	evidence
experience	facet	fact	factor
feature	form	issue	item
manner	method	objective	occurrence
phase	period	plan	practice
problem	process	program	project
purpose	reason	result	scenario
shortfall	stage	step	subject
system	task	technique	tendency
term	topic	trend	type

Some of these nouns have very similar meanings and can be used interchangeably to form cohesive ties in many contexts.

Lexical Substitutions of Enumerative "Catch-all" Nouns

aspect – facet	category – class
characteristic – feature	disadvantage – drawback
element – item	phase – stage
process – system	approach – method
difficulty – problem – issue	task – project

Everyone Has Something: Indefinite Pronouns

Indefinite pronouns that consist of **every-**, **no-**, **some-**, and **any**-words (**everybody**, **everything**, **nothing**, **anyone**) are markedly more frequent in L2 academic texts than in comparable L1 prose (Hinkel, 2002, 2011).

- *Every-* and *no*-words are extremely rare in formal writing, and they are usually associated with overstatement and exaggerations (Quirk, et al., 1985; Hinkel, 2005b).

- *Some-* and *any*-words are often so vague that they may have little semantic content.

Here's an example:

> People hear the word "information" **_everywhere any_** day and usually define "information" as news, facts, knowledge, data, and so on. **_Everyone_** wants to have as much information as they can when they make business decisions. However, in **_every_** field of business, information is different for many people, and it depends on what people specialize in. **_Every_** student using the internet as the information system tries to search for **_something_** that they want to gain through it. And the information systems transmit **_something_** to learners. People have heard the concepts of facts, data, and knowledge. Although these concepts have different meaning, facts are **_something_** that have happened or have been done. This is the type of information that is valuable for **_everyone_** in **_any_** business.
>
> (From a student's academic paper on
information technology)

Studies of written English-language corpora have shown that *every-* and *no-*words are marked exaggeratives, and they are hardly ever found in academic prose. Quantifiers such as *some* and *no* are encountered occasionally (2.5 occurrences per hundred thousand words, that is, 0.0025%) (Biber, et al., 1999). In conversations and speaking, however, *every-* and *no-* words occur with greater frequency in overstatements, inflation of facts, or hyperboles.

Research into L2 text demonstrates that in L2 prose overstatements and exaggerations are employed as a means of rhetorical persuasion common in rhetorical traditions other than Anglo-American (Hinkel, 2003b; Hu & Cao, 2011; Hyland, 2008).

In many cases, *some-* and *any*-words (*someone, something, anybody*) function as hedges that express vague general truths and commonly held opinions, together with uncertainty and imprecision.

- In some discourse traditions, indefiniteness and hesitation are considered to be desirable characteristics because they allow writers to state their opinions indirectly, without the risk of offending or losing rapport with the reader.
- In Anglo-American academic prose neither exaggerations nor vagueness are valued highly.

For instance, in the example above, the *-body* and *-one* pronouns can be relatively easily replaced with nouns, such as *business managers/researchers/students/community*, and *-thing* pronouns with contextually relevant nouns.

> It is important for L2 writers to learn vocabulary substitutions and use only sparingly **every-** and **no-** pronouns and **some-** and **any-** words.

Chapter Summary

On the whole, the uses of specific personal pronouns differ by genre and text types.

> Work on pronouns represents only one aspect of a bigger picture of teaching L2 writers to identify their audience and adjust their text accordingly.

- First person pronouns are rare in academic prose, but they are common in personal narratives and, occasionally, fiction.
- Second person pronouns are hardly ever found in written academic prose. They are associated with direct appeals to and/or establishing common ground with the audience.
- Third person pronouns can be useful in avoiding repetition of proper nouns. However, uses of third person pronouns require care to ensure that they refer to specific and easily identifiable nouns in the preceding text.
- *It*-cleft constructions are common in academic text because they project objectivity, depersonalization, and authorial distance. Such constructions represent a persistent problem for L2 writers and may require additional and specifically focused work and practice.
- Because demonstratives, *this, that, these, those,* represent the simplest cohesive device, they are frequently overused in L2 text. The popularity of demonstratives can be reduced to some extent by expanding the vocabulary range to include enumerative "catch-all" nouns.
- Indefinite pronouns, *some-, any-, every-, no-* words, with their exaggerative or vague meanings, are extremely infrequent in formal writing.

Strategies and Tactics for Teaching and Teaching Activities

Teaching Activities

The goal of the teaching suggestions and activities presented below is to promote academic noun learning and retention.

- Noticing the uses and meanings of nouns (see chapter 3).
- Explicit and incidental learning of words (see chapter 3).
- Discussing contextualized occurrences of nouns and their vocabulary substitutions.

It is very important that the teacher follow up on the assigned exercises and vocabulary learning tasks: review, review, review. And more review.

- Learning 10 new words per hour is not an unreasonable rate (see chapter 3).
- It is through discussion and activities that words are actually learned.
- In-class discussions and/or follow-up work with nouns and other words provide the most important benefit because they give students additional opportunities for review.

All teaching activities exemplified in this chapter and other chapters have been used for decades with L2 writers at various levels of proficiency, from beginning to advanced. The teaching suggestions presented here are based on using texts easily obtainable online, e.g. advertisements, book cover descriptions, and news reports. Example texts are easy to find.

As a general rule, if text simplification is needed, it is best to eliminate rare words rather than those that are frequent, even if they are lexically and structurally complex.

Various written genres can be relatively easily identified by their text features. The goal of the activities below is to help learners to identify and notice pronouns (and other textual characteristics, such as adjectives and adverbs) that distinguish various types of prose.

Genres and Pronouns: Personal Narratives or Academic Text

(1) A couple of pages from memoirs or juvenile romantic fiction can be analyzed for the uses of personal pronouns and, for example, determine the frequency count of first, second, or third person pronouns in a paragraph or a page.

(2) Then a similar analysis and/or computation can be performed with a text excerpt of a proximate length from an introductory level textbook or a science or business report.

Questions to guide the class or small group discussion

- Why do pronoun counts differ?
- What is the author's purpose in either text? Is it to tell a personal story or present impersonal information?
- How many occurrences of the impersonal pronoun *it*, for example, can be identified in each text?

Preparing to work on an assignment

- What is the assignment's rhetorical purpose?
- If it is to tell a personal story, then certainly the use of first person pronouns is necessary.
- If it is not, then how should the writers approach the text?

In group activities, different types of text can be analyzed and discussed, e.g. a student essay/personal narrative may be contrasted with a published argumentation/position essay, an opinion or an editorial article with company promotional materials, or excerpts on textbooks on philosophy and business/economics.

Topics of the materials can differ widely to match students' interests and can range from those on fashion, cars, and computer games to pollution, nutrition, and regional history. After students analyze various genres of text, depending on the students' proficiency level, they can present their results to another group or the entire class, or they can write a short report to describe their findings and observations.

> Part of the benefit of this exercise is helping students develop their noticing skills when they are reading or working with text.

Demonstratives and Enumerative Nouns in Text Cohesion

(1) Work with demonstrative pronouns needs to address their limited cohesive power in English and the requisite noun–pronoun agreement in number, e.g. *employees – these workers, the author's argument/claim – this position.*

> Most demonstratives require the presence of identifiable noun or phrase references in the immediate proximity to the pronoun.

(2) Demonstratives can refer only to nouns, noun phrases, or clauses, but they cannot be used to refer to entire contexts or implied referents.

(3) For this purpose, learners can be asked to identify the specific nouns or phrases to which demonstratives in texts refer.

For example, drawing connecting lines or arrows in texts or their own essays can help students understand the highly limited cohesive power of demonstratives in English. If a demonstrative pronoun does not point at any particular noun, phrase, or clause, then this pronoun probably cannot be used as an effective cohesive device.

(a) The textual uses and functions of enumerative nouns can also be discussed. Students can be similarly asked to draw the connecting "strings" to establish lexical ties between particular words or phrases.

(b) For instance, nouns such as *advantage, factor, problem, reason, stage, term, type* are expected to have specific identifiable referents in text, to which these nouns are "connected."

(c) Ask students to "tie" each of the enumeratives to the structures, text elements, or text excerpts to which these nouns refer.

(d) If such structures or short contexts cannot be easily identified, then enumerative nouns may not be the best choice of cohesive device.

For activities to work with indefinite pronouns, see chapter 12 on Hedges.

Endnote

1 In some contexts, *this* can refer to several points provided that a restatement/paraphrase noun is used to apply to all points covered by *this*, e.g. *Senator Smith called members of his*

party useless civil servants, and <u>*this gaff*</u> *is likely to cause his resignation* (<u>this</u> tip was suggested by Marcella Frank, New York University).

Further Reading

Celce-Murcia, M. & Olshtain, E. (2000). *Discourse and context in language teaching.* New York, NY: Cambridge University Press.

An excellent and teacher-oriented book on the importance of discourse and its components in spoken interactions and written texts. Language features that characterize different genres and socio-cultural factors are essential for comprehension and production of different types of texts and talk. Language teaching necessarily entails an awareness of discourse and pragmatics that can be applied to course curricula and assessment.

Hinkel, E. (2001). Matters of cohesion in L1 and L2 academic texts. *Applied Language Learning, 12*(2), 111–132.

A comparative analysis of median frequency rates of cohesive devices employed in academic texts of L1 and L2 students who are speakers of English, Japanese, Korean, Indonesian, and Arabic. The study focuses on the median rates of phrase-level coordinators, sentence transitions, logical-semantic conjunctions, demonstrative pronouns, and enumerative and resultative nouns. The study shows that, regardless of their first languages, L2 texts employ sentence transitions and demonstrative pronouns at significantly higher median frequency rates than do basic L1 texts.

Swales, J. (1990). *Genre analysis.* Cambridge: Cambridge University Press.

A seminal work on the connections between sociolinguistics, text linguistics, and discourse analysis to shed light on the language characteristics of various genres, with a focus on academic writing and teaching. This book is important reading for L2 professionals who work in teaching English for academic purposes and college writing.

References

Ädel, A. (2006). *Metadiscourse in L1 and L2 English.* Amsterdam: John Benjamins.

Biber, D., Johansson, S., Leech, G., Conrad, S., & Finegan, E. (1999). *Longman grammar of spoken and written English.* Harlow: Pearson.

Carter, R. & McCarthy, M. (2006). *Cambridge grammar of English: A comprehensive guide.* Cambridge: Cambridge University Press.

Harwood, N. (2006). (In)appropriate personal pronoun use in political science: A qualitative study and a proposed heuristic for future research. *Written Communication, 23*(4), 424–450.

Hinkel, E. (1999). Objectivity and credibility in L1 and L2 academic writing. In E. Hinkel (Ed.), *Culture in second language teaching and learning* (pp. 90–108). Cambridge: Cambridge University Press.

Hinkel, E. (2001a). Matters of cohesion in L1 and L2 academic texts. *Applied Language Learning, 12*(2), 111–132.

Hinkel, E. (2001b). Giving examples and telling stories in academic essays. *Issues in Applied Linguistics, 12*(2), 149–170.

Hinkel, E. (2002). *Second language writers' text*. New York, NY: Routledge.

Hinkel, E. (2003a). Simplicity without elegance: Features of sentences in L2 and L1 academic texts. *TESOL Quarterly, 37*, 275–301.

Hinkel, E. (2003b). Adverbial markers and tone in L1 and L2 students' writing. *Journal of Pragmatics, 35*(2), 208–231.

Hinkel, E. (2005a). Analyses of L2 text and what can be learned from them. In E. Hinkel (Ed.), *Handbook of research in second language teaching and learning* (pp. 615–628). New York, NY: Routledge.

Hinkel, E. (2005b). Hedging, inflating, and persuading in L2 academic writing. *Applied Language Learning, 15*, 29–53.

Hinkel, E. (2011). What research on second language writing tells us and what it doesn't. In E. Hinkel (Ed.), *Handbook of research in second language teaching and learning, Volume 2* (pp. 523–538). New York, NY: Routledge.

Hinkel, E. (2015). *Effective curriculum for teaching L2 writing: Principles and techniques*. New York, NY: Routledge.

Hu, G. & Cao, F. (2011). Hedging and boosting in abstracts of applied linguistics articles: A comparative study of English- and Chinese-medium journals. *Journal of Pragmatics, 43*(2), 2795–2809.

Hyland, K. (1999). Disciplinary discourses: Writer stance in research articles. In C. Candlin & K. Hyland (Eds.), *Writing texts, processes and practices* (pp. 99–120). London: Longman.

Hyland, K. (2000). *Disciplinary discourses: Social interactions in academic writing*. London: Longman.

Hyland, K. (2008). Academic clusters: Text patterning in published and postgraduate writing. *International Journal of Applied Linguistics, 18*(1), 41–62.

Johns, A. (1997). *Text, role, and context: Developing academic literacies*. Cambridge: Cambridge University Press.

Leedham, M. (2016). *Chinese students' writing in English: Implications from a corpus-driven study*. London: Routledge.

Leedham, M. & Fernandez-Parra, M. (2017). Recounting and reflecting: The use of first person pronouns in Chinese, Greek and British students' assignments in engineering. *Journal of English for Academic Purposes, 26*(1), 66–77.

Leki, I., Cumming, A. & Silva, T. (2008). *A synthesis of research on second language writing in English*. New York, NY: Routledge.

Paltridge, B. (2014). Genre and second language academic writing. *Language Teaching, 47*, 303–318.

Paltridge, B. & Starfield, S. (2011). Research in English for specific purposes. In E. Hinkel (Ed.), *Handbook of research in second language teaching and learning, Volume 2* (pp. 196–121). New York, NY: Routledge.

Quirk, R., Greenbaum, S., Leech, G. & Svartvik, J. (1985). *A comprehensive grammar of the English language*. New York: Longman.

Swales, J. (1990). *Genre analysis*. Cambridge: Cambridge University Press.

Swales, J. (2005). Attended and unattended "this" in academic writing: A long and unfinished story. *ESP Malaysia, 11*, 1–15.

Swales, J. & Feak, C. (2012). *Academic writing for graduate students* (3rd edn). Ann Arbor, MI: University of Michigan Press.

Verb Tenses and Active–Passive Constructions in Text Cohesion

7

Overview

- Tenses and aspects.
- Tense and time.
- The simple present tense.
- The past tense.
- The future tense.
- Aspect.
- Typical problems with the uses of tenses and aspects.
- Active and passive voice in academic writing.

Much earlier research has demonstrated that in general English tenses are often difficult for L2 learners to use appropriately (Hinkel, 1992, 1997, 2004, 2017). However, errors in the uses of tenses are considered to be among the most egregious problems in the quality of academic L2 text (Celce-Murcia, 2002; Ferris, 2009, 2011; Horowitz, 1986; Vaughan, 1991).

Tenses and Aspects

Although grammar textbooks describe around 12 tenses or more (e.g. the present progressive, the present perfect, or the present perfect progressive), the simplest way to teach tenses is to start by separating tenses and aspects (see also chapter 4).

- There are three tenses in English: the **past**, the **present**, and the **future**.
- There are also two aspects: the **progressive** and the **perfect**.
- The **tenses and aspects can combine and create a nice stew** that includes such ingredients as the past perfect or the present perfect progressive.

Fortunately, in effect, only a few combinations of tenses and aspects are used in academic writing, as opposed to, for example, conversational discourse or grammar classes. For academic writers the task of using tenses and aspects correctly is greatly simplified. For example, past tense constructions are relatively infrequent in academic prose, compared to, for instance, press reportage, personal letters, or face-to-face conversations.

In formal academic writing, the tense system provides an important means of textual cohesion (Hinkel, 2005; Swales & Feak, 2012) (see also chapter 11). Inconsistent uses of tenses and aspects represent highly common types of errors in L2 academic writing. The reasons that in L2 academic writing tenses are often employed inconsistently are usually based on L2 writers' logical analyses of the sequence of events along the time continuum.

Tense and Time

- Errors with inconsistent uses of tenses and aspects are highly prevalent in L2 academic writing.
- In the long run, it may be helpful and effective to address these problems in teaching to provide L2 writers the means of correcting or preventing such errors in their own writing.

In all human languages, time (but not necessarily tense) is divided into three large categories: **now** (the present), **before now** (the past), and **after now** (the future).

Timeline

| before now | now | after now |

←————————————————|————————————————→

In English, as in other languages, the **tense** marks the time and connects an action or event to a particular time.

Here's an example.

Tense Meanings

The Past Tense	
*Scientists **sought** knowledge.*	A **finished** action that took place before now – ~~ marked by the past tense verb ***sought***
The Present Tense	
*Scientists **seek** knowledge.*	A **general** action that took place in the past, takes place in the present, and is likely to continue into the future – ~~ marked by the present tense verb ***seek***
The Future Tense	
*Scientists **will seek** knowledge.*	An action that **did not take** place in the past, **does not take** place in the present, but is **certain** to take place in the future (the time forward from now) –~~ marked by the future tense ***will***

English Tenses on a Timeline

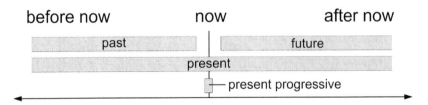

Tenses in Academic Writing

---

(1) The present tense is used more than three times more frequently than the past tense.

(2) Phrases with modal verbs (***can/may/might go***), and hence no overt tense markers, represent 10–15% of all verb phrases (Biber, et al., 1999; Carter & McCarthy, 2006).

This chapter focuses primarily on uses and functions of the present tense due to its prevalence, and to a smaller extent, on those in the past tense and verb aspects.

The Simple Present Tense

Meanings and Forms

The simple present tense refers to actions and events that are general, that is, they have no specific (or definite) time to which they refer (Leech, 2004; Quirk, et al., 1985).

Present Tense Meanings

---

(1) The present tense refers to actions and events that take place generally – including the present, but not necessary at the present moment or time.

*Sociologists **study** social experiences in each stage of life.*

- The action ***study*** refers to general time, that is, it took place in the past, takes place in the present, and is likely to continue to take place in the future.
- ***Study*** may not necessarily take place at this moment if none of the sociologists are at work, at this moment, studying social experiences.

(2) In academic writing, the present tense refers to states or habitual (and repeated) activities. It typically occurs with:

- ***Be***-verbs, e.g. *Rice **is** normally an annual plant, and its edible seed **is** the grain.*

- Linking verbs (**become, seem, appear**), e.g. *Cooking rice **seems** very easy, but in some cases, it **is** not.*
- Stative verbs, e.g. **consist, believe, know**, e.g. *The rice grain **consists** of an outer covering, the hull, and the fruit.*

Present Tense Verb Markers

With plural, and 1st and 2nd person subjects	Ø	*Scientists, I, we, you, they* **studyØ.**
With 3rd person singular subjects	**-s** or **-es**	*The scientist, he, she, it* **studies.**

Uses and Functions

Generally, in academic writing, the present tense is strongly associated with stative and mental verbs (*believe, **know**, **require**, **think**, **understand***), while the past tense denotes specific actions and events in the past time, such as case studies (Quirk, et al., 1985).

> For L2 writers, the present tense provides a relatively safe grammatic venue: in academic text the uses of the simple present tense are highly conventionalized and appropriate in various contexts.

One of the contexts where the past tense can be appropriate – but entirely optional – is in citations of earlier research. However, even in these constructions, the present tense can be used appropriately (Swales, 1990; Swales & Feak, 2012).

Smith (2020)   **found / investigated / reported** . . .
Johnson (2015)   **finds / investigates / reports** . . .

> - The uses of **"citational present"** are very common in the academic genre, e.g. in presentations of general facts, opinions, or research findings.
> - Citing, reviewing, paraphrasing, and referring to sources allows writers options in their choice of tenses.

Here are a few examples:

Bobson (2025) __points__ to the recent decreases in employment rates among high school students.

Jane Peterson (2026) also __examines__ the socialization processes in medical school.

It __is__ difficult to estimate the number of youngsters involved in home schooling.

Most adolescents in the United States __live__ in or just outside an urban area. Urban children __are__ more likely than rural children to have access to community or recreation. Nevertheless, rural children __are__ more likely than other children to share a meal with their family every day of the week.

(www.hhs.gov/ash/oah/facts-and-stats/changing-face-of-americas-adolescents/index.html)

With the exception of references to specific actions and events that occurred in the past, for L2 writers, the task of constructing academic text can be greatly simplified when large portions of their assignments and papers (if not entire assignments and papers) can be written in the simple present tense.

- L2 writers should be encouraged to use the simple present tense whenever possible in their prose.
- The academic present tense, however, requires establishing the subject–verb agreement and doing so correctly in most occurrences.

The example below is excerpted from a student's paper on gender and reasoning skills.

Present Tense Uses in Student Academic Writing: An Example

Women __are__ a minority in school science classes and in the scientific society in the US, which __are__ well-known phenomena. Research on gender and science __shows__ us that gender differences in science education __come__ from achievement, attitude, and motivation, or science course selection. The purpose of the study by John Smith, a professor in the Department of Education, __is__ to investigate gender-related differences between gender-related reasoning skills and learning interests during the early adolescence stage. His study __hopes__ that the result *can help figure out explanations to the differences that **exist** in school courses participation.*

*In this research, a videotaped group test **is** used to measure students development. This test **contains** 12 videotaped simple experiments and demonstrations. At the end of each demonstration, students **answer** questions and **justify** their solutions. Students with correct answers **receive** two points. Then students **are** categorized by their points into concrete, transitional, or formal reasoners. Students also **have** to write down two subject fields which they **are** most interested in. . . .*

The simple present tense is employed throughout the text – beginning with a general introduction and in the discussion of a specific experiment. Swales and Feak (2012) refer to what they call "citational present," often considered to be useful and appropriate in, for instance, introductions and citations from sources. The flexible academic present tense allows L2 writers to avoid pitfalls and complications associated with the use of other more complex English tenses.

> The flexibility of the conventionalized simple present tense can help simplify tense uses in L2 writing – with the exception of references to time-specific events, such as case studies, historical analyses, or biographical descriptions.

A handful of verbs tend to occur predominantly in the simple present tense, and these are easy to learn.

Verbs Predominantly Used in the Present Tense

care	differ	doubt	imply	know	matter
mean	mind	suppose	tend	want	

Important Caveats

➢ The simple present tense cannot be used to refer to actions and events that take place at this very moment or at any specific moment.

> In academic writing, a lack of grammatically correct subject-and-verb agreement is considered to be a serious error.
> For L2 writers, dealing with subject–verb agreement is made more complex because many learners have trouble identifying the main (head) subject noun in a subject noun phrase.

(See chapter 3 for teaching techniques on how to locate the head subject noun).

Talking Shop

In 1946, in his widely acclaimed article, Edward Calver provided the following definition of the present tense that has since served as a foundation for much of the subsequent work in English grammar.

> The basic meaning of the simple present tense is the constitution of things, logical, physical, psychological, essential, etc.; of the present progressive, mere occurrence. The distinction between them is not a time-distinction.
>
> (Calver, 1946, p. 317)

In contemporary publications, English **tenses and aspects** are sometimes referred to as **abstract and symbolic concepts** because their occurrences in language often defy explanations in terms of real time and time measurements.

Many L2 learners attempt to establish reasoned and sensible connections between tense and aspect meanings, and time divisions that are a universal construct in most human societies. In teaching, it can be very helpful to explain that such connections do not necessarily prevail in English, e.g.

- *A British fleet under Admiral Nelson **defeats** a French and Spanish fleet in 1805.*
- *The Pharaoh **will resist** the demand.*
- *When they finally **land**, the Pilgrims **are** hungry and cold.*
- *Next week, we **leave** on Tuesday and **return** on Friday.*

The Past Tense

Meanings and Forms

- In the teaching of grammar, much attention is usually devoted to the formation and meanings of the past tense.
- In academic writing, past tense verbs represent less than 18% of all verbs that have tense (Biber, et al., 1999).
- Most past tense verbs denote specific, limited-time activities.
- The English past tense is sometimes called the **definite past**, employed largely in "historical or biographical statements which have specific people, places, or objects as their topics" (Quirk, et al., 1985, p. 184).

Past Tense Verb Markers

-ed or **The past forms of irregular verbs** e.g. *brought, sang, sent, taught,* *thought, took, wrote*	*The scientist, he, she, it* **studied**. *The exam, I, he, she, it* **began**.

Complete lists of irregular verbs are found in practically every grammar textbook or dictionary (and for this reason, the form of the past tense verb is not examined here in any detail).

Past Tense Meanings

(1) In past tense constructions, time adverbs play an important role and can greatly assist in identifying the time of the action or event.

   In early American history, the family **assumed** *responsibility for educating its children.*

   – The sentence is marked by the past time adverb phrase *in early American history*.

(2) However, when the adverb phrase is omitted, the action remains in the past time.

   The family **assumed** *responsibility for educating its children.*

– The meaning of the past tense verb **_assumed_** indicates that the action was performed or a state existed in the past and was finished in the past.

Uses and Functions

The verbs used in the past tense refer to actions, events, or states that took place or existed in the past and no longer continue in the present (Quirk, et al., 1985).

- The past tense <u>necessarily</u> marks an action or a state for the past time, no longer continuing at the present time.
- The past tense usually refers to specific and finished (as in completely finito, done and over with) past time actions, events, and states.

In academic writing, **past tense uses necessarily require a past time marker**, such as an adverb, phrase, or clause, that warrants the uses of the past tense, e.g. *last month, five years ago*.

The past time marker **applies to an entire text excerpt** – until a new time marker is used to flag that the time and the tense can be switched.

Contextual Tense Markers and Tense Switches: An Example

> The past tense marker

In the 1840s, *Dr. John Gorrie of Florida* **_proposed_** *the idea of cooling cities to relieve residents of "the evils of high temperatures." Gorrie's medical practice* **_showed_** *that cooling* **_was_** *the key to avoiding diseases like malaria and making patients more comfortable, but his system for cooling hospital rooms* **_required_** *ice to be shipped to Florida from frozen lakes and streams in northern locations. Although Gorrie* **_was_** *unsuccessful at bringing his patented technology to the marketplace, his invention* **_created_** *the foundation for modern air conditioning and refrigeration.* **_In modern times_**, *the air conditioner* **_is_** *one of the most important inventions – cooling homes, businesses and systems that* **_are_** *critical to our world.*

> The tense switch to the present after the present tense marker

(www.energy.gov/articles/history-air-conditioning)

In the excerpt, the past time adverb phrase _**In the 1840s**_ marks the beginning of the past tense use that continues throughout the text until the present time adverb is encountered: _**In modern times**_. The present time adverb marks the beginning of the present tense use and shifts the entire text to the general present.

> - In academic writing, a consistent use of tense is needed to establish textual cohesion.
> - A specific-tense context is framed by time markers – until a new tense marker allows a tense "switch." For example, past-time adverbs flag the past tense uses and apply to the entire context – until another time marker comes up.

Inconsistent uses of tenses in students' writing is discussed in the section on Trouble Spots later in this chapter.

Case Studies and Specific Past Events

In academic writing, the past tense can be useful in specific and limited contexts, for example:

- Case studies in business or environmental studies.
- Specific experiments in, say, psychology or sociology.
- Examples of specific past-time events.

For example, the text below refers to a specific event that took place in 1904.

At the St. Louis World's Fair _**in 1904**_, _organizers_ _**used**_ _mechanical refrigeration to cool the Missouri State Building. The system_ _**used**_ _35,000 cubic feet of air per minute to cool the 1,000-seat auditorium, the rotunda and other rooms within the Missouri State Building. It_ _**marked**_ _the first time the American public_ _**was**_ _exposed to the concept of comfort cooling. A big breakthrough in comfort cooling technology came in the 1920s, when Americans_ _**flocked**_ _to movie theaters to watch Hollywood stars on the silver screen. Air conditioning_ _**is**_ _**now**_ _in nearly 100 million American homes, representing 87% of all households._

> The tense switch to the present with the present tense marker

(www.energy.gov/articles/history-air-conditioning)

In contextual examples and descriptions of past-time events or states, the uses of the past tense are framed by means of adverbs or adverbial prepositional phrases that specifically "switch" the time to the past, e.g. **_in 1904_**. Within the past-time context, the discourse continues in the past tense until it is switched to the present tense by means of another marker, e.g. **_now_**.

In another example, the "switch" marker is not an adverbial phrase of time, but a past-time event flagged by the past tense verb **_was + a time_** – even though the adverb today begins the paragraph.

> The tense switch to the past after the past tense marker

*Practically unimaginable today, there **was a time** when cell phones **didn't** exist. The first modern cell phone **was** demonstrated in a call from Chicago to Alexander Graham Bell's grandson, in Berlin, Germany almost 40 years ago. The 1983 phone's price **was** $3,995. In 1990, there **were** just over 5 million people in the country with cell phones. In 2000, that number **was** nearly 110 million. **Now**, close to 100 percent of Americans **have** cell phones or smart phones.*

> The tense switch to the present with the present tense marker

(www.census.gov/library/audio/profile-america/
profileeven/profile-even-13.html)

In this excerpt, the discourse switches from a general-present statement, **_Practically unimaginable today_**, to a specific past-time event, **_was a time_**, which supports the claim that now cell phones are everywhere. Then the text reverts to a present tense general statement, **_close to 100 percent of Americans have cell phones_**.

The "switch" time markers can take a few forms, but in text, these are usually explicit:

- Adverbs and phrases, e.g. *now/then, today/at that time, currently/in the past, in today's society/in the early days.*
- Adjectives, e.g. *new/old, recent/past, current/previous/early.*
- Other verbs with a different tense, e.g. *the study continues/the author states/the findings indicate.*

In some disciplines, however, such as history and philosophy, required academic assignments seem to employ more uses of the past tense than those in the natural sciences, political science, psychology, sociology, or economics.

Like the list of verbs used predominantly in the present tense, the list of specific verbs that occur mostly in the past tense is also very limited.

Verbs Predominantly Used in the Past Tense

bend	bow	lean	light	remark
reply	set off	shake	turn away	wrap

(Adapted from Carter & McCarthy, 2006)

The Future Tense Functions and Uses

Meanings and Forms

The future tense marks the future time that follows <u>**now**</u>. The future tense is marked by auxiliary verbs, as well as time adverbs.

Future Tense Verb and Other Markers

High certainty/definiteness/ predictions	**will** + the base form	*Scientists/I/we/you/ they **will** study.*
Plans/intentions – informal	**be + going to +** the base form	*Scientists **are going to** travel.*
Future-time adverbs, e.g. **tomorrow, next month, in 2025**	verb + **-s** or **-es**	*Tomorrow, the flight* **leav<u>es</u>** *at 6.*

Present tense uses to refer to the future are particularly prevalent with subordinate clauses of time and condition, marked by conjunctions *if*, **whether**, **when**, **before**, e.g.

- *The interest rates* **<u>will rise</u>** **when** *the Federal Reserve Board* <u>approves</u> *the new fiscal policy.*
- *If passengers* <u>miss</u> *their flight connections, they* **<u>will need</u>** *to contact an airline agent.*

> Future tense markers are never used in clauses of time and con-
> dition, with *if*, *whether*, *when*, *before*, and other time clause
> markers.
>
> Constructions, such as *When the Federal Reserve will increase the
> prime rate*, are unambiguously ungrammatical and unidiomatic
> sentences.

(See chapter 10 for further and more emphatic discussion.)

Uses and Functions

The general function of the future tense is to refer to future actions, events,
or states.

- With the auxiliary verb **_will_** or the simple present tense (**_begins tomorrow,
  ends on Monday, departs at 3 pm_**).
  - o "A marked future of **unusual definiteness**, attributing to the future
    the degree of certainty" usually associated with the present and the
    past (Quirk, et al., 1985, p. 215).
  - o Definitive references to future activities or states are **extremely rare**
    in academic writing: the writer is usually expected to project "proper
    caution" and anticipate negative reactions to the "claims being
    advanced" (Swales, 1990, p. 175).

- The **_be + going to_** construction has not been widely accepted in formal
  written prose.

In written academic corpora, the future tense marked by any type of future
verb forms, such as **_will_**, **_going to_**, or the simple present tense, is often considered to be extremely definite, or conversational and colloquial. Instead, modal
verbs, such as **_may_**, **_can_**, or **_could_**, represent the hedging devices of choice to
project an appropriate amount of hesitation and cautious claim-making (see
chapter 12).

Studies of L2 writing and text have noted that students' academic prose
often conveys a high degree of certainty (Hinkel, 2005; Hyland & Milton, 1997).

> Definitive future markers occur significantly more frequently in L2 than L1 college-level writing.

For example, the differences in the degree of certainty and definiteness expressed by means of the future marker <u>**will**</u> and the modal verbs <u>**may**</u> and <u>**can**</u> is readily apparent in the following contrasting sentences:

(a)   *When goals are hard to define, managers <u>**may**</u> tell employees to do their best.*
(b)   *When goals are hard to define, managers <u>**can**</u> tell employees to do their best.*
(c)   *When goals are hard to define, managers <u>**will**</u> tell employees to do their best.*

The sentence in (c) clearly expresses definitively what the manager will do, as opposed to noting a possibility in (a) or an ability in (b).

> Due to definiteness and certainty constraints in the usage of the future tense, it is hardly ever employed in academic writing.
>
> Instead, L2 academic writers should be encouraged to employ modal verbs, such as *may*, *can*, *could*, and *might*.

How to Teach It

Trouble Spot

The definitive certainty future tense marker <u>**will**</u> is used instead of modal verbs, such as *can, could, may, might,* that are conventionally required in academic prose.

Examples of trouble-spot sentences:

*In countries like Costa Rica, political decisions are based on the economic model. Under this model, the market competition <u>**will**</u> increase, and the market* *economy **will** solve most problems in an efficient way without any interruption of the government. When markets don't work well, the government **will** try to fix them, but they **will** fail because the market cannot be fixed by the government. The market **will** solve its own problems, and it **will** benefit the people and create a stable economy. In turn, the stable economy **will** lead the country to political stability, and the political order **will** give the people peace for a long time.*

(From a student's paper on the role of the
government in a market economy)

In this excerpt, the future tense uses project a high degree of definiteness in the success of the implementation of a market economy without government interference. That is, the writer appears to be certain in the outcomes of the market policies, which in reality, however, may not be nearly as certain.

Teaching Tip

Students' textbook excerpts, for example, can be compared and analyzed to determine which displays a higher degree of definiteness and certainty in the future outcomes of events.

> The easiest route is to replace the future tense markers with modal verbs **may**, **can**, **might**, and **could** with less definite meanings, as is the convention in academic writing. Varying the modals can avoid repetition and redundancy.

*In countries like Costa Rica, political decisions are based on the economic model. Under this model, the market competition **may** increase, and the market economy **can** solve most problems in an efficient way without any interruption of the government. When markets don't work well, the government **may** try to fix them, but they **may/are likely** to fail because the market cannot be fixed by the government. The market **may/can** solve its own problems, and it **may/is likely to** benefit the people and create a stable economy. In turn, the stable economy **can** lead the country to political stability, and the political order **may** give the people peace for a long time.*

This text is slightly re-worded without the uses of the future tense. In combination, the modal verbs <u>*can*</u> and <u>*may*</u>, as well as the hedge <u>*to be likely to*</u>, help to project academic possibility rather than certainty.

(For "future in the past" constructions, e.g. **Sam Walton predicted that Walmart <u>would turn</u> into the largest discount chain in the US**, see chapter 10, Subordinate Clauses.)

Aspect

The time of an activity or a state is denoted by means of the verb tense – the past, present, or future. The verb **aspect** additionally marks actions and events for continuity and completion. The aspect – progressive and/or perfect – marks the progression of an activity during a period of time

- **Progression or continuity** <u>during</u> a particular marked period of time – **the progressive aspect.**
- Occurrence during the time period <u>leading</u> up to or prior to another **specific time** marker, activity, or event – **the perfect aspect.**

- The time period is always overtly or implicitly marked – up to a particular specific time / event.

> In academic writing, a large majority of verb phrases with the **progressive** and **perfect** aspects are used in the **present** tense, but not in the past or the future. It may be more helpful, therefore, to spend more teaching time focused on the **present perfect** than on teaching the past or the future perfect.

Aspect Markers

Aspects	Markers	Examples
No marked aspect (zero) With the general present tense and the past tense	Ø	*Students/I/we/you* **travelØ**. *The chef/he/she/it* **cooks**. *The teacher/I/we/he/she* **smiled**. *The bird/I/we/he/she* **flew**.
Progressive	**be** + verb + **ing**	*The teachers/I/you/we* **are smiling**. *The student/he/she/it* **is reading**. *The birds/we/they* **were flying**.
Perfect	**have/has** + verb **past participle** (**flown, seen, written**) (also called the 3rd form of the verb)	*The movie/he/she/it* **has begun**. *Researchers/I/we/you* **have left**.

Present Tense and Aspect Meanings

Example	Tense and Aspect Meanings	Markers
Television **socializes** *its viewers to become mass consumers.*	The general present tense: no progression or completion is marked.	Ø

*Television **is socializing** its viewers.*	The present tense – marked by the present tense of the auxiliary verb **is** – combined with the progressive aspect to refer to the progression of the activity **at the present moment.**	**be** + verb + **ing**
*Television **has socialized** its viewers.*	The present tense – marked by the present form of the auxiliary verb **has** – combined with the perfect aspect to refer to the activity **up to (or relevant to) the present moment.**	**have/has** + verb **past participle**

Past Tense and Aspect Meanings

Example	Tense and Aspect Meanings	Markers
*Television **socialized** its viewers.*	The past tense and zero aspect. No progression or completion is marked.	Ø
*Television **was socializing** its viewers . . . in 2020 and 2021.*	The past tense – marked by the past tense of the auxiliary **was** – combined with the progressive aspect to refer to the progression **during a marked period, 2020 and 2021.**	**be** + verb + **ing**
*Television **had socialized** its viewers . . . prior to 2020.*	The past tense – marked by the past of the auxiliary *had* – combined with the perfect aspect to mark the completion **up to the time marker, 2020.**	**had** + verb **past participle**

(For a detailed discussion of tense and aspect auxiliaries in English, see chapter 4.)

A great deal of time and effort is expended on teaching students how to use English tenses and aspects correctly. The point of fact is that this instruction may not be particularly necessary for the purposes of academic writing. According to corpus analyses, in various types of language use, e.g. news reportage or academic writing, about 90% of the most common verb phrases have zero aspect (Biber, et al., 1999; Carter & McCarthy, 2006).

- In academic prose, the perfect aspect is encountered in only a small fraction (around 7–8%) of all verb phrases.
- The progressive aspect is employed with even fewer verbs.
- The combination of the perfect and the progressive aspects in all tenses (e.g. **_have/had been writing_**) is encountered extremely rarely at around 0.5% of all verb tense and aspect markers.

After learning English grammar in language courses, sometimes for years, L2 writers frequently employ various tense and aspect constructions that are as likely to be rare and unusual as they are to be common. Even at first glance, it is not difficult to figure out that tense and aspect combinations can be highly error prone. On the whole, the teaching of perfect progressive verb forms and their uses may not be worth the instruction time. Furthermore, devoting class time, work, and effort to the teaching of the forms and meanings associated with the various uses of the progressive aspect in general may be of limited benefit.

The Progressive Aspect

Progressive verb phrases consist of at least two elements: (1) the auxiliary verb **_be_** and (2) the main verb + -**_ing_**. The tense of the verb phrase is marked in the form of the auxiliary verb, e.g. **_is/are_** (present) and **_was/were_** (past).

The usage of the progressive aspect is predominately in conversational and informal registers but can be encountered in personal and/or expressive narratives (Chafe, 1994).

- The progressive aspect is used to refer to action and events that are **in progress during a particular specified period of time** or at the time of another specific action and event.

- When the progressive aspect is combined with the present tense, the activity takes place **at the present moment**, and this meaning is implicit.

For example:

- *The students **are conducting** an experiment* [at the present moment].
- *The water **was boiling** steadily from 1:05 to 1:10* [past progressive; time duration/period specified].
- *The technician **was mixing** the solvents when the chemical reaction took place* [past progressive; the time of another event overtly specified].

As has been mentioned, progressive tenses very rarely occur in academic prose, and the number of verbs that are useful in the teaching of L2 academic writing is actually very small.

Verbs That Often Occur in Progressive Tenses

bring	buy	carry	do	hold	listen	look
make	move	say	stand	take	wait	watch

Stative and other types of non-progressive verbs, however, are practically never used with the progressive aspect in any tense[1] (Quirk, et al., 1985). Broadly defined, progressive verbs can refer to actions and events that, by virtue of their meaning, can take place in progression.[2]

The meanings of non-progressive verbs fall into three groups:

(1) States rather than actions, e.g. *believe, know, understand, possess*.
(2) Actions that are momentary (and, therefore, cannot have progression), e.g. *doubt, note, notice*.
(3) Perceptions that are involuntary, that is, the doer of the action (the grammatical subject) has little control of the action, e.g. *consist (of), contain, hear, resemble, perceive*.

> In teaching, whenever possible, it is very helpful to contrast the non-progressive uses of some verbs in **formal** prose with progressive uses of **activity** verbs with similar meanings.

Here's an example:

know – learn	**is/was knowing –* ***is/was learning***
see – look – watch – observe	**is/was seeing –* ***is/was looking/watching/observing***
hear – listen	**is/was hearing –* ***is/was listening***
contain – place/put (into)	**is/was containing –* ***is/was placing***

The complex meanings of non-progressive and stative verbs may make them difficult for L2 writers to use appropriately. However, the few common items can be simply learned.

Frequent Non-progressive Verbs

agree	*appear*	*appreciate*	*associate*	*attain*
attribute	*base*	*believe*	*belong*	*concern*
conclude	*consist (of)*	*contain*	*correlate*	*cost*
desire	*dislike*	*dissolve*	*doubt*	*equal*
exist	*fear*	*find*	*guarantee*	*have*
hear	*include*	*initiate*	*interest*	*invent*
know	*like*	*matter*	*mean*	*need*
owe	*own*	*perceive*	*possess*	*prefer*
promise	*realize*	*recognize*	*resemble*	*see*
seem	*sound*	*surprise*	*understand*	*weigh*

Non-progressive verbs are important for L2 writers to know because these items can be used only in the simple present or the simple past.

- Progressive tenses are very rare in academic prose.
- However, they are common in conversations and spoken discourse.
- For this reason, the usage of progressive verbs may impart a somewhat conversational flavor to academic writing.
- In formal academic writing, simple present (and occasionally simple past) tenses can be much more effective and easier for students to use.

Research has demonstrated that the meanings of aspects create an additional level of complexity. In teaching tenses for L2 writing, it seems that simpler is indeed better.

The Perfect Aspect

As was mentioned, the perfect aspect combines with tenses to create complex verb phrase forms and meanings, e.g. the present perfect, **has developed**, or the past perfect, **had come**. The most common present perfect verbs in academic writing, such as **have/has been** or **have/has shown**, occur at frequency rates between 0.1% to 0.004%, that is, at most, 1 per 1,000 words (computed based on Biber, et al., 1999).

Frequency Rates of Perfect Verbs in Academic Writing

have/has	been	0.1% – 1 in 1,000 words
	shown	0.01% – 1 in 10,000 words
	had, made, seen, become	0.004% – 4 in 100,000 words

In addition to the relatively infrequent uses of the present perfect, **past perfect** verb phrases are hardly ever found in academic writing. Practically all entail **be-** verbs that occur with frequency rates of 0.01% per million words, e.g. **Prior to the 2020s, public service announcements had been aimed at adults, informing them of possible environmental or military dangers**. In formal academic writing, however, past perfect verb phrases tend to occur in the adjective clauses of complex sentences (see chapter 10 for more information).

Verbs Rarely Used in Perfect Tenses

accommodate	afford	aim	base
believe	boil	compete	comprise
connect	consist	constitute	contain
correspond	denote	depend	differ
distinguish	ensure	excuse	glance

illustrate	induce	inhibit	lean
matter	need	protect	quit
reflect	regulate	relate	remember
represent	require	resemble	suppose

(Adapted from Carter & McCarthy, 2006; Swales & Feak, 2012)

- On the whole, the teaching of verb tenses and aspects in L2 academic writing needs to focus first on the meanings and uses of the **simple present**.
- The meanings and uses of the **simple past** represent the next order of priority, followed possibly by the **present perfect** tense.

Based on the frequencies of occurrences in formal academic writing, the teaching of other verb tenses and aspects may be of reduced value compared to the top three tenses.

Typical Problems with the Uses of Tenses and Aspects

In L2 academic writing, the forms and functions of verb tenses usually require ongoing work and effort.

Inconsistent Contextual Uses of Tenses

The uses of tenses in academic writing are highly conventionalized, and their uses do not necessarily reflect objective reality of time, actions, and events. For this reason, the conventional use of the "academic" present tense often appears untruthful and incorrect to L2 writers.

One of the most common causes of L2 tense and aspect errors is that conventionalized uses of tenses in academic writing do not follow logic and common sense.

A few typical and logical reasons for tense and aspect errors are illustrated below.

> ### Trouble Spot
>
> Past tense verbs are used to refer to activities that took place prior to activities denoted by present tense verbs.

An example of a trouble-spot sentence:

> *Last quarter, the student **studied** hard, and he **gets** good grades.*

Logically speaking, in the sequence of activities, an earlier action that precedes another is marked for the past tense, and this is a common sense choice to indicate to the reader that one action took place before another. In academic writing, however, the sentence does not seem correct due to the inconsistency of tenses.

TEACHING TIP

To correct these types of errors, a past-time adverbial marker needs to be inserted to re-frame the context for the present time and tense, e.g.

> *Last quarter, the student **studied** hard, and **now** he **gets** good grades.*

> ### Trouble Spot
>
> With mixed present and past tenses, one verb may refer to an activity that takes place in the general present, but another verb denotes past tense activity.

An example of a trouble-spot sentence:

> *When the market **moves** up and down **every day**, the fund manager **issued** a new policy.*

In this sentence, both tenses, the present and the past are used logically: **the market moves every day** refers to an action that is generally true while the fund manager took a one-time, past tense action to issue a new policy.

TEACHING TIP

In this case, the inconsistent use of tenses can be corrected in one of two ways:

1) By inserting an adverbial or other marker (such as an adjective) to re-frame the context for a different tense (and time), as was discussed earlier.
2) By changing the past tense to the general present tense, to match the other verb(s).

> When the market **moves** up and down every day, the fund manager **issues** a new policy.

The problem with merely changing the tense of the verb, as in (2), is this correction may appear factually untruthful to the writer – if it is known that the past time action of the manager's issuing a new policy is a factual past-time event.

In teaching, two points need to be emphasized:

•   The uses of the general present tense are highly conventional-ized in academic writing in English.
•   The verb tenses must meet the requirements of the conventions even when they may appear to be somewhat factually incorrect.

The extended example below demonstrates various inconsistent uses of tenses in an excerpt from a student's paper on efficiency in public administration.

> Every country in the world **has** present many problems such as pollution, unemployment, crime, war, and so on. And in most modern countries, the government **takes** present a role to solve these problems. It **is** present due to the fact that any individual or organization **can't afford** present to manage

costs to do this. As society **_becomes_** [present] more complicated, the government **_expanded_** [past] its role dramatically.

The fundamental services, which we **_use_** [present] every day such as water, gas, electricity, public transportation **_were produced_** [past] by individual vendors. But there **_was_** [past] a critical problem with these individual suppliers, and in industrial societies the government **_provides_** [present] these services. It **_is_** [present] a question whether the government really **_provides_** [present] these services as efficiently as possible. Actually, it **_was_** [past] the fundamental question in public administration, since public administration **_began_** [past] as an independent discipline.

As one solution to this problem, John Smith **_presents_** [present] some principles of public administration to improve efficiency. According to his suggestion, a higher level of efficiency **_can be achieved_** [present] by specialization of tasks. Smith's principles also **_mentioned_** [past] how to improve efficiency in public administration, such as unity of command, process, and clients. These principles **_are called_** [present] the principles of efficiency, and they **_became_** [past] the focus of research. Many scholars **_present_** [present] new principles every day, when public **_demanded_** [past] more public services and goods from the government.

(From a student paper on efficiency in
public administration)

Throughout the text, present tense verbs are mixed with those in the past tense. Most of the inconsistent uses of tenses can be corrected (or prevented) by employing the types of corrections discussed earlier.

(1)   Change the tense to be consistent:

As society **_became_** more complicated, the government **_expanded_** its role . . .
As society **_becomes_** more complicated, the government **_expands_** its role . . .

(2)   Use overt markers to signal time and tense changes:

(a)   The fundamental services, which we **_use_** [present] every day such as water, gas, electricity, public transportation **_were_** [past] → **_originally/initially produced_** [past] by individual vendors.

(b)   But → **_in those days/at that time/during that period_**, there **_was_** past a critical problem with these individual suppliers, and in → **_today's/current/ modern_** industrial societies the government **_provides_** [present] these services.

(c)   → **_Today/These days/Currently_** it **_is_** [present] a question whether the government really **_provides_** [present] these services as efficiently as possible.

(d) *Actually, it **was** [past]* → *the **initial/early/original/old** fundamental question in public administration, since* → *the **time/the beginning (when)** public administration **began** [past] as an independent discipline.*

Exercises for correcting inconsistent tense errors in actual student writing can be highly productive and useful.

Progressive Aspects with Non-progressive Verbs

Trouble Spot

A common type of error occurs when non-progressive verbs are used with progressive tenses.

A text excerpt with trouble-spot sentences.

*This essay ***is concerning** the studies that have shown a sharp decline in the number of recycling plants in the New York area and other US cities. Those people who listen to the news ****are hearing** about the high cost of recycling that makes it too expensive for the industry to continue collecting metal and paper. The news quote recycling plant owners and operators who ****are depending** on recycling for their jobs and who **are complaining** that there is simply not enough material to recycle for them to earn a living and that operating too many plants ****is costing** too much. So, the plant owners propose to close down some of their collection centers and reduce recycling. However, the plant owners and news media **are dealing** with this problem totally incorrectly. They need to educate the public to recycle more instead of closing down plants that will lead to the public recycling less.*

(From a student paper on how to educate the public on recycling)

Progressive tenses are especially rare with verbs such as ***concern***, ***hear***, ***depend***, and ***cost***.

Thus, the use of non-progressive verbs in progressive tenses needs to be avoided, and non-progressives can be used instead. However, in real contexts, the issue may seem to be more complex than just simply changing the aspect of the non-progressive verbs because other verbs, such as **_complain_** and **_deal_**, found in the same context are perfectly acceptable in the progressive form: **_are complaining_** and **_are dealing_**.

Two points are important to remember:

* Progressive verbs occur very seldom in academic writing.
* Frequent and important academic verbs are not used in the progressive aspect, and these verbs need to be learned.

The Active Voice and the Passive Voice in Academic Writing

The form and grammatical derivation of passive constructions can be found in all grammar textbooks. For example:

The student bought the book.	$\rightarrow$	*The book was bought by the student.*
John helped the boy.	$\rightarrow$	*The boy was helped by John.*

Because passive derivations are highly regular in their form, L2 learners generally quickly figure out how to convert active constructions into passive ones. Then, when it comes to fill in the blank exercises on sentence converting, learners fill in all the blanks, and their learning of how to use the passive voice is thus completed.

Unfortunately, however, as is often the case with other English structures, the uses of passives in real academic writing are far more complex than doing exercises in a grammar textbook or filling the blanks.

The Uses and Functions of Passives in Academic Writing

The passive voice is extraordinarily common in academic writing, and to a large extent, the prevalence of the passive voice is determined by academic discourse conventions (Celce-Murcia, 2002; Hinkel, 2004; Swales, 1990; Swales & Feak, 2012).

The usage of the passive voice in formal writing has a number of important textual functions. One of these is to project an **academic indirectness, detachment, and objectivity**, in what Johns (1997) calls "the author-evacuated prose" considered to be requisite in the Anglo-American scientific tradition, and particularly so in natural sciences and engineering. However, in reaction to the conventionalized use of the passive in rigidly structured academic discourse, in the US much writing instruction and many composition texts discourage the use of the passive voice, except on rare occasions.

In addition to creating an impression of detachment and objectivity, a more sophisticated function of the passive voice is to develop cohesive text by means of organizing information in connected sentences:

Known/old information – → – New/important

Here are a few examples.

*New Orleans has a unique history and culture that is rooted in the **colonial period**.*

*The city **was founded** in 1718 as part of the French **Louisiana colony**.*

*The **Louisiana** territories **were ceded** to Spain in 1763 but **were returned** to **France** in 1803.*

***France** almost immediately sold the **colony** to the United States in the **Louisiana** Purchase.*

*The appeal of the **New Orleans sound** knew no boundaries. By 1919 the Original*

*Dixieland **Jazz Band** performed in England and Bechet was in **France**; their **music***

***was** wholeheartedly **welcomed**.*

(www.nps.gov/jazz/learn/historyculture/history_early.htm)

In these examples, the passive voice constructions shift the new/important idea to the end of the sentence and thus help to create **lexical and semantic**

cohesive chains by connecting the end of the first sentence to the beginning to the next (see chapter 11).

There are probably few constructions in writing and writing instruction that have been subject to as much debate and controversy as the passive voice. Its opponents claim that the active voice is more emphatic, vigorous, and clear than the passive, that in the active voice the doer of the action is placed in the sentence subject position, and that active verbs are usually more effective, clearer, simpler, and easier to read. All these evaluations are undoubtedly true.

> Corpus analyses of academic prose show that, in real academic writing, outside of the teaching of composition, the passive voice is ubiquitous and remains a prevalent feature of academic text in various disciplines.

A common sense recommendation is provided in a writing guide specifically geared toward efficiency and clarity in writing (Williams & Bizup, 2017, pp. 54 and 56) (see also chapter 11 on Cohesion):

> "Some critics tell us to avoid the passive everywhere because it adds words and often deletes the agent, the 'doer' of the action. But the passive is often the better choice." The "important use of the passive" is that it allows the sentence to focus on what is done rather than who does it and that it can be of great value in developing cohesive text, by means of "shifting the most important and new information to the end of the sentence."
>
> **To put it simply, if the passive works better than the active in a particular context and for a particular discourse purpose, then use it, and if not, then don't.**

The Contexts and Uses of the Active vs. the Passive Voice in English

Several studies of the uses of passive constructions in English have shown that the passive voice is very difficult for L2 learners to use appropriately because, generally speaking, many passive structures are lexicalized (Hinkel, 2002a, 2004; Owen, 1993). That is, many passive constructions and specific contextual uses are **idiomatic** and cannot be structurally derived in some cases.

> It may be practically impossible to avoid using the passive voice in academic writing: 25% of all sentence predicate verbs are employed in the passive (Hyland, 1996; Swales, 1990).

Analyses of L2 academic text have shown, however, that compared to first-year L1 university students, L2 writers even at advanced levels of proficiency do not use passive structures nearly as frequently (Hinkel, 2002b). (As a side note, *get*-passives, such as *get confused/finished/married*, are extremely rare and occur only in conversation, and even then they seem to be highly infrequent.)

For L2 writers, another important complication arises in regard to learning to use passive constructions in English. Passive-like structures exist in many languages, such as Spanish, Chinese, Japanese, Arabic, or Russian. However, also in many languages, the doer of the action expressed by the verb must be a person or an animal, that is, some type of a living being that is actually enabled to perform the action (Hinkel, 2002a; Master, 1991).

In such languages, it would be correct to say *The man writes well* but incorrect to use a subject that is not capable of acting on its own, e.g. *The pencil writes well*. The problem with such structures is further compounded by the fact that **instruments** and **abstract concepts** as subjects (rather than alive beings) of **active** verbs are highly common in academic writing, e.g. *the chapter discusses/reviews/presents, the program/machine runs, the factory produces, the office develops, the process begins, the forecast compares.*

> For L2 writers, a key issue with passive constructions is that, in English, it does not really matter whether the subject of the active verb is alive or not, or whether it has the capacity to perform the action expressed by the verb.
>
> Thus, all such structures and sentences are grammatical, no matter whether the subject of the active verb actually and effectively performs the action.

In addition, a small number of verbs are never used in the passive voice and are always encountered in the active. These verbs need to be learned because verbs with similar meanings exist in other languages in which they can be and often are used in the passive voice (e.g. Arabic, Polish, Russian, Spanish, or Tagalog). Hence, L2 writers need to be particularly careful when employing these verbs in their text.

Verbs That Are Always (or Almost Always) Used in the Active Voice*
(in descending order)

appear*	arrive	belong	consist	come	die
happen	**fall**	**lack**	**last**	**occur**	**resemble**
rest	**remain**	**seem**	stay	wait	

*The verbs in bold font are **always** used in the active voice.
(Adapted from Biber, et al., 1999; Swales & Feak, 2012)

Transitive Verbs, Direct Objects, and Agents

In teaching, it is important to emphasize that only transitive verbs – that require direct objects – can be used in the passive voice. The reason that only the structures with transitive verbs can be converted from active to passive is that only the direct object can be moved to make it the subject of the passive verb:

Managers __considered__ [past] the price →
The price __was__ [past] __considered__ (by managers)

To derive a passive construction, the following steps need to take place:

(1) The direct object moves to the subject position.
(2) Add a _be_-verb – and the **tense** stays the **same**.
(3) The main verb is used in the past participle form, e.g. **_written_**, **_gone_**, **_shown_**, **_considered_**.
(4) The subject of the active verb moves to the back of the sentence and into the _by_-phrase.

Here's an illustration.

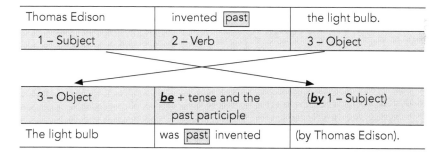

Thomas Edison	invented $\boxed{\text{past}}$	the light bulb.
1 – Subject	2 – Verb	3 – Object
3 – Object	**_be_** + tense and the past participle	(**_by_** 1 – Subject)
The light bulb	was $\boxed{\text{past}}$ invented	(by Thomas Edison).

A Side Note: In passive constructions, the nouns and noun phrases in the _by_-phrase are sometimes called **agents** (and the entire phrase is called the **agentive phrase**).

In the English passive construction, all **_by_**-phrases are optional. In fact, some of them can be downright incorrect (see below).

A quick check to see if a verb can be used in the passive is to place it in a structure with a direct object, e.g.

report →	The book/article/xxx **_reports_** the finding.
	If the verb can be used with a direct object, the verb can be converted into the passive.
	The verb **_report_** can be used in the passive.
	The finding **_is reported_** (*by the book/article).

hold →	*xxx* **holds** *the book →* Passive constructions are possible → *The book* **is held** *(by xxx).*
appear →	**The book* **appeared** *the page →* Passive constructions are not possible.
last →	*The rain* **lasted** *(two hours) →* Passive constructions are not possible: **two hours** is adverbial of time and not a direct object.

Analyses of written academic texts have demonstrated that *by*-phrases occur infrequently, and the presence of a *by*-phrase depends on whether it is needed for cohesion and the continuity of new information from one sentence to the next by means of cohesive chains, e.g.

> *Most consumer goods are sold by* **retailers**. *→*
> *Many in the* **retail** *trade industry have a size standard of 3.5 million in average annual receipts.*

In most contexts, however, the *by*-phrase is usually omitted.

In contexts where the agent is unknown, unimportant to the discussion, or easily understood from the context, the **by**-phrase needs to be omitted.

---

(1) *?The fuel injector was designed* **by us** *to show it at the Engineering Senior Fair.*
(2) *?We were told* **by someone** *that a company in Everett has a similar fuel injector.*
(3) *?When their original design was developed* **by them***, they had to re-do it because at first the injector did not work, but the one developed* **by us** *worked from the start.*

    (From a student assignment in engineering)

In (1), the *by*-phrase can be understood from the context of a written group assignment; in (2) the writers did not know or did not care to mention the agent, and the sentence can easily do without the by-phrase. In (3), both *by*-phrases, the *by them* and *by us*, are unnecessary because the agent in each phrase can be understood from the context.

> A vast majority of passive sentences in formal academic writing do not include the *by*-phrase.

To summarize, L2 writers encounter a number of difficulties with appropriate uses of passive constructions in English. Some have to do with various complexities in the meanings and uses of passives and others with the influence of the first language grammar on the learners' uses of passive in English. However, due to the prevalence of the passive voice in academic writing in English, L2 writers need to learn to employ passive constructions correctly.

> Several important considerations must be taken into account in instruction on the passive voice in academic writing.
>
> - The greatest difference between active and passive constructions is stylistic, and in English, passives have no additional meanings compared to active structures.
> - Many passive constructions in English are idiomatic, and these need to be learned.
> - In English sentences, instruments and abstract concepts can be the subject of active verbs, even when the sentence subject does not actually perform the activity expressed by the verb.
> - For this reason, structures such as **the book fell, the door is sliding**, or **the mail arrives late every time** are perfectly grammatical.
> - Only transitive verbs that require direct objects can be used in the passive voice.
> - The **by**-phrase is always optional in English sentences, and it's rarely used in academic writing.

Working with Passive Constructions

In light of the many complexities associated with the contextual uses of the passive voice in English, one of the easier techniques that L2 writers can rely on with great effect is to select the verbs that almost always occur in the passive and learn and practice using them (Nation, 1990, 2013; Swales & Feak, 2012).

The Most Common Passive Verbs in Academic Writing (in declining order):
be *(is/are/was/were)* + the Past Participle Form of
the Main Verb (as listed)

made	given	seen	used	found	done	considered	shown

These especially common passive verbs are usually familiar to L2 writers at intermediate and higher levels of proficiency simply because they are encountered in most academic reading and other types of textbooks. For this reason, practice with common passives can be combined with other verb constructions, such as modal verbs or infinitive complements, e.g. ***can/may be found***, ***is considered to be***, or ***was shown to be*** (see additional suggestions for teaching at the end of this chapter).

In addition to these highly common verbs, other important academic verbs include a large number of those noted in chapter 8.

Some of these verbs are often accompanied by relatively fixed prepositions, which can be also learned and practiced in context.

Other Academic Verbs Predominantly Used in the Passive Voice: **be *(is/are/ was/were)* + the Past Participle Form** of the Main Verb (as listed)

achieved	aligned (with)	applied	approved
asked	associated (with)	attributed (to)	based (on)
born	brought	calculated	called
carried	chosen	classified (as)	compared
composed (of)	coupled (with)	deemed	defined
derived	described	designed	determined
discussed	distributed	documented	drawn
entitled (to)	estimated	examined	expected

explained	expressed	extracted	flattened
formed	given	grouped (with/by)	held
identified	illustrated	inclined	intended
introduced	involved	kept	known
labeled	left	limited (to)	linked (to/with)
located (at/in)	lost	measured	needed
noted	observed	obtained	performed
plotted	positioned	prepared	presented
recognized	regarded	related (to)	replaced
reported	represented	required	said
situated	stored	studied	subjected (to)
thought	told	transferred	treated
understood	viewed		

Typical Problems with Passives

> **Trouble Spot**
>
> Incorrect verb forms – many, many errors in passive constructions have to do with verb forms.

Examples of trouble-spot sentences:

> *The articles on the sociology of crime **was write/wrote** by John Smith.*
> *Psychology studies **were conduct** at Harvard University.*

- **The past participle form** of the verb is **required** in passive constructions, following *be*-verbs.
- Many L2 writers, even those who are highly advanced, do not attribute sufficient importance to the distinctions between the past tense and the past participle forms of irregular verbs. **Both forms need to be learned**.

Other similar types of problems occur simply due to the fact that even at the college-level, L2 writers have not learned the basic three forms of irregular verbs.

Cheaters are usually __catched__ by their professors.

When such ugly constructions are encountered in academic assignments and term papers, they usually prove to be highly embarrassing, whether or not L2 writers are actually embarrassed by them.

Learning the forms of irregular verbs is one of the **basic essentials** in university-level studies, similar to learning the multiplication table to be able to do basic math operations.

Trouble Spot

Intransitive verbs (that do not have a direct object) in passive constructions – a very common type of error includes perfectly correct passive structures with verbs that can **never** be used in the passive.

Examples of trouble-spot sentences:

This problem __was happened__ in my country.
The change in climate __was occurred__ in coastal areas.

Only transitive verbs (those that require direct objects) can be used in passive. The verbs that never occur in the passive must be learned (see the very short list earlier in this chapter).

Trouble Spot

Agentive (who does it) is used instead of **instrumental (by means of)** in **by**-phrases. These types of errors are encountered occasionally and may be worthwhile mentioning when necessary.

Examples of trouble-spot sentences:

*The students are taught **by the Silent Method**.

If this sentence is converted back from the passive to the active voice, the following structure results:

***The Silent Method teaches** the students.*

In passive sentences, agentive **by**-phrases are located at the end and include nouns and noun phrases that would be subjects of parallel active constructions, e.g.

*The solution was mixed **by the student** [passive] →*
***The student** mixed the solution [active].*

- In this case, the test question can be used to identify the **doer** of the verb action:

    *Does **the subject noun** of the sentence perform/do the action?*

- If the answer is no, then the passive cannot be used, e.g. **Teachers teach the students.**

Thus, the sentence may need to be completely re-written, e.g.:

*Teachers taught the students **by means of** the Silent Method [instrumental meaning].*
*Students were taught **by means of** the Silent Method [instrumental meaning].*

When working with passive sentences, it is important to identify the differences in meaning and function between the two constructions:

(1)   The agentive meaning of the **by**-phrase

[the action was done by **whom?/who** did the action?].

(2)   The instrumental meaning in the **by means of** phrase

[**How** was the action done?/**By what means** was the action done?].

(a) **The agentive *by*-phrase refers directly to the doer** of the action and the sentence subject that did the action can be always reconstructed when the passive sentence is converted back to active.

(b) BUT instrumental ***by means of*** (prepositional) phrases can never be the subjects of any sentence.

> The uses of tenses and aspects in English are complex, and tense-related errors are considered to be one of the most grievous in L2 writing.

- Written academic discourse and text are relatively rigid and conventionalized.
- From this perspective, L2 writers do not need to become excellent users of the entire range of tenses in English, but only some of them.
- A great proportion of contextualized verb phrases in academic prose employ the present tense.
- The present tense is probably one of the simpler tenses in English in terms of its attendant verb forms and contextual application.
- The past tense is also not particularly complicated to use.
- By consistently maintaining these two tenses in appropriate and overtly marked contexts, L2 writers may be able to construct a large variety of reasonably accurate contexts, at least in terms of tenses.

> The contextualized uses of the active and passive voice present a number of problems for L2 writers, who need to become proficient with passive verb forms and meanings.

The **form of passive verbs** can become easier to employ with some practice. On the other hand, the meanings and functions of the passive voice in sentences and broader contexts require a great deal of work from the students, and attention, effort, and knowledge from the teacher.

Chapter Summary

English tenses are often difficult for students to understand and use appropriately. The simplest way to teach tenses is to start by separating tenses and aspects.

- There are three tenses in English: the **past**, the **present**, and the **future**.
- There are two aspects: the **progressive** and the **perfect**.
- The **present** tense is very flexible, and its uses are highly conventionalized.
- For this reason, the **present** can be employed even in contexts where, logically speaking, the past tense should be used, e.g. citations from and references to earlier publications.
- The **past** tense can be used in specific contexts of historical and biographical descriptions of specific people, events, and/or places, such as case studies.
- The **future** tense is rarely used in academic writing – more commonly modal verbs (e.g. *can*, *may*, *might*) are used to express future expectation.
- **Progressive aspects** with tenses are rarely found in academic writing, and **perfect aspects** are employed only occasionally and mostly with a limited class of verbs.

> The **passive voice** is common in academic writing, even though some composition books advise against its use.

- Judicious uses of the **passive** voice are essential in academic writing.
- Only **transitive verbs that have a direct object** can be used in the passive voice.
- The *by*-phrase is optional and rarely used in academic writing.
- Many passive constructions are idiomatic and must be learned independently of general rules.

Strategies and Tactics for Teaching and Teaching Activities

Teaching Activities

The following six exercises and practice assignments can help students with verb tenses and voice.

- Noticing the typical and frequent errors in verb phrases and preventing them – in as many cases as possible.

- Learning to use and figure out the strange English active verbs that occur with sentence subjects that can't actually "do" anything because they are **inanimate (lifeless) objects**, such as books, tools, or furniture, as in *the chair fell*.
- Functions and uses of the passive voice in academic writing.

Learning to Notice Typical Errors in the Verb Phrase and Articulate the Reasons for the Errors

- This exercise is very similar to those found in many grammar textbooks.
- The primary benefit of this practice is that the students need to explicitly indicate what the problems with the sentences are and devise a general rule to avoid making similar errors in their own writing.
- Students can work in pairs or small groups, and then compare their generalizations to decide on the most accurate and the easiest to remember.

INSTRUCTIONS FOR STUDENTS

Correct the errors in the following sentences and create specific rules that can be followed to avoid making such errors in writing. What types of errors have you noticed in these sentences? How many?

(1) College graduates will earning more money than people without college degrees.

(2) The Internet has everything, the news, shopping, and gossip, and the Internet has reach every aspect of our lives. When I searched for the information for my classes, I have find all the facts I need.

(3) The purpose of my essay will be to focus on the work of Pendelton's early paintings that has been giving the credit for founding the still-art school.

(4) It is not Pendelton's style that was widely imitating among the local group of painters in the 16th century, but the style of his pupil Johnson (1479–1559).

(5) Johnson didn't just only learned painting from Pendelton; he was also often imitated the styles of earlier artists, such as Ellison, Dickerson, and Morris.

(6) Abraham Maslow did identified the order of human needs from the lowest to the highest.

(7) The interviewer have not spoke to the study subjects in detail, but he should.

(8) The topic of the causes of Second World War has been discussing in many articles.

English Is a Strange Language: Strange Subjects of Active Verbs and Strange Active Verbs

> This exercise often leads to very interesting – and somewhat unexpected – discussions for pairs or small groups of students.
>
> It is important, however, that the teacher follow up with a whole-class discussion and explanation.

INSTRUCTIONS FOR STUDENTS

- *In your opinion, which of the following sentences are grammatical, which are a little strange, and which are not grammatical?*
- *Explain why you think that some of the sentences seem strange or incorrect, and how they can be corrected.*

(1) It was a dark and stormy night, and students studied in the library because they will have a test tomorrow.

(2) (a) Engineers will make a decision about the design for the bridge.
   (b) They will choose one of the three designs: a floating bridge, a suspension bridge, or an arch bridge.
   (c) The public vote will approve their choice.

(3) (a) The dog ate my homework.
   (b) The food processor ate my homework.
   (c) The vacuum cleaner ate my homework.

(4) (a) The tree is growing.
   (b) John's paper is growing.
   (c) The city is growing.
   (d) The child is growing.

(5) (a) The man is running.
 (b) The water is running.
 (c) The car is running.
 (d) The test is running.
 (e) The tape is running.
 (f) Time is running.
(6) (a) A barometer predicts the weather.
 (b) A TV station predicts the weather.
 (c) A meteorologist predicts the weather.
(7) (a) The weather is predicted (by a barometer).
 (b) The weather is predicted (by a TV station).
 (c) The weather is predicted (by a meteorologist).

"English Is Not My Native Language and I Can't Write Like Native Students" Practice

The purpose of this practice is to provide L2 writers examples of tenses and passive uses in authentic L1 **student** writing. Published pieces of writing almost always go through many rounds of editing and polishing before they see the light of day, and these are not realistic examples for students, L1 and L2 alike. L2 writers often believe that the quality of language usage (and discourse organization) usually found in L1 texts is superb and that the standards of quality expected of L2 writing can be unfair and unreasonable.

- Typically, these beliefs are based on a simple lack of facts: L1 students' writing often leaves a great deal to be desired in both the quality of language and discourse organization.
- An important teaching objective, however, is to demonstrate to L2 students that the fact that a student is an L1 writer does not guarantee "superb" writing and that L1 student writing, like L2 writing, varies widely in quality.

Samples of L1 students' writing can be requested from the Writing Center, a mainstream composition/writing instructor, or even individual students on campus. If the teacher has access to the writing of several L1 students, the best way to proceed is to collect three or four pieces of L1 writing: one not-so-good, one passable (and passing), and one good piece.

- If the L1 papers/essays are written on the same topic (or in similar disciplines), text and discourse analysis can be very profitable for L2 writers.

- Most importantly, however, the analysis of L1 essays can address a number of points, simultaneously or in the course of a couple of class meetings.

  o Discourse organization and structure (including thesis and topic supports and the amount of elaboration – see the appendix to chapter 11).
  o Uses of tenses and passives, as well as adverbial time (and tense) markers and frames, and tense shifts.
  o Uses of adjectives and descriptive adverbials, such as prepositional phrases (see chapter 6).
  o Vocabulary range, e.g. nouns and verbs (see chapters 4 and 8).
  o Any useful/relevant type of discourse or text features.

> In addition to highlighting how L1 writers of similar academic backgrounds employ text features, one of the main benefits of this exercise is that it helps to take away the illusions of L1 writing perfection that many L2 academic writers have regarding L1 academic papers.

Functions of the Passive Voice in Academic Writing

- The goal of this activity is to help students identify the functions of the passive in academic writing and develop their skills as astute users of the active and passive voice.
- An attendant objective is to practice revising and editing skills with tenses and passive/active constructions.

INSTRUCTIONS FOR STUDENTS

- *Read the following excerpt from a student assignment. Some constructions used in it contain errors that need to be corrected.*
- *Some other constructions are grammatically correct, but they can be written better.*

  (1) Identify both types of structures.
  (2) Correct the errors.

(3) *Explain which sentences should be improved and why.*

(4) *Show how they can be re-written.*

(5) *When you are finished with the revisions, please explain the various functions of the passive voice that you have noticed while working to improve this essay.*

As a part of our marketing assignment, we had to go to a small cheese farm where the husband and wife own it. The husband and the wife sent a letter to our marketing professor, and they requested that someone come there to analyze their marketing techniques to help them improve their sales. We went through their entire production chain, and we tried to figure out two things: how they can cut their costs and how they can improve their sales.

In this paper, we analyze how they can cut their costs. We found out that each cheese is poured into a container for ripening and storage. The containers cost 9 cents each and the lid costs 4 cents. So, if they store the containers one on top of the other than they do not need lids, and they can save 4 cents on each lid. Of course, the container on the top needs to have a lid.

Then we analyzed how they can cut their storage costs. They keep all the cheese in a huge refrigerator for ripening, and when it is ready, they take to the market. They keep the new cheese for at least two months and the aged cheese for up to 18 months. They keep the temperature between 40° and 45°. So, we performed a little calculation and figured out that if they keep the temperature at 45° instead of 40°, then they can save about a dollar a day on their electric costs.

Then we analyzed their shipping costs. We asked them to tell us how much they pay for shipping. They told us that the shipping of each cheese is costed them $4.80 because they have to ship the cheese in a special container so it does not warm up and spoil in the truck or when it is waited for the customer to come home and take it inside. Each container costs $2.80, and they have to pay $2.60 for transportation. So, we did some research, and we found out that they can find a cheaper supplier for their containers, and the new supplier will sell them the container for $2.50. We are told them that they can save 30 cents on each container if they will buy it from the new supplier we found. But they said that they have a relationship going with their old supplier and that the new supplier will not like it if they switch.

When we heard that we said to them do you care if your old supplier will not like it or do you care to save money? And then we said that if they will have trouble in their business in the future than their old supplier will have to sell them fewer containers because they will ship fewer cheeses. We recommended that they talk to their old supplier and explain the problem with the price. We said maybe your old supplier will match the price of the new supplier then you'll be in good shape. But they said that they always buy from the old supplier for almost 30 years and that they cannot talk to them about a new price after all this time.

(Extracted from a group student
assignment in marketing)

Subjects of Active Verbs

The goal of this activity is help learners become adept with using active verbs with subjects that are not live beings and that are seemingly unable to perform the verb action.

INSTRUCTIONS FOR STUDENTS

Complete the following sentences. The main verbs are provided.

(1) Hot weather [lead] _____
(2) Ice cream and diary consumption [increase] _____
(3) In some regions, climate [change] _____
(4) The chapter in the book [lack] _____
(5) Human eyes [adapt (to)] _____
(6) Mixing colors [produce] _____

Mixing Active and Passive Constructions in Academic Writing

The goal of this exercise is to help L2 writers employ both active and passive constructions to best advantage in their text, e.g. employ varied structures in a reasonably cohesive text.

- This practice can be particularly useful for paired work when students can discuss their suggested revisions and changes.
- The teacher needs to be sure to follow-up with a whole-class review when students are finished working.
- Exercises of this type can also be assigned as homework with a follow-up in class discussion.

- *Decide which structures should be used in the active or the passive voice to improve the text.*
- *Pay special attention to various types of errors and the uses of **by**-phrases.*
- *Some structures should be converted from active to passive; others from passive to active. Some should be left unchanged.*
- *It is your decision how to improve this text, but your goal is revise it to help its author write as well as possible.*
- *Be ready to explain why you think a particular structure should be re-written and how your revision improves the original.*

Excerpt #1

When the world population increases dramatically, more food is demanded by all people. Only a few decades years ago, the world population was counted at 4 billion, then it was 5.3 billion, and it expects to grow to 9.8 billion by the year 2050. However, the speed of food production cannot be kept up the rate of growth of population under the limited farmland, and it is already fallen far behind the demand. This problem could solve by the development of engineered foods. The new biotechnology can be contributed by increasing the productivity of crops and improve diversification in food sources.

It is clear that to eliminate hunger is involved expansion of crop production. The potential yield of existed crops is necessary to decrease or eliminate hunger, and in the process, the environment cannot be destroyed. This be required further scientific advances in food production, and plant biology will play an important role in it. Growing new crops requires the use of various pesticides and irrigation, in addition to fertilizing. Creating new foods is requires changing the local crops by the agricultural scientists because it is possible to obtained certain plants that will made more productive and better adaptive. A "miracle rice" was developed under this process at the founded International Rice Research Institute in the Philippines in the 1970s by biologists. The researchers created a new shorter rice plant with better crops. The new rice was matured more quickly so farmers did not lost their crops to floods. Engineered plans also have the ability to reduce the use of chemicals. The cost to farmers will be reduced, and the pollution will be decreased as well.

Opponents argue that engineered foods offended nature. They think that the creation of a new type of life form should be leave alone and evolution will be taken care of that by itself. They have these ideas only because people are always distrusted new products, particularly food. We should know that traditional creating of new crops is almost as old as agriculture. The first farmer who was bred the best bull with the best cow in the heard to improve the stock, was implemented agricultural engineering in a very simple way. The first baker who used yeast to make bread pie was also used a lining thing to produce an improving product. Science always finds new ways for them to introduce quickly and directly a specific crop, and animal improvements will lead to more people with food by technology. These days, it can take a decade to produce something that was taken by generations of farmers to come up with.

(Extracted from a student assignment on
world hunger and biotechnology)

Excerpt #2

Instructions for students

- *Identify the tense-related (and other types of) errors.*
- *Clearly explain these errors so that other students can correct them independently, without having to rely on the teacher's corrections.*

Around the world, there are numbers of people with diseases that were inherited from their ancestors. Every day, approximately 14% of newborn infants were afflicted by some sort of inherited physical or mental problems when they were born. The diseases dealing with genes are very hard to know who will inherit it. Gene therapy is a medical procedure that treats a disease by replacing a faulty gene. Though many people thought that gene therapy has some side effects, I believe that gene therapy will be important to us for our future. Nowadays, scientists are trying to solve the problem of cancer and AIDS. Gene therapy researchers are trying to find a cure for the disease that many infants inherited from their mothers when they were born. There are many developments that were occurred in gene therapy recently that will bring the world around.

(From a student assignment on the influence of
technology on health care)

Endnotes

1 Some verbs that denote momentary actions, e.g. **blink, bounce, explode**, are used in the progressive aspect to refer to a succession of momentary actions.

2 In such constructions as *Mary is seeing John* or *John is seeing a new doctor*, see has the meanings of *date* or *visit*, both of which can take the progressive tense. Also, in conversational register, it is possible to say, *I am hearing you*; such structures, however, may be inappropriate in most contexts.

Further Reading

Celce-Murcia, M. (2002). Why it makes sense to teach grammar in context and through discourse. In E. Hinkel & S. Fotos (Eds.), *New perspectives on grammar teaching in second language classroom* (pp. 119–133). New York, NY: Routledge.

A clear and well-rounded presentation on the influence of context on grammar and verb tenses based on examples of academic grammar structures. According to the chapter, grammar needs to be taught within a discourse context. That is, English grammar can be explained only partly at the sentence level, but for full understanding of grammatical structure, a context at the discourse level is required. For this reason, grammar instruction has to move beyond the sentence and to the discourse level.

Hinkel, E. (2002). Teaching grammar in writing classes: Tenses and cohesion. In E. Hinkel & S. Fotos (Eds.), *New perspectives on grammar teaching in second language classrooms* (pp. 181–198). New York, NY: Routledge.

The suggested teaching activities are easy to implement in most instructional contexts. Text examples and excerpts from news media articles show how text and discourse move among an array of tenses and verb forms, such as present, simple past, present perfect, and passive, and use adverbials to establish cohesion and coherence throughout the text. In most formal writing, verb tenses change within a single paragraph, and L2 learners can analyze different examples of shifting tenses in context, instead of working with them in isolation and in textbook exercises.

Ur, P. (2011). Grammar teaching: Research, theory, and practice. In E. Hinkel (Ed.), *Handbook of research in second language teaching and learning, Volume 2* (pp. 507–522). New York, NY: Routledge.

An excellent and insightful overview of the key role of grammar in language teaching curricula, across various teaching methods and different schools of thought. Historically, grammar instruction has been scorned and promoted, but regardless of methodological fashions and pendulum swings, grammar has retained its central position in instruction and language skills. Despite the currently dominant focus on communicative and task-based methodologies, grammatical explanations and exercises continue to be prominent in curricula and classroom teaching.

References

Biber, D., Johansson, S., Leech, G., Conrad, S., & Finegan, E. (1999). *Longman grammar of spoken and written English*. Harlow: Pearson.

Calver, E. (1946). The uses of the present tense forms in English. *Language, 22*(4), 317–325.

Carter, R. & McCarthy, M. (2006). *Cambridge grammar of English: A comprehensive guide.* Cambridge: Cambridge University Press.

Celce-Murcia, M. (2002). On the use of selected grammatical features in academic writing. In M. Schleppegrell & M. Colombi (Eds.), *Developing advanced literacy in first and second languages: Meaning and power* (pp. 143–158). New York, NY: Routledge.

Chafe, W. (1994). *Discourse, consciousness, and time.* Chicago, IL: University of Chicago Press.

Ferris, D. (2009). *Teaching college writing to diverse student populations.* Ann Arbor, MI: University of Michigan Press.

Ferris, D. (2011). *Treatment of error in second language student writing* (2nd edn). Ann Arbor, MI: University of Michigan Press.

Hinkel, E. (1992). L2 tense and time reference. *TESOL Quarterly, 26*(3), 556–572.

Hinkel, E. (1997). The past tense and temporal verb meanings in a contextual frame. *TESOL Quarterly, 31*(2), 289–313.

Hinkel, E. (2002a). Why English passive is difficult to teach (and learn). In E. Hinkel & S. Fotos (Eds.), *New perspectives on grammar teaching* (pp. 233–260). New York, NY: Routledge.

Hinkel, E. (2002b). *Second language writers' text.* New York, NY: Routledge.

Hinkel, E. (2004). Tense, aspect and the passive voice in L1 and L2 academic texts. *Language Teaching Research, 8*(1), 5–29.

Hinkel, E. (2005). Hedging, inflating, and persuading in L2 academic writing. *Applied Language Learning, 15*(1), 29–53.

Hinkel, E. (2017). Prioritizing grammar to teach or not to teach: A research perspective. In E. Hinkel (Ed.), *Handbook of research in second language teaching and learning* (pp. 369–383). New York, NY: Routledge.

Horowitz, D. (1986). What professors actually require: Academic tasks for the ESL classroom. *TESOL Quarterly, 20*(4), 445–462.

Hyland, K. (1996). Talking to the academy: Forms of hedging in science research articles. *Written Communication, 13*, 251–281.

Hyland, K. & Milton, J. (1997). Qualification and certainty in L1 and L2 students' writing. *Journal of Second Language Writing, 6*(2), 183–205.

Johns, A. (1997). *Text, role, and context: Developing academic literacies.* Cambridge: Cambridge University Press.

Leech, G. (2004). *Meaning and the English verb.* New York, NY: Routledge.

Master, P. (1991). Active verbs with inanimate subjects in scientific prose. *English for Specific Purposes, 10*(1), 15–33.

Nation, I.S.P. (1990). *Teaching and learning vocabulary.* Boston, MA: Heinle & Heinle.

Nation, I.S.P. (2013). *Learning vocabulary in another language* (2nd edn). Cambridge: Cambridge University Press.

Owen, C. (1993). Corpus-based grammar and the Heineken effect: Lexico-grammatical description for language learners. *Applied Linguistics, 14*(2), 167–187.

Quirk, R., Greenbaum, S., Leech, G., & Svartvik, J. (1985). *A comprehensive grammar of the English language.* New York: Longman.

Swales, J. (1990). *Genre analysis.* Cambridge: Cambridge University Press.

Swales, J. & Feak, C. (2012). *Academic writing for graduate students* (3rd edn). Ann Arbor, MI: University of Michigan Press.

Vaughan, C. (1991). Holistic assessment: What goes on in the raters' minds? In L. Hamp-Lyons (Ed.), *Assessing second language writing in academic contexts* (pp. 111–126). Norwood, NJ: Ablex.

Williams, J. & Bizup, J. (2017). *Style: Ten lessons in clarity and grace* (12th edn). New York, NY: Pearson.

Appendix to Chapter 7

Discourse-driven Sentence Stems with the Present Perfect Tense

The increasing interest in xxx has heightened the need for . . ./to . . .

Recently, there has been growing interest in . . .

The possibility of xxx has generated wide interest in . . .

The development of xxx has led to the hope that . . .

The xxx has been/become a favorite topic for analysis/discussion/ examination . . .

Knowledge of xxx has become an important aspect of . . .

(The) xxx has been extensively studied in recent years.

Many educators/scientists/analysts have recently turned to . . .

The relationship between xxx and yyy has been investigated/studied by many researchers.

Many recent articles/reports have focused on . . .

(From Swales & Feak, 2012)

Lexical Classes of Verbs   **8**

Meanings and Text Functions

Overview

- The most essential academic verbs.
- 350 foundational verbs.
- Text functions and grammatical properties of lexical verb classes.
- Activity verbs.

  - Reporting verbs.
  - Mental process verbs.
  - Linking verbs.
  - Relationship verbs.

Verbs represent one of the most important elements in sentences and in the construction of text. In addition to these grammatical properties of verbs (chapter 7), verb meanings and textual functions play a prominent role in building academic text.

This chapter covers the functions and uses of lexical classes of verb and their specific contextual meanings. As with nouns, the prominent role of verbs in academic writing and text cannot be underestimated. As has been mentioned throughout this book, it may not be possible to express many ideas within the confines of a 500-word vocabulary. To help L2 writers expand their range of accessible academic verbs, they need to be explicitly and persistently taught.

This chapter covers the indispensable verbs in the following order:

- The most essential "academic" verbs.
- A foundational set of approximately 350 verbs: these are key to college-level language production.

- Context and discourse functions of lexical verb classes to lead to a noticeable improvement of L2 writers' academic prose.

Verb Classification Caveats

➤ In general terms, there are probably more lexical classifications of English verbs that one could shake a stick at.

➤ Some analyses of verb meanings identify as many as 30 or more semantic classes, and others fewer than a dozen.

➤ Typically, large classes of verbs are assigned different labels, depending on the purpose of a particular classification.

➤ For teaching L2 academic writing, the specific classifications and terms are probably immaterial.

➤ Whenever possible, the verb terminology follows that in many student textbooks.

➤ Many classical terms were developed by Quirk, et al. (1985), Leech and Svartvik (2003), and Leech (2004).

➤ In L2 teaching, the transparency of the terminology is of the greatest importance.

Lexical Verb Classes

Five major verb classes are particularly important in L2 instruction (modal verbs are discussed in chapter 12 on hedging):

- Activity verbs.
- Reporting verbs.
- Mental process verbs.
- Linking verbs.
- Relationship verbs.

A few notes to get started:

(1) Different types of verbs do not play the same role in teaching L2 academic writing, and some are more important than others.
(2) Few activity verbs (*eat, walk, run*) and mental process verbs (*believe, feel, think*) are actually encountered in academic text, but linking and relationship verbs (*appear, seem, include*) are very frequent.

(3) Activity and mental process verbs are relatively rare in academic writing, but these are very common in conversations.

(4) Reporting verbs (***state, comment, explain***) and relationship verbs (***change, combine, increase***) are far more academic and advanced, and they need to be taught.

Spelling!
A Tremendously Important Point about Academic Verbs

- It is a well-known fact that even advanced university students continue to make numerous mistakes in the spelling of irregular verbs.
- The number of academic irregular verbs is not very large, but such spelling mistakes are at best profoundly embarrassing.
- Even in the age of ubiquitous spellcheckers, students need to learn to spell irregular verbs. Without knowing the correct verb form, it is difficult to figure out which suggested form should be accepted and which can make the text almost incomprehensible.

L2 writers have to learn the correct spelling of common academic verbs and their forms.

In many cases, about a month of persistent practice can do the job.

The Most Essential Verbs

Various studies of academic prose have determined that certain verbs consistently recur in academic texts ranging from introductory course books to publications of innovative research (Biber, et al., 1999; Leech, et al., 2001; Nation, 1990, 2013; Webb & Nation, 2017).

Recurrent and highly frequent academic verbs are essential for students to know and use in their writing. These number fewer than a hundred, and they may not be especially difficult to learn, particularly because they are encountered repeatedly.

Such relatively simple and highly frequent verbs as *make, bring, take, use,* and *show* predominate across all written genres as single words or in combinations with particles as two- or three-word verbs (*bring about, make up, take on*). These extremely common verbs are not included on the list of the academic must-have verbs below because they can be easily learned in routine exposure to English. Other highly common academic verbs, e.g. *describe, imply, refer,* are also not included because they are familiar to practically all L2 college-bound students: these are included dozens of times in test questions and instructions, e.g. on the TOEFL, IELTS, or ACT.

Thus, *The Most Essential Verbs* below constitute a somewhat reduced list of core verbs. Without at least some of these, it may not be possible to write an academic essay or paper in any discipline or on any topic.

The 40 Most Essential Verbs

affect	allow	appear	apply	(a)rise (from)
assume	cause	change	consider	constitute
contain	determine	develop	emerge	find
follow	form	include	increase	indicate
investigate	involve	lack	leave	matter
obtain	occur	produce	prove	provide
reach	reduce	reflect	relate	remain
represent	require	result (in)	seem	tend

(Adapted from Biber, et al., 1999; Leech, et al., 2001; Nation, 1990, 2013)

(1) Learning many essential verbs may take very little effort because they can be encountered in all kinds of settings that are not necessarily academic, e.g. *alter, find, follow,* or *leave*.

(2) These can be practiced in speaking activities, reading, or listening exercises.

(3) Others have been traditionally difficult for students to learn and use appropriately, e.g. *affect, cause, form, lack,* or *matter*.

(4) In part, the reason for learners' difficulties with these verbs stems from the fact that they have identical noun–verb forms.

(5) The similarity in the spelling of these dual noun–verb forms can make identifying their syntactic functions particularly confusing.

> Identical spelling and divergent syntactic functions of nouns, verbs, and adjectives have to be explicitly addressed in teaching.

Dealing with ambiguous noun–verb forms:

- To determine whether a particular word is a noun or a verb, one needs to look around the sentence to see the context of the word.

  o For instance, if an article or a possessive pronoun is in front of the word, it is probably a noun.

- If in the sentence the word follows something that looks like a noun, it is likely to be a verb.

Contrasting nouns and verbs that have identical spelling, for example, *change*, *form*, *lack*, and *matter*, can clarify their uses as nouns or verbs:

[Noun] *A lack of rain in the past few days has caused an increase in water consumption.*
[Verb] *The companies lack funding for a new venture.*
[Noun] *A change in the weather pattern may bring us a welcome precipitation.*
[Verb] *The weather patterns will change in the next few days.*

For instance, *a lack* is preceded by the article *a*, and therefore it is a noun. On the other hand, *the companies* is probably a noun phrase – the article again, followed by *lack* and *funding*. In this case, *lack* is likely to be a verb, and *funding* – a gerund because *-ing* verbs require an auxiliary *be* to be present (*are funding*). Similarly, *a change* is a noun, and *will change* is a verb phrase with the future auxiliary *will*.

Verbs such as *change*, *form*, *lack*, and *matter* are very common in all manner of texts. To highlight the high frequencies of words with identical **noun–verb–adjective** forms, students can be assigned to find and bring examples to class for discussion: for example, three uses of these words as nouns and three as verbs.

Foundational Academic Verbs

Foundational verbs are required to construct academic writing. That is, it may simply not be possible to construct academic text if one's vocabulary range is fewer than 1,000 words (Nation, 1990, 2013).

A list of approximately 350 foundational verbs[1] is presented below, and the words in bold are found most frequently and in highly varied texts across all academic disciplines.

Highly Frequent Verbs in Introductory University Texts

abandon	accelerate	access	accompany	accomplish	accumulate
achieve	acquire	adhere	adjust	administer	advocate
affiliate	agitate	aid	align	allege	allude
alter	**analyze**	appeal	append	appraise	appreciate
approach	arouse	ascribe	assemble	assert	**assess**
assign	assimilate	assist	**assume**	assure	attach
attain	avail	benefit	bore	breed	cancel
capture	cater	cease	challenge	circulate	clarify
coincide	collide	commit	communicate	compel	compensate
complement	complicate	**comply**	compound	comprehend	comprise
compute	conceive	concentrate	**conclude**	condense	conduct
confer	confine	conflict	conform	confront	conserve
consist	console	constitute	**construct**	construe	**consult**
consume	contact	contaminate	contemplate	contend	contract
contradict	contrast	contribute	convene	converge	converse
convert	cooperate	coordinate	correlate	correspond	create
debate	decline	dedicate	defect	defer	**define**
deflect	degenerate	degrade	deliberate	demonstrate	**denote**
deny	depress	deprive	**derive**	design	detect
deviate	**devise**	devote	dictate	diffuse	digest
discern	dispense	disperse	displace	dispose	dispute
dissipate	dissolve	distinct	distort	distribute	diverge
dominate	edit	elaborate	elevate	elicit	eliminate
emancipate	embody	embrace	emerge	emphasize	enable
enhance	enlighten	enrich	ensure	enumerate	**equate**
err	**establish**	estimate	**evaluate**	evaporate	evoke
evolve	exclude	execute	exert	exhaust	expand
expel	exploit	export	expose	extract	facilitate
factor	fare	feature	fluctuate	focus	forgo
formulate	found	frustrate	fuel	fulfill	function
fund	fuse	generate	grant	**guarantee**	harbor

identify	ignore	illuminate	**illustrate**	**impact**	implement
imply	import	impose	impress	incline	incorporate
indicate	induce	infer	inhibit	injure	insist
inspect	institute	instruct	integrate	interact	interlock
interpret	interrelate	intersect	interview	intervene	invade
invest	investigate	invoke	**involve**	irrigate	isolate
issue	justify	label	launch	lecture	legislate
liberate	locate	maintain	manifest	manipulate	migrate
modify	notate	oblige	obtain	occupy	occur
orientate	oscillate	overlap	participate	perpetrate	persist
pervade	plead	plot	postulate	precede	precipitate
predict	**presume**	**prevail**	**proceed**	process	proclaim
procure	prohibit	project	propagate	prosper	protest
provoke	**publish**	purport	**pursue**	quote	react
rebel	recur	reform	refute	reign	reinforce
reject	release	rely	remove	render	repress
reproduce	repudiate	**require**	research	respond	restore
restrict	retain	retard	reveal	reverberate	**reverse**
revise	revive	revolt	revolve	rotate	route
saturate	schedule	scheme	score	seek	select
shift	shrink	signify	sketch	**specify**	speculate
starve	stimulate	stipulate	stress	structure	subdivide
subside	subsidize	subtle	**suffice**	sum	superimpose
supplement	suppress	survey	suspend	sustain	switch
sum	tape	team	tire	tolerate	trace
transact	transfer	transform	transmit	transport	undergo
underlie	undertake	utilize	utter	**vary**	verify
violate	withdraw				

(Extracted from the University Word List: Nation, 1990)

As with nouns, expanding the vocabulary range of verbs can take place by means of learning small numbers of verbs with similar meanings. Having choices of similar verbs increases a writer's options. For this purpose, two- or three-word verbs and formal multiword expressions can be also practiced in context, together with other verbs with similar meanings (Hinkel, 2016, 2017a, 2017b, 2019).

Essential Verbs and a Small Number of Very Close Synonyms

abandon – give up – leave	accelerate – speed up – quicken
access – enter – go in(to)	accompany – go hand in hand (with)
accomplish – achieve – attain	appear – emerge – show up
choose – select – pick out	continue – go on – keep on
discover – find out – learn – determine	discuss – take up – raise
finish – complete – conclude	investigate – research – examine
leave – go away – depart	maintain – continue
reject – dismiss – turn down	remove – take off – take away
review – look over	search (for) – look for

The verbs with synonyms can be practiced in editing or contextualized substitutions. The following example of a student text can benefit from an expanded range of verbs and a bit of editing.

> As a **development** of science and technology, the research fields of human beings are **changing** into more variety. Medical technology is also **changing**, and computers are **changing** everything. Most of the projects cannot be completed by the person who just **knows** the one field. These projects require the researcher who **knows** many disciplines. This produces a contemporary scientific research approach that is also **changing**. With the **development** of microelectronics, much progress has been achieved in electrical engineering. The research area of electrical engineering has increased much more. On the other hand, people **change** to care about themselves more and more. There is much **development** in medical fields in recent years. Research has given us a lot of information that is always **changing**.
>
> (From a third-year term paper on technological advancements)

In a 122-word extract, the word *change* is repeated six times, *development* three times, and *know* twice. In this case, as in numerous other cases of L2 academic text, rudimentary vocabulary work can lead to a direct, even if superficial, improvement. For instance, both nouns and verbs can be somewhat more diverse at a relatively low cost in terms of time and work.

- **change** [verb] – expand – develop – transform – modify – alter – advance
- **produce** [verb] – create – bring about

- *know* [verb] – *be informed/educated* – *be familiar with* – *have experience in* – *work in*
- *increase* [verb] – *grow* – *broaden* – *spread* – *enhance* – *expand* – *rise*

While few of these substitute expressions are lexically and syntactically sophisticated, their uses in L2 academic prose can make a noticeable difference in the linguistic variety of textual features.

Talking Shop

<u>Collocations</u> are combinations of words, e.g. **look up, look into, turn upside down, bring about, bring up, bring together, bring out,** that frequently occur and re-occur together in speaking and writing. Collocations are extremely frequent, and most are language- and culture-specific. According to various corpus analyses, up to 67–70% of spoken and written discourse consists of collocations. The meanings and grammar elements of multiword units can be difficult to piece together due to their lexical and syntactic irregularity.

The meaning transparency or opaqueness of collocations represents a continuum that can range from expressions that are almost always deducible to those with fully idiomatic meanings, and these have to be learned and memorized. Many short recurrent phrases, for instance, can have transparent meanings that can be surmised – at least to some extent, as in **make a living/mistake/difference/trouble/speech/observation/plans**, but not ***make homework**, ***make an accident**, or ***make a feeling**.

However, a majority are semantically opaque, e.g. **hotdog, a hot potato, the hot seat, at the drop of a hat, hold on to your hat, cut corners, cut to the chase, cost an arm and a leg, last straw, on the ball, hit the sack/hay, a dime a dozen, a toss up, buy a lemon, right as rain,** or **piece of cake** (not to be confused with **easy as pie** with a similar meaning that is often misused, as in ***easy as a piece of cake**).

Activity Verbs

Activity verbs comprise the largest class of verbs, and some of the verb classes below are basically subclasses of activity verbs, (e.g. see the sections on Reporting Verbs and Relationship Verbs below).

- Activity verbs refer to physical actions, e.g. *eat, give, take; precipitation falls, the river overflows.*
- Two- or three-word verbs also belong in this class, e.g. *give up, look into, make up.*

Activity verbs can be transitive and intransitive, that is, used with or without direct objects. They can be used with animate subjects, e.g. *the sociologist adheres to . . ., the teacher writes/travels,* or inanimate subjects (*the valve turns, the conclusion sums up*).

- Activity verbs are not particularly frequent university textbooks and formal academic writing.
- Corpus analyses of English-language academic prose demonstrate that activity verbs are far less common than stative or linking verbs, e.g. *be, appear, seem, exist.*
- Activity verbs predominate in conversations, fiction, and news reports.

For example, in Nation's (1990) University List, activity verbs largely refer to physical actions, but not necessarily in their literal meanings, e.g.

abandon [a direction/venture]	*accelerate [growth/development]*
access [information/facilities]	*accompany [innovation/change]*
accumulate [resources/capital]	*acquire [meaning/business]*
adhere [to rules/guidance/direction]	*adjust [figures/course of action]*

The Most Frequent Activity Verbs in Academic Writing
(in declining order, left to right)

make	*give*	*take*	*use*	*deal with*	*show*
move	*produce*	*provide*	*apply*	*form*	*obtain*
reduce					

These verbs are also common in two- and three-word verbs or collocations.

Verbs, Synonyms, and Frequent Collocations

Verbs & Synonyms	Collocations
make up – consist (of) – form	*make a difference, make do, make time, make way, make [something] up*
take up – start *take out – remove – omit* *take on – undertake*	*take place, take part, take time/money/ space, take something well/badly*
give off – emit – produce *give up – stop – leave – abandon*	*give a thought, give time, give an impression, give credit, give authority*

Practice materials for these common verbs can be found in various types of print media and used for group or individual work in context. For example, news headlines, articles titles, and other authentic materials provide a wealth of opportunities for exposure to activity verbs. Here are a few examples of headlines.

Headlines with Activity Verbs

- *Heinz Will <u>Catch Up</u> in California.*
- *<u>Making Way</u> for the New Student Center.*
- *New Clam <u>Showing Up</u> in Oregon.*
- *More College Students <u>Drop Out</u> than Graduate.*

Highly frequent basic activity verbs such as **buy, put, pay, catch, meet, play, run,** or **wait** are hardly ever encountered in academic prose, even though they are prevalent in conversation and fiction (Jordan, 1997; Leech, et al., 2001).

Action Point

A **Phrasal Verb** is defined in the *Cambridge Dictionary* as "a combination of a verb and an adverb or a verb and a preposition, or both, in which the combination has a meaning different from the meaning of the words considered separately."

In lexical classifications, phrasal verbs have deservedly received much attention. For one thing, their numbers are so large that exact or even proximate counts are unknown. An excellent case in point is that two highly regarded and classical dictionaries published by Cambridge

University Press and Oxford University Press, since the 1980s and to this day, have released dictionaries of phrasal verbs as separate volumes to supplement their main dictionaries of English.

Phrasal verbs have traditionally presented a great deal of difficulty for language learners and, by extension, for teachers and material writers. For example, a phrase such as *__go on__* has at least a dozen main meanings, (e.g. *happen, continue, operate, talk, move to, pass*) and *__turn around__* can be a noun or a verb, and spelled together or separately, each with different meanings.

By and large, learners do not notice or learn phrasal verbs in text because their vocabulary components may not be new, but word combinations are likely to be, e.g. *account for, deal with, look up, look into, look for, come about, come around, come up, turn down, turn out, turn off.*

Pointing out, identifying, and discussing phrasal verbs in context is an essential step in teaching these verbs. Teachers need to explicitly focus students' attention on their form, structure, and meaning.

Reporting Verbs

Lists of reporting verbs can be found in most grammar books, beginning with those for intermediate level students. Reporting verbs denote such simple acts as *ask, say, speak,* or *tell.* Indeed, these reporting verbs predominate in informal spoken discourse. On the other hand, in academic prose, the most frequent reporting verbs are more lexically and semantically complex.

The Most Frequent Reporting Verbs

acknowledge	address	admit	advise	announce	appeal
argue	call (for)	carry out	challenge	deny	describe
determine	discuss	emphasize	encourage	explain	express
indicate	inform	mention	note	offer	point out
propose	publish	question	quote	recommend	remark
report	respond	specify	state	suggest	teach
urge	warn	write			

- Reporting verbs are particularly important in paraphrasing, reviewing readings, and citing from sources.
- Reporting verbs are used to introduce indirect and reported statements in noun phrases or noun clauses.

Here are a few examples.

- *Sandra Johnson **has shown** that fraternal twins who resemble one another enough to be mistaken for identical twins have more similar personalities than other twins.*
- *The researchers **reported** finding a gene nearly identical to the mouse obesity gene in humans.*
- *This research **indicates** that people really are born with a tendency to have a certain weight.*
- *A new study at Famous University **notes** a connection between better grades and exercise.*

- Citations of data, research findings, and scholarly studies are a ubiquitous means of demonstrating one's familiarity with readings and sources.
- References to external sources of knowledge represent a requisite means of supporting one's position in rhetorical argumentation (Swales, 1990).
- For L2 writers, it is paramount to develop a varied stock of expressions to cite information from readings.

It is important for students to know that in English, the subject **noun animacy** (a degree of being alive) makes no difference in the functions of reporting verbs used as predicates. That is, *Smith (2025) shows* or *the study/research shows* are equally grammatical and can be used in similar contexts (Hinkel, 2002a; see also chapter 7).

To many L2 users, the use of inanimate (lifeless) subjects with active verbs can seem ungrammatical. Animate subjects with active verbs may be a better place to start, e.g. ***Jones (2030) states that . . .* or *According to Jones (2030), . . .***

Frequent Phrases and Sentence Stems for Citing Information from Sources

Sentence Subjects	Reporting Verbs	*That*- Clauses, Etc.
The First Mention of the Source		
Smith (2029) *Smith and Johnson (2029)*	*state(s)* *note(s)* *mention(s)* *comment(s)* *remark(s)* *indicate(s)* *explain(s)*	*(that . . .)/[noun/* noun phrase, e.g. *a change]*

Inanimate (lifeless) Subjects
 Smith's (2030) study/findings/
    data
 The analysis of xxx
 The investigation of xxx/
    data, information, examples,
    illustrations, facts, statistics,
    study results, observations
	show(s)
	 demonstrate(s)
	 emphasize(s)
	 maintain(s)
	 argue(s)
	 deny/(-ies)
		(that . . .)/[noun/
		 noun phrase]

The Second or Subsequent Mention of the Source		
The *author(s)/researcher(s)/studies*	*propose(s)* *report(s)* *comment(s)* *point(s) out* *remark(s)* *suggest(s)*	*(that . . .)/[noun/* noun phrase]
The Second or Subsequent Mention in a Paraphrase from the Same Source		
The *researcher(s)/***This** *scholar*	*go(es) on to say* *further write(s)* *additionally state(s)*	*(that . . .)/[noun/* noun phrase]
Adverbial Constructions and Hedges		
According to Smith (2029), *Based on Johnson (2030),*		

The uses of reporting verbs in references to sources, citations, and paraphrases can be presented in columns to show clearly how syntactic regularities can work to the learners' advantage. That is, by simply replacing the subject noun or the verb with various proximate alternatives, L2 writers can actually come up with a great number of diverse and contextually appropriate expressions.

<table>
<tr><th colspan="3">Advanced Frequent Phrases and Sentence Stems</th></tr>
<tr><th>Sentence Subjects</th><th>Reporting Verbs</th><th>Dependent Clause Markers, Etc.</th></tr>
<tr><td colspan="3">Dual Reporting Verbs with Infinitives **to**</td></tr>
<tr><td>Smith/The author(s)</td><td>describe xxx <u>to show</u>
explain xxx <u>to demonstrate</u>
present xxx <u>to emphasize</u></td><td>(that . . .) /
[noun/noun phrase]</td></tr>
<tr><td colspan="3">Reporting Verbs with Object Complements (Noun Phrases)</td></tr>
<tr><td>The author(s)</td><td>presents <u>the opinion</u>
holds <u>the position</u>
advocates <u>the view</u></td><td>(that . . .) /
[noun/noun phrase]</td></tr>
<tr><td colspan="3">Reporting Verbs with Noun Clauses and Object Complements</td></tr>
<tr><td>Their results
The study results
The new findings</td><td>explain
challenge
offer</td><td>that/how/why

the reasons that
the view
the position that
the argument that
the claim that
(the) explanation(s) that</td></tr>
</table>

Realistically speaking, few students may need a supply larger than five or six citational expressions, and practicing reporting verbs in the context of references to sources may help L2 writers become comfortable with their uses.

Mental Process Verbs

In general, mental process verbs refer to intellectual states, e.g. *know*, *learn*, *think*, and non-observable intellectual acts, e.g. *notice*, *suspect*, *trust*. Other verbs in this class refer to cognitive processes, e.g. *compare*, *calculate*, *recognize*.

> Mental verbs are not very popular in academic writing, and their rate of use in academic prose stands at approximately less than one half of a percent (0.39–0.42%) in large English-language corpora.

The teaching of mental verbs needs to proceed judiciously. While some of the verbs in this class are relatively common in academic writing, others are hardly ever encountered because they often impart a personal and subjective tone to formal discourse. In classroom teaching, mental and reporting verbs can be combined, but a good range of reporting verbs is of the essence in academic writing (Simpson-Vlach & Ellis, 2010; Quirk, 1995).

The most frequent **mental process verbs** found in academic text actually include fewer than ten (listed here in declining order of frequency, left to right).

The Most Frequent Academic Mental Verbs

see	find	consider	know	think
assume	determine	mean	read	

A majority of mental verbs found in published academic text largely refer to cognition, e.g. *enjoy, face, hate*, and *want*, and in rare cases, receiving information, e.g. *observe, read, recognize*.

In addition to the most frequent verbs, other mental verbs found substantially **less often** in large English-language corpora include other verbs that refer to cognitive processes (Leech, et al., 2001).

Less Frequent Academic Mental Verbs

accept	appreciate	assess	calculate	compare
conclude	decide	determine	discover	distinguish
doubt	establish	estimate	identify	intend
interpret	judge	learn	notice	prefer
prove	realize	recognize	solve	study

> Mental verbs are far more prevalent in informal discourse and fiction than academic in text. Verbs such as *attempt, plan, try, want* refer to the future time and are often employed in tentative or personal constructions with an element of uncertainty.

In Anglo-American academic prose, projecting hesitation and avoiding overly confident propositions and claims is considered to be desirable and appropriate. On the other hand, in many other discourse traditions, authoritative, direct, and confident assertions are valued more highly. Many studies have demonstrated that direct assertions and strong arguments (e.g. *assure*, *claim, reject*) occur significantly more frequently in L2 writing than in L1 academic text. By and large, informal and conversational vocabulary (e.g. *believe*, *feel, know, think*) is very common in L2 writing because most learners have a great deal more exposure to casual interactions than academic prose (Hinkel, 2002b, 2003; Hyland & Milton, 1997; Shaw & Liu, 1998).

> In addition to working with common academic verbs, it is also important to alert L2 writers to the fact that conversational verbs are hardly ever encountered in formal academic text.

Conversational Verbs Usually **Not** Found in Academic Prose

attempt	believe	desire	expect	feel
hear	like	listen	love	plan
remember	suppose	try	want	wonder

The uses of these verbs may seem somewhat subjective in formal academic writing, when discourse is expected to project academic objectivity and distance (Swales, 1990; Swales & Feak, 2012). Here are a few examples of informal vocabulary found in L2 academic assignments.

> *Many American scholars have studied the history of American education. They have **tried** to find out what made education change. I **feel** that there are different causes for that.*
>
> (From a student text on early American history and education)

> *Biologists **like** to work with each other because they **feel** that they need knowledge from other fields, such as chemistry and physics. They **think** that one person cannot work alone. We can **notice** the same in other fields, such as geology, when they share information, and everyone **likes** to take part that is related to his major. When biological research starts a new project, we **want** to **listen** to one another and **plan** what we will do because we **expect** to get results together. Knowledge grows rapidly in this world, and biologists **try** to*

*keep up with the current knowledge by working together to design research. After research design is evaluated, we can **recognize** what went well and what didn't.*

(From a student paper about research design in biology)

Due to the preponderance of conversational verbs in this text, it may need to be thoroughly edited to make the text appear more academic. (Also, repeated uses of first person pronouns, characteristic of formal written discourse in various non-Anglo-American rhetorical traditions, may not be the best academic choice.)

Linking Verbs

Linking verbs refer to a **syntactic** "link" that exists between the subject on the left-hand side of the verb phrase and the subject complement on the right-hand side of the verb.

(1) Food safety **is** very important.
(2) Food handling safety risks **are** more common than most people think.
(3) The evolution of mechanical refrigeration **was** a long, slow process originally introduced in the late 19th century.
(4) Symbols **are** basic representations of human behavior. Road signs, images, icons, or numbers **are** everyday examples of how symbols can communicate information.

(www.census.gov/library/stories/2018/12/why-does-the-american-community-survey-ask-the-questions-it-does.html)

In these texts, the subject phrase *food safety* is linked to the adjective *important*. Similarly, *food handling safety risks* is connected to *more common*, and the subject phrase *symbols* refers *basic representations*.

> In many cases, the function of the verb **be** or other linking verbs, such as **seem** and **appear**, can be taught as the sentence subject approximately equal to (≈) or directly referring to the complement – located on the other side of the link.

Linking Verbs to Connect Sentence Elements

Sentence	Linked Complements	Connections
Jane **is/seems** tall.	tall → Jane	One of Jane's characteristics (≈) *tall*
John **is** a student.	a student → John	One of John's characteristics (≈) *student.*
Symbols **are** basic representations.	symbols ↔ representations	symbols (≈) basic representations

In English, there are fewer than a dozen linking verbs, but they are far more predominant in academic text than in any other genre (Swales & Feak, 2012).

> The most common linking verbs are *be* and *become*, and *be* is used over 20 times more frequently than any other linking verb.

Highly Common Academic Linking Verbs

appear	be	become	grow	prove	seem

Academic text uses of linking verbs:

- The verbs *be* and *become* are followed by adjective phrases in the vast majority of cases, e.g. *be important, become necessary.*
- The linking verbs *seem* and *appear* are prevalent in academic writing. These verbs refer to likelihood or strong possibility (e.g. *the economy seems stable*), or conclusions that may not be completely certain (Chafe & Nichols, 1986).
- Adjectives of subjective evaluation such as *nice, good, wonderful, terrible, good, pleasant, terrific,* or *terrible* are generally **not** employed in academic writing.

The Most Common Academic Adjectives That Follow Linking Verbs

true	different	important	difficult	possible
likely	necessary	available	useful	remain

In academic writing, the verb *be* is very frequently followed by **a noun phrase**. Additionally, linking verbs can be followed by **noun clauses** and, rarely, prepositional phrases (Leech & Svartvik, 2003).

- *Gross domestic product (GDP)* ***is*** <u>*a comprehensive measure of US economic activity.*</u>
- *The reasons for housing relocation* ***are*** <u>*that individuals change their marital status, take new jobs or job transfers, or find cheaper housing.*</u>
- *Retail shopping in general* ***seems*** <u>*in decline.*</u> *The estimated retail sales by the nation's department stores* ***are*** <u>*clear examples*</u> *of annual sales figures from the month of December each year.*
  (www.census.gov/library/working-papers/
  2016/demo/SEHSD-WP2016-22.html)

Impersonal *it*-cleft constructions are prevalent in academic writing and are almost always followed by a linking verb (Quirk, et al., 1985; Quirk, 1995).

- ***It is*** *large retail businesses that usually provide part-time and full-time employment in regional hubs.*
- ***It is*** *the dozens of small retail businesses that often make up the character of the shopping center.*
- ***It is*** *these shopping events that are important to retailers and the national economy as a whole.*
- ***It is*** *the increase of 42.2 percent from e-Commerce sales that has boosted the revenue in the third quarter.*

In teaching, a small chart may be helpful in explaining the syntactic regularities of the structure and uses of linking verbs.

The Most Frequent Academic Structures with Linking Verbs

Subject Noun(s) & Examples	Linking Verbs	+ Adjective
	be, become, seem, appear	
The problem	*is*	*important, and . . . necessary/*
A solution	*is*	*available.*

	Linking Verbs	+ Noun Phrase, Prepositional Phrase, or Noun Clause
	be, become, remain	
Harry S. Truman	*was*	*a US president.*
The definition	*is*	*in Chapter 1.*
The main point	*is*	*that culture is a social fact.*
It-Cleft Constructions	**Linking Verbs**	**+ Adjective or + Noun Clause**
	be, become, seem, appear, remain	
It	*is/seems*	*reasonable.*
It	*appears/remains*	*clear + that societies evolve.*

In L2 writing, structures with **linking verb + adjective** are often overused, and such constructions may appear to be relatively basic and descriptive.

> *In history, science __grows__ more __complex__, and it __grows__ from general to specific. When science __is__ still __new__, scientists do not have to have a special kind of knowledge. They work in general knowledge. But when knowledge __is__ more __complex__, scientists begin to choose special part from knowledge as a whole. Their jobs __become__ more __specialized__. This special approach in science __is__ __important__ because scientists can accurately make conclusions. The new approach in research __is__ __important__ because by this approach scientists can explain a phenomenon or solve a complicated problem. When science __is__ __mature__, then research needs more special knowledge, and technical knowledge __becomes__ __essential__.*
>
> (From a student paper on the history of science)

To deal with a high number of **linking verb + adjective** structures, the issue of sentence **compactness** needs to be explicitly addressed. For example, if the predicative adjective is moved and placed in front of the subject noun, the second half (the predicate) of the sentence can be "freed up" to include more information. Here are a few examples.

science is complex	→	*complex science* *(requires specialized knowledge)*
science is mature	→	*mature science*

technical knowledge becomes essential	→	essential technical knowledge (can lead to accurate conclusions)
jobs become specialized	→	specialized jobs

The teaching of the uses and functions of linking verbs is relatively uncomplicated and can be well suited for beginning and intermediate proficiency levels.

Relationship Verbs

The function of **relationship verbs** is to refer to causes, effects, proofs, or changes in the state of affairs. Although the lexical content of some of these verbs is advanced, their contextual uses do not need to be.

Essential and Frequent Relationship Verbs

accompany	account (for)	allow (for)	alternate (with)
approximate	arise (from)	belong to	cause
change	combine (with)	complement	conflict
consist of	constitute	contain	contradict
contrast (with)	contribute (to)	decrease	depend on
develop	differ from	follow	illustrate
imply	include	increase	indicate
involve	lead (to)	occur	precede
reflect	replace	represent	resemble
result (in)	sum		

> Presenting collocations (recurrent phrases) with relationship verbs and having students learn them in contextualized expressions and chunks represents a highly practical – if not the most productive – teaching technique.

Collocations with relationship verbs typically occur in combinations with nouns, prepositions, or other verbs. A few examples are presented below (for teaching techniques, see the next section of this chapter).

Identical Verb and Noun Forms with Collocations

cause	verb	cause concern
		cause problems, cause inconvenience
	noun	a root cause, an underlying cause
		with good cause, without cause
		a cause for concern
		a common cause; a lost cause
		a cause of death
change	verb	change color
		change (from xxx) to yyy (change from stocks to bonds)
		change jobs
		change direction, change course
		change gears (conversational)
		change the subject (conversational)
		change sides
		change one's mind
		change hands (one million shares changed hands)
		change places with
	noun	to be/represent a change
		(the new law represents a dramatic change)
		a change for the better
		a change of heart (= to change one's mind)
		in change, loose change, small change

> For many L2 writers, it is more effective and efficient to learn rela-
> tionship verbs and their collocational expressions as whole entities
> rather than trying to assemble phrases from basic vocabulary and
> grammar components (Hinkel, 2015, 2019; Howarth, 1998; Nation,
> 2013; Nation & Webb, 2011).

For example, collocational practice can consist of, say, news reportage and information restatements from business articles, e.g. *and now we bring you the latest from the stock market,* formal business plans, presentations to **the board of directors** or a company president, or poster sessions with formal explanations for **stock holders** or potential investors.

Examples for Practice: Frequent Relationship Verbs and Formal Expressions

Verb	Derived Noun	Formal Expressions
combine	*combin + ation*	*combine to do xxx* *combine business with pleasure* *combined with xxx (acid combined with alkali)* *combined effort/action, combined income* *in combination with a winning/perfect combination* *a combination of factors,* *combinations of (numbers/variables)*
develop	*develop + ment*	*develop an idea/option, a plan (of action),* *develop a relationship (with customers)* *develop into (a long-lasting peace, a new cell)* *(designed/created/positioned) to develop (markets)* *develop land* *develop an illness/a treatment* *developed middle class* *child development, skill development* *housing/budget/project development* *a new/recent/significant/important development* *research and development*

The key consideration is to give learners an opportunity to use the vocabulary and grammar structures that they would not otherwise have in their casual and informal interactions. In this case, many relationship verbs can be useful in somewhat formal academic writing and presentations.

Action Point

In English language textbooks and dictionaries, multiword expressions are regularly provided for cultural distinctiveness and eccentricity, regardless of their frequency or practicality, e.g. *in a pickle, a cold fish, a hill of beans, a dirty look, in the bag, a leg up,* or *a fat chance*. However, the most useful and commonplace multiword units are those that are less exotic, and they tend to consist of high frequency words, e.g. *make an appointment/a mistake/a call/a stop*.

By far, the most frequent single-word vocabulary items, such as the verbs *have, take, make, do,* and *go,* serve as the basis for the most statistically common multiword units (Webb & Nation, 2017). Carefully selecting collocations for learning can become an ongoing task for both teachers and learners.

Based on long-established research findings, flash cards or electronic applications and tools (e.g. mini self-quizzes, review lists, or phrase collections) represent the single most efficient way of learning and practicing vocabulary and collocations for retention. Numerous electronic applications send automatic and timed review notifications and reminders – a great convenience for teachers and learners. (This list is adapted from Simpson-Vlach & Ellis, 2010.)

Top 10 Most Frequent Collocations in Academic Writing

in the first	*(on) the other hand*	*it should be noted*
due to the fact that	*it is (not) possible to*	*there are a number of*
in such a way that	*(as) can be seen*	*a wide range of*
it has been	*take into account the*	*is likely to*

Vocabulary and multiword unit notebooks are also a very useful, efficient, and practical learning aid because reviewing the items that have been covered and learned previously can be made easier when they are collected in one place (Hinkel, 2013, 2019).

Teaching a Few Prefixes and Suffixes

A popular venue for learning and using academic verbs is the traditional work with prefixes and suffixes. However, the teaching of prefixes and some types of suffixes may need to account for a few **caveats**.

Important Caveats

➢ Most academic prefixes, roots, and suffixes have Latin or Greek origins, and teaching them creates an additional learning burden (Nation, 2013).

➢ There are many (many!) English words with meanings that do not represent the sum of their semantic parts (Schmitt, 2000).

   o For example, does the **de-** in **demonstrate** have the same meaning as it does in **denounce** or **deliberate**? Also, is the prefix in **antipollution** related to the one in **antiquity**?

➢ The ability to identify meanings of prefixes, word roots, and suffixes requires learners to divide words into parts correctly – a difficult job for both L1 and L2 writers.

➢ Working on new L2 vocabulary by means of learning word parts is likely to be of limited value and effectiveness.

A number of academic prefixes, suffixes, and word roots are so common, however, that it may be difficult to do without them, e.g. *non-*, *il-*, *intro-*, *post-*.

> Productive word parts with transparent meanings should be selected carefully. Devoting effort to learning many others may not be worth the requisite labor and time.

Relationship verbs include several with widely used prefixes *con-*, *de-*, and *in-*, and helping learners notice them and apparent similarities in verb meanings can create an additional opportunity for learning. Learning highly frequent word parts can help expand a student's essential academic vocabulary range.

Highly Frequent Verb Prefixes and Academic Verbs

Prefix	Meaning	Frequent Verbs
con- (also: *col-*, *cor-*, *co-*)	*with, together, inside*	*conflict, constitute, construct, contain* *contradict, contrast* *collaborate, correspond, correlate*

Prefix	Meaning	Frequent Verbs
de-	*not, away from, down from*	*decrease* (vs. *increase*) *decline* (vs. *incline, recline*)
in- (also: *im-, il-, ir-*)	*into or not*	*illustrate* (*explain, clarify*) *imply* (vs. *comply*) *include* (vs. *exclude*) *insert* *indicate, involve*
re- (also: *retro-*)	*back, again, backwards*	*reflect* (vs. *deflect, inflect*) *replace, represent* *resemble* (vs. *semblance; similar*) *return* *result* (as a consequence/outcome)

> To circumvent the tedium of learning a high number of English affixes, the most expedient technique is to learn whole words without parsing them into constituent parts.

Numerous teaching materials are available for prefixes and suffixes practice. Lists, exercises, classroom activities, and homework assignments can be found in practically all reading and vocabulary textbooks, as well as test and college preparation textbooks.

English derivational **suffixes** (*-tion, -ment, -ness, -able, -ship*) are less numerous than lexically abstract Greco-Latinate prefixes, and teaching derived deverbal nouns, e.g. *compete – completion*) is comparatively easier. Most dictionary entries for verbs, as well as other words, provide all possible derivational suffixes, derived word forms, and essential grammar information, as well as collocational expressions and sentence examples (see the dictionary exercise later in this chapter).

Morphologically complex relationship verbs are a good place to start work on derivational forms and suffixes. In general terms, nouns derived from verbs (gerunds with *-ing* and nominalizations with *-tion, -ment,* or *–ity – reading, writing, contradiction*) play a prominent role in academic writing, and learning noun-forming derivational suffixes is essential for L2 academic writers (see also chapter 5).

The examples below of such verbs as *alternate* and *approximate* and their attendant forms and other words with similar meanings illustrate only a few of the numerous possibilities.

Working with Academic Verbs and Derived Word Forms

Verb		Derived Words
alternate		*alter – alternate* (adj.) *alternative* (adj./noun) *alternatively – alternating (current)*
	Noun relatives	*alternative* (adjective above) *alteration – alternation*
	Similar meanings	**Verbs**: *modify – change – vary* **Nouns**: *alternation – modification – change – variation*

approximate		*approximate* (adj.) *– approx.* (written abbreviation) *– approximately*
	Noun relatives	*approximation* (**phrases**: *close/rough approximation*)
	Similar meanings	*about, nearly, roughly, close to*

Effective research-based techniques for learning academic vocabulary:

- A small number of words that are **closely** related in meaning and/or form are easier to learn and recall than unrelated words or antonyms.
- When learning academic words, only a couple of near-synonyms are needed, and not necessarily every word in a synonym cluster. For example, if the word *approximately* does not immediately come to mind, then easier words, such as *about* or *nearly*, may also work well in context (Nation, 1990, 2013; Schmitt, 2000).

Chapter Summary

Constructing university-level L2 academic text places great demands on students' vocabulary and grammar skills. In addition to approximately 40 essential verbs that recur in formal academic prose across various genres and disciplines, 350 foundational verbs need to become a focus of L2 vocabulary teaching.

- Overall, most verbs employed in academic texts can be roughly divided into five lexical classes:

  o   Activity verbs.
  o   Reporting verbs.

o   Mental process verbs.
o   Linking verbs.
o   Relationship verbs.

In L2 writing, lexical verb classes do not have an equal importance, and activity verbs and mental verbs play a less central role than reporting, linking, and relationship verbs.

- Reporting verbs play an instrumental role in referring to and paraphrasing from sources.
- Linking verbs and relationship verbs are far more common in formal written prose than in any other genre.
- Teaching relatively uncomplicated linking verbs and a handful of relationship verbs is crucial in vocabulary and grammar instruction.

A variety of effective pedagogical approaches to vocabulary teaching have been developed during the decades of vocabulary research.

- The most valuable techniques entail helping learners build small sets of very close synonyms that can provide vocabulary substitutions.
- Teaching verb collocations with nouns, prepositions, and other words represents another important technique in vocabulary instruction.
- For L2 academic writing, a highly efficient technique is to learn recurrent phrases and lexical chunks as whole units, instead of incrementally assembling academic constructions piece by piece.

Vocabulary teaching can additionally focus on two- or three-word verbs and idioms, as well as a few derivational prefixes and suffixes.

Strategies and Tactics for Teaching and Teaching Activities

Teaching Activities

The following six exercises are designed to increase students' mastery of academic English verbs. All these exercises can be assigned as individual or group tasks, or homework with a follow-up in-class discussion.

The learning goals of the teaching suggestions and activities presented below are to promote academic verb learning and retention, expand vocabulary, and work with collocations and phrasal verbs.

- Navigating dictionary entries and dictionary work.
- Learning academic verbs, phrasal verbs, and lexical substitutions.
- Practicing with a small number of prefixes.

The teaching suggestions presented here are based on using texts easily obtainable online, e.g. statistics, numerical data, business reports, and encyclopedia entries.

The single most important factor in all vocabulary learning:
Review, review, review.
Practice and review.

Dictionary Exercise

- Any online dictionary entry can be discussed in class to show learners how to use an English–English dictionary to their best advantage.
- An example of the entry for the verb *occur* can be reasonably interesting to present and explain.
- Discussion points are added in boxes.

oc·cur
verb
verb: **occur**; 3rd person present: **occurs**; past tense: **occurred**; past participle: **occurred**; gerund or present participle: **occurring**

the spelling of the past and *-ing* forms requires two *-rr-*'s

(1) happen; take place

the first and frequent meaning – these can be used as replacements/synonyms

"the accident occurred at about 3:30 p.m."
synonyms: **happen**, take place, come about, **transpire, materialize, arise,** crop up; *informal*   go down

more examples: *The event occurs/takes place annually/frequently/in the fall.*

(2) **exist or be found to be present in a place or under a particular set of conditions.** the second most common meaning

"radon occurs naturally in rocks such as granite"

synonyms: be found, be present, **exist**, **appear**, present itself, turn up possible replacements for the second meaning

"the disease occurs chiefly in tropical climates"

(3) **(of a thought or idea) come into the mind of (someone).**

"it occurred to him that he hadn't eaten"

synonyms: enter one's head/mind, cross one's mind, come to mind, spring to
mind, strike one, hit one, dawn on one, suggest itself, present itself

"an idea occurred to her"

In learners' dictionaries, additional information is also available.

o Prepositions, *occur in/among*, e.g. *Viral infections occur mainly among school children.*

o Collocations, e.g. *it occurs to somebody that, It occurred to him that new sports drinks may be popular among baseball fans.*

o Distinctions between formal and informal uses, e.g. *occur is formal and not common in spoken English.*

In general, dictionary exercises can provide learners the necessary skills to navigate English–English dictionaries that are daunting for many L2 writers, even when they have outgrown their bilingual dictionaries. Teacher guided dictionary practice can also help learners notice occurrences of important words in reading.

Building Meaning Clusters and Vocabulary Substitutions

- A list of verbs with various clusters of similar meanings is provided in random order.
- Working in pairs or small groups, learners need to sort out the verbs into clusters according to the similarities of their meanings, e.g. Change Verbs or Organize Verbs.
- Students need to supply additional verbs from their own knowledge to bring the number of verbs in each cluster to 10 (or some other number).
- The student groups should be prepared to defend their classification choices during the extension portion of this verb practice.

Here's an example. The verb meanings can be divided into several options, such as those below or some other broader or narrower combinations of these.

Verb Groupings (in any combination)

Change Verbs	Restate Verbs	Organize Verbs	Study Verbs	Differentiate Verbs

The starting set can include the most frequent verbs:

analyze	*investigate*	*decline*	*classify*	*decrease*
elaborate	*conclude*	*distinguish*	*structure*	*identify*
note	*rise*	*reduce*	*examine*	*alter*
modify	*propose*	*debate*	*observe*	*expand*
notice	*arrange*	*enlarge*	*broaden*	*complete*
precede	*advocate*	*remove*	*follow*	*mention*

More than one reasonable clustering of verbs is possible when the clusters are based on abstract vocabulary meanings, such as *organize, function,* and *differentiate*. For example, the verb *observe* can fit well into the clusters Study Verbs and Restate Verbs, or *precede* and *follow* into Organize and Differentiate. However, the teacher can take advantage of this conceptual fluidity and move to the next step of this exercise (see below).

Here is one version of the verbs grouped by meaning (various possible options are listed in parentheses) – an example.

Change Verbs	Organize Verbs	Restate Verbs	Differentiate Verbs
decline	distribute	elaborate	distinguish
reduce	schedule	conclude	separate
expand	(balance)	(identify)	(structure)
(arrange)	(structure)	(note)	(identify)
enlarge	(identify)	view	(note)
broaden	(coordinate)	propose	extract
(complete)	(arrange)	(observe)	divide
decrease	organize	notice	
remove	precede	(expand)	
(move)	follow	mention	

(1) **Beginning levels**. Action verbs with concrete – but not particularly academic – meanings work well to expand vocabulary as a starting point.

- o *giggle, laugh, cackle, chuckle*
- o *continue, go on, carry on*
- o *reduce, lower, cut down*
- o *state, explain, discuss*

(2) **High-intermediate levels**. Students can work in groups or complete the assignment as homework, followed by a substantial class discussion of verb meanings and their vocabulary choices. Usually, the preparation for this exercise as homework, class work, and the final discussion combined lead to almost immediate and noticeable productive uses of these verbs in students' academic writing.

- The time for this practice should allow a few minutes for the final verb list review and last minute reshuffle ("time to huddle").
- Then student pairs (or groups) can compare their verb list clusters and defend their choices, which invariably differ among groups.
- Students who are familiar with secondary and non-literal meanings of abstract verbs have an opportunity to teach other students and verbalize their knowledge explicitly.

> Much productive direct and incidental learning takes place when students need to explain meanings of verbs to other students and the reasons for their choices.
>
> The greatest benefit of the exercise lies in the follow-up discussion of verb meanings and the students' reasons for placing them in particular clusters.

Editing practice and word replacements

- Lists of sentences and/ or text excerpts with conversational or colloquial words (nouns or verbs)[2] are provided.
- The conversational vocabulary has to be replaced with **academic – and grammatically correct** – equivalents.
- A few possible replacements are noted in square brackets.

(1) *These days, education is the most important thing* [objective, achievement, opportunity for advancement] *in people's lives since without education we*

cannot do [accomplish, attain, carry out] *anything* [our objectives, goals, advancement] *in our lives.*

(2) *People* [individuals, students, youth] *who get* [acquire, obtain, receive] *better education will* [may, can] *get* [find, secure, compete for] *a better job, and people who get* [have] *less education will get* [have] *a hard time* [trouble, difficulty] *getting a job* [position, employment, job opportunities].

(3) *Students use telecommunication and try* [attempt, undertake] *to search for* [find, learn, locate, obtain] *something* [information, facts, data] *that they want* [aspire, seek] *to gain* [benefit from, increase their knowledge].

(4) *When we discuss* [describe, examine, undertake to study, take a look at] *the history of western music, we discuss* [analyze, classify, categorize] *the music history by dividing it into several parts* [styles, genres, eras, types, groups, categories, classes].

(5) *Many scholars think* [find, have the opinion, hold the view] *that since ancient times, music has not had a direct relation* [connection] *to painting.*

Describing graphs/charts and writing data analysis

- The students work in pairs or small groups to write a report that presents the data, graphs, or charts, and includes the verbs from the list.
- Similar or different lists of verbs for each data set or graph can be provided.
- The data examples: Country A, Country B, Country C, online statistics, encyclopedia entries, company business graphs, the stock market overviews, and other numerical data.
- As an extension activity and in a discussion, students can also produce speculative explanations for the distribution of data in their data sets.

(An alternative: In writing practice, after students produce a paragraph or an essay, the teacher can underline verbs or phrases in the student texts to be replaced with other words with similar meanings.)

Frequent Verbs for Various Graphs/Data

combine	decline	decrease	deduce	determine
deviate	drop (off)	fall	grow	hold (up)
increase	judge	lead	level	notice
observe	precede	raise	reduce	reflect
resemble	result	rise	sink	slip
speculate	supplement	sustain		

College Enrollments and Tuition Costs in State and Private Universities:
Topic Specific Verbs

apply (for)	admit	afford	charge	drop out	employ
enroll	fail	graduate	pay	retain	teach

Normal High and Low Temperatures and Precipitation in Two to Four States:
Topic Specific Verbs

coincide	compound	cool down	cool off	deviate	dry out/up
fall	flood	form	freeze	heat up	rain
rise	snow	warm (up)			

50 (or 5) Top Grossing Movies/Video Games in a Year/Decade:
Topic Specific Verbs

award	come out	earn	hold	generate	gross
import	market	produce	reign	release	sell (out)
shoot (shot)	show	stream	take in	top	win

Large US Centers of Population 2020–2030 (Year-to-Year):
Topic Specific Verbs

arrive	decline	decrease	expand	gain	grow
increase	inhabit	leave	locate	lose	maintain
move (in/out)	populate	relocate	reside	reverse	revive
seek	shift	stabilize	stimulate	supplement	sustain

Word, Verb, or Prefix Competitions

To maximize learning, students should be told a few days in advance of the competition when it is scheduled to take place. In this way, students have the opportunity to study and review their words, verbs, and affixes for an extended period of time.

(1) **Intermediate levels**. Individual students or pairs of students receive a list of verbs, where each represents a close synonym cluster as a starting point.

> *Report*   *Research*   *Develop*

- Students need to present as many close synonyms, collocational phrases, or sentences for each verb in a limited amount of time, say, 5 or 10 minutes.
- Then students can count and compare their lists to see which students won the competition.

(2) **High-intermediate and advanced levels**. With prefixes, students receive a list of similar starting points.

> *Re-*   *Con-*   *De-*   *In-*   *Pro-*

- Students need to create as many verbs, phrases with verbs, or sentences with these prefixes to see who can top the class counts.

At the completion of each competition, the winning student or team read out their list to the rest of the class. If the winners missed some verbs or phrases, the rest of the class can supplement them, and as a result of the cooperative effort, the entire class arrives at the complete accessible list. The list can be later distributed to the entire class for all students to have and review.

Omitted Verbs

- In an excerpt from an academic text or textbook, all verbs should be deleted or blocked (see chapter 5 for a similar exercise).
- The list of the omitted verbs should be given to students separately.
- Individually or in pairs, students can replace all the omitted verbs.
- To add a level of complexity, students may be asked to confirm that verb tenses are used correctly in the replaced structures.
- When the task is completed, verb replacements can be compared among groups to see who has correctly replaced the most verbs.
- When comparing the replaced verbs, students or pairs of students discuss their reasons for making particular verb choices.

Endnotes

1 In many cases, noun and verb forms can be identical (e.g. *access, aid, influence, advocate*). These are included on both the list of common nouns and the parallel list of common verbs.
2 I am grateful to Bruce Rogers, Ohio State University, for this exercise.

Further Reading

Hinkel, E. (2019). Teaching strategies and techniques: Collocations and multiword units. In E. Hinkel (Ed.), *Teaching essential units of language: Beyond single-word vocabulary*, (pp. 107–133). New York, NY: Routledge.

A short synopsis of strategies, techniques, and activities for teaching collocations. Recurrent phrases and multiword units are so frequent and ubiquitous that they can be found anywhere. Instruction in collocations can take place in the teaching of listening, speaking, reading, and writing, and their uses can be highlighted in practically any context. Because practically all collocations and phrases are idiomatic and highly conventionalized, their instructional applications can contribute to learners' strategic language development in receptive and productive skills in various instructional settings.

Leech, G. (2004). *Meaning and the English verb* (3rd edn). New York, NY: Routledge.

A classic work on the meaning and use of verb constructions in English. A lively and practical discussion of most interesting insights and problems in the area of verbs and verb phrases, as well as tenses and aspects. With language teachers and teaching in mind, this concise volume presents up-to-date examples. The discussion shows clearly how meanings and uses of verb constructions are reflected in British and American English. An excellent and well-organized reference that covers learning trouble spots that are not addressed in most style and usage guides.

Ur, P. (2012). *A course in language teaching: Practice and theory* (2nd edn). Cambridge: Cambridge University Press.

A through and clear comprehensive introduction to English teaching that combines theory, practice, and hands-on classroom instruction. The book is well suited for teachers in a variety of educational settings, including secondary and post-secondary education. The material surveys essential and new topics for the modern English language teacher, such as English as an international language, content-based teaching, corpus analysis, and digital techniques. The book is an efficient and clearly written reference guide for novice and practicing teachers.

References

Biber, D., Johansson, S., Leech, G., Conrad, S., & Finegan, E. (1999). *Longman grammar of spoken and written English*. Harlow: Pearson.

Chafe, W. & Nichols, J. (Eds.) (1986). *Evidentiality: The linguistic coding of epistemology*. Norwood, NJ: Ablex.

Hinkel, E. (2002a). Why English passive is difficult to teach (and learn). In E. Hinkel & S. Fotos (Eds.), *New perspectives on grammar teaching* (pp. 233–260). New York, NY: Routledge.

Hinkel, E. (2002b). *Second language writers' text*. New York, NY: Routledge.

Hinkel, E. (2003). Simplicity without elegance: Features of sentences in L1 and L2 academic texts. *TESOL Quarterly, 37*(2), 275–301.

Hinkel, E. (2013). Research findings on teaching grammar for academic writing. *English Teaching, 68*(4), 3–21.

Hinkel, E. (2015). *Effective curriculum for teaching L2 writing: Principles and techniques*. New York, NY: Routledge.

Hinkel, E. (2016). Practical grammar teaching: Grammar constructions and their relatives. In E. Hinkel (Ed.), *Teaching English grammar to speakers of other languages* (pp. 171–191). New York, NY: Routledge.

Hinkel, E. (2017a). Teaching idiomatic expressions and phrases: Insights and techniques. *Iranian Journal of Language Teaching Research, 5*(3), 45–59

Hinkel, E. (2017b). Prioritizing grammar to teach or not to teach: A research perspective. In E. Hinkel (Ed.), *Handbook of research in second language teaching and learning* (pp. 369–383). New York, NY: Routledge.

Hinkel, E. (2019). Teaching strategies and techniques: Collocations and multiword units. In E. Hinkel (Ed.), *Teaching essential units of language: Beyond single-word vocabulary* (pp. 107–133). New York, NY: Routledge.

Howarth, P. (1998). Phraseology and second language proficiency. *Applied Linguistics, 19*(1), 24–44.

Hyland, K. & Milton, J. (1997). Qualification and certainty in L1 and L2 students' writing. *Journal of Second Language Writing, 6*(2), 183–205.

Jordan, R. (1997). *English for academic purposes*. Cambridge: Cambridge University Press.

Leech, G. (2004). *Meaning and the English verb* (3rd edn). New York, NY: Routledge.

Leech, G., Rayson, P., & Wilson, A. (2001). *Word frequencies in written and spoken English*. London: Routledge.

Leech, G. & Svartvik, J. (2003). *A communicative grammar of English* (3rd edn). London: Routledge.

Nation, I.S.P. (1990). *Teaching and learning vocabulary*. Boston, MA: Heinle & Heinle.

Nation, I.S.P. (2013). *Learning vocabulary in another language* (2nd edn). Cambridge: Cambridge University Press.

Nation, P. & Webb, S. (2011). Content-based instruction and vocabulary learning. In E. Hinkel (Ed.), *Handbook of research in second language teaching and learning, Volume 2* (pp. 631–644). New York, NY: Routledge.

Quirk, R. (1995). *Grammatical and lexical variance in English*. London: Longman.

Quirk, R., Greenbaum, S., Leech, G., & Svartvik, J. (1985). *A comprehensive grammar of the English language*. New York, NY: Longman.

Schmitt, N. (2000). *Vocabulary in language teaching*. Cambridge: Cambridge University Press.

Shaw, P. & Liu, E. (1998). What develops in the development of second language writing? *Applied Linguistics, 19*(2), 225–254.

Simpson-Vlach, R. & Ellis, N. (2010). An academic formulas list: New methods in phraseology research. *Applied Linguistics, 31*(4), 487–512.

Swales, J. (1990). *Genre analysis.* Cambridge: Cambridge University Press.

Swales, J. & Feak, C. (2012). *Academic writing for graduate students* (3rd edn). Ann Arbor, MI: University of Michigan Press.

Webb, S. & Nation, P. (2017). *How vocabulary is learned.* Oxford: Oxford University Press.

Adjectives and Adverbs in Academic Discourse 9

Overview

- Adjectives and adverbs in academic writing.
- Essential academic adjectives and adverbs.
- Expanding the vocabulary range.
- How to distinguish adjectives and adverbs.
- Academic comparatives and superlatives.
- Prepositional phrases as adjectives and adverbs.
- Participles and infinitives.
- Adjectives in thesis statements.
- Writing from sources and evaluative adjectives.

In academic writing, adjectives and adverbs can perform key rhetorical functions. Although adjectives and adverbs are not as numerous as nouns and verbs, adjectives are extraordinarily frequent in academic writing – much more so than in conversational discourse or other types of writing (Bhatia, 1993; Carter & McCarthy, 2006; Huddleston & Pullum, 2002).

> Practically every sentence in academic prose includes adjectives and/or adverbs, as corpus analyses have long established.

In L2 writing, adjectives and adverbs often present several challenges. Numerous studies on academic writing demonstrate clearly that the L1 and L2 uses of adjectives and adverbs are markedly distinct in their frequencies and grammatical characteristics (Hinkel, 1997, 1999, 2003a; Hyland, 1998, 2008; Hyland & Milton, 1997; Swales, 1990).

A few prominent examples of the differences between L1 and L2 academic prose of similar writing types and levels have been identified in research.

- L2 writing includes significantly fewer **descriptive (attributive) adjectives**, e.g. *leading/primary/sole indicator*.
- L2 prose relies on far greater frequencies of **predicate adjectives**, e.g. *the solution is necessary/important/promising*.
- L2 texts contain particularly high rates of intensifying adjectives and adverbs, e.g. *absolute, complete, really, very, totally*.
- Markedly low frequencies of **hedging (softeners)** to limit the strength of generalizations and claims, e.g. *many/most, possible/possibly*.

In addition, irregularities of grammatical constructions and forms can make academic adjectives and adverbs particularly error-prone. Some of these are probably familiar to many language teachers:

- o *to work hardly and walk fastly*, instead of *to work hard and walk fast.*
- o *Students are confusing about the assignment*, instead of *Students are confused.*

Although L2 errors and misuses of adjectives and adverbs can appear to be a curse that cannot be broken, many of these problems can be addressed in instruction. For instance, *hard* and *fast* are adverbs, but they do not take the *-ly* suffix. To find out whether a word is an adjective or an adverb, one needs to ask the following questions:

When? Where? How? or *Why?*

All words and phrases that answer these questions are adverbs.

To see whether an adjective can or cannot become an adverb, a command can be used: *Be blue/long/tall!* If the command does not work, then an adverb cannot be derived.

Similarly, answers to such ubiquitous student questions are actually not complicated:

- – *Why can't I say *in this month or *in last year?*
- – *Why is I am boring incorrect, if the movie is boring is perfectly fine?*
- – *What's wrong with *it is a good time for going shopping? I can say *it is a good day for going shopping, can't I?*

The truth of the matter is that many of the constructions that lead to these types of errors and questions are actually not very difficult to address. These and other adjectival and adverbial mysteries are clarified in this chapter.

An Adverb – The Definition

This is the only accurate definition that is ever needed in language teaching and learning.

An Adverb is:
A When, Where, How, or Why.

Academic Adjectives and Adverbs

Adjectives are modifiers of nouns. **Adverbs** are modifiers of adjectives, adverbs, verbs, and entire sentences.

- The syntactic function of adjectives is to describe, refer to, and modify nouns and noun phrases.
- Adverbs refer to and modify verbs, adjectives, and whole sentences.
- Thus, because nouns predominate in academic prose, adjectives to describe them are also prevalent.

The example below contains a short paragraph from an introductory overview on farmers' markets and mobile produce marketing. This excerpt consists of 98 words and contains three definitions, all of which pivot on at least 15 attributive and predicative adjectives.

> At **_farmers markets_**, two or more **_farmer-producers_** sell their **_own_** **_agricultural_** products directly to the **_general_** public at a **_fixed_** location, and these include fruits and vegetables, meat, fish, poultry, dairy products, and grains. Farmers markets provide **_direct_** connections between **_urban_** centers and farms and have continued to rise in popularity, mostly due to the **_growing_** consumer interest in obtaining **_fresh_** products. The **_mobile_** **_agricultural_** **_market model_** enhances cost **_effective_** community access to **_fresh_** produce, as **_numerous_** communities have begun to experiment with **_neighborhood_** delivery of **_fresh_** food as a **_possible_** solution to their **_existing_** food access issues.
>
> (www.fns.usda.gov / ebt / definitions-farmers-markets-direct-marketing-farmers-and-other-related-terms)

From this short excerpt, it is easy to see that neither the definition of a **_farmers market_** or a **_farmer-producer_** can be constructed without the crucial role of adjectives.

On the other hand, <u>adverbs</u> are far less frequent. The next example is similarly extracted from an introductory overview of the direct marketing of farm products. The text below contains 102 words, one definition, and five adverbs, and four adverbial phrases (**_at their disposal_**, **_in their vehicles_**, **_by offering the products_**, and **_to make a complete meal_**).

> An additional consideration is that the residents of communities that mobile markets try to serve **_typically_** have limited time **_at their disposal_** to

purchase and prepare food. __Even__ *if they have access to transportation, they* __often__ *lack the time to purchase groceries from multiple outlets. To accommodate the needs of neighborhood residents, some of the* __more successful mobile__ *markets have put in refrigeration* __in their vehicles__ *to provide milk, eggs and meat. Others offer grains, cereal and basic household staples. These mobile markets hope to make the shopping experience* __more__ *convenient for neighborhood residents* __by offering the products to make a complete meal__.

(www.ams.usda.gov/publications/content/potential-demand-local-fresh-produce-mobile-markets)

The most important difference between the uses of adjectives and adverbs is that it may not be possible to define the terms a *__farmers market__, __farmer-producers__*, or a *__mobile market model__* without adjectives, while the brief description of *__mobile markets__* in the second excerpt is likely to remain clear even if most adverbs are dropped.

> Academic adjectives play an important role in classifications, cohesion, and evaluations.

For example, abstract nouns with broad meanings are highly frequent in academic prose, e.g. *concept, decision, recommendation*, or *development*, can be narrowed down by means of adjectives and be made more specific to fit in particular contexts (Bhatia, 1993; Swales, 1990; Swales & Feak, 2012):

- *new – innovative/difficult – complex/clear – transparent* + *concept*
- *positive/negative/radical/creative*   +   *decision/recommendation/development*

Adverbs play a similar focusing role for the meanings of semantically broad verbs or entire sentences. For example, the meanings of the verbs from the University Word List *dissipate, establish*, or *rely* can be delimited to make them very different in their contextual implications:

dissipate	**quickly/immediately**	– or –	**slowly/eventually**
expand	**broadly/widely**	– or –	**narrowly/slightly**
rely	**primarily/greatly**	– or –	**sporadically/occasionally**

Adjectives have two main grammar functions:

(1) Attributive/descriptive, e.g. *a* **tall** *order*, *an* **important discovery**.
(2) Predicative after **be** or linking verbs, e.g. *is* **tall**, **seems important**.

- Attributive – descriptive – adjectives precede nouns and noun phrases and modify them, e.g. **human and financial** *capital*.
- Predicative adjectives mostly occur as subject complements following linking verbs, e.g. *Computer chip markets are* **competitive/profitable**. A few frequent adjectives are always predicative: *afraid, asleep, aware, unable*.

Predicative adjectives actually belong to a different type of syntactic structures than attributive adjectives (the teaching of predicative adjective uses is discussed in some detail in chapter 4).

A Bit about the Syntax of Adverbs and Adjectives

Most adverbs, like descriptive adjectives, represent optional phrase or sentence elements (the only exceptions are those that function as subject or object complements).

- The primary function of adverbs is to modify (restrict or add to) adjectives, other adverbs, and entire sentences, e.g.:

  with adjectives   – *highly/somewhat desirable*
  with other adverbs – *very/particularly quickly*
  in entire sentences – *Occasionally/Usually, economists disagree about their conclusions.*

- In academic writing, adverbs are the least frequent among the main parts of speech, that is, less frequent than nouns, verbs, and adjectives.

Adverbs are usually classified by their meanings, such as time, place, reason, manner, and duration. However, regardless of their meanings, adverbs are sentence components that answer these questions:

When? Where? How? Why? How long? How often? To what extent?

Both adjectives and adverbs can have simple or more complex forms.

- Simple one-word adjectives and adverbs can also be combined to form compounds, e.g. *tall/short, quickly/slowly*, and *nice, fragrant, and delicious*.
- More complex, such as prepositional and other types of phrases, e.g. *the partridge **in the pear tree** and **In the pear tree**, we have a partridge*.

> **A Side Note on Terminology**: Complex modifiers of nouns are usually referred to as **adjectivals**, while **adverbials** modify everything that adverbs do. Both terms – the **adjectival** and the **adverbial** – refer to **functions**, rather than parts of speech.

Corpus analyses demonstrate that adjectivals of all types, as well as nouns, are particularly frequent in academic writing, while adverbials and verbs are common in conversation and fiction, that is, non-academic text (Hunston, 2011; Hunston & Thompson, 2000; Simpson-Vlach & Ellis, 2010).

Furthermore, extensive research in L2 academic writing provides clear evidence that a reasonable range of adjectives and adverbs is essential to construct academic text and express the meanings that the writer intends to express (Hinkel, 1997, 2003b, 2005; Hyland, 1998, 2004; Jordan, 1997). To put it simply, focused instruction is essential to help L2 academic writers to expand their vocabulary ranges of simple and complex adjectivals and adverbials that they can use in their writing.

The Essential Adjectives and Adverbs

Similar to the lists of nouns and verbs (see chapters 5 and 8), a number of adjectives and adverbs have been identified as foundational and recurrent in introductory texts across various disciplines (Coxhead, 2000; Nation, 1990, 2013). In fact, most of these lexical items are so common that it may be difficult to imagine doing without them in practically any context, including academic, e.g. *annual, appropriate, classic, constant, identical*, or *principal*.

In English, it may be a little tricky to tell an adjective from an adverb or an adjective from a noun or a verb without context,[1] e.g. *an abstract painting – the article abstract, a novel idea – a great novel*. This is one of the disadvantages of word lists. On the other hand, if L2 learners are aware that a particular word can have different syntactic functions and notice these words in context, learning new and recurrent vocabulary and grammar structures can be made productive and directly relevant.

Most English adverbs are derived from corresponding adjectives and are marked by the suffix -*ly*, with the exception of those that have identical adjective/adverb forms and masquerade as either adjectives (e.g. *fast, hard, high*) or adverbs (e.g. *costly, early, friendly*). Because adverbs require an addition of the suffix -*ly*, adjectives are considered to be lexically and morphologically simpler than adverbs because they are the base forms from which adverbs are derived, e.g. *accurate – accurately, annual – annually, approximate – approximately*.

The University Word List (Nation, 1990), in fact, includes just the adjective form for both adjectives and corresponding adverbs. In many analyses of large text corpora, word frequency counts rarely distinguish between adjective and adverb forms of the same lexical base (also called **word root**).

> Learning the 160 adjectives of the list works to expand one's vocabulary by approximately 250–260 words (not every adjective has a corresponding adverb). Based on research findings, for a majority of L2 learners, learning and practicing 10–15 new words per day represents a reasonable and attainable learning goal (Nation, 2013).

In fact, the entire list of the essential academic adjectives can actually be learned in slightly under two weeks.

The 160 Most Essential Academic Adjectives

abnormal	abstract	academic	accurate	adequate
adjacent	amorphous	angular	annual	anonymous
appropriate	approximate	automatic	averse	aware
capable	civic	classic	cogent	colloquial
concentric	consequent	constant	contingent	contrary
corporate	credible	crucial	crystal	cumbersome
deficient	definite	dense	distinct	diverse

divine	domestic	drastic	dynamic	efficient
elaborate	elicit	eloquent	empirical	equidistant
equivalent	evident	eventual	explicit	external
feasible	federal	fertile	final	finite
fluent	fundamental	genuine	homogeneous	hostile
huge	identical	imperial	implicit	incessant
incompatible	inconsistent	indigenous	ingenious	inherent
initial	innate	intelligent	intense	intermediate
internal	inverse	judicial	kindred	legal
legitimate	liable	linguistic	magnetic	major
material	maternal	mature	mental	military
minor	mobile	moist	negative	neutral
novel	nuclear	obvious	odd	partisan
passive	perpendicular	perpetual	pertinent	physical
positive	potential	pragmatic	precise	preliminary
previous	radical	random	rational	reluctant
respective	rigid	rudimentary	rural	scalar
secure	similar	simultaneous	solar	sophisticated
spatial	spontaneous	stable	stationary	subjective
subordinate	subsequent	subtle	superficial	superior
supreme	synthetic	tangible	temporary	tense
tentative	thermal	tiny	transparent	trivial
tropical	ultimate	unduly	urban	utter
vague	valid	vast	verbal	vertical
virtual	visual	vital		

(Adapted from Nation, 1990)

Contextual substitutions of adjectives represent one of the easiest techniques to produce diverse vocabulary constructions and text. In some cases, however, close synonym replacements may not be easy to find. For example, it would be difficult to come up with flexible and relatively context-independent substitutions for, e.g., **abstract, angular, civic, concentric, divine, synthetic,** or **vertical.** On the other hand, numerous other highly common adjectives can have a variety of approximate and contextually suitable descriptors, including words on the list, e.g. *amorphous – vague, definite – positive*, or *radical – drastic – dramatic*.

In teaching, a few sets of vocabulary substitution for frequent adjectives would not require much special preparation. It is easy to derive adverbs from most adjectives on the Essential Adjective list, as well as their substitutions. Here are several examples:

Adjectives and Adverbs	Examples of Vocabulary Substitutions
accurate	correct, precise, exact
accurately	correctly, precisely, exactly
adequate	satisfactory, sufficient, acceptable
adequately	satisfactorily, sufficiently, acceptably
adjacent	adjoining, next, nearby
adjacently	next, nearby
amorphous	vague, unclear
amorphously	vaguely, unclearly
annual	yearly, per year, per annum
annually	yearly, per year, per annum
appropriate	suitable, fitting, relevant
appropriately	suitable, fitting, relevant

The most common adjectives used in academic corpora of English number fewer than 25 (Biber, et al., 1999). These can be used both in attributive and predicative functions.

The Most Frequent Academic Adjectives

able	available	better	clear	common
different	difficult	great	high	important
impossible	large	likely	long	low
necessary	new	possible	small	sure

In academic writing adverbs are not nearly as common as adjectives, and even the most common are encountered at the rate of less than 1% (Biber, et al., 1999). A handful make up the vast majority of adverbs and have the function of intensifiers, hedges (softeners), delimiters, or additives (Hoye, 1997).

The Functions of Highly Frequent Academic Adverbs

Text Functions	Adverbs
Intensifiers	*even, very, quite, more, well*
Hedges	*sometimes, often, usually, relatively, probably, perhaps, generally*
Delimiters	*only, especially, particularly*
Additive (one)	*also*

Most single-word adverbs or adverbial phrases in academic text occur in the middles of sentences, rather than at the beginning or the end, e.g.

— *Measuring the temperature* **by hand** *and* **at uneven intervals** *proved to be*

. . .

— *It is* **often** *noted that air-born particles do not* **usually** *move in predictable patterns.*

Telling Adjectives and Adverbs Apart

Although most adverbs are marked by the suffix *-ly*, many are not. **Adverbs without markers** are prevalent in academic prose.[2]

Frequent <u>Adverbs</u> without *-ly*

almost	already	here	next	now	often
quite	rather	seldom	sometimes	then	there
today	tomorrow	yesterday	yet		

On the other hand, some **adjectives have the *-ly* suffix.**

Frequent <u>Adjectives</u> with *-ly*

costly	early	elderly	friendly	likely/unlikely	lively
lovely	sickly	silly	ugly	yearly	

Some words can have the **functions of both adjectives and adverb** without changes in their form:

Adjectives and Adverbs with the Same Forms

deep	early	fast	hard	hardly	high	late	long	low	near

> To determine whether a particular word or phrase is an adjective or an adverb, answer the questions:
>
> **When, Where, How**, and **Why** (as well as **How Often/Long**)

Here's an example:

Every business must operate (**how?** –) *profitably to stay around* (**when/ how long?** –) *for a while*.

Non-Adverbables and Non-Comparables

Adjectives can be divided into various semantic classes, such as **stative** and **dynamic**, and **gradable** and **non-gradable**. These classifications are important only because these adjectives and adverbs are grammatically quirky and, for this reason, highly error-prone (Hinkel, 2002, 2003a, 2003b, 2005).

Stative and **dynamic adjectives** are highly common in academic text. They usually denote shapes, measurements, colors, or nationalities.

- **Stative adjectives** refer to qualities that <u>cannot be changed by the person or object that possesses these characteristics</u>, e.g. people or buildings cannot make themselves more or less *tall* or *short* or *old, young, red, yellow, German,* or *Korean*.
- **Dynamic adjectives** refer to those qualities that <u>people or objects can control or change about themselves</u>, e.g. one can choose to be *careful, quick, quiet, reasonable,* or *thorough*.

Stative adjectives do **not have corresponding** manner adverbs with similar meanings. Adverb forms of these adjectives that do exist have completely different meanings.

Different Meanings of Adjective and Adverb Forms

Adjectives	Adverb Forms and Their Meanings	
short	shortly	[soon]
hard	hardly	[almost not]
broad	broadly/largely	[generally]
wide	widely	[in many places/among many people]
late	lately	[recently]

> The most frequent academic stative adjectives are: **long, small, high, low**, and **large**. These do not have corresponding adverb forms.

To test if an adverb form of an adjective exists, it can be used in an imperative sentence, e.g. **Be tall/short/old/young/round/long.*

On the other hand, dynamic adjectives can be converted to adverbs by adding the suffix -*ly*, e.g. *anonymous – anonymously, arbitrary – arbitrarily, fair – fairly, feasible – feasibly, legal – legally, neutral – neutrally, objective – objectively, rational – rationally.*

Two additional classes of quirky adjectives include **gradable** and **non-gradable**.

Gradable adjectives can be used for comparisons, and non-gradable adjectives cannot.

<u>Gradable</u>	*more/most*	*complex/drastic/fluent/flexible/intense*
<u>Non-gradable</u>	**more/*most*	*potential/total/uncountable/main/wrong*

- **Non-gradable** adjectives refer to **everything-or-nothing** qualities of nouns (either you are total or you are not).
- Non-gradable adjectives **cannot be used with <u>very</u> or have sentence predicate functions** with linking verbs.

The new project is **more potential/main and **very right/principal**.*
This year's profits are **more excellent, but then they are **more domestic**.*

Comparatives and Superlatives

Comparative and superlative adjectives are used for comparing nouns, e.g. *big difference – bigger difference*. In academic writing, comparatives and superlatives occur only in three constructions (Biber, et al., 1999; Hunston, 2011; Hyland & Milton, 1997).

(1) Comparative/superlative degree forms with the markers *-er/est*.
(2) Phrasal comparatives with *more/most*, e.g. *more/most complex*.
(3) Rarely, structures with comparative clauses *than* and *as . . . as*, e.g.

   – *The report is longer than I expected* [it to be].
   – *The prices for commodities are (not) as high as analysts predicted* [them to be].

> Comparative constructions are more common in academic writing than in fiction or news. Comparative adjectives with **-er** are the most frequent.

For **monosyllabic and two-syllable adjectives** with *-y, -ly*, or *-le* endings, comparatives and superlatives are marked by *-er* and *-est*, and discussed in practically every grammar textbook, e.g. *hot – hotter – hottest, pretty – prettier – prettiest*. Other comparative adjectives adhere to a phrasal pattern with *more/most* + adjective, e.g. *more accurate, most prominent*.

> **More** and **most** phrases with both adjectives and adverbs are also found more frequently in academic text than in any other.

• All adverbs with the *-ly* suffix take *more/most* forms of comparative and superlative degrees.
• Adverbs with *more* and *most* are far more numerous than those that take *-er/-est* comparatives simply because more adverbs end in *-ly* than those that do not.
• The adjectives and adverbs with identical form follow the adjective comparative pattern, e.g. *early – earlier – earliest, friendly – friendlier – friendliest, fast – faster – fastest, late – later – latest, low – lower – lowest*.

What Not to Teach

Spending a lot of class time on the following is not the best use of limited resources:

- Highly infrequent constructions with **comparative clauses,** such as *-er than* and *as . . . as* – even though they are addressed in most grammar textbooks. In corpus research, both these types of clauses are identified at the rate of approximately 0.03% per one million words of academic text (Biber, et al., 1999).
- **Superlative adjectives and adverbs,** e.g. *best, most, heaviest.* The frequency rate of superlatives is only 800 per one million words (0.08%). This finding can be contrasted with a much greater frequency of superlatives in news reportage or conversation

> Superlative adjectives and adverbs are extremely rare in formal prose, e.g. ***most impressive(-ly)**, **most clean(-ly)**, **most clear(-ly)***.

Occasionally and in specific contexts, simple adverbs without *-ly* can be used in superlative degree, but largely not in academic essays, e.g. ***at your earliest convenience, at the earliest/soonest, most nicely***, or ***most pleasantly***.

What to Teach

In academic prose, comparative and superlative adjectives and adverbs occur in only a few – but very frequent – constructions (Biber, et al., 1999; Swales & Feak, 2012; Simpson-Vlach & Ellis, 2010).

The Most Frequent Comparatives and Superlatives (in declining order)

One-word Comparatives and Superlatives	One-word Comparatives Only	**More** and **Most** Phrases
better – best	earlier	most important
greater – greatest	easier	more difficult
higher – highest	lower	more important
larger – largest	older	more likely
	smaller	most likely
	wider	

The Second Most Frequent **More** and **Most** Phrases

most common	more complex	more complicated
more convenient	more detailed	most effective
more frequent	more general	more powerful
more recent	most significant	more sophisticated
most suitable	more useful	most useful

Only a handful of attributive adjectives persistently recur in academic writing, and these can be learned and used interchangeably in L2 writing.

Adjectival and Adverbial Prepositional Phrases

> In academic writing, prepositional phrases are highly, highly frequent – more so than in any other type of writing.

Their functions can be either **adjectival** and **adverbial**, depending on the word or phrase they modify.

- An **adjective** function when it modifies a **noun**, e.g.

    a dinner **_at a restaurant_**, a book **_on English grammar_**, peas **_in a pod_**

- An **adverb** function when it describes a **verb** or an entire **sentence**, e.g.

    *Important clients eat **_at a restaurant_**.*
    At a restaurant, *we can observe an important separation of goods and services.*

English prepositional phrases are famously – notoriously, extremely – difficult to teach, learn, and use correctly. Even for highly advanced and proficient L2 writers prepositions represent an ongoing problem. There are many reasons that make prepositions onerous to use correctly, but at least a couple may be worth mentioning (Hinkel, 2017, 2019).

> - Almost all uses of prepositions are idiomatic and lexicalized, and they do not follow grammar and vocabulary rules.
> - Many (most?) uses and functions of prepositions are un-derivable, illogical, and opaque, that is, their meanings cannot be guessed from context.

At the very least, L2 writers need to recognize prepositional phrases when they occur in the texts they read and their own writing.

Academic writing is particularly packed with prepositional phrases because they allow a writer to structure a great deal of information compactly. In fact, several adverbial phrases can occur in one sentence, and often do. It is this particularly high density of prepositional phrases in academic writing that makes them essential in teaching and learning.

(1) A number studies have demonstrated that L2 writers use adjective and adverb prepositional phrases significantly differently than L1 writers do (Hinkel, 2002, 2003b, 2005; Hyland, 1998, 1999; Hyland & Milton, 1997).

(2) Prepositional phrases serve key modifying functions of nouns and verbs and play a crucial role in constructing specific and clear sentences (Jordan, 1997; Swales, 1990).

(3) Prepositional phrases located in various sentence slots can change the meaning of the sentence or a phrase. For example, in many sentences, prepositional phrases occupy the obtrusive position between the subject and the verb and make it difficult to identify the main subject noun and construct grammatical sentences.

There are only a few prepositions that are frequent in academic writing.

> The six most common prepositional phrases with any type of function account for 90% of all uses:
>
> **of   in   for   on   to   with**

The second most frequent set of prepositions consists of only two: *at* and *by*.

Prepositional phrases with adjective functions predominate in academic and collocational phrases with *of*:

- Quantifiers, e.g. *one/two/of the . . ., a set/number of . . .*
- Possessives, e.g. *the door of the house, the light of the . . .*
- Noun classes, e.g. *type/kind/class of books.*
- Containers, e.g. *a box of chocolates, a can of soda.*
- Measures, e.g. *a gallon/liter of gasoline, two ounces of fluid.*
- Direction or position, e.g. *the back of the foundation of the building.*
- Time, e.g. *the beginning of the experiment.*

Like adjectives, prepositional phrases with *of* have an important function of **delimiting** broad **meanings** of nouns, e.g.

- *the style of communication*
- *the mode of rhetoric*
- *the function of nouns*
- *the role of verbs*
- *the psychology of dreams*

Recurrent phrases with *in* also proliferate but to a smaller extent than those with *of*. The phrases with *in* often follow a large number of nouns that deal with physical location and logical relations between two nouns/noun phrases. *In*-phrases are extremely common in academic text.

Frequent Academic Phrases with the Preposition *in*

Noun		Noun
increase	*in*	profit
decrease		sales
gain		crime
growth		the number of incidents
involvement	*in*	politics
participation		markets
part		research
role		the study/investigation of . . .
lead		

factor issue component element	*in*	*the (this) decision/development/* *plan/choice*
difference *similarity* *variation* *contrast*	*in*	*the meaning* *the (their) performance* *the level of . . .*
difficulty *success* *progress* *delay*	*in*	*the analysis* *determining . . .* *identifying . . .*

> Prepositional phrases play the role of adverbs in practically all academic writing. They represent the most frequent form of adverb modification, followed by single-word adverbs.

- **Adverbs of manner** predominate and describe **how** an action occurred or something was done, e.g. **with care, by air/water, piece-by-piece.**
- The second most common type consists of **agentive/instrumental adverbials**, e.g. **by users/software developers, with/for this purpose.**
- Adverb phrases of **time, place, and condition** are **infrequent** in formal academic writing, e.g. **in January, at the lab/in this city**, and **if the company sells . . .**

Research has demonstrated that in L2 academic prose, adverbials are often overused and can be repetitious (Hinkel, 2002; Hyland & Milton, 1997). Here's an example from a student's assignment on knowledge explosion and technology.

> <u>*Nowadays*</u>, *knowledge explosion is a term we often hear of. Knowledge explosion in technology* <u>**today**</u> *means massive accumulation of data.* <u>**A hundred**</u> <u>**years ago**</u>, *there is even no computer, but* <u>**these days**</u> *there is computer science and technology. Computers are* <u>**now**</u> *used* <u>**everywhere,**</u> <u>**in laboratories,**</u> <u>**on**</u> <u>**assembly lines,**</u> *and* <u>**in offices.**</u> *Computers are used to control production*

*on assembly lines and **at the factory**. **If we need computers**, we need to know how they work. **Nowadays in offices**, most paperwork can be done on computers. **If computers do not function well**, our society cannot work well either.*

This short excerpt from a student's text contains seven adverbials of place, six adverbials of time, and two conditional clauses, not to mention two manner adverbs, an intensifier, and a frequency adverb. Clearly, the redundant adverbials of time and place need to be omitted and, possibly, replaced with other information.

Another large and important class of adverbials consists of various hedging devices that express hesitation (***possibly***, ***perhaps***), an element of doubt and uncertainty (***probably***, ***quite likely***), attribution of knowledge and information (***according to the article***), and limitation (***in this case***, ***in my view***). These are discussed in chapter 12.

Trouble Spot

Misplaced descriptive adjective prepositional phrases.

Example trouble-spot sentences:

In the experiment, the first speaker is shown in a professional suit **with long hair.*
****With reading materials**, class assignments require looking up many words in the dictionary.*

> Descriptive adjective prepositional phrases must immediately follow the noun or pronoun that they describe.

Teaching Tip

First, the prepositional phrase has to be identified and then moved directly to follow the noun that it describes or refers to.

(a) *In the experiment, the first speaker **with long hair** is shown in a professional suit.*

(b) *Class assignments **with reading materials** require looking up many words in the dictionary.*

In teaching, a few sentences with the prepositional phrases located in different slots in the sentence can be demonstrated for contrast. In most cases, the differences in the meaning of the contrasting sentences are easy to notice and figure out. Here's an example.

— *__With the professor__, students discussed their problems.*
— *Students discussed their problems **with the professor**.*
— *__*With the book__, students discussed their problems.*
— *Students discussed their problems **with the book**.*

Noun Phrases of Time, Manner, and Frequency

> Time phrases with **this, that, these,** and **those**, as well as **every, last, next, all,** can be particularly difficult to learn and use correctly, e.g. *in this/that/last week or *in every next month/year.

This type of error occurs when these time phrases are formed in a similar way to other time adverbials, such as *in March/2025*.

The main point about these constructions is that *this, that, these, those, every, last, next,* and *all* + **time phrase** do not take the prepositions *in* or *on* (**on this Monday*, **in next week*), even though it is possible to say *on this __day__* or *__during__ this/that/the last month/year*.

> As a general rule, nouns function as adverbs in contexts when they can answer the questions – **When? How often? How long?**

With all prepositional phrases, it is important recognize and learn to use them in varied constructions. To construct coherent and grammatical sentences, L2 writers have to separate – optional – prepositional phrases from the required key sentence elements, such as subjects, verbs, and objects/complements. In academic text, the placement of the prepositional phrase in a particular sentence slot can change the meaning of the sentence (more on this later in the chapter).

Trouble Spot

The placement of adverb prepositional phrases changes the sentence meaning or leads to confusing meanings.

Examples of trouble-spot sentences:

- ?*In Chinese and Japanese, professors have tried so hard to explore where Japanese originated from and whether it originated from Chinese.*
- ?*Engineers usually try different models to improve quality, productivity, and less wasted product, during the drying process.*

After the prepositional phrase has been located, it is important to figure out what exactly it refers to, that is, a specific noun or phrase, or the entire sentence. If the prepositional phrase refers to the entire sentence, then it has an adverb function, and the easiest place to put it is at the very beginning.

Similar to the contrasting sentences with adjective phrases (above), a number of various phrase placements can be considered and discussed. The different meanings can become clear when the prepositional phrase is moved around in sentence locations.

- *The experiment was conducted, and the book was published later at the end of the year.*
- *At the end of the year, the experiment was conducted and the book was published later.*
- *At the end of the year, the experiment was conducted and later the book was published.*
- *The experiment was conducted at the end of the year, and the book was published later.*

Participles and Infinitives as Adjectives and Adverbs

Present and past participles (*confusing, increasing, written, blown*) and infinitives (*to summarize, to mention*) represent other frequent types of adjectival and adverbial modifiers. For example, in the phrase *developing countries,* the present participle modifies the noun *countries* and therefore has an adjective function, as does the past participle in <u>*industrialized*</u> *nations* or the infinitive in *a method <u>to check</u> the water level.*

On the other hand, such constructions as *a solution emerged to simplify . . .,* *to calculate the temperature, we . . ., compared to the average increase,* or *by drawing a straight line* all have adverb functions because they modify verbs or entire sentences.

Participial Adjectives and Adverbs

Participial adjective phrases are very common in academic writing, far more so than the adjective clauses from which they are derived (Hunston & Thompson, 2000; Swales & Feak, 2012), e.g. *the thermostat controlling the temperature . . .* or *the temperature held constant at 50°F.*

The terms *present and past participle* actually have little to do with the present or past.

- Present participles with -*ing* (e.g. *amazing, boring, leading*) actually mark **active** adjectives. That is, **the noun that they describe performs the action expressed by the participle.** In fact, typically, these constructions are shortened (reduced) adjective clauses.

  - *nations [that are] developing → developing nations*
  - *the research [that is] amazing → the amazing research*

- Past participles with -*ed* or -*en* (e.g. *reported, lost, hidden*) mark <u>**passive**</u> **adjectives.** That is, **the noun that they modify does not perform the action but some other entity does.**

  - *the data [that are] reported → the reported data*
  - *the continent [that is] lost → the lost continent*

The distinction between -*ing* and -*ed* forms of participial adjectives is often difficult for students. Errors with these constructions are extremely common.

  - **I am boring with this book.*
  - **I am confusing about the homework.*

Emphasizing active or passive (doing and receptive) functions of these adjectives is very productive and can clarify a great deal of misunderstanding about the usage of these adjectives. Here's an example of how to work with the structures: *I am boring* or *I am confusing*.

> – *Are you __performing/doing__ the action?*
> – *Are you __boring/confusing__ (to) __someone__?*
> – *Or is something else performing the action? In this case, are you __boring__ or __bored__? __Confusing__ or __confused__?*
> – *Looking at the pairs __boring teacher__ – __bored students__ and __boring students__ – __bored teacher__, can you tell me how this boring/bored structure works?*

Most active or passive participial adjectives in English are idiomatic and lexicalized, that is, they do not follow particular syntactic rules and can be impossible to derive.

The constructions that are used frequently simply have to be learned as fixed phrases and expressions, e.g. **a winding road, a long-winded speaker, an interesting book, I am interested in chemistry.**

- One-word adjectives of any type precede the noun they describe, as in *reported data* or *forgotten legends*.
- Adjective phrases are placed after the noun and do not move from their original position.

> the objects *[that are]*   *moving slowly* approach one another   →
> the objects   *moving slowly* approach one another
>
> the couples *[that are]*   *described in the journal article*   →
> the couples   *described in the journal article*

- Present or past participles can also perform the function of **active or passive adverbials** (also called reduced adverb clauses).

> *Revolving around the earth*, the moon is revered in many religions or
> *Revered in many religions*, the moon revolves around the earth.

- Participial adverbial phrases are **__singularly rare__** in student academic writing and are not worth expending time and effort on teaching them.

The Most Common Active and Passive Participles in Academic
Writing (in any function)

Active Participles		Passive Participles		
being	concerning	based	caused	obtained
containing	involving	given	concerned	produced
using	having	used	made	taken

Talking Shop

There are three types of *-ing* constructions in English:

(1) The progressive verb aspect, e.g. *I/he am/is singing*.
(2) The gerund, that is, in fact, a noun derived from a verb, e.g.
     Singing is enjoyable/Peter enjoys *singing*.
(3) The present participle that can perform the function of an **adjective**,
     e.g. *a singing bird*, or an **adverb**, e.g.
     While singing, the bird . . .

To tell the difference between the progressive verb aspect, the ger-
und, and the present participle, the **sentence function** of an *-ing* word
needs to be determined.

- An *-ing* word in the **verb phrase** is likely to be a progressive verb, e.g.
  The cake is baking.
- An *-ing* word in a **subject or object sentence** position is a gerund, e.g.
  The key to learning is reading and writing.
- An *-ing* word that describes a **noun** or is a subject/object **comple-
  ment** is likely to be an adjective, e.g.
  an amazing story or *the story is amazing* (to me).

In many cases, however, it is impossible to tell the difference between
the functions of various *-ing* words, e.g. *I am confusing* vs. *I am confusing you right now*.

Also, for example, in the phrase ***reading books***, the function of the
word ***reading*** can be identified only when it is placed into a sentence, e.g.

Reading books _are_ expensive (adjective) vs. **_Reading_ books _is_ important** (gerund).

Being aware of the various sentence roles of **-ing** words can help identify at least a couple of their important functions, such as gerunds or active/passive adjectives.

Infinitives as Adjectives and Adverbs

Infinitives have a large number of functions, e.g. as nouns when they are subjects and objects, or as adjectives and adverbs (Hunston & Thompson, 2000; Quirk, et al., 1985; Swales & Feak, 2012). Some researchers identify as many as 10, and others up to 20 functions (Biber, et al., 1999; Huddleston & Pullum, 2002). In this section, only the adjective and adverb functions of infinitives are discussed.

- The most common function of infinitives, noted in practically every grammar book, is that of a noun-like (nominal) in the subject and/or object position, e.g.

  - _To see_ is _to believe_.
  - _To err_ is _human_.

- Another ubiquitous type of infinitive is that with **verb + noun/gerund/infinitive** constructions, e.g.

  - _Young consumers prefer **denim/wearing** sports shoes/**to wear** sports shoes._

In academic writing, only two types of infinitives occur in **adjective** functions (Hunston & Thompson, 2000; Simpson-Vlach & Ellis, 2010):

a/the **way** to + verb _a/the **time** to_ + verb

Infinitives with adverb functions adhere to several idiomatic and lexicalized patterns that simply need to be learned.

INFINITIVES WITH ADVERB FUNCTIONS

(1) Infinitives of purpose with omitted *[in order]* + *to* constructions, e.g.

> *The experiment was conducted [in order] to . . .*
> This type of construction can be relatively easy to teach. If the phrase *[in order to]* can be inserted after the verb, then an infinitive can be used. If not, then a gerund may be an alternative.
> For example, which structure is correct: **Students went to the library** *for studying* or *to study*? In this sentence, the insertion works: **Students went to the library** *[in order] to study*. Therefore, the infinitive is correct.

(2) Infinitives after linking verbs, *be, seem, appear, tend*, e.g.

> *The water level seems* **to increase/be constant/be held at** *. . .*

> This is the most frequent type of construction in academic writing.

(3) Infinitives following frequent academic verbs:[3] *try, attempt, fail, allow, continue, enable, require*, e.g.

> *The market continues* **to drop/rise**.

(4) Infinitives after frequent academic adjectives: *possible/impossible, easy, difficult*, and *hard*.

> o   <u>Necessity adjectives</u>: *important, essential, necessary, vital*, e.g.
>
> > *Heat is* **essential** *to boil the water.*
> > *It is* **necessary** *to calculate . . .*
>
> o   <u>Evaluation adjectives</u>: *better/best, appropriate/inappropriate, desirable, interesting, logical, reasonable/unreasonable, surprising, useful/useless, wise, wrong*, e.g.
>
> > *The power of nonverbal communication can be* **useful** *to notice in routine interactions.*
> > *By the age of twelve, most children know when it is* **appropriate** *or* **inappropriate** *to establish eye contact with another person.*

On the whole, infinitives with adverbial functions are much more common in written than in conversational discourse. They are so prevalent in practically any type of writing that it may not possible to produce a written assignment without them.

Action Point

There is a clear and inflexible order of organizing adjectives and adverbs in English sentences. However, the ordering of adjectives, adverbs, and phrases is often skipped in language textbooks. The sequence is rigid and does not permit any rearrangements, but all descriptive adjectives and adverbs are optional.

> Evaluation/Opinion – Size – Age – Shape – Color – Origin – Material – Purpose + **Noun**

For example:

> a **shiny, large, new, brown American sports** car
> a **brilliant, extensive, widely available marketing** study
> **– but not –**
> *a **Japanese red** car or *a **grammar interesting** book

Adverb phrases also follow this rigid order.

> **(1)** **In 2023** + **(2)** **at The Big University** + **(3)** **in their research** +
> the scientists conducted the experiment.

In many languages other than English, the order of organizing modifiers differs substantially and in addition can be far more flexible. For L2 writers, an explicit and clear-cut explanation of the adjective and adverb order usually proves very useful in the long run.

The-Rich-and-the-Poor Constructions

> The conversion of adjectives to noun phrases is actually quite rare and occurs only in limited contexts, such as highly general texts in the humanities.

In fact, some analyses call these constructions generic (Huddleston & Pullum, 2002): *the young, the elderly, the impossible*. Because on the whole these constructions are rare in academic texts, only a couple of their characteristics need to be mentioned.

(1) *The-rich-and-the-poor* phrases that refer to **groups of people never take singular verbs**, e.g. **the rich gets richer*. These structures, in fact, refer to concrete nouns, that is, <u>those people</u> who are rich or <u>those people who are poor</u>.

(2) *The-impossible* phrases, such as *the unlikely* or *the ridiculous*, can take **singular verbs** because they have abstract meanings, that is, <u>what is impossible</u> or <u>that which is ridiculous</u>.

> **These structures are exceptionally rare in academic writing**, e.g. *the impossible/the unthinkable has happened*. These structures may not be worth the time and effort expended on teaching them.

(3) Adjective-to-noun phrases are very inflexible and can only add the intensifier *very*, e.g. *the <u>very</u> old* and *the <u>very</u> young*. In fact, they cannot even take demonstratives or possessives, e.g. **these rich, *those very poor, *our old*.

Key Adjectives in Thesis Statements

As was noted at the beginning of the chapter, adjectives play a defining role in academic prose.

> While frequent descriptive adjectives are found practically anywhere in academic text, noun modifiers play a key role in thesis statements and statements of purpose.

- Adjectives (and adjective phrases) can be used specifically for marking/ signaling thesis statements – typically considered to be obligatory in academic papers and essays (Swales, 1990; Swales & Feak, 2012).
- Thesis statements are crucially important to provide coherence in academic prose. Their function is to highlight and summarize the central idea of the paper, usually in a single and clear sentence.

In many cases, thesis statements in L2 academic papers appear to be very broad and general, and one of the persistent areas that teachers need to work with students on is how to narrow the thesis down and make sure it has a clear focus.

> Adjectives are a very practical and useful tool for delimiting the power of nouns and narrowing down a broad thesis statement.

Research into academic writing has shown that topics and thesis statements can be narrowed down in two ways:

(1) By explicitly stating the strategic plan for the essay, e.g.

  two main arguments, **different** theories, three **central points**

(2) By restricting the breadth of abstract nouns ubiquitous in academic writing, e.g.

  the main character's story of **natural and personal** disaster

Corpus analyses of academic prose have shown that the most common adjectives used to outline essay structure and thesis statements number slightly over a dozen (Biber, et al., 1999).

The Most Frequent Adjectives to Narrow Thesis Statements

The top two:	same, different
The second five:	whole, general, major, main, single
Other possibilities:	basic, common, following, individual, particular, similar, specific, various

Here are a few examples of topic delimiters that can be used in various contexts.

(1) *The **main** point of this paper is to discuss **two/three major/different** influences on/factors in . . .*

(2) *This paper evaluates the **general/basic principles** of Keynesian economics/economic injustice . . .*

(3) *In this essay, I will argue that the **single** most important **factor** in the success of recycling/the increase of sports gambling is . . .*

Topic and thesis delimiters are usually derived from nouns e.g. *finance – financial* or *politics – political*. These are also ubiquitously used in introductory and opening paragraphs, when writers need to orient the reader to the main points made in the essay (Swales, 1990).

The Most Frequent Adjective Topic Classifiers

economic	human	international	local	national
political	public	social	informative	

These adjectives have the function of narrowing down the scope of the main topic **noun**. Here are a few examples.

(1) *My essay discusses and outlines the **political beliefs** held by Americans prior to/before the fall of the xxx regime/Soviet Union.*
(2) *This essay describes and explores **social impact** of social media on **public attitudes and behaviors.***
(3) *This paper explains the **human** and **economic outcomes of/factors in/ considerations of** teen marriage.*

Writing from Sources and Evaluations

Most academic papers and assignments of any length are expected to be based on information obtained from published sources, such as books, articles, reports, or news. Thus, following the thesis statement, the discourse moves to supporting information that takes the form of summaries, paraphrasing, or citations from sources (Swales, 1990; Swales & Feak, 2012).

> Analyses of written academic corpora in English have shown that evaluative adjectives belong to the largest class of adjectives, followed by descriptors of size.

Usually in academic papers or assignments, in addition to simply making summaries and paraphrasing information, writers are expected to evaluate their sources and the opinions expressed in them critically. According to Swales and Feak (2012), for instance, in literature overviews and summaries, evaluative adjectives represent an integral part of the writer's description of a work or source.

> Particularly in student assignments in social sciences and humanities courses, after summarizing the information, writers are expected to signal their own views on the topic, issue, or the author's tone.

Evaluations of the material obtained from sources require uses of evaluative adjectives and adverbs. Familiarity with these modifiers can allow L2 writers to recognize them in text when they are reading and then use them in their own writing.

In academic prose, evaluations of information and the author's tone can be positive or negative, depending on whether the main thrust of the **paper supports or rejects the ideas expressed in a particular source.** For this reason, **evaluative adjectives/adverbs can be positive or negative**.

(1) *In the history of the United States, the struggle for women's rights plays a very **important/special** role.* [**positive**]

(2) *The author **accurately** presents a clear picture of today's life in Japan.* [**positive**]

(3) *The currently popular account of causes of youth violence appears to be based on **incomplete** facts.* [**negative**]

(4) *The articles blame the threat of overpopulation on **controversial/misguided/questionable** data.* [**negative**]

A number of both positive and negative evaluative adjectives and adverbs have been identified as more common in academic prose than in any other type of genre (Biber, et al., 1999; Hunston, 2011; Swales & Feak, 2012).

The Most Frequent Positive Adjectives and Adverbs

accurate(-ly)	careful(-ly)	clear(-ly)	competent(-ly)
good/well	important(-ly)	impressive(-ly)	innovative(-ly)
interesting(-ly)	right(-ly)	significant(-ly)	special(-ly)
thorough(-ly)	useful(-ly)		

The Most Frequent Negative Adjectives and Adverbs

controversial(-ly)	inaccurate(-ly)	incomplete(-ly)	inconclusive(-ly)
limited(-ly)	minor	misguided(-ly)	questionable(-ly)
restricted	unconvincing(-ly)	unsatisfactory(-ly)	

Chapter Summary

The syntactic function of adjectives is to modify nouns and noun phrases, and similarly adverbs modify verbs, adjectives, or entire sentences. However, these descriptions do not convey the complexities L2 writers encounter with actual uses of adjectives and adverbs in context.

- The most frequent academic adjectives and adverbs need to be learned together with their closest alternatives.
- For adverbs, a simple rule of thumb is to test if a particular word or phrase answers the questions: **When, Where, How,** or **Why.**
- The comparative and superlative degree adjectives and adverbs that occur in academic writing are actually limited to only a few frequent items, and these are easy to learn.
- Prepositional phrases with adjective or adverb functions are particularly prevalent in academic text.
- Instruction and practice should explicitly address placement and use of prepositional phrases.
- Active and passive adjectives (e.g. _**bored/boring**_) are confusing and often misused. Many of these constructions are idiomatic and lexicalized, and they cannot be derived based on grammar and vocabulary rules, but asking the questions of who is doing the action can be very helpful, e.g. **The boring/bored teacher** – who is boring and who is bored?
- Evaluative adjectives are useful for narrowing the focus of thesis statements and writing from sources.

Strategies and Tactics for Teaching and Teaching Activities

Teaching Activities

The learning goals of the teaching suggestions and activities are to focus on adjectives and adverbs and to promote academic learning and retention. These exercises can be used for learning any type of academic vocabulary and are not necessarily confined to adjectives and adverbs.

A variety of adjectives and adverbs can be found in academic textbooks, materials, or test preparation exercises. The activities presented below can be made graded, that is, adjusted for difficulty and complexity levels, beginning with easier ones and progressing to the more complex.

All these can be assigned as homework, or for pair and group work, with follow-up discussions. Occasionally, these can be collected and graded to evaluate students' progress.

When working with sets of adjectives and adverbs for academic writing (e.g. *new – innovative – novel, careful – thorough*), the number of phrases, sentences, or contexts in each set should range between 5 and 10.

The activities and learning practice has to provide ample opportunities for vocabulary review. And more review.

Expanding the Vocabulary Range for Adjectives and Adverbs

(1) The first step is to locate new adjectives and adverbs in sentences and remember their meanings in the sentences/contexts.

(2) Then the same sentences are recycled with some vocabulary omitted, when learners need to recall the new words and complete the sentences as close to the originals as possible.

(3) If this short practice can be repeated two or three times per week, the new vocabulary will continue to grow over time.

(4) To provide students opportunities for vocabulary review, sentences can include a growing number of combinations, for example, with new items, as well as the vocabulary learned earlier.

An <u>alternative</u>: For additional flexibility or challenge, learners may be able to complete the sentence with vocabulary substitutes or list the new lexical item **and** additional substitute items. When the work is completed, students can discuss new words and the substitutes in small groups or the whole class.

INSTRUCTIONS FOR STUDENTS

Part 1. Read the sentences/texts, identify the new words, and do your best to remember them. Some vocabulary items are repeated in different sentences.

(1) *When faced with the need to identify an __odor__ (smell), people are __surprisingly imprecise__ and __inconsistent__.*

(2) *The experiment that resulted in a __rather low__ identification of 20 recognizable smells required participants to note as many __unfamiliar__ odors as they could.*

(3) *Even with corrections from the experimenters, the probability that the same __vaguely familiar__ smell would be recognized remained __low__.*

(4) *__Perhaps__ the most __dramatic__ change in the US economy over the past six decades has been the __increasing__ importance of international trade and finance.*

(5) *__Technological__ progress has also led to growth in trade in __raw__ materials, such as steel and wood products, and __perishable__ goods, such as food, by making transporting goods less __costly.__*

(6) *Goods produced by __modern__ technology are often __light__ and easy to transport because they have __low__ weight and __relatively compact__ size.*

(7) *__Clearly__, international trade policies of a __particular__ country also affect __financial__ and __political__ decisions made by its government and often lead to important changes in the market place.*

Part 2. Students receive sheets of paper with approximately half of the original sentences. However, the sentences on the sheets can include various combinations, e.g. Sentences 1, 3, 5, and 7, **or** 2, 4, and 6.

Some of the lexical items in each sentence are omitted, and students have to complete the sentences with the original lexical items or their substitutes. When students complete the work on their first sheet, with, for example, Sentences 1, 3, 5 and 7 they receive the second sheet with the other set of sentences, e.g. 2, 4, and 6.

For pair or group work, when all sheets are completed, both sheets can be handed back to their "authors", and students can discuss their results. Pairs or groups of students can be additionally asked to come up with as many substitutes as they can for each filled-in word.

Version 1. Sentences 1, 3, 5, and 7

(1) *When faced with the need to identify an odor (smell), people are _____ imprecise and _____.*

(3) *Even with corrections from the experimenters, the probability that the same _____ familiar smell would be recognized remained low.*

(5) *_____ progress has also led to growth in trade in _____ materials, such as steel and wood products, and _____ goods, such as food, by making transporting goods less costly.*

(7) *Clearly, international trade policies of a _____ country also affect _____ and _____ decisions made by its government and often lead to important changes in the market place.*

Version 2. Sentences 2, 4, and 6

(2) *The experiment that resulted in a _____ low identification of 20 recognizable smells required participants to note as many _____ odors as they could.*

(4) *_____ the most _____ change in the US economy over the past six decades has been the increasing importance of international trade and finance.*

(6) *Goods produced by modern technology are often _____ and easy to transport because they have low weight and _____ compact size.*

What is your function?

(1) Modifiers are slippery characters because they occupy various slots in the sentence structure and, depending on their position, have the function of modifying nouns, verbs, entire sentences, or other constructions.

(2) Practice with identifying the functions of modifiers can be particularly suitable for pair or group work. When the exercise is completed, pairs or groups can compare their results and discuss them.

INSTRUCTIONS FOR STUDENTS

Part 1. Identify the function of the underlined modifying phrase(s) and indicate what word(s) or phrase(s) it modifies. Explain whether it is possible for this modifying phrase to be moved to a different position in the sentence.

If so, how would the meaning of the sentence change? Be ready to discuss and explain your choices.

(1) *In the old days, mothers used to purchase clothes for their daughters. However, that approach didn't work anymore, because **a few decades ago** girls started to want independence **at a younger age.***

(2) *Good health care and maintenance, balanced diet, regular exercise, and sufficient amounts of sleep can lead to tangible benefits **in the long term**.*

(3) ***Long-term** success of sales often depends on the ability of advertising and the sales personnel to build a good relationship with the buyer.*

(4) *Advertising consists of any type of communication carried **by a mass medium** to promote products or services. When consumers think of advertising, they normally think of television, the internet, and social media, but any mass medium may be used **for advertising over the long term**.*

(5) *The ability to convey messages **to a large number of people at once** is the major benefit of advertising.*

(6) ***In the mass media**, such as television and web services, advertising companies have to follow strict legal guidelines and a number of federal regulations designed to control the types of messages intended **for the public.***

(7) *Publicity can also appear to be similar to advertising **in the mass media**. However, publicity is free, while advertising is not. Advertisers have a great deal of control over the content of promotional and sales messages, and **mass-media** advertising has its disadvantages.*

Part 2. Locate possible positions/places where a prepositional phrase or a couple of prepositional phrases can be placed to make the sentence meaning as precise and clear as possible. Be ready to explain your choices.

(1) *Two psychologists interviewed 50 newlywed couples.*

in several states   in an experiment

(2) *Happily married couples sat close, looked at each other, and talked to their spouses.*

together   during the interview   frequently

(3) *It turned out that the style of being together seems to continue.*

over time   in a follow-up study   nine months later

(4) *The concept of self plays an important role, and today's lecture explores two questions: "Who am I?" and "Why I am here?"*

basic   in interpersonal communication   for this reason

(5) *We will move to the third question, "Who are these others?"*

to complete the discussion   then   necessary   all

(6) *Social psychologists work with data on the formation of self-concepts beginning with first interactions.*

at a young age   in peer groups   with others

(7) *Our self-concepts are affected.*

during childhood   by others   deeply   in addition

Restatement and paraphrase

In Part 1, the adjectives need to be replaced to restate the phrase, and in Part 2, the entire sentences need to be paraphrased. (Optional definitions for students: Restatement uses different words to say the same thing in a short phrase or sentence. Paraphrasing means taking one or two sentences from the text and expressing their meaning in a different way. Good paraphrasing contains all the necessary information from the original text, but uses a different sentence structure and vocabulary.)

INSTRUCTIONS FOR STUDENTS

Part 1. Replace the adjectives in the phrases or the entire phrases. Be sure that the meaning of the phrase remains close to the original.

(1) *a precise measure* _____
(2) *a negative impression* _____
(3) *an explicit statement* _____
(4) *believable evidence* _____
(5) *huge profits* _____
(6) *a contrary view* _____
(7) *an elaborate design* _____
(8) *pertinent information* _____

(9) *a potential improvement* _____

(10) *indigenous people* _____

Part 2. Paraphrase the following entire sentences.

(1) *In modern America, news correspondents are employed to gather and analyze events and provide information to the public.*
Paraphrase _____
_____

(2) *Numerous technological developments that affect the speed of news dissemination require reporters to adapt continuously to the pace of innovation.*
Paraphrase _____
_____

(3) *Modern technology began radically revolutionizing news reportage as early as the 1970s.*
Paraphrase _____
_____
_____

(4) *Although news outlets remain a strong presence in disseminating information, a number of significant concerns have been raised about their future.*
Paraphrase _____
_____

(5) *In recent decades, the development of faster means of communication have created intense demand for expedient and faster ways of transmitting various forms of data.*
Paraphrase _____
_____

Endnotes

1 When adjective and noun forms or adjective and verb forms are identical, they are included on both lists.
2 Words such as **now**, **today**, **tomorrow**, or **yesterday** can have either a noun or an adverb function depending on their sentence syntactic role. For example, **now** and **today** are subject nouns in such sentences as *Now is a good time* or *Today is a wonderful day*, but adverbs in other cases, *Now, what's for lunch* or *Today, we are having cakes*.
3 Some of these frequent verbs can be used with infinitives that function as nominals, e.g. *fail to pass the test, continues to fall/its decline*, or without modification/complementation, e.g. *The experiment failed, The downturn continues*.

Further Reading

Coxhead, A. (2019). Working with multi-word units in ESP/EAP. In E. Hinkel (Ed.), *Teaching essential units of language: Beyond single-word vocabulary* (pp. 36–54). New York, NY: Routledge.

A down-to-earth overview of the reasons that multiword units are important in EAP and ESP. This teacher-oriented work discusses the types of academic multiword units together with excellent examples of word lists that consist of practical and useful multiword units necessary for L2 writing and other college-level skills. Some advantages and disadvantages for teachers and learners when working with such lists are examined from a pedagogical perspective. The material also focuses on how teachers can integrate specialized multiword units into their planning, testing, and teaching.

Folse, K. (2016). Selecting grammar lessons and activities based on actual learner needs. In E. Hinkel (Ed.), *Teaching English grammar to speakers of other languages* (pp. 63–83). New York, NY: Routledge.

The chapter covers a range of important considerations in how and why teachers need to choose to teach specific grammar points while excluding others. Learners' needs are key when designing grammar courses that are geared toward individual L2 learning goals, such as writing better academic papers, passing a high-stakes exam, and improving personal conversational skills. Recent applications of corpus linguistics research techniques can help teachers make better informed decisions about which grammar points to emphasize as well as those to skip.

Hinkel, E. (2003). Adverbial markers and tone in L1 and L2 students' writing. *Journal of Pragmatics, 35*(7), 1049–1106.

A quantitative analysis of L1 and L2 university student writing is presented, with a focus on modifying and intensifying adverbs, as well as several semantic classes of adverb clauses. The greatest pronounced differences between the L1 and L2 texts are identified in the frequency rates of amplifiers and emphatic adverbs that are very common in informal conversations, but not in formal written prose. Because L2 academic writers have a great deal of exposure to conversational discourse, the frequency rates of adverb clauses in L2 texts is determined by the frequency of a particular clause type in conversations.

References

Bhatia, V. (1993). *Analyzing genre: Language use in professional settings*. London: Routledge.

Biber, D., Johansson, S., Leech, G., Conrad, S., & Finegan, E. (1999). *Longman grammar of spoken and written English*. Harlow: Pearson.

Carter, R. & McCarthy, M. (2006). *Cambridge grammar of English: A comprehensive guide*. Cambridge: Cambridge University Press.

Coxhead, A. (2000). The new academic word list. *TESOL Quarterly, 34*(2), 213–238.

Hinkel, E. (1997). Indirectness in L1 and L2 academic writing. *Journal of Pragmatics, 27*(3), 360–386.

Hinkel, E. (1999). Objectivity and credibility in L1 and L2 academic writing. In E. Hinkel (Ed.), *Culture in second language teaching and learning.* (pp. 90–108). Cambridge: Cambridge University Press.

Hinkel, E. (2002). *Second language writers' text.* New York, NY: Routledge.

Hinkel, E. (2003a). Simplicity without elegance: Features of sentences in L1 and L2 academic texts. *TESOL Quarterly, 37*(2), 275–301.

Hinkel, E. (2003b). Adverbial markers and tone in L1 and L2 students' writing. *Journal of Pragmatics, 35*(2), 208–231.

Hinkel, E. (2005). Hedging, inflating, and persuading in L2 academic writing. *Applied Language Learning, 15,* 29–53.

Hinkel, E. (2017). Prioritizing grammar to teach or not to teach: A research perspective. In E. Hinkel (Ed.), *Handbook of research in second language teaching and learning* (pp. 369–383). New York, NY: Routledge.

Hinkel, E. (2019). Teaching strategies and techniques: Collocations and multiword units. In E. Hinkel (Ed.), *Teaching essential units of language: Beyond single-word vocabulary* (pp. 107–133). New York, NY: Routledge.

Hoye, L. (1997). *Adverbs and modality in English.* London: Longman.

Huddleston, R. & Pullum, K. (2002). *The Cambridge grammar of the English language.* Cambridge: Cambridge University Press.

Hunston, S. (2011). *Corpus approaches to evaluation: Phraseology and evaluative language.* New York, NY: Routledge.

Hunston, S., & Thompson, G. (Eds.) (2000). *Evaluation in text: Authorial stance and the construction of discourse.* Oxford: Oxford University Press.

Hyland, K. (1998). *Hedging in scientific research articles.* Amsterdam: John Benjamins.

Hyland, K. (1999). Disciplinary discourses: Writer stance in research articles. In C. Candlin & K. Hyland (Eds.), *Writing texts, processes and practices* (pp. 99–120). London: Longman.

Hyland, K. (2004). *Disciplinary discourses: Social interactions in academic writing.* Ann Arbor, MI: University of Michigan Press.

Hyland, K. (2008). As can be seen: Lexical bundles and disciplinary variation. *English for Specific Purposes, 27*(1), 4–21.

Hyland, K. & Milton, J. (1997). Qualification and certainty in L1 and L2 students' writing. *Journal of Second Language Writing, 6*(2), 183–205.

Jordan, R. (1997). *English for academic purposes.* Cambridge: Cambridge University Press.

Nation, I.S.P. (1990). *Teaching and learning vocabulary.* New York, NY: Heinle & Heinle.

Nation, P. (2013). *Learning vocabulary in another language* (2nd edn). Cambridge: Cambridge University Press.

Quirk, R., Greenbaum, S., Leech, G., & Svartvik, J. (1985). *A comprehensive grammar of the English language.* New York, NY: Longman.

Simpson-Vlach, R. & Ellis, N. (2010). An academic formulas list: New methods in phraseology research. *Applied Linguistics, 31*(4), 487–512.

Swales, J. (1990). *Genre analysis.* Cambridge: Cambridge University Press.

Swales, J. & Feak, C. (2012). *Academic writing for graduate students* (3rd edn). Ann Arbor, MI: University of Michigan Press.

Appendix to Chapter 9

Frequent Evaluative Adjectives and Noun Phrases

Evaluative Adjective	+ Main Noun
good	judges, readers, separation, communication, relations, fortune, indication e.g. good judges, good fortune
important	changes, advances, step, part, consequences, respect, role, point, factor e.g. important changes, important step(s)
special	process, regulations, class, types, method e.g. special cases, special process(es)
right	principles, level, relation, direction, answer, criteria e.g. right principles, right level(s)

(Adapted from Carter & McCarthy, 2006; Hunston, 2011)

Contrasting Pairs of Adjectives for Paraphrasing

large – small	low – high	general – particular	primary – secondary
long – short	final – initial	same – different	necessary – possible
young – old	previous – following	simple – complex	positive – negative

Highly Frequent Academic Prepositional Phrases and Multiword Units

the end of the	*the beginning of the*	*a number of the*
~ at the end of	*~ at the beginning of*	*~ a large/small number of*
~ at the end of the	*~ at the beginning of the*	*the*
		~ in a number of
		(in) a total number (of)
one of the	*at the same time*	*the size of the*
~ one of the most	*for the first time*	*the amount of the*
most of the	*at this/that time*	*the type of the*
some of the	*at the time of*	*the rate/frequency of the*
(a) part of the		*the value of the*
		the form of the
(is/are) the same as	*is similar to*	*as well (as)*
the same way (as)		*as well as the*
a wide range of	*based on (the)*	*in addition*
	~ is/are based on the	*~ in addition to the*
	on the basis of the	*~ in addition to this/that*
as a result (of)	*for this reason*	*because of (the)*
		~ due to (the)

(Adapted from Biber, et al., 1999 and Simpson-Vlach & Ellis, 2010)

Part III

Text and Discourse Organization
The Sentence and Beyond

The chapters in Part III move from the major sentence elements to clauses and rhetorical features of text.

- Chapter 10 covers the construction and discourse functions of adverb, adjective, and noun clauses, and how these subordinate clauses can be taught. Working with subordinate structures in L2 writing is complicated, but it can greatly benefit the quality of text.
- Chapter 11 focuses on rhetorical features of text that can improve the cohesion and coherence in L2 writing. The building of academic prose covers cohesive ties and vocabulary substitution, phrase-level conjunctions, parallel structure, and sentence transitions. The uses and functions of rhetorical questions and examples in academic writing are also discussed.
- Chapter 12 takes a close look at how to teach academic hedging (softening devices) to help L2 writers work with careful and formal written prose. The requirement for hedging and limiting the breadth of statements, generalizations, and claims in academic prose is not an obvious consideration for many L2 writers. This prominent characteristic of academic writing in English has to be explicitly addressed in teaching.

Backgrounding Discourse and Information

10

Subordinate Clauses

Overview

- Adverb clauses:

  o Time.
  o Condition.
  o Concession and Contrast.
  o Cause.

- Adjective clauses and participial phrases.
- Noun clauses and reporting verbs.
- Writing from sources.

Coordinating conjunctions, such as ***and***, ***but***, and ***or***, conjoin two or more simple sentences into more compound constructions. Similarly, subordinate clauses can conjoin two or more simple sentences into much more complex sentence units. For example, these two simple sentences can be conjoined by various means and turned into a number of compound or complex sentences:

Two Simple Sentences

(1) *Facial expressions are the most obvious emotional indicators.*

(2) *Some emotions are easier to express facially than others.*

(1)	Compound Sentences with Coordinating Conjunctions (a) Facial expressions are the most obvious emotional indicators, **and/but** some emotions are easier to express facially than others. (b) Some emotions are easier to express facially than others, **and** facial expressions are the most obvious emotional indicators.
(2)	Compound Sentences with Sentence Transitions (a) Facial expressions are the most obvious emotional indicators; **however,** some emotions easier to express facially than others. (b) Some emotions easier to express facially than others; **however,** facial expressions are the most obvious emotional indicators.
(3)	Complex Sentences with Cause Clauses (a) **Because** facial expressions are the most obvious emotional indicators, some emotions are easier to express facially than others. (b) **Because** some emotions are easier to express facially than others, facial expressions are the most obvious emotional indicators. (c) Facial expressions are the most obvious emotional indicators **because** some emotions are easier to express facially than others.
(4)	Complex Sentences with Time Clauses (a) **When** facial expressions are the most obvious emotional indicators, some emotions are easier to express facially than others. (b) Facial expressions are the most obvious emotional indicators, **when** some emotions are easier to express facially than others.
(5)	Complex Sentences with Concession Clauses (a) **Although** facial expressions are the most obvious emotional indicators, some emotions are easier to express facially than others. (b) Facial expressions are the most obvious emotional indicators, **although** some emotions are easier to express facially than others.
(6)	Complex Sentences with Adjective Clauses Facial expressions are the most obvious emotional indicators **that** some emotions are easier to express facially than others.

Depending on how sentences are conjoined, the contextual meaning can change in dramatic ways.

- In uncomplicated compound constructions in (1), the mere order of simple sentences in compound sentences (a) and (b) results in two slightly different meanings.
- In the two compound sentences in (2) the order of simple sentences and the placement of the conjunction **_however_** changes the meanings of the contrast.
- Important meaning differences can be noted among sentences with **_because_** (3a, b, and c). The order of the sentences and the placement of the cause conjunction can completely alter the sequence of a cause and its result.
- The placement of the concessive conjunction **_although_** in (5a and b) can differently mark two ideas for their importance in the context, and possibly contextual continuity.
- The most dramatic structural and meaning differences can be noticed in the complex sentence in (6) with a descriptive subordinate clause . . . **_that some emotions are easier to express facially than others_**, where the clause actually explains what the **_indicators_** are.

In general terms, most grammar books identify three types of subordinate clauses: **adverb**, **adjective** (also called relative), and **noun** (also called nominal) **clauses**. In complex sentences, **adverb** clauses usually perform the function of simple adverbs or adverb phrases. For example, the function of the time adverb can be performed by simple adverbs or complex adverbs alike:

Examples of Adverb Phrases and Clauses with Similar Functions

Soon/Now/Today,   *most water is lost to plants due to runoff.*

During spring/ **In** the fall/   *most water is lost to plants due to runoff.*
 After the rain,

When the vegetation on   *most water is lost to plants due to runoff.*
land is removed,

Similarly, adjective clauses perform the functions of simple adjectives or adjective phrases, all of which describe nouns or noun phrases:

Ditto for Adjective Phrases and Clauses

Soil erosion and soil   in the ecology of the entire region.
 loss cause a change

Soil erosion and soil   **that** affects the ecology of the entire region.
 loss cause a change

Following the line of similarity, **noun clauses** perform the functions of nouns and noun phrases. Thus, noun clauses, like nouns, can be sentence subjects or objects, as well as objects of prepositions.

> *Experience tells us **that males and females differ considerably*** [noun clause – direct object] ***in** **how they express emotion*** [noun clause – object of the preposition ***in***].

Subordinate clauses of all types represent advanced syntactic constructions. Thus, it is not particularly surprising that they are more common in academic writing than in speech or conversations (Biber, et al., 1999; Carter & McCarthy, 2006). On the other hand, analyses of L2 writing have shown that L2 texts include significantly fewer subordinate clauses of most types than those identified in the academic writing of L1 first-year students (Hinkel, 2002a, 2011, 2015).

For L2 writers, however, it is important to use complex sentences in academic text at the college or university level, because a writer cannot credibly build an entire assignment or a term paper using only simple or compound sentences. It is not just that L2 writers have to use complex sentences, but they have to use subordinate clauses correctly. Using complex constructions is not likely to win any accolades if the assignment contains numerous errors (Ferris, 2011; Frodesen, 2014; Hamp-Lyons, 1991).

Practically all grammar and writing textbooks provide explanations, recommendations, directions, and exercises for using subordinate clauses in academic writing to improve the organization of information and connections between ideas (Hinkel, 2002b, 2005; Swales & Feak, 2012).

> Only a few varieties of subordinate clauses are usually employed in academic writing. For L2 writers, it may not be necessary to become excellent and proficient users of all the types of complex sentences that can be found in grammar books.

Among the three types of subordinate clauses, adverb clauses are probably easier to teach and learn than adjective or noun clauses, and the material in this chapter is organized in the order of the easier first.

Adverb Clauses

In general, adverb clauses are more common in speech than in writing. On the other hand, in teaching academic writing and argumentative writing in particular, various types of adverb clauses, such as cause, concession, and condition, are often recommended in explanations, reasoning, and analysis.

> Many studies demonstrate that in L2 academic writing similar types of adverb clauses are used repeatedly and without much variation.
>
> For this reason, the use of complex sentences with subordinate clauses needs to be encouraged in L2 writing. Becoming familiar and practicing with a range of subordinate clauses can lead to improvements in L2 text complexity.

Meanings and Types

Adverb clauses modify the entire sentence found in the main (independent) clause and express various contextual relationships that can refer to time, cause, contrast, and condition. Some adverb subordinators, such as *while*, *since*, and *as*, are ambiguous because they can be found in clauses of cause, time, and contrast. However, for L2 writers, being able to name the types of particular clauses is not very important, and the fact that some of them are ambiguous does not matter a great deal.

Grammar books and writing guides usually classify adverb clauses by the meanings of subordinators and typically include the following.

- <u>Time</u> clauses with subordinating conjunctions such as *after, as before, when, while, until*.

  - <u>*When*</u> *water tables drop, water flow from springs and seeps diminishes.*
  - <u>*As*</u> *the air rises, it cools.*

- <u>Cause</u> clauses with the highly frequent subordinator *because*, and an occasional *as* and *since*.

  - <u>*Because*</u> *oceans cover about 70% of the earth's surface, the largest amount of water enters the atmosphere by evaporation from the ocean surfaces.*

- **Concessive** clauses, also called concession or contrast clauses, with subordinators, such as *although*, *even though*, or *though*.

  - *Although water evaporates from lakes and rivers, large amounts of water enter the atmosphere by transpiration from plants.*

- **Condition** clauses, in most cases marked by conjunctions *if*, sometimes *unless*, and <u>rarely</u> *even if* or <u>*whether or not*</u>.

  - *If a river is diverted, ecological impacts may be difficult to predict.*
  - *Academic journals specify the word limit* <u>**whether or not**</u> *a submission is accepted for publication.*

A Few Key Points for Teaching

- Structurally, adverb clauses of all types are conjoined with – or attached to – the main clauses.
- Although adverb clauses are peripheral to the structure of the independent clause, they play an important role in marking primary and secondary information in text.
- The **meaning** of the subordinate clause is always **external** to the meaning of the main. Adverb clauses are always optional because simple sentences can be conjoined in a variety of ways.
- A pivotal function of adverb clauses is to frame discourse for time and/or place, for example, and present background information relevant to that in the independent clause.

Because adverb clauses are functionally optional components that are not integral to the main clause structure, various types of syntactic sentence errors, such as fragments, can be encountered in L2 academic writing.

Essentially, when working with adverb clauses, L2 writers need to decide what information is important in their sentences.

The most important information goes into the main clause, and secondary/background information goes into the adverb clause.

In academic writing, the most common adverb clauses can have various meanings, but their prevalence differs a great deal. In teaching, particularly when time is a concern, the teacher needs to determine what structures are more useful and practical, and which are less so. For example, clauses of place or purpose are not very frequent in academic writing but clauses of time and condition are worthwhile to address and learn (Hinkel, 2005, 2015, 2017; Hoye, 1997; Hunston, 2011).

Frequent Academic Adverb Clauses

- **Condition** clauses in introductions and argumentation.

    If a problem cannot be denied or repressed completely, some individuals distort its nature so that they can handle it more easily.
- **Concession** clauses as hedges to limit generalizations and claims, as well as account for opposing points of view.

    Although irrigation can be costly, drip irrigation greatly reduces water use and waste.

A Caveat: Concession clauses with **_whereas_** are hardly ever encountered in student-level academic texts.

Less Frequent Clauses

- **Time** clauses.

    When the Etruscans expanded their territory in Italy during the seventh and sixth centuries BC, they controlled the monarchy in Rome.
- **Cause** clauses – mainly conversational (Leech, et al., 2001).

    Because marketing is primarily responsible for conception and development of products, marketing analysts also test and refine product ideas.

A Note: Cause clauses may not very popular in real academic writing – as opposed to cause/effect compositions usually assigned in composition courses – because direct and clear-cut causes of events and developments may be difficult to identify (Biber, 1988).

On the other hand, cause clauses are relatively frequent in student academic writing, possibly due to the fact that they are common in the conversational discourse. Other important adverb clauses, such as **concession** and **condition**, are rarely encountered in L2 student writing, and it may be that the importance of their contextual and academic uses needs to be emphasized in instruction (Hinkel, 2002a, 2005).

Important Caveats

➤ Cautionary notes should be made in regard to the lists of adverb sub-ordinators ubiquitously found in composition textbooks and writing guides.

➤ Some of them are hardly ever found even in real-life academic prose, e.g. *as if, every time that, for* (purpose, e.g. *?for I need to study hard*), *in case, in the event that, in order that, now that, provided that, so that, whereas.*

➤ The long lists of seemingly redundant subordinators with similar meanings, as they are typically listed, can be confusing and discouraging to L2 writers.

➤ The best approach may be to **focus on a smaller number** of practical sub-ordinators that L2 writers can use in various contexts.

The Most Frequent Adverb Subordinators (in declining order)

Condition	*if* (and rarely, ***unless***)
Time	***when*** (and occasionally, ***as, after, before, until***)
Concession	***although, while, though*** (declining order)
Cause	***because*** (and occasionally, ***since***)

In general terms, concessive clauses can be employed as sophisticated hedging devices that can also help writers give a balanced perspective on the issue / topic at hand.

Prefabricated sentence stems with concessive clauses can be highly useful in introductions, thesis statements, topic sentences, and generalizations:

Although/While xxx,   *yyy* (thesis/topic/generalization)

It is important for L2 writers to remember that their main point should be placed in the main clause (Quirk, et al., 1985).

— **_Although_** _many among minorities do not have money to go to school_, they need to get education to win the struggle for power in society.
— Need for achievement varies widely from person to person, **_although_** _psychologists suggest a learned achievement motive_.

On the other hand, cause clauses may need to be used sparingly and with caution.

A good rule of thumb for academic sentences with adverb clauses:

The-main-for-main.
The main information goes in the main clause.

Uses and Functions

The mobility of adverb clauses, just as that of adverbs and adverb phrases, can be used to the writer's advantage (Celce-Murcia & Olshtain, 2000, 2005; DeCarrico, 2000; see also chapter 11).

- When the subordinate clause is placed at the **beginning** of the sentence, it helps establish a cohesive link between the text that immediately precedes the clause and the new information that follows.
- Adverb clauses at the ends of sentences expand the information in the main clause.

Here's an example.

> The increase in the mobile consumption of news is fueled in part by the proliferation of smartphones. One study found that the top 10 mobile devices used for news and information access were either smartphones or high-end feature phones. **_Because_** _smartphones can capture still images and many can record digital video footage_, they are becoming critical to the distillation of newsworthy events.
>
> (Adapted from https://transition.fcc.gov/osp/
> inc-report/INoC-5-Mobile.pdf)

In this excerpt, the **sentence-initial** position of the *because*-clause connects the information in the preceding sentence to that in the main clause:

> smartphones – mobile devices – phones, news and information access – newsworthy events, smartphones – they, capture – news

Adverb clauses at the beginning of sentences connect ideas and serve as transitions to maintain the pattern of **old-information-first-and-new-information last**. Research has found that the majority of all initial clauses consist of *if*-conditionals that have the function of organizing discourse, as well as establishing and maintaining topics. On the other hand, corpus analyses of various genres have demonstrated that conditional clauses are less common in academic writing than in conversation or fiction (Biber et al., 1999; Leech et al., 2001).

The **sentence-final** adverb clause expands the information in the main clause where the information in the clause provides an example for the point made in the main clause.

> *The market for smartphones, tablet computers, laptops, PCs, and TVs is evolving rapidly,* **as the distinctions between these devices become increasingly blurred**.

In addition to the sentence-initial and sentence-final position, adverb clauses can also occur in the middles of sentences. However, these types of constructions require a break in the flow of information in a sentence, resulting in syntactically complex constructions that most (if not all) L2 writers probably would not miss a great deal.

Tenses in Clauses of Time and Condition

Two essential grammar rules:

(1) In clauses of **time and condition**, only the **present and the past tense can be used**.

(2) In complex sentences with time and condition clauses, **only the main clause can be marked for the future tense**.

Here are a couple of examples.

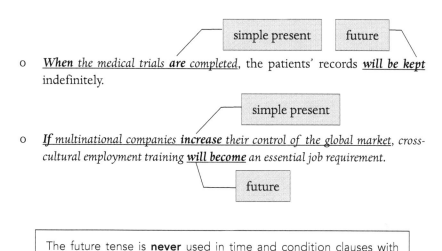

o *When the medical trials **are completed***, the patients' records ***will be kept*** indefinitely.

o *If multinational companies **increase** their control of the global market, cross-cultural employment training **will become** an essential job requirement.*

> The future tense is **never** used in time and condition clauses with subordinate conjunctions **after, as, as soon as, before, when, while, until, whether**, and **if**.

In time and condition clauses, **perfect tenses are also singularly rare**. As was discussed in chapter 7, in general the uses of the future and the perfect tenses are rare in academic writing.

Position and Punctuation

As earlier, complex sentences with adverb clauses in effect represent two conjoined simple sentences, which can be moved around freely, until they are conjoined.

Two Simple Sentences

In the past, colleges and universities were primarily the domain of students in their late teens and early twenties.

Now increasing numbers of older students are returning to school.

These two sentences can be combined in various ways, depending on the writer's ideas and desired context. **The main point of a sentence is placed in the main** clause, and **secondary** information in the **adverb clause**.

The two sentences can be sequenced in a way that best fits the context.

(1) The adverb clause first.

> _**Although** in the past, colleges and universities were primarily the domain of students in their late teens and early twenties_, now increasing numbers of older students are returning to school.

(2) The adverb clause follows the main clause – the same basic meaning.

> Now increasing numbers of older students are returning to school, _**although** in the past, colleges and universities were primarily the domain of students in their late teens and early twenties_.

(3) The main and background information is switched – the meaning is different from that in (1) and (2).

> _**Although** now increasing numbers of older students are returning to school_, in the past, colleges and universities were primarily the domain of students in their late teens and early twenties.

(4) The meaning is the same as in (3), and both (3) and (4) are different from (1) and (2).

> In the past, colleges and universities were primarily the domain of students in their late teens and early twenties, _**although** now increasing numbers of older students are returning to school_.

In L2 academic writing, there are only a couple of important things to remember about the placement and the **punctuation** of adverb clauses:

> If adverb clauses are placed at the **beginning** of a sentence, a **comma** must be used to separate them from the main clause. **No comma** is necessary when the clause is in at the **end** of the sentence.

Typical Errors with Adverb Clauses

Trouble Spot #1

"Three Steps Back": **Although** . . . **but** errors. Using **although** or **even though** and **but** in one complex sentence.

Example trouble-spot sentences:

> *__Although__ managers believe that a worker's salary is everything, __but__ they for-get to think about other benefits.
>
> *__Even though__ art was very important in the 18th century, __but__ it is not so important now because technology is where the future is.

The main function of *although* and *even though* concessive clauses is to hedge (limit or soften) the generalization or statement in the main clause and present a balanced position by accounting for other perspectives.

> __Although__ not all communities and groups accept society's institutions, a majority of the citizens in any country do not challenge the social order and accepted social patterns.

> Economic descriptions of buying decision making assume buyers' purely ratio-nal purchase decisions, __even though__ many buying decisions have emotional aspects.

Concessive clauses play a role analogous to "**one step back**," and the **main** clause, "**two steps forward**."

In L2 text, however, when writers misunderstand the "one step back" func-tion of concessives, they additionally employ the conjunction *but* with main clauses.

Teaching Tip

In effect, *although . . . but* constructions result in double concession, and the thrust of the writer's main point does not seem to advance. In teaching, a very useful and visually clear teaching technique is to demonstrate the con-cession clause and the main clause "steps" that take place in expressing ideas in such sentences. The main clause gets 2 steps of value, being the main point, and the concession clause gets 1 step of value.

Here's an illustration.

__Although__ cell phones seem to be a new service, **but** *they were invented in the 1970s.*
    one-step-back ~*although* + two-steps-back ~*but* in the main clause = three steps back

---

With a bit of practice, this type of error is usually short-lived, but it does require occasional repeating and a few reminders.

Trouble Spot #2

Sentence fragments. The most frequent types – separated adverb clauses or prepositional phrases.

Example trouble-spot sentences:

> *__Because__ engineering is a practical field of the application of science and math.*
> *__Although__ education and training are an investment.*
> *__When__ students earn more knowledge and hospital experience in nursing.*

In L1 and L2 writing alike, such errors are frequent because separated adverb clauses are acceptable and highly common in conversations, e.g.

— *Why did you decide to study engineering?*

    — *__Because__ engineering is a practical field of application of science and math.*

— *Education is expensive these days. Hmmm.*

    — *Education and training are an investment* **though**.

— *So, when do students get a chance to do clinical training?*

    — *__When__ students earn more knowledge and hospital experience in nursing.*

- Subordinate conjunctions, such as *because*, *although*, *when*, and *if* conjoin the main and subordinate clauses.
- Thus, when conjunctions are used, they need to have two clauses to conjoin.
- In a sense, conjunctions play the role of "glue" to join **two** sentences together.

If a sentence includes only one simple sentence and a bit of glue, there is nothing for the conjunction to conjoin.

To correct separated adverb clauses, two options are possible:

(1) The glue must be removed (and the conjunction deleted).

OR

(2) Another sentence needs to be added to make use of the "gluing" conjunction power.

Other types of sentence fragments, such as separated prepositional phrases, are also highly common in conversations, e.g.

— *Where did you read about xxx?*

   — *In an article about visual art in advertising.*

— *When did World War I begin?*

   — *On the day when the Austrian crown prince was assassinated in Sarajevo.*

In written text, separated prepositional phrases are more difficult to notice and correct than abandoned adverb clauses. Fortunately, however, lonely prepositional phrases are less common.

Teaching Tip

Every English sentence must have at least a subject and a verb to be grammatical (see chapters 4 and 9).

- Thus, to identify separated prepositional phrases, the **first** step is to **find the sentence verb**.
- If there is **no verb**, it is a safe guess that there is probably **no sentence**.
- On the other hand, if one merely inserts a verb into a prepositional phrase to turn it into a sentence, the next step is to **find the subject**.

A Cardinal Rule – Always Correct in All Cases and at All Times: In English Prepositional Phrases Cannot Be Sentence Subjects. No Exceptions.

The last step is to give the sentence **a subject, in addition to the verb**. If the subject and the verb "agree" in number – singular or plural, then the sentence is finally complete. Finally.

Adjective (Relative) Clauses

Adjective clauses have functions similar to those of simple adjectives or adjective phrases, and these complex constructions are pretty frequent in academic prose (Tse & Hyland, 2010).

- Single-word adjectives or even a series of single-word adjectives (**big, bright, and red**) precede the noun they describe.
- Adjective phrases (**very happy**) and adjective clauses follow the noun.

A few examples:

— *Yellow ribbons play an important symbolic role in American culture.*
[a single-word adjective]
— *Contemporary educational reform is an issue for the public debate.*
[serial single-word adjectives]
— *A study **carried out at the University of Kansas** focuses on TV viewing among adolescents.*
[an adjective phrase that describes the *study*]

— *Today, a typical American couple consists of a husband and wife, <u>who both</u>*
   <u>*work outside the home*</u>.
   [an adjective clause that describes *a husband and wife* noun phrase]
— *Many of the children <u>who attend day care centers</u> do not seem to pay much*
   attention to their mothers' departure and return.
   [an adjective clause that describes the noun phrase *the children*]

In academic writing, an advantage of using adjective clauses, as
opposed to descriptive adjectives, is that the amount of information included in a clause can be greater than that conveyed by
single-word adjectives.

Adjective clauses can modify practically any type of noun or noun phrase.

The **relative pronouns *that*, *who*,** and ***which*** replace the noun that
the adjective clause modifies.

— *Rembrandt, **who** [~~Rembrandt~~] <u>**was**</u> Dutch and never <u>**went**</u> abroad, was*
   considerably influenced by the work of the Italian masters.
— *Livia (58 BC-AD 29), <u>**who**</u> [~~Livia~~] <u>**was**</u> Octavian's third wife, <u>**was**</u> admired*
   for her wisdom and dignity.
— *In search of spices <u>**that**</u> [~~spices~~] <u>**were**</u> in extraordinarily high demand, the*
   Portuguese went directly to the source, to India.

In academic writing, ***who, that,*** and ***which*** are used far more frequently
than ***whom***,[1] ***whose, when***, or ***why***. The fourth common relative pronoun is
where to modify nouns that refer to places or nouns in prepositional phrases
of place, e.g. ***the regions where, in the city where***, or ***at the site where***. Other
types of relative pronouns – ***in which*** and ***to which*** – are only occasionally
found in academic writing (Biber, et al., 1999). (A list of frequent phrases
and sentence stems with nouns and relative pronouns that follow them in
frequently encountered adjective clauses is included in the Appendix to this
chapter.)

For L2 writers, only a couple of points are important to learn and practice.

> Relative pronouns, e.g. *that*, *who*, and **which** "copy" the grammatical information from the noun phrase they replace. That is, if the noun phrase is plural, then the relative pronoun remains plural and requires the plural verb.

In the examples above, *Livia* is a singular noun, therefore, the pronoun *who* is also singular, and therefore, the verb *was* is also singular, whereas the noun *spices* is plural, therefore, the pronoun *that* is also plural, and therefore the verb *were* is plural.

In addition to these relatively simple adjective clauses, one more type of these constructions exists, and it is not as simple as in the examples with Rembrandt, Livia, and spices. In adjective clauses, the verb immediately follows the relative pronouns *who (was)* and *that (were)*. Thus, a conclusion can be made that *who* and *that* are subjects of the adjective clauses in *who was Dutch, who was Octavian's third wife*, and *that were in extraordinarily high demand*.

Relative Pronouns as Clause Objects

Adjective clauses can become far more complex and far more error prone when the **relative pronoun is the object** of the adjective clause verb.

(1) *European expansion advanced outside the continent with the development of the sail and the gun. Western Europeans combined* **the sail and the gun** *in the form of the gunned ship.*

(2) *European expansion advanced outside the continent with the development of the sail and the gun,* **which** *Western Europeans combined [*the sail and the gun*] in the form of the gunned ship.*

In (1) and (2), the adjective clause modifies the noun phrase that actually has the function of the **verb object**.[2]

> When the **verb object** in the adjective clause is turned into **a relative pronoun** (e.g. *who*, *that*, *which*), two things happen:

- The relative pronoun is moved to the first position in the clause – directly to follow the noun it describes, e.g. *Rembrandt painted extraordinary* **portraits+ that** *his contemporaries admired.*
- The relative pronoun (**that**, **which**) is omitted, e.g. *Rembrandt painted extraordinary* **portraits** [~~that~~] *his contemporaries admired.*

The following points are important to address in teaching and for practice.

Trouble Spot #3

Too many pronouns in the adjective clause when the object pronoun is left behind.

Example trouble-spot sentences:

*Rembrandt painted extraordinary **portraits that** *his contemporaries admired* ***them****.*
*European expansion advanced outside the continent with the development of the sail and the gun, **which** *Western Europeans combined ****them*** *in the form of the gunned ship.*

In L2 writing, many, many object pronouns in adjective clauses are left behind when the relative pronoun is moved to the beginning of the clause.

*Rice is the most widely consumed food **that** *traders export* ⟶ **it** ⟵ *world-wide.*

The structure is incorrect because it includes **two pronouns – *that* and *it* – to refer to only one** and the same **noun phrase**. Not a good idea to leave remnant pronouns behind.

When it comes to pronouns in adjective clauses, there should only be one pronoun for each noun or noun phrase. A **one-for-one exchange**.

Adjective clauses and relative pronouns of any kind always follow the noun phrase they describe.

Restrictive and Non-restrictive Adjective Clauses

All grammar textbooks that deal with adjective clauses invariably mention **restrictive and non-restrictive** adjective clauses. **Restrictive** clauses, by means of narrowly identifying a particular noun, "restrict" the range and type of nouns they modify to one specific noun or a type of nouns, e.g.

> *A primary family consists of a small number of people <u>who live together or</u> <u>stay in regular contact, have close personal ties, and are committed to the</u> <u>relationship</u>.*

In this example, the rather vague noun phrase *a small number of people* is "restricted" or limited by the specific definition in the adjective clause. Restrictive adjective clauses are never separated by commas because the information in the adjective clauses is necessary (and cannot be separated out) to define and identify the noun.

On the other hand, **non-restrictive** clauses are those that supply additional information to describe nouns that are already known or well defined, e.g.

> *In agrarian communities, primary interactions occur among the members of the group, close friends, and **family**, <u>which can include the spouse, parents,</u> <u>grandparents, siblings, aunts and uncles, cousins, and other relatives</u>.*

The adjective clause in this sentence largely defines the word **family** that actually may not need a specific definition and that is likely to be known to most L1 or L2 users of English. Non-restrictive clauses do not delimit the noun to one specific object or types of objects because a narrow identification of this specific noun is not needed, e.g. *low rainfall regions, which. . .; the Romans, who . . .; feudal law, which . . . .* In this case, the adjective clause is separated by commas: it provides helpful but inessential information.

The greatest issues with the ever-popular discussions on restrictive and non-restrictive adjective clauses, included in every grammar and composition book, is that they are extraordinarily difficult for L2 writers to identify.

In an earlier example, for instance, the L2 writer would have to know that the meaning of the word _family_ applies to different types of relatives in English than it does in other languages, e.g. _Is one's third cousin twice-removed family or not? What is a third cousin anyway?_ And then, one has to be able to figure out that this word already has a relatively limited meaning in English, and therefore be able to conclude that the adjective clause has to be separated out by commas.

> The teaching of the distinction between restrictive and non-restrictive adjective clauses and their punctuation may simply not be worth the time and work expended on their conceptual (and vague) definitions and the ambiguous rules.

In formal academic writing, only 15% of all adjective clauses are non-restrictive, and the information included in them is usually tangential and somewhat unnecessary (Biber, et al., 1999). Undoubtedly, the quality and the types of prose in the formal academic writing research in English language corpora is different from that in student writing. Nonetheless, in teaching academic L2 writing, the distinction between restrictive and non-restrictive clauses, as well this particular aspect of punctuation, may simply occupy a very low priority. In light of the vocabulary and conceptual complexities associated with restrictive and non-restrictive clauses, one general rule of thumb may be useful for L2 writers, however.

> ### A Practical Punctuation Rule of Thumb
>
> Adjective clauses with **that** relative pronouns are never separated by commas.

Adjective Participial Phrases

Adjective participial phrases are derived by means of reducing an adjective clause to an adjective phrase. The functions of participial phrases are largely the same as those of single-word adjectives and adjective clauses, that is, to modify nouns and noun phrases.

In formal academic writing, the main purpose of these advanced constructions is to package information as compactly as possible (Biber, 1988). In various studies of written discourse and the assessment of L2 writing, reduced clauses and participial phrases are often identified with formal written discourse and advanced facility in writing and grammar (Hamp-Lyons, 1991).

> Participial phrases of any type are hardly ever found in L2 academic writing, but using them occasionally – and correctly – may project a certain degree of linguistic sophistication.

Adjective participles can be active or passive (see also chapter 7), e.g.

- *Most water __flowing in irrigation canals__ comes from nearby rivers.* [active participial phrase]
- *Water __stored in artificial lakes__ evaporates during dry and hot summers.* [passive participial phrase]

When teaching **advanced** L2 or EAP writing classes, teachers need to be familiar with the mechanisms for adjective clause reductions, even if they are not explicitly taught (see chapter 7). For instructors, familiarity with the participial phrase derivation may come in very handy when working with common student errors in the uses of active and passive adjectives.

Adjective clauses are reduced by means of just a few steps.

In Brief

(1) The relative pronoun that is the adjective clause subject *who, **that, which*** is deleted.
(2) The clause verb is converted to a **participle**.

Active verbs

- o   The tense/person morpheme is deleted.
- o   The base verb + *-ing*, e.g. *flow + ing, contain + ing, include + ing.*

Passive verbs

- o   The auxiliary *-be* verb is deleted.
- o   The past participle stays unchanged, e.g. *[is/are] found, [was/were] reduced.*

Some examples:

Active Participial Phrase

The un-reduced sentence, the starting point:

*Most water **that flows in irrigation canals** comes from nearby rivers.*

(1) *Most water [~~that~~] **flow** [+ s] **in irrigation canals** comes from nearby rivers.*
(2) *Most water **flow** [~~+ s~~] **in irrigation canals** comes from nearby rivers.*
(3) *Most water **flow + ing in irrigation canals** comes from nearby rivers.*

Passive Participial Phrase

The un-reduced sentence, the starting point:

*Water **that is stored in artificial lakes** evaporates during dry summers.*

(1) *Water [~~that~~] **is stored in artificial lakes** evaporates during dry summers.*
(2) *Water [~~is~~] **stored in artificial lakes** evaporates during dry summers.*
(3) *Water **stored in artificial lakes** evaporates during dry summers.*

Here are a couple of additional examples.
Active

> *In regions **~~that~~ face** water shortages, about 85% of the water comes from canals.*
> *In regions **face + ing** water shortage, about 85% of the water comes from canals.*

Passive

> *The volume of ground water **~~that is~~ found** underground exceeds that of all surface water.*
> *The volume of ground water **found** underground exceeds that of all surface water.*

According to a detailed study by Master (2002), the prevalence of adjective clause reduction depends on the discipline to some extent. For example, in biology, chemistry, psychology, computer science, geology, math, and physics, adjective clauses are reduced far more rarely than in the humanities. On the whole, however, discipline-related distinctions are not very pronounced. Most importantly, Master (2002) found that **a vast majority of clause reductions occurs with relative pronouns**, e.g. *who, that, which,* **as the clause subjects,** e.g. *the river flowing* . . . . These types of participial phrases are far easier to teach and learn than those with clause objects (fortunately indeed).

A small number of active or passive adjective participles are recurrent in formal academic writing, and these are derived from highly frequent academic verbs (see chapter 8). The frequent participles can be learned and used as needed in academic writing.

> With the exception of constructions with **using**, the **-ing** participles hardly ever occur as progressive verbs. Thus, L2 writers do not need to be concerned about confusing them.

Frequent Academic Participles

Active (in declining order)

containing	*using*	*concerning*	*having*	*involving*
arising	*consisting*	*corresponding*	*relating*	*requiring*
resulting				

Passive (in declining order)

based	*given*	*used*	*caused*	*concerned*
made	*obtained*	*produced*	*taken*	

Some examples of the phrases with these participles can be taught in combinations with catch-all and other academic nouns (see chapter 4).

Frequent Collocations with Academic Nouns + Participles

the issue concerning	*the experiment involving*	*the problem relating to/resulting from*
the data containing/using	*a solution requiring*	*the result produced*
the information taken (together)	*given these facts*	

Generally speaking (this is a participial phrase), the reduction of adjective clauses to adjective participial phrases is an optional and advanced syntactic operation. For this reason, it can be useful for teaching advanced L2 writing or when working on grammar errors.

Noun Clauses

Noun clauses are extraordinarily frequent in academic writing, and they are probably the most common type of subordinate construction. As the information below demonstrates, they are also by far the most structurally complex.

As noted earlier, the functions of nouns can be performed by single words, phrases, full clauses, and reduced clauses (such as infinitive or gerund phrases – see chapter 4). Noun clauses occupy the noun slot in a complex sentence, e.g. the subject, the object, the subject complement, or the adjective complement (Biber, et al., 1999; Swales & Feak, 2012; see chapter 3).

> Noun clauses in the object slot are by far the most frequent in academic writing.

Here's an example:

Psychologists know <u>that information in short-term memory must be repeated</u>.
[Psychologists know **noun**, e.g. the fact / something / xxx].

The sentence pattern with noun clauses as objects, following the main verb phrase, is highly, highly frequent.

- *Millions of students have learned <u>that they need to repeat the multiplication table to remember it</u>.*
- *Bartlett's research shows <u>that material in long-term memory interacts in interesting ways</u>.*

Uses and Functions

The most important **discourse function** of noun clauses is to present and paraphrase information from sources.

> Noun clauses are particularly prevalent in academic writing after **reporting verbs** in summaries, restatements, and citations.

Other types of constructions where noun clauses occur is following a specific and **limited class of adjectives**, such as:

- *It is apparent/clear/evident/well known/true/vital <u>that students learn vocabulary</u>.*
- *The author is certain/clear/correct/right <u>that students need to practice</u>.*

Noun clauses also serve as extensive cohesive ties to recap the information stated earlier or outline the discourse structure, so particularly in introductions.

- *It was stated/mentioned previously/above **that** . . .*
- *This essay/I will show/argue/prove **that** . . .*

> As opposed to adverb clauses, in **noun clauses**, the secondary information is presented in the main clause.
>
> **The most important information is presented in the subordinate clause**, which is – almost always – placed at the end.

Noun clauses in the subject position are found in every grammar book, e.g. *That students study hard is a well-known fact*, but these are **very rare** in formal academic prose, and they practically never occur in student academic writing of any kind (Hinkel, 2002a).

Meanings and Forms

SIMPLE SENTENCES

Practically all simple sentences and questions can become noun clauses. Simple sentences are embedded into complex sentences and are marked by the subordinate – and occasionally optional – conjunction **that**, e.g.

| Some psychologists believe | *(that)* | *changes occur in steps and stages.* |
| Others maintain | *(that)* | *changes take place in smooth, steady progression.* |

> Although officially the clause marker **that** is optional, its important function is to mark a noun clause.
>
> In formal writing, the omission of **that** can lead to confusing constructions that are somewhat informal. In L2 writing, it's best to keep the **thats** in.

By far the most common pattern of noun clauses entails reporting and mental process verbs followed by *that* clauses (see also chapter 8). Additional lists of reporting and belief verbs are included in the appendix to this chapter.

The Most Frequent Reporting Verbs Followed by **That** Clauses
(in declining order)

state	show	suggest	know	see	find
ensure	indicate	think	believe	mean	feel

(Adapted from Leech, et al., 2001)

The second type of construction with *that* noun clauses is when the clause follows an adjective. In these constructions, noun clauses have the function of adjective complements, e.g.

- *It is **apparent** that the current recycling policy is not working.*
- *The author is **correct** that the American public needs to be educated about waste.*

Such constructions are far more common in conversations than in any type of written prose, and they are relatively rare in formal academic writing. However, they occasionally appear in evaluative student writing, possibly due to the fact that these structures occur in conversations, e.g.

- *I am **angry/glad/happy/pleased/sorry/sure** you had problems.*
- *It is **nice/great/incredible/shocking/terrible** that he was elected.*

The number of frequent adjectives followed by noun clauses is actually small.

The Most Frequent Academic Adjectives Followed by **That**-Clauses

General Purpose

accepted/ acceptable	apparent	certain	clear	correct
doubtful	evident	likely/unlikely	possible/ impossible	probable
right	true	well known		

Evaluative Adjectives

critical	crucial	desirable	essential	important
necessary	vital	interesting	disappointing	notable
noteworthy	noticeable	preferable	sufficient	understandable
unusual				

(Adapted from Swales and Feak, 2012, and Leech, et al., 2001)

WH- QUESTIONS

Wh- noun clauses represent embedded **wh-** questions. They also delay the most important and new information to the secondary position and introduce the topic. The topic-introduction function of **wh-** clauses is particularly important in developing **cohesive ties from the old-to-the-new** information organization.

> In noun clauses, the constructions with **wh-** questions and subordinators, such as **what, where, who,** are typically error-prone.

In direct questions, subjects and verbs are inverted, and an auxiliary verb is added in almost all cases (with the exceptions of **who** and **what** questions to sentence subjects – below). For example:

— What <u>*are some problems*</u> with Bentham's utilitarian theory?
— How <u>*does the need*</u> for political theory <u>*arise*</u>?
— What <u>*does Aquinas mean*</u> by "motion" and why <u>*cannot something be*</u> both "moved" and "mover"?

To convert direct **wh-** **questions to noun clauses** – and make them indirect questions – the questions need to be turned into statements.

- In statements, the word order is **the subject first and the verb second.**
- In noun clauses, when **wh-** questions are converted to indirect questions, **all wh- words must be retained and cannot be omitted.**

When paraphrasing direct **wh-** questions, most of the work takes place inside the noun clause.

Converting Embedded Questions into a Noun Clause

Main Clause	Noun Clause with Embedded Question
The author asks	**what** [are] some problems **are** with Betham's utilitarian theory.
The article discusses	**how** [doe**S**] the need for political theory **arise + S**.
Philosophers continue to debate	**what** [doe**S**] Aquinas **mean + S** by "motion" and **why** [cannot] something **cannot** be both "moved" and "mover."

In Short

- *Be-* and modal verbs (e.g. *can, may, might*) are moved after the subject slot.
- With other types of verbs, **auxiliary verb** information, such as tense, person, number (e.g. *does, do, did*) is "merged" with the main verb, e.g.

  *doe**S** . . . mean → means**S***
  *did . . . mean → mean**T***
  *did . . . arise → **arose***

For teaching **wh-** questions to noun clause conversions, the steps are:

(1) Identify the **entire subject slot** and determine where to put *be-* or modal verbs.
(2) Locate the **head noun** in the subject slot to figure out if it is singular or plural to attend to subject–verb agreement.

Here's the easy part. Embedding questions with **subject wh- words immediately followed by main verbs** does not require moving any elements of the noun clause, e.g.

	*What **determines** status or class within society?*
Hegel's theory explains	*what **determines** status or class within society.*

	*What **distinguishes** philosophy from theology?*
This essay presents Burke's views on	*what **distinguishes** philosophy from theology.*

A Caveat. In examples such as *What **are some problems** with Bentham's utilitarian theory?*, the sentence subject is the noun phrase *some problems*, and not the pronoun *what*. As stated earlier, it is necessary to identify **the entire subject noun phrase** and the head noun to convert *wh-* questions to noun clauses.

How to Locate the Subject and the Head Noun

The Litmus Test: A Full-Sentence Response to the Question

What are some problems with Bentham's utilitarian theory?
   Some problems with Bentham's theory are xxx.
What distinguishes philosophy from theology?
   YYY distinguishes philosophy from theology.

A point to make in teaching: after direct questions are converted into statements, **no question mark is needed**. It is replaced by **a period, to mark the end of the sentence**.

The concept of a sentence and marked sentence boundaries is difficult for L1 and L2 writers alike. To add to the mix, in many languages,[3] the **syntactic** distinctions between questions and sentences are marked by intonation alone – and without grammatical operations, as in English. The statement-to-question conversions to ask a mere question (*Where **is Bob**? What **time is it**?*) – and then additional question-to-statement conversions in noun clauses (*I don't know **where Bob is***) can be particularly puzzling to speakers of the languages without such numerous grammatical perturbations, e.g. what's all with the inverted subject and verb order, not to mention the separation of verbs into various parts, and the to-dos with questions marks.

YES/NO QUESTIONS

> With yes/no questions that have **no wh- words** (e.g. *Does utilitarian theory explain xxx?*), a **wh- word must be added** – **whether**.

Here are a couple of examples of embedded yes/no questions.

No one knows	**Is** <u>government in civil society</u> *a necessary evil?* [**yes/no**] **whether** [I̶s̶] <u>government in civil society</u> **is** *a necessary evil.*

	Does anarchy arise *in the absence of government?* [**yes/no**]
Smith investigates	**whether** [D̶o̶e̶S̶] <u>anarchy **ariseS**</u> *in the absence of government.*

Contrary to explanations found in many grammar books that **whether** and **if** can be equally well employed in noun clauses, in academic writing, **if** occasionally occurs with only three verbs:

> *see (if)   determine (if)   find out (if)*

As the examples demonstrate, to convert a question into a noun clause correctly, the first thing is to **identify the entire subject noun phrase** in the subject slot (***government in civil society***) because the verb follows the subject. Then it is necessary to **identify the head noun, with which the verb must agree in number.** Clearly, noun clause construction is not a trivial task.

Three Types of Noun Clauses
(Who Can Learn This Language Anyway)

(1)   With **statements** – the easiest task.

- Build the main clause, add **that**, and then add the statement.

  Biologists claim   **that**   *cellular theories can explain aging.*

(2) With **wh- questions**.

- Build the main clause, keep the **wh-** word, and identify the whole subject slot.

  After years of research, it is still not known **what** <u>**the causes of depression**</u> **are**.

- Move **be-** or modal verbs (**can**, **may**) to follow the entire subject slot.
- In the case of **the auxiliary-and-main verb split**, merge the verbs.
- **If the verb follows the wh-word, do not move anything.**

  Entomologists continue to investigate <u>**what eradicates** pests in food crops</u>.

- Locate **the head noun** in the subject slot and make sure that the number of the head noun agrees with that of the verb phrase elements (including auxiliary verbs).

  <u>**What doeS**</u> *carbon dating* <u>**show**</u> *researchers?*

  The article discusses <u>**what**</u> *carbon dating* **showS** *researchers*.

(3) With **yes/no** questions.

- Build the main clause and add **whether** after the main clause.
- Identify the <u>whole subject slot</u> and move **be-** or modal verbs to follow the entire subject slot.
- In the case of the auxiliary and main verb split, **merge the verbs**.
- Locate the head noun and make sure that the number agrees with that of the verb phrase elements, including auxiliary verbs, e.g. <u>**does**</u> **not show**, <u>**are**</u> **not included**.

A Rule of Thumb for Noun Clauses

When questions become clauses, they are no longer questions – they are clauses. Clauses are actually sentences.

For this reason, the question word order (the verb before the subject) and separated verbs, e.g. <u>**what does**</u> **it** <u>**do**</u>**?** <u>**does**</u> **it** <u>**do**</u> **. . .?**, cannot be used in statements, even when a larger sentence includes a question in it.

A useful analogy can be a pencil box/pouch, a ring binder, a file folder, or any type of a container that includes smaller items in it. The main clause can include all sorts of items in it, such as noun (or adjective) clauses, but what is seen on the outside is the container and not its contents. So, when the larger "container" is a sentence, the entire structure is a sentence. Helping L2 writers to **learn to notice** their own errors in the word order and the verbs in embedded noun clauses can take the form of simple prompting: *Is this a question or a sentence? Is this a question? This is a sentence, right?*

TENSES IN NOUN CLAUSES

As has been mentioned throughout this book, the distinctions between conversational language and formal academic writing need to be explicitly addressed in teaching (Hinkel, 2002a, 2005, 2019).

> In English-speaking settings, most L2 learners have far greater exposure to conversational than to written academic discourse, and many structures that may be commonplace in casual interaction find their way into formal writing.

— *John **said** that he'**ll** call me tomorrow; ?Mary **told** me that she'**ll** be here at 8.*

Although the uses of the past and the future tenses with noun clauses is ubiquitous in conversation, this usage is not typically acceptable in formal written English (see also chapter 7).

> The usage of tenses in formal writing is highly conventionalized. A formal system of rules, also called the sequence of tenses, governs the uses of tenses in noun clauses.

Formal Sequence of Tenses in Noun Clauses

- When the **main verb is in the past tense**, then the **subordinate clause can only take past or present tenses**, e.g.

    - *The study **reported** that children between the ages of 8 and 12 **spent/spend** up to 8 hours a day on social media.*
    - *The survey **showed** that over 85% of those aged 14–17 **had** cell phones.*

- **Future markers** and **modal verbs** undergo some of the following changes. These are only about half of all the rules (also called "reported speech" or "indirect speech").

  o The future marker _**will**_ is turned into _**would**_ or _**would have**_ in <u>negative</u> with the meaning of _**did not . . .**_, e.g.

    – _He **said** that he **would study** for the test_ [and he did].
    – _He **said** he **would have studied** for the test_ [he actually did not].

  o The modal _**can**_ turns into _**could**_ in positive constructions, and _**could have**_ in negative also with the meaning of _**did not . . .**_, e.g.

    – _She **told** me that she **could help** me._
    – _She **told** me that she **could have helped** me_ [but she did not].

  o _**May**_ becomes _**might**_, e.g. _They **mentioned** that they **might come**._
  o _**Should**_ and _**might**_ do not change, e.g. _We **said** that we **should/might go**._
  o _**Must**_ (obligation) becomes _**had to**_, e.g. _They **told** us that we **had to go**._

Given these rules, it is not difficult to see how implementing them may become hairy indeed. However, the conventionalized uses of tenses in academic writing can be used to L2 writers' advantage because the range of tenses and aspects in written prose is far more limited than that in conversational discourse (or most grammar books).

> In academic writing, the large number of rules and specific verb conversions in noun clauses can be simplified to a great extent.

A Practical Simplification for Using Tenses

(1) If the **main** clause is in the **past**, the **noun** clause can take the **present** or **past** tenses.
(2) The **present tense is far easier to use in both main and noun clauses** than to change verbs to past tense forms (no positive/negative worries).

The Past Tense

Researchers **noted** that the experiment **did** <u>not include</u> a control group.

The Present Tense

> Researchers **note**Ø that the experiment **does** not include a control group.

Both the past tense and the present tense constructions are perfectly usable, although their meanings differ slightly.

The Gist

- Whenever possible, the easiest academic way to go is to stick to the present tense in both the main and the noun clauses.
- Exceptions – case studies and historical or biographical contexts, which are specifically "flagged" for the past tense, e.g. past time adverb phrases.

In the following two examples, the present tense and the past tense in the main and noun clauses work equally well.

The Past Tense

> — *Nancy Smith* **showed** *that shyness* **represented** *a relative, culture-bound label. She* **found** *that no differences* **existed** *in the reactions of four-month-old babies.*

The Present Tense

> — *Nancy Smith* **shows** *that shyness* **represents** *a relative, culture-bound label. She* **finds** *that no differences* **exist** *in the reactions of four-month-old babies.*

> The flexibility of meanings and functions in the present tense makes it highly versatile and practical for L2 writing. Simple is as simple does.

In light of structural complexities in the uses of the noun clause, it is hardly surprising that even advanced L2 writers continue to make errors in these structures. Most importantly, what is needed for these students is practice, practice, and practice.

Action Point

The rigid rules of formality in academic writing apply to numerous language features that include vocabulary and grammar choices. For instance, clear distinctions between the levels of formality can be highlighted in the teaching of reporting verbs, referring to sources, and presenting information. Due to the fact that most L2 learners have a great deal of exposure to conversational language, informal vocabulary often finds its way into academic writing.

> <u>**Informal Reporting Verbs:**</u> *answer, ask, chat, feel, guess, look at, pass on, pick up/out, say, see, stick to, talk, tell, think, want to know, wonder*
>
> <u>**Other Informal Verbs:**</u> *bother, check (out), come down, come up with, deal with, dislike, disturb, get, go down/through/up, keep, like, love, pull down/up, skip, throw, try*

The differences between **formal and informal language** should be addressed in teaching and explicitly identified. Here are examples of a few sentences that can be discussed in terms of language informality or formality in academic writing.

- *The author says that many second language writers hate learning vocabulary, and it bothers language teachers.*
- *The researcher feels that learning to write academic essays takes a lot of work for all students.*
- *Copernicus knew that the Earth revolved around the Sun, but his contemporaries didn't believe him.*
- *In Wisconsin and other Great Lake states, snow storms can bring water in the form of snow, and the farmers there love it even though it closes the roads.*
- *At a recent meeting, the proponents and opponents of conservation were angry, and they *are argued, as the report tells us.*

Talking Shop

In English, the pronoun **_that_** can serve many masters and do many things, and for this reason, its functions are typically very confusing.

(1) The easiest form of *that* is **demonstrative**, as in *this*, *that*, and *the other*.

   That article was on achievement and learned motives.

To identify the demonstrative *that*, it can be simply replaced by *this* or *the other*.

(2) The least useful – an optional – form of *that* introduces noun clauses but does not have a function in them.

   *The author thinks **that** the earth is flat.*

In this sentence, *that* can be simply omitted without any damage.

   The author thinks Ø the earth is flat.

In noun clauses that occupy the entire subject position, the introductory *that* cannot be omitted:

   That students have trouble with noun clauses is understandable.

(3) The third form of *that* is probably the most complex. It replaces subject or object noun phrases in **adjective clauses** and, thus, takes over the functions and the grammatical features of the noun phrases it replaces.

   *Social interaction **that** is found in many human activities is key to socialization.*

The pronoun *that* as the subject is easy to identify because it is immediately followed by the sentence verb. When *that* is not followed by the sentence predicate, it is the object of the adjective clause.

   *Emotions **that** people are not willing to discuss include aggression and envy.*

In this example, *that* is the verb object of the adjective clause: it is followed by the subject *people* and the verb *are*. When that is the subject or the object of the adjective clause, it cannot be merely dropped, as is the case with *that* in noun clauses. Without it, the sentence would be ungrammatical.

Chapter Summary

Subordinate clauses of all types represent advanced syntactic constructions. These clauses are essential and highly frequent in academic writing. Subordinate constructions can be complicated and error-prone.

- **Adverb clauses** are probably the easiest subordinate clauses for L2 writers to master. They express a variety of contextual relationships that refer to time, condition, cause, and concession.

  o Adverb clauses are separate from the main clause of a sentence, and contain supplemental information to the primary information in the main clause.

- **Adjective clauses** perform the same function as adjectives and adjective phrases. But where single-word adjectives precede the nouns they describe, adjective clauses follow the nouns. Adjective clauses can be used to modify practically any type of noun or noun phrase, and the relative pronouns *that*, *who*, and *which* replace the noun that the adjective clause modifies.

  o Adjective clauses are easier when the relative pronoun is the subject in the clause. When the relative pronoun is the object, the relative pronoun needs to be moved to the beginning of the clause, and the object noun is omitted.

- **Noun clauses** are probably the most common type of subordinate construction, but, unfortunately, they are also the most structurally complex. In addition to embedding simple sentences as clauses in the subject or object position, converting **wh-** questions and **yes/no** questions into statements requires complex grammatical operations that are not for the squeamish.

Strategies and Tactics for Teaching and Teaching Activities

Teaching Activities

The exercises and extended teaching activities are designed to help students improve their use of subordinate clauses for academic writing. The practice with complex sentences can take place with writing-from-readings, as is typically required in college/university academic assignments.

Short or long readings can be chosen depending on students' interests and proficiency levels: articles from news sources or professional journals, or reviews of books, movies, games, or, say, electronics. Alternatively, the teacher can select the articles.

- If students choose their own readings, an approximate word count should be specified, e.g. 150–200 words.
- To count an approximate number of words in a text, the number of words in the first line (say, 13 words) is multiplied by the number of lines (say, 10 lines), for about 130 words total (13 x 10 =130 words).

A Caveat. A common complaint is "But I couldn't find a suitable/interesting/good article." Usually, such issues are easy to counter if the teacher has a small stock of articles – possibly saved from previous classes.

The learning goals of the teaching suggestions and activities presented below are to work with sources and data, as well as use complex sentences, reporting verbs, and evaluative adjectives.

- Focusing on reporting verbs and their contextual meanings that establish the writer's position.
- Identifying the author's position in the opinions, arguments, and points of others.
- Academically evaluating arguments and positions in text.

All these exercises can be assigned as individual or group tasks, or homework with a follow-up in-class discussion.

Reviewing the Reviewer

- **Reporting verbs** and **evaluative adjectives** (see also chapters 8 and 9) can be organized into groups, such as <u>Positive – Negative, Supporting – Rejecting, or Neutral</u>. An example of a starter list is presented below, e.g. *state, assert, claim, suggest, indicate*.
- Then, students add their own verbs and adjectives to supplement the lists, e.g. Positive Reporting Verbs, Positive Evaluative Adjectives, Negative Reporting Verbs, or Negative Evaluative Adjectives.

- In pairs or individually, students write evaluations of their readings. This task can be assigned several times throughout the term or a couple of times per week when the lists are continually expanded to increase vocabulary range.
- Extended Practice. The same task can also include identifying the implications or possible outcomes of the argument/position expressed in the article/review.

Here's an example of a starter list for students to begin making their own.

Positive Reporting Verbs	Negative Reporting Verbs	Neutral Reporting Verbs
agree	deny	maintain
confirm	claim	demonstrate
contend	allege	conclude

Discussing and Analyzing Data

> This activity can take 2–3 hours of class time and can be carried out in intermittent phases with gaps of 1 to 3 days between phases.

- Descriptions and explanations of data in graphs, charts, tables, or texts works very well for this writing practice.
- The data should deal with issues that most students find useful and interesting. A few examples of data sources:
    o The US Census website (www.census.gov) contains a wealth of information and data on immigrants and immigration, education, men and women, college enrollments, cost of housing in a particular area of the country, or food.
    o Sociological and demographic data can also be useful for practicing academic vocabulary in writing (see chapters 4, 8, and 9).
- Discussing the data in graphs or texts **without explanations** may be helpful before students begin writing.

Example #1 – Data Points and Discussion Prompts
The graph shows that annual temperature variations in London are far less dramatic than in Toronto or Sydney. The winters are not as cold, and

the summers are relatively mild. Clearly, since Sydney is located in Australia, January and February there are the height of the summer. What can be the reasons for the mild English temperatures? Why are January and February hot in Australia? What can be said about the Toronto weather?

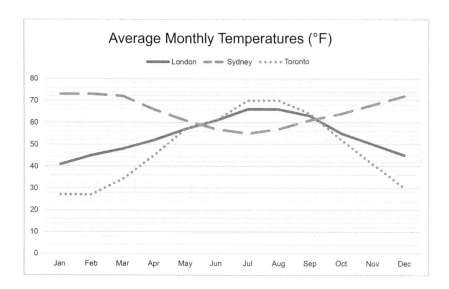

Example #2 – Data Points and Disparities

Based on the temperature graph, it hardly ever freezes in London with the low temperatures declining only as far as 40°F. The London summers seem very different from those in Toronto when the highs rise above 70°, and Sydney appears to have similar highs during the winter months. In addition, in Sydney, the low temperatures in July and August do not exceed greatly the London highs during the same months. Approximately 30° or 40° differences can be observed between the summer and the winter months in Toronto.

INSTRUCTIONS FOR STUDENTS

<u>Assignment Part 1</u>

(a) Discuss and analyze the data from a practical or business perspective. Several suggestions are presented for you to consider.

  o How can the weather data be valuable for regional economists and government agencies?

For example, a great deal of electricity is required for air-conditioning in large cities. How can increased residential and commercial power consumption affect electricity prices and so on?

   o   How can the temperature data be useful for employers in tourism, car rental agencies, and hotel management?
   o   How can conference organizers or meeting planners use the temperature data in their jobs?
   o   What marketing plans can ice-cream producers and distributors make based on the weather data?

(b)   Use some or all of the following verbs (or any other types of verbs) to help you construct your text. Do not forget important modal verbs such as *can, may,* or *might* (see chapter 12).

assume	conclude	conjecture	deduce	demonstrate
expect	explain	hypothesize	illustrate	imply
infer	mean	note	reason	report
reveal	show	suggest	suppose	

Assignment Part 2

(c)   When you are finished with data discussion, exchange your proposed analysis with another pair of students. Read the alternative proposed by other students and write a brief evaluation.

   o   What can you say about the discussion offered by another student/ pair of students?
   o   What good points are noted in the alternative discussion?
   o   What possible points or issues does an alternative presentation overlook?
   o   What broad conclusions can be made about the data, if both your own and alternative explanations are combined to write a general overview?

(d)   Do not forget some of the useful evaluative adjectives and adverbs (see chapter 9):

Positive Evaluative Adjectives and Adverbs

accurate(-ly)	careful(-ly)	clear(-ly)	correct(-ly)
good/well	important(-ly)	impressive(-ly)	interesting(-ly)
right(-ly)	significant(-ly)	special(-ly)	thorough(-ly)

Negative Evaluative Adjectives

inaccurate(-ly)	inconclusive(-ly)	limited(-ly)	minor
misguided(-ly)	questionable(-ly)	unconvincing(-ly)	unsatisfactory(-ly)

Error Correction and Editing

The goal of this activity is to help students to articulate and explain their editing of text.

INSTRUCTIONS FOR STUDENTS

- Correct the errors and explain what you think needs to be corrected.
- Some of the text needs to be completely re-written. In this case, provide possible re-writes.

Text #1

The biologists and zoologists who study the environment where we live in they are called environmentalists. But in addition, social scientists who work in sociology, education, and public science, they also examine how do we talk about environment. Our thinking reveals more about what don't we understand about nature than about what can we count on as we study. How to carry out the effective advocacy approach. I will take an environmental issue which is solid waste management to make an example to utter clearly how does the process of environmental education work on it.

Solid waste management defining as that an area of study associate with the control of generation, storage, collection, and disposal in a manner that are in accord with the principles of economics, public health, conservation, and other environmental consideration, and that are also responsibly to the public. Solid waste management includes administrative functions involving in the whole solution to the problems of solid waste thrust the community by its inhabitants. Because it is important for our future and for the life.

According to EPA Journal, last year, it provided a general introduction to solid waste management and served as a way for understanding. To solve specific solid waste problems, the various elements that are combining in what is usually knows as a solid waste management system. In most cities, a solid waste management system that is existed for collection of solid waste. In below, these are relationships among four functional elements and solid waste concerns.

(From a student paper on the importance of solid waste management for the environment)

Text #2

The reason of I mention the culture of poverty can be relate with work incentive although different opinion for different people. In labor economics and with public assist that is providing in the field of social work, the author of the article states that as a dominating social perspective seen by higher social class on the poor people.

Because the brightest focus about this matter is that was put in our society in the dilemma that we should provide economic assist with the poor who are not working or not. Another matter that we should look for it further is if the culture of poverty is really existed in them and is maintaining generation by generation.

(From a student assignment on the culture of poverty)

What is Your Point?

For writing-from-reading practice, paraphrasing and summarizing can also be included with high-intermediate or advanced L2 writers (see also appendix to chapter 11).

- If students find their own readings, they should be required to submit their work together with the copies of their articles.
- If the work is done in class, an additional copy should be also handed in together with the written assignment.

An Alternative. Readings can consist of two articles on a similar topic, particularly when some "hot" issue is discussed in the media or on news sites, and articles are relatively easy to find.

> A variety of sentence stems for summary-writing is presented in the appendix to this chapter.

INSTRUCTIONS FOR STUDENTS

Assignment Part 1

(1) Read the article, identify the author's thesis and the main points that support the thesis. Underline them.
(2) Then paraphrase of the author's main points, point by point. Be sure to use your own words and avoid those used in the article. Here's an example.

A Skeleton Summary

- *The author's main point is that . . .*
- *The article also states/notes/observes that . . .*
- *In addition, the author believes/thinks that . . .*
- *The conclusion of the article is that . . .*

Assignment Part 2

(3) Decide which of the author's points are valid and which are not.
(4) Then explain your support or disagreement with each of the author's points.
(5) Do not neglect to make your arguments balanced by acknowledging the argument validity even though you may disagree with a particular point.
(6) Expand on your *Skeleton Summary* and give it some argumentation muscle.

Here's an example.
A Muscular Summary and Solid Argumentation

- o *The author's main point is that . . . . Although I can see her point, xxx is not the only issue in yyy.*
- o *The article also states/notes/observes that . . . . I also think/believe that zzz.*
- o *In addition, the author believes/thinks that . . . . She supports her position based on xxx, but she may remember that zzz.*
- o *The conclusion of the article is that . . . . Other authors/reports/articles state that . . . . In my opinion, the author may need to consider that . . . .*

An Alternative. Students can exchange articles and do it all again, Round 2, based on an article chosen by their classmates.

Then, when both Summaries and Argumentations are completed, students can compare (1) how they identified the article author's main point(s), and (2) what points in the article they chose to support or argue against.

Endnotes

1 The pronoun **whom** is required only when it follows a preposition, e.g. **to whom**, **for whom**, **about whom**. In all other cases, **who** would be appropriate (Leech & Svartvik, 2003; Quirk, et al., 1985).

2 In some languages, such as Arabic, Hebrew, or Amharic, the repetition of the object noun or pronoun is required, and L2 writers who are speakers of these languages may make this type of error particularly frequently.

3 In many nontonal languages, such as Russian, Ukrainian, and Arabic, questions are into-nation marked, e.g. *You are tired* ↓ – a falling tone for statements, and *You are tired* ↑ – a rising tone for questions.

Further Reading

Hinkel, E. (2019). A short preamble: A bit of history in the life of phrases and multiword units. In E. Hinkel (Ed.), *Teaching essential units of language: Beyond single-word vocabulary* (pp. 1–16). New York, NY: Routledge.

A brief overview of historical perspectives and classifications of idiomatic phrases and expressions in English, as well as their uses in conversations, speaking, writing, and teaching. For L2 learners, conventionalized recurrent phrases and constructions have almost always presented an area of difficulty. In speech and writing, phrases and expres-sions are typically culture-specific with implicit references to abstract or metaphorical constructs that may or may not exist in learners' natal cultures or first languages.

Nation, I.S.P & McAlister, J. (2021). *Teaching ESL/EFL reading and writing* (2nd edn). New York, NY: Routledge.

Based on well-researched principles of language teaching and learning, this user-friendly guide for in-service and pre-service teachers provides a broad range of strategies and tech-niques for helping learners develop their reading and writing skills. The teaching principles are organized around the four instructional strands: meaning-focused input, meaning-focused output, language-focused learning, and fluency development. Drawing on research findings, teachers can design well-rounded language courses in reading and writing.

Richards, J. & Reppen, R. (2016). 12 principles of grammar instruction. In E. Hinkel (Ed.), *Teaching grammar to speakers of other languages* (pp. 151–170). New York, NY: Routledge.

Learning and using grammar effectively applies directly to making grammar and vocabulary choices work together to create texts that are well suited for various con-texts and that accomplish different functions. The objective of grammar teaching is to develop learners' awareness of the types of texts and the functions of grammar within them. Hands-on instruction can expand the grammatical options that learners make use of when they work to produce spoken and written texts.

References

Biber, D. (1988). *Variation across speech and writing*. Cambridge: Cambridge University Press.

Biber, D., Johansson, S., Leech, G., Conrad, S., & Finegan, E. (1999). *Longman grammar of spoken and written English*. Harlow: Pearson.

Carter, R. & McCarthy, M. (2006). *Cambridge grammar of English: A comprehensive guide*. Cambridge: Cambridge University Press.

Celce-Murcia, M. & Olshtain, E. (2000). *Discourse and context in language teaching*. New York, NY: Cambridge University Press.

Celce-Murcia, M. & Olshtain, E. (2005). Discourse-based approaches: A new framework for second language teaching and learning. In E. Hinkel (Ed.), *Handbook of research in second language teaching and learning* (pp. 729–742). New York, NY: Routledge.

DeCarrico, J. (2000). *The structure of English: Studies in form and function for language teaching.* Ann Arbor, MI: University of Michigan Press.

Ferris, D. (2011). *Treatment of error in second language student writing* (2nd edn). Ann Arbor, MI: University of Michigan Press.

Frodesen, J. (2014). Grammar in second language writing. In M. Celce-Murcia, D. Brinton, & M. Snow (Eds.), *Teaching English as a second or foreign language* (4th edn) (pp. 238–253). Boston, MA: Cengage.

Hamp-Lyons, L. (1991). Reconstructing academic writing proficiency. In L. Hamp-Lyons (Ed.), *Assessing second language writing* (pp. 127–153). Norwood, NJ: Ablex.

Hinkel, E. (2002a). *Second language writers' text.* New York, NY: Routledge.

Hinkel, E. (2002b). Teaching grammar in writing classes: Tenses and cohesion. In E. Hinkel & S. Fotos (Eds.), *New perspectives on grammar teaching in second language classrooms* (pp. 181–198). New York, NY: Routledge.

Hinkel, E. (2003). Adverbial markers and tone in L1 and L2 students' writing. *Journal of Pragmatics, 35*(2), 208–231.

Hinkel, E. (2005). Analyses of L2 text and what can be learned from them. In E. Hinkel (Ed.), *Handbook of research in second language teaching and learning* (pp. 615–628). New York, NY: Routledge.

Hinkel, E. (2011). What research on second language writing tells us and what it doesn't. In E. Hinkel (Ed.), *Handbook of research in second language teaching and learning, Volume 2* (pp. 523–538). New York, NY: Routledge.

Hinkel, E. (2015). *Effective curriculum for teaching L2 writing: Principles and techniques.* New York, NY: Routledge.

Hinkel, E. (2017). Prioritizing grammar to teach or not to teach: A research perspective. In E. Hinkel (Ed.), *Handbook of research in second language teaching and learning* (pp. 369–383). New York, NY: Routledge.

Hinkel, E. (2019). Teaching strategies and techniques: Collocations and multiword units. In E. Hinkel (Ed.), *Teaching essential units of language: Beyond single-word vocabulary* (pp. 107–133). New York, NY: Routledge.

Hoye, L. (1997). *Adverbs and modality in English.* London: Longman.

Hunston, S. (2011). *Corpus approaches to evaluation: Phraseology and evaluative language.* New York, NY: Routledge.

Leech, G., Rayson, P., & Wilson, A. (2001). *Word frequencies in written and spoken English.* London: Longman.

Leech, G. & Svartvik, J. (2003). *A communicative grammar of English* (3rd edn). London: Routledge.

Master, P. (2002). Relative clause reduction in technical research articles. In E. Hinkel & S. Fotos (Eds.), *New perspectives on grammar teaching second and foreign language classrooms* (pp. 201–231). New York, NY: Routledge.

Nation, P. (2013). *Learning vocabulary in another language* (2nd edn). Cambridge: Cambridge University Press.

Quirk, R., Greenbaum, S., Leech, G., & Svartvik, J. (1985). *A comprehensive grammar of the English language.* New York, NY: Longman.

Swales, J. & Feak, C. (2012). *Academic writing for graduate students* (3rd edn). Ann Arbor, MI: University of Michigan Press.

Tse, P., & Hyland, K. (2010). Claiming a territory: Relative clauses in journal descriptions. *Journal of Pragmatics, 42,* 1880–1889.

Appendix to Chapter 10

Reporting and Mental Process Verbs for Academic Writing

Frequent Academic Reporting Verbs

affirm	allege	argue	assert	assume	claim
contend	describe	discuss	examine	exemplify	explain
illustrate	imply	maintain	present	presume	reveal
state					

Other Academic Reporting Verbs

add	agree	allege	announce	assume	comment
concede	confirm	convey	deny	describe	discuss
examine	imply	mention	object	present	presume
promise	remark	report	reveal	say	suggest
write					

Mental Process and Belief Verbs Common in Academic Writing

accept	assume	believe	conclude	conjecture	consider
decide	deduce	deem	determine	doubt	establish
expect	forget	hold (the view that)	imply	infer	mean
note	presume	presuppose	prove	realize	reason
understand					

(Adapted from Quirk, et al., 1985)

Reporting Verbs and Noun Clause Phrases for Summaries

The author goes on to say/state/show that xxx.
The author further argues/explains/shows that . . .
The article further states that . . .
(Smith) also states/maintains/argues/asserts that . . .
(Smith) also believes/concludes/feels that . . .
The article/report concludes that . . .
In the second half of the article/report, (Johnson) presents xxx to show/ explain that . . .

(Adapted from Swales & Feak, 2012)

Academic Adjective Clause Stems and Phrases

Frequent Noun + Adjective Clause Phrases

Place			
area(s) where	area(s) in/to which	situation where	situation in/to which
point where	case(s) where	country where	conditions where
examples where			

Time			
time(s) when	time(s) in/at which	case(s) when	period(s) when

Other Frequent Noun + Adjective Clause Phrases

the way in which (the)	the ways in which	way in which the	such a way that
the extent to which (the)	extent to which the	the fact that the	the fact that it
the degree to which	and the extent to which the		

Academic Nouns Most Frequently Modified by **That**-Clauses
(in declining order, **_the fact that_** pattern)

fact	possibility	doubt	belief	assumption	idea
suggestion	conclusion	claim	grounds	view	sense
notion	hypothesis	observation	report	sign	

(Adapted from Nation, 2013)

Rhetorical Features of Text   **11**

Cohesion and Coherence

Overview

- Cohesive ties and lexical substitutions.
- Teaching text and discourse cohesion.
- Expanding the range: synonyms, near-synonyms, and general words.
- Phrase-level conjunctions and parallel structure.
- Sentence transitions and idea connectors.
- Complex prepositions.
- Clarifying and giving examples.
- Structures not to use or to use sparingly.
- Punctuation.

This chapter addresses a number of rhetorical features of L2 academic writing, largely focusing on those that specifically require attention in teaching. Various studies have found that in academic writing cohesion represents an essential characteristic of text and discourse flow, and constructing cohesive texts requires focused instruction (Dong, 1996; Hamp-Lyons, 2011; Hinkel, 2001a, 2002a, 2002b, 2003, 2011; Leki, Cumming, & Silva, 2008; Tadros, 1994).

In general, **cohesion** refers to the connectivity of ideas to create a unified flow. In writing and composition textbooks, cohesion can also refer to the ways of connecting sentences and paragraphs. Although the terms **cohesion** and **coherence** are often used together, they do not refer to the same properties of text and discourse. For example, the presence of an introduction, a thesis statement, rhetorical support, and a conclusion can create a coherent essay that is not necessarily cohesive (Carrell, 1982; Chafe, 1994; Scollon, Scollon, & Jones, 2012).

Cohesion usually refers to connections between sentences and paragraphs.

Coherence can also refer to the **logical** organization of discourse with all elements present and fitting together.

Since the 1970s, a great deal of research has been carried out into the effects of text features on discourse. Many studies have determined that the types of syntactic and lexical constructions used in text, as well as how and when they are used, alter the text's clarity, cohesion, formality or informality, and communicative effectiveness (Halliday & Hasan, 1976; van Dijk, 2009, 2010).

The descriptions of a text's qualities, however, are constructed in abstract terms, and it is not always possible to define text clarity, cohesion, or effectiveness with any degree of precision. Any two well-educated individuals may disagree (and often do) about whether a particular written text is clear, cohesive, or developed.

The rhetorical characteristics of academic text addressed in this chapter predominantly discuss matters of lexical (vocabulary) and semantic (meaning) cohesion, the grammar and discourse functions of phrase coordinators, sentence transitions, and the academic types of examples and L2 trouble spots. Numerous studies of L2 writing have identified the specific features of L2 text that can benefit from focused instruction.

Cohesive Ties and Lexical Substitution

The term "**cohesive ties**" (also called cohesive chains) was originally developed by Halliday and Hasan (1976) to explain how cohesive elements act to conjoin text from one sentence to the next. In the example below, a few cohesive chains span the entire text excerpt by connecting words and meanings: the first to the last mention of *automobile*, as well as added cohesion in *travel – distances – commuting, work – workplace – workforce*, and *center – decentralization*.

*The flexibility and speed afforded by **automobile travel** has contributed to urban forms vastly different from the dense and walking-oriented population **centers**. The **automobile**, among other forces, contributed to the **decentralization** of the workplace and greater physical **distances** between home and work. Many **automobile**-oriented landscapes include residential and commercial spaces not easily accessible by other means. The **automobile** is the predominant **commuting** mode for all metro areas, even those with comparatively low rates of **automobile travel**.*

(Adapted from www.census.gov/
library/publications.html)

Vocabulary substitutions can work to establish cohesion across several sentences. A lexical item can be replaced by a pronoun, a near synonym, or a **superordinate word** with a broad meaning that refer to an entire class of similar words (also called general words), e.g. *automobiles* for *cars, trucks and vans*, or *children* for *boys, girls, and infants*.

Here's another example with vocabulary cohesive ties and superordinates:[1]

  — *bicycling and walking – commuting activity – **these travel modes***
  — *walking – **pedestrian and bicycle travel** – foot traffic – walking and biking*
  — ***strategies – these efforts – changes – options***

  ***Bicycling and walking** make up a relatively small portion of **commuting activity**, but **these travel modes** play important roles in many local transportation systems. Several state and urban agencies have taken steps to promote **pedestrian and bicycle travel**. **Strategies** to accommodate **walking and biking** vary across communities, but may include sidewalk modifications, **foot-traffic** commercial centers, or **bicycle** lanes. **These efforts** reflect ongoing **changes** in infrastructure and travel **options** across the nation's dynamic transportation systems.*

Even in short texts, several cohesive chains and vocabulary connections can come into play without a great deal of overlap and interference.

By and large, vocabulary cohesion follows the predictable pattern of lexical substitutions, related word forms (e.g. **bicycle – biking**), near-synonyms, and general words.

Teaching Text Cohesion

The importance of lexical substitutions to expand the L2 writer's vocabulary range has been emphasized throughout this book. This section offers a few teaching techniques and tricks that have the goal of simplifying matters of text cohesion as much as they can be simplified without a great deal of damage.

An intelligent and intelligible system for teaching text cohesion to anyone was originally created by Joseph M. Williams in 1981 (Williams & Bizup, 2017). This system was based on a few highly useful and accessible principles.

The Essentials of Text Cohesion

(1) The **subject, topic,** or **familiar ideas go first** – at the beginning of a sentence. That is, first, what is **known** about the topic.
(2) If a few sentences have more than one topic, then the topics have to be consistent and hold together, e.g. ***commuting – biking and walking***, but not *****commuting – eating a sandwich**.
(3) The **newest and the most important idea goes to the end** of the sentence because it will be expanded upon in the next sentence.

A Few Caveats

- It is more difficult to begin a sentence well than to end it well.
- Two decisions have to be made at the outset:

   o What is known about the topic.
   o Which idea is the newest and the most important.

- The beginning of the sentence needs to be constructed carefully: the beginning of the sentence strongly sets up the reader's expectations about what follows.

The diagram below illustrates the organization of **old–new** information in a succession of several sentences. The first sentence starts with **known** information, for instance, a noun phrase that refers to the topic of the readings, or mentioned in the text or the title.

These techniques to accomplish the goals of constructing cohesive text are practical and straightforward (Williams & Bizup, 2017).

Building Sentences for Cohesion

(1) <u>Adverbs first</u> – to frame the sentence and connect it.

    (a) Preliminary contexts and evaluative adverbs, e.g. *in many ways, generally speaking, it is important to note that, perhaps*.

    (b) Then adverb connectors, and/or time and place adverbs, e.g. *in the 20th century, during the experiment, at the time of the Reformation, in Rome, in American social structure*.

(2) After the preliminaries, <u>the sentence</u> – what is already <u>known</u> and <u>the new information at the end</u>.

    (a) Sentence topics that are usually the grammatical subjects.

    (b) The rest of the sentence – new information about the topic.

Here's an example.

The Text

Sentence 1. *Called the world's most popular food, pizza has experienced growth in sales at both big chain and independent restaurants.* **Sentence 2.** *In addition, frozen and chilled pizza also reported growth.* **Sentence 3.** *Overall, on any given day, 13% of the US population aged 2 years and over consumes pizza.*

(www.ars.usda.gov)

The Analysis

Sentence 1 →

Adverbs First	Subject/Topic	New Information about the Topic
Called the world's most popular food,	***pizza***	*has experienced growth in sales at both big chain and independent restaurants.*

→ **Sentence 2** →

	Repeated/Old Info	
In addition,	*frozen and chilled **pizza***	*also reported growth.*

→ **Sentence 3** →

		Sticking to the Topic/New Info
Overall, on any given day,	*13% of the US population aged 2 years and over*	*consumes **pizza**.*

Sentence Building Techniques

(1) **Repeating short and specific sentence subjects/topics** creates a cohesive text, particularly in sentences with long predicate phrases, as in Sentence 1.

(2) For L2 writing, to simplify the construction of a cohesive chain, the next sentence should **repeat at least one word from the preceding sentence** or provide its lexical/semantic substitute, e.g. a near synonym or a pronoun.

(3) The third sentence similarly **repeats or substitutes one word from the second sentence** to create an identifiable cohesive chain.

For example, in the excerpt from a L2 text below, the cohesive chain is relatively easy to identify, and several **cohesive chains** are developed simultaneously without interfering with one another.

The Text

Coastal erosion [1] *is a problem throughout the United States, and it* [1] *occurs on the east coast and the west coast* [1]*. The coastal erosion* [1] *will directly influence the environment and society* [2] *in the coastal area* [1]*. Cities and villages* [2] *that* *are located in <u>coastal areas</u> [1] will experience <u>changes</u> [3] in the shape of the <u>shoreline</u> [1]. When <u>shorelines</u> [1] have <u>changed</u> [3] shapes, <u>fishing</u> [4] in tide pools and from boats will also need to become <u>different</u> [3]. So, the <u>local people</u> [2] who <u>make their living</u> [4] by <u>fishing</u> [4] will also have to <u>adjust</u> [3] their traditional ways of doing <u>their jobs</u> [4] every day.*

(From a student paper on People and
Environment: Coastal Erosion).

The Analysis

Cohesion →

<u>Chain</u> [1] →   *coastal erosion* → *it* and *then* → *east coast and west coast* → *coastal erosion* → *coastal area* → *coastal areas* → (related & repeated →) *shoreline/shorelines.*

<u>Chain</u> [2] →   *environment and society* → *cities and villages* → *local people.*

<u>Chain</u> [3] →   *changes* → *changed* → *different* → *adjust*

<u>Chain</u> [4] →   *fishing* → (related → *local people*) → *make their living* → *fishing* → *their traditional ways* → *their jobs*

Although the text is slightly repetitive, it is highly cohesive and unified.

> The technique of repeating a word from the immediately preceding sentence is easy to use for L2 writers at most levels of language proficiency.

Enumerative "Catch-all" Nouns

Much research on text cohesion emphasizes the key role of general – superordinate – words with such broad and vague meanings that they can function as lexical substitutes in a range of contexts, e.g. *fact, factor, reason, effect, explanation, result*.

Analyses of written academic corpora in English have found that a vast majority of general words are in fact nouns. In research, these are also called **enumerative nouns**, shell nouns, signaling nouns, carrier nouns, or advance/ retrospective labels (Hunston & Francis, 2000; Mahlberg, 2005; Tadros, 1994).

> Enumerative nouns are far more common in academic than other types of writing, and many are highly frequent.

Frequent Academic Catch-all Nouns

approach	aspect	category	challenge	change
characteristic	circumstance	class	difficulty	event
experience	fact	facet	factor	feature
form	issue	item	manner	method
phase	problem	process	purpose	reason
result	stage	subject	system	task
tendency	topic	trend	type	

These nouns can be very useful establishing cohesive chains in academic text:

> *approach – method, subject – topic, problem – difficulty, tendency – trend*

> Catch-all nouns can be employed interchangeably as lexical substitutes for other nouns with more specific meanings.

A few examples from student papers illustrate the usefulness of enumerative "catch-all" nouns in text.

> *The author mentions pollution, water shortage, and loss of soil **issues** concerning the threat of overpopulation. In his article, he mostly talks about the environment but does not mention the health and nutrition **problems**. The health **challenges** are created when there are too many people in the world.*

> Lexical ties/substitutions: ***issues – problems – challenges***

> *For a long time, philosophers have been discussing the **factors** that create a happy marriage. We find **characteristics** of happy marriages in the work of Aquinas, Singer, and sociologist Wallerstein, who argue about the **aspects** of marriage to show which ones are happy and which ones are not and why.*

> Lexical ties/substitutions: ***factors – characteristics – aspects***

> *Americans are getting more and more uninterested in politics, and political scientists and educators have been trying to understand the **trend** that Americans do not care about politics. In my country, people think that they are powerless*

*to control the political system, and they don't care about politics either. So, American researchers have been studying the **tendency** that many people do not even go to vote.*

<u>Lexical ties:</u> ***trend – tendency***

On the whole, the number of enumerative nouns in English probably does not exceed a hundred, and learning them is well worth the time and the effort because of the breadth of their meanings and their flexible contextual uses.

Demonstrative Pronouns

Demonstrative pronouns, such as ***this, that, these***, and ***those***, are also a prominent feature of cohesive discourse.[2] Demonstratives can be effectively used to connect nouns and ideas across sentences.

Similar to articles or possessive pronouns, demonstrative pronouns belong in the class of determiners and play a prominent role in text cohesion. Demonstratives have referential functions in written English (Halliday & Hasan, 1976), that is, they "point" to particular objects or events discussed in earlier text. There are several functions of demonstratives in discourse,

and these pronouns are often ambiguous in their referential and determinative properties (Quirk, et al., 1985; Swales, 2005). Because demonstrative pronouns are relatively easy to use, L2 writers frequently employ too many of them in their writing (Hinkel, 2001a, 2002a, 2015). For this reason, the limitations of demonstratives as a cohesive and "pointing" device need to be addressed in teaching (see chapter 6).

Phrase-level Conjunctions and the Parallel Structure

Officially, the function of conjunctions is to mark connections between ideas in discourse and text, and conjunctions are the most ubiquitous and probably the most lexically simple means of developing text cohesion (Halliday & Hasan, 1976; Swales & Feak, 2012).

> Among the various types of conjunctions, coordinating conjunctions in particular determine a parallel relationship of ideas and syntactic units.

*According to a smartphone-user study, 95 percent of "mobile searchers" have used their smartphone to look for local information. The most popular topic accessed was <u>weather</u>, followed by <u>local restaurants, businesses</u>, <u>general local news</u>, <u>sports scores/updates</u>, <u>traffic **and** transportation</u>, <u>local coupons, discounts</u>, **and** <u>news alerts</u>.*

(Adapted from https://transition.fcc.gov/osp/
inc-report/INoC-5-Mobile.pdf)

Unofficially, however, coordinating conjunctions can be used to make sentences of practically any length one wishes. Here's an example.

*Some people seem to disagree with some of the aspects of advertising because they feel that some advertisements are too dangerous for their children, **and** one of the examples is alcohol advertisement, **but** according to the advertisers, the purpose of the advertisers is to attract more customers, **and** unique and attractive advertisements will lead people to buying more products, goods, **and** services, **and** companies attract their consumers by advertising in magazines **or** newspapers **or** TV, **and** most advertisements are shown on TV, especially*

*during breaks of sports events **and** popular shows, **and** the customers can see these advertisements **and** find out about new products.*
(From a student paper on social impacts of advertising)

Parallel phrases can operate at multiple levels, for example, ***traffic and transportation*** are parallel nouns that are a part of a much larger parallel construction in ***local restaurants, businesses, general local news, sports scores/ updates, traffic and transportation**, local coupons, discounts, and news alerts.* Similarly, the phrase ***coupons, discounts, and news alerts*** consists of parallel nouns that are a part of a longer noun phrase.

Coordinating conjunctions – most frequently **and**, **but**, **yet**, **so** – can establish parallel relationships between and among virtually any types of syntactic units: nouns, pronouns, verbs, adjectives, adverbs, phrases, and sentences.

Two simple parallel sentences or two subordinate clauses can also be conjoined into parallel constructions (see also chapter 4 for punctuation rules). Here are a couple of examples.

o   Parallel Simple Sentences

*The cellular phone was invented at Motorola in 1973, **and** it became commercially available in the United States a decade later.*

o   Parallel Subordinate Clauses

*Cicero adopted the Stoic belief that natural law governs the universe **and** that all belong to a common humanity.*

The flexibility of the coordinating conjunctions that allows them to conjoin practically any types of parallel words, phrases, or sentences is unquestionably a wonderful characteristic. However, it is this very characteristic that can cause much turmoil among the parallel syntactic elements, when sentences do not seem to end.

Another problem with coordinators is that, as has been mentioned, they are by far the most common and simple of all cohesive devices in English, and no matter how long one's sentences are, they do not fool many people into thinking that their author is a sophisticated writer.

Corpus analyses of spoken and written English have determined that *and* is one of the most frequent words and that it occurs at the rate of approximately 27,000 times per million words. *But* and *so* are also fairly prevalent with the rates of approximately 5,000 occurrences each (Leech, Rayson, & Wilson, 2001). Coordinating conjunctions are particularly common when they conjoin parallel phrases and simple sentences, while *but* is **least frequent in academic text**.

> In academic writing, slightly over 30% of all occurrences of *and* conjoin simple sentences, but the large majority connect parallel phrases.

When it comes to developing cohesion between sentences in formal academic text, employing coordinating conjunctions may not be the most impressive way to proceed. In fact, as has been mentioned, *and, but*, and *so* are greatly overused in L2 writing to not-so-good effect (Hinkel, 2001a, 2002a, 2017). Simply including coordinating conjunctions in the text without connecting meanings of sentences and phrases results in a simple chaining of ideas and a fragmented writing style (Chafe, 1985, 1994).

However, the conjunction *or* finds many more uses in academic writing than in other types of text mostly because academic definitions, explanations, and discussions often provide descriptions of alternatives and options.

Correlative conjunctions, such as *both . . . and, either . . . or*, and *neither . . . nor*, though widely popular in grammar textbooks are actually rare in any types of discourse, including spoken and/or written (Leech, Rayson, & Wilson, 2001). For instance, Biber, et al. (1999) found *nor* to be far less common than all other coordinators in academic prose. In addition, according to their analysis, *both . . . and* occur with the frequency rates of 0.1%, *either . . . or* with the rates of 0.05%, and *neither . . . nor* hardly at all.

The Rigidity of Parallel Structure

Using coordinating conjunctions that develop cohesion between sentences and sentence elements is not without pitfalls. L2 written text often contains various parallel structure errors that are actually relatively easy to teach because parallel sentence elements are highly regular and predictable in their rigidity.

Parallel Structure with Coordinating Conjunctions

- Identical or repeated sentence elements are omitted.
- Coordinated elements are conjoined – **and, or, but**.

(1)   ?We measured   <u>the thickness of the bar</u>   **before**   <u>applying the solvent,</u>

and
<u>we measured</u>   <u>the thickness</u>   **after**   <u>applying the solvent.</u>

Repeated Elements: The subject, the verb, and the object, as well as the
gerund **applying the solvent** – following the preposition **after**.

(2)   ??We measured the thickness of the bar   **before** applying the solvent,

and . . .   Ø   **after . . .**   Ø

(3)   We measured the thickness of the bar   **before and after** applying the
solvent.

It is possible to think of these repeated elements as simplifying a basic alge-
braic expression $2a + 2b = 2(a + b)$, that is, common elements between the
two sentences are placed at the beginning of the sentence and apply equally
to all subsequent elements. Here are a few additional examples.

can be measured and **can be** increased   →   can be measured and . . .
                                                            increased

*the **metal** spoon and **the metal** bowl   →   the metal spoon and . . .
                                                            bowl

large factories, wholesalers, and **big** retailers   →   large factories, wholesal-
                                                            ers, and retailers

> Coordinating conjunctions can conjoin **series** of elements that have
> to be of the same type, e.g. nouns or noun phrases, adjectives or
> adjective phrases, verbs or verb phrases, or prepositional phrases.

The term **parallel structure** refers to "a string" of elements that are similar to beads in a necklace: they can be a little bit different but not dramatically so. Several examples from authentic texts are presented below (adapted from www.faa.gov/about/history/brief_history/;www.nps.gov/articles/modern-aviation.htm).

o   Parallel noun phrases in the subject and object positions.

   −   *Community size, design, infrastructure, and climate influence the availability, attractiveness, and affordability of various transportation modes.*

o   Parallel verb phrases – both in the past tense.

   −   *Charles Lindbergh flew nonstop from New York to Paris and touched off an enormous surge of interest in aviation.*

o   Parallel adjectives in a noun phrase and parallel predicate adjectives.

   −   *Early aviation remained a dangerous and difficult business, and fatal accidents were frequent and routine.*

o   Parallel nouns phrases and prepositional phrases.

   −   *The magnetic compass was one of the first flight instruments together with a wind meter, a map, and a stop watch.*
   −   *However, the compass was a necessity for flying over the terrain without recognizable landmarks, during night time, or over water.*

> If the string of parallel elements consists of more than two phrases, commas are used to separate them.
>
> The conjunction, **and**, **but**, **or**, comes before the last item. This is how readers know that they have arrived at the last item in the string.

*The Wright brothers were two American aviators who **invented, engineered, built, refined, and flew** the world's first successful airplane. Although not the first to build experimental aircraft, the Wright brothers were the first to invent **aircraft controls, steering, and the three-axes model** that made fixed-wing powered flight possible.*

> In sentences with parallel noun clauses – or more rarely adjective clauses – clause markers *(e.g. that, who, which)* must be retained even when they are identical in form and function.
>
> Parallel subordinate clauses are marked as clauses by means of these subordinators.

Here are a couple of examples:

o   Parallel nouns clauses.

  – *Benjamin Franklin's experiments demonstrated **that** lightning was static electricity, **that** the electric charge was conducted by metal, **and that** the charge could be safely conducted into the ground.*

o   Parallel nouns clauses and noun phrases.

  – *Charles Lindbergh's flight proved **that** air travel was possible, **that** commercial aviation had a viable future, **and that** the primary obstacle to long-distance aviation was not the technology **but** public opinion.*

Usually parallel noun clauses occur following reporting verbs, e.g. *caution, demonstrate, holds, mention, note, prove, state*, and in general, in these and other contexts, parallel clauses are not very common (see also chapter 8). In L2 prose, parallel nouns clauses may be particularly rare (Hinkel, 2002a, 2017).

Typical Errors in Parallel Structures

Typical errors found with the parallel structure largely involve similar problems when their parallel elements – head words or phrases – belong to different types and/or parts of speech. In most cases, they can be easy to correct and explain.

Trouble Spot #1

Faulty Parallelisms: Infinitives with gerunds (*-ing* nouns, *reading, writing, listening*) and other verb phrase elements.

Example trouble-spot sentences:

> *The article describes how today young people <u>do not like</u> **reading** but **to play** computer games.*
>
> *Many experts insist on **discussing** <u>the types of language tests</u> **and** **to review** <u>their advantages and disadvantages</u>.*

Teaching Tip

The errors in these two sentence are very similar:

- o   *reading* is not parallel with *to play*.
- o   *discussing* does not align with *to review*.

1) The coordinating conjunctions have to be located – *but* in the first sentence and *and* in the second.
2) Then the forms of the two parallel elements joined by the conjunction have to be made identical:

- o   *reading – but – playing.*
- o   *discussing – and – reviewing.*

Trouble Spot #2

Un-parallel nouns, noun phrases, and prepositional phrases.

Example trouble-spot sentences:

> *Pascal was a <u>philosopher,</u> law <u>scholar, educator, scientist,</u> **and** <u>he studied mathematics</u>.*
>
> *A solar cell is an electrical device that converts the energy of light directly <u>into electricity</u> **and** <u>don't worry about using it up</u>.*

Teaching Tip

In the first sentence, the series of nouns, **philosopher, scholar, educator,** are not parallel to the sentence **he studied mathematics**. The elements in the parallel phrase have to be grammatically similar, that is, nouns.

- o   *he studied mathematics* → *mathematician*

In the second sentence, the construction is a little more complicated: the prepositional phrase *into electricity* is not parallel to the sentence *don't worry about using it up*.

(1) To make the structures parallel, first the conjunction has to be located – _and_.

(2) Then the elements that need to be parallel are identified:

   o   A prepositional phrase *into electricity*.
   o   The sentence *don't worry about using it up*.

(3) The sentence *don't worry about using it up* has to become a prepositional phrase, as well: *without [preposition] + worrying +about using it up*.

Trouble Spot #3

Un-Parallel Simple Sentences in a Compound Sentence.

Example trouble-spot sentence:

   For the public, this definition is obscure, **and** exists the belief that engineers are technical people who don't have much knowledge in anything.

Teaching Tip

In this sentence, the second construction ***exists the belief*** is a sentence without the subject that attempts to be parallel to the complete simple sentence ***this definition is obscure***.

The sentences do not align because the second sentence does not have a subject:

o   *This definition is obscure.*
o   *   ø   exists the belief . . .

Two corrections are possible: **there exists [a] belief that** or **many believe that . . .**

Trouble Spot #4

Un-parallel adjectives, noun + noun modifiers, and **be**-verbs with activity verbs.

Example trouble-spot sentence:

> *In <u>urban</u> **and** <u>high-expense</u> settings, a proper treatment of wastewater <u>is necessary</u> **and** <u>preserve</u> a healthy environment.*

Teaching Tip

The sentence contains two different parallelism errors:

(a) Modifiers – **urban and high expense** – do not form very good parallels because one is an adjective and the other one is a noun. The phrase **high-expense** can become **highly expensive** (or simply **expensive**).

(b) **Be**-verbs with predicative adjectives – **necessary** – do not get along with activity verbs, e.g. **read**, **write**, **preserve** (see chapter 4).

The phrase **is necessary** does not match the verb in **and preserve + a healthy environment**. The second element of the predicate phrase may need to be re-written without the conjunction **and**. There are two possibilities here with slightly different meanings.

o   *for the preservation of a healthy environment*

   or

o   *to preserve a healthy environment*

Trouble Spot #5

Un-parallel comparisons with too many omitted elements – a very common error.

Examples of trouble-spot sentences:

- *The precipitation rates in Portland are lower **than** Seattle.
- *The conventional treatment of wastewater is more expensive **than** mechanical equipment.
- *Math teaching in Japan is more **than** the US.

One of the most confusing and difficult types of errors with the parallel structure entails faulty parallelism in complex comparisons in two conjoined sentences with omitted elements (see also chapter 4). In comparative constructions, which elements to omit, which to retain, and which to replace can cause a variety of problems.

Teaching Tip

In all these constructions, the necessary parallel (or replacement) elements have been omitted, that is, the subject noun **those/that + in** or **by means of** (see complex prepositions below).

(1) First, the coordinating conjunction needs to be located – **than**.
(2) Then two conjoined parallel elements have to be identified and made similar.

- The precipitation rates **in** Portland are lower **than [those + in]** Seattle.
- The **conventional treatment** of wastewater is more expensive than **[that + by means of]** mechanical equipment.
- Math teaching **in Japan** is more **[intensive/thorough]/[better] than [that+ in]** the US

Replacing the omitted elements can usually correct the errors. In teaching; however, it is important to highlight the complex comparative parallel structures with **than**.

Action Point

Text cohesion is fundamentally a culturally and linguistically bound social construct that is closely intertwined with literacy, education, and socialization. In academic writing in English, it may be presumptuous to assume that the writer and the reader share a good deal of common knowledge and are equally familiar with certain universal truths.

Yet, to some degree, such an assumption must be made in order for the writer to produce practically any piece of writing, and for the reader to grasp its meaning. Novice writers, L1 and L2 alike, are faced with the complex – and sometimes daunting – task of striking a balance between explaining too much and not providing enough information for the reader to understand their text.

Matters of lexical, semantic, and culturally bound cohesion are worth teaching, demonstrating, and discussing, with immediate and long-term benefits for academic writers and the quality of their writing.

Here are examples of a few sentences that can be discussed in class for their cohesive properties or lack thereof. It is a safe bet that not all the connections between these sentences pairs can be easily grasped or their contexts transparent even though their authors considered them pretty obvious.

- *The end-of-the-year sales are a boon for merchants. The spring merchandize begins to ship in early February.*
- *Florida's Apalachicola Bay is one example of pollution dangers. In economic terms, water contamination means that various sea products are threatened.*
- *A few thousand people came to the opening night. The players were devastated.*
- *This paper will discuss the decline in the importance of the Constitution and the standards of behavior expected of government officials.*
- *Americans are greatly dependent on their cars. According to the recent data, close to 80% drive alone to work, and almost 90% of American adults have licenses issued by the local authorities.*

All textbooks for teaching writing and writing guides alike emphasize particular elements of cohesion, such as sentence conjunctions and transitions, and give examples. However, cultural, linguistic, and contextual factors that in fact determine text cohesion are rarely addressed in instructional materials. There are many good reasons for that.

Sentence Transitions and Idea Connectors

Sentence transitions (also called sentences connectors or linking adverbs) have the primary function of connecting ideas between sentences and identifying the relationship between ideas (Swales & Feak, 2012). Practically every textbook on teaching writing presents detailed lists of sentence transitions, in which they are classified by their meanings.

Most textbooks encourage the use of sentence transitions because, as most textbook authors believe, they help novice writers establish clear cohesion between the ideas and clearly mark the discourse flow. Teachers also emphasize these sentence linkers because they are relatively easy to explain and also because the ideas in writing may occasionally seem so disjointed that every little bit can help.

Two Points about Sentence Transitions Found in Every Writing Guide:

(1) The major problem with sentence connectors is that because these linkers are easy to understand and use, in L2 prose there are typically far too many of them.
(2) The use of sentence transitions does not necessarily make the academic writing cohesive or the information flow easy to follow (Hinkel, 2001a, 2002a, 2015).

The following example from a student's text illustrates these points.

> **_First_**, the teenage crime rate is increasing very fast. **_Besides_**, the age of criminals is going down. **_Therefore_**, this is a serious problem. The society structure is toward the money principle, and **_moreover_**, everybody thinks that money is the most important thing. **_But_**, it is about the source of crime. **_In addition_**, the common crime for teenagers is stealing because they lack money. **_Nevertheless_**, sociologists have debated how to prevent teenage crime. **_Conclusively_**, family is the basic component of society, and family problems can cause teenagers to do maleficent things because their family cannot let them feel warm. **_Thus_**, they lack parents' love and care.
>
> (From a student paper on the causes of youth crime)

In light of the emphasis on sentence transitions in writing instruction, the misuse and overuse of these cohesive devices is not particularly surprising.

> In teaching, an important point to stress is that sentence transitions cannot make the text unified when the ideas in discourse flow are disjointed, no matter how many transitions are used.

Sentence Transition Uses

- In academic writing, the rate of sentence transitions is higher than in any other types of writing.
- Sentence connectors account for less than 10% of all academic adverbials.
- Conversational discourse employs far more sentence transitions than academic writing does.

(Biber, et al., 1999)

In academic writing, the most frequently encountered sentence transitions are actually not *first(-ly)*, *second(-ly)*, *third(-ly)*, *or moreover*, as, undoubtedly, many teachers have noticed in their students' writing.

The Most Frequent Transition Functions

(1) Contrast and concession, e.g. *however, on the other hand, instead, nevertheless, yet*.
(2) Enumerative, additive and summative, e.g. *as a result, to begin with, for one thing, in addition, further, also, then, similarly, in sum, to summarize, all in all*, and *overall*.

(Adapted from Shaw, 2009; Simpson-Vlach &
Ellis, 2010; Tadros, 1994)

The most common transitions number fewer than half a dozen. The most frequent linker *however* occurs at the rate of 0.10%, followed by *thus* and *therefore* at the rates of 0.07% and 0.06% per million words (Biber, et al., 1999).[3] Other sentence connectors, with frequency rates of 0.01% each, include *first, finally, furthermore, hence, nevertheless, rather, yet, in addition, on the other hand*, and *that is*.

> In formal academic writing, sentence transitions are actually not common at all.

The Most Frequent Sentence Transitions in Formal Academic Writing
(in declining order)

however	thus	therefore	then	so

Complex Prepositions and Other Alternatives

In general, the grammar function of prepositions is to express a relationship between two entities. In this, they are similar to coordinating conjunctions and sentence transitions that mark a relationship between ideas in two sentences. **Complex prepositions** are those that consist of more than one word – usually of two or three words, e.g. *as for, except for, in line with*.

Prepositions vs. Conjunctions

Sentence and discourse functions of prepositions, as well as complex prepositions as a subclass, have much in common with those of conjunctions and adverbs. **Both prepositions and conjunctions have connecting functions**, e.g.

— *the time <u>when</u> Ireland experienced a population crash in 1845*
— *the time <u>of</u> a population crash in Ireland in 1845*
— *the time <u>of</u> the 1845 population crash in Ireland*
— *the time <u>of</u> the 1845 Irish population crash*

In fact, many prepositions and conjunctions have identical forms and, for this reason, can be confusing for learners,[4] e.g. *after, as, before, since, until*.

The Key Differences between Conjunctions and Prepositions

• Prepositions are always followed by a noun, a noun phrase, a nominalization (*-tion, -ment, -ness*), or a gerund (*-ing*).
• Conjunctions conjoin the main and subordinate clauses – that necessarily have a predicate verb or verb phrase.

Thus, if the constructions following such words as *after* or *before* contain a verb, then these are subordinate clauses. If no verb can be identified, then the word is the preposition in a prepositional phrase.

Telling Apart Prepositions and Conjunctions with Identical Forms

after	Preposition	<u>no verb</u> **After a landslide**, *vegetation begins to grow at the site.*
	Conjunction	<u>verb – **occurs**</u> **After a landslide <u>occurs</u>**, *vegetation begins to grow at the site.*
as	Preposition	<u>no verb</u> **As a start**, *a few tough species invade the area.*
	Conjunction	<u>verb – **begins**</u> **As the ecosystem <u>begins</u> to restore itself**, *a few tough species invade the area.*
before	Preposition	<u>no verb</u> **Before the restoration of the ecosystems**, *the pioneer species change the soil.*
	Conjunction	<u>verb phrase – **are restored**</u> **Before the ecosystems <u>are restored</u>**, *the pioneer species change the soil.*
since	Preposition	<u>no verb</u> **Since the 1960s**, *urban growth has declined.*
	Conjunction	<u>verb phrase – **began to attract**</u> **Since suburbs <u>began to attract</u> urban residents**, *employers also relocated to smaller cities.*
till/until	Preposition	<u>no verb</u> **Until the increase in suburban job markets**, *most urban residents lived in city centers.*
	Conjunction	<u>verb – **emerged**</u> **Until manufacturing job markets <u>emerged</u> in the early 1800s**, *only 5% of Americans lived in cities.*

In addition to one-word (simple) prepositions and conjunctions with identical forms, many complex prepositions and subordinating conjunctions also have similar meanings and text functions. In academic writing, some can be used interchangeably, provided that verbs are NOT included in prepositional phrases.

Two- and Three-word Prepositions

Complex prepositions can be divided into two groups: **two-word and three-word** units.

- Two-word prepositions: <u>a word + a preposition</u>, e.g. *according to, because of, due to, except for*.
- Three-word prepositions: <u>a preposition + a noun + a preposition</u>, e.g. *in spite of, by means of, in light of*.

> The uses of complex prepositions can provide a large number of options among phrase and sentence connectors, in addition to transitions and clause subordinators.

Many two- and three-word prepositions have similar connective functions and grammar features. Connectives of all sorts can be used interchangeably, provided that the syntactic constructions they conjoin are used accordingly, e.g. only nouns and noun phrases following prepositions, complete sentences with transitions, and subordinators in clauses. Here are a few examples.

Examples of Sentence and Phrase Connectors

Connector	Sentence or Phrase #1	Sentence or Phrase #2
In spite of	*initial setbacks,*	*Lindbergh continued his flight training.*
Despite	*recent rainfall,*	*the drought is far from over.*
Nevertheless/ However,	*meteorologists calculate that a moist air mass is on the way.*	
Although/Even though	*heavy precipitation seems likely,*	*predicting its occurrence remains challenging.*

Most Frequent Two- and Three-Word Prepositions, and Their Substitutions

Two-word Prepositions	Three-word Prepositions	Sentence Transitions, Subordinators, Etc.
according to	in accordance with, in line with, based on	
ahead of prior to [time]	in front of [place] prior to [time]	before [place/time] until
along with together with	in addition to	also, further, furthermore
because of, due to		therefore, as a result, so because . . ., since . . .
contrary to	in contrast to/with	however, on the other hand, on the contrary
except for apart from, aside from	with the exception of	
instead of	in lieu of, in place of	
subsequent to		after, following

Frequent Three-Word Prepositions, and Their Substitutions

Three-word Preposition	Other Prepositions	Sentence Transitions, Subordinators, Etc.
by means of	with [instruments/tools only]	
in (the) case of		if, as long as, unless, provided that
in (the) process of	during	while, when meanwhile, in the meantime
in spite of	despite	though, although, even though nevertheless, nonetheless
in view of, in light of	because of, due to	

Numerous research reports find that particular sets of connectives are employed repeatedly in L2 writing, e.g. *first, second, according to, moreover, therefore*. However, the quality of academic writing is often evaluated based on vocabulary and grammar variety, and providing writers options may help create a greater lexical diversity (Cotterall & Cohen, 2003; Hinkel, 2005, 2011; Laufer & Nation, 1995; Read, 2000). The usage of complex prepositions in addition to sentence transitions and subordinate clauses can provide at least some degree of variation among lexical connectives and syntactic structures.

Clarifying and Giving Examples

In academic writing instruction, giving examples is often strongly advocated. In most textbooks, among other types of supporting evidence, examples and illustrations are presented as a classical and accessible means of rhetorical support. Instructional guides consistently point out that the examples need to be representative and understandable with relevant facts, statistics, descriptive details, and elaborate explanations.

> In academic prose, what can serve as representative examples, relevant facts, "descriptive details," and "elaborate explanations" is not clear cut.

Although giving examples is referred to as a prevalent rhetorical support strategy in English, teachers and researchers have found that academic L2 writers rarely employ this strategy successfully and in keeping with the guidelines in writing instruction (Dong, 1998; Nesselhauf, 2004; Paquot, 2008).

In fact, in many cases, the strategy is counter-productive and leads to L2 prose that seems to be particularly un-academic with high frequencies of discourse and text features incongruous with typical characteristics of formal writing in English (Gilquin, Granger, & Paquot, 2007; Jordan, 1997). Some examples of incorrect and unsuitable examples found in student writing can include:

- — *For example, my brother/my country/my case.*
- — *For example, I do too.*
- — *For example, I agree/I hate it.*
- — *Take my example, for instance.*

Other studies have found that L2 writers frequently misunderstand how to provide appropriate exemplification and use brief mentions of situations or events, and lengthy, highly personal narratives in lieu of "representative" examples (Hinkel, 2001b, 2002a; Shaw, 2009).

How to Construct Academic Examples

	To Support a Generalization
(1)	Provide information from **published and citable sources,** such as statistical or factual data, research findings, or opinions of experts, e.g. – *For example, Peters (2030) has a different view and states that . . .* – *For example, for children, 44% of pizza consumption occurred at lunch and 42% occurred at dinner.* – *For example, the average daily high in San Francisco in July and August is between 62 and 68 °F (17 and 20 °C).*
(2)	Explicitly state that generalizations indeed apply to **most (or many) cases/people/situations/events,** e.g. – *For example, 42% of all high school students have part-time jobs.* – *For instance, in US universities today, only a minority of students are male at 48%.* – *For example, a higher percentage of males (15%) than females (11%) consumed pizza on any given day.*
	To Clarify and Explain Unfamiliar Terms and Abstract Concepts
(3)	Refer to **specific** cases that **demonstrably** apply to **most (or many) cases/people/situations,** e.g. – *For example, when a coastline changes its shape, the tide pools where the local people fish will also become different.* – *For example, large cities with dense populations are likely to have public transportation and pedestrian sidewalks.* – *For example, in small towns, where people can reach their destination on foot, car traffic may be very light.*
(4)	Present expanded – a sentence or two – descriptions of **the documented and factual events/developments/groups/communities/circumstances/public figures,** e.g. – *For example. when the Wright brothers made their first flights, they used a stopwatch to time how long their airplane stayed in the air, and they also had a tape to measure the distance.* – *For example, most widely available pickles are made from cucumbers and cabbage that are kept in salt water with vinegar and spices. The salt water makes it impossible for any spoiling bacteria to multiply.*

> In academic writing, examples and extended examples present factual information that is clear and well organized.

Examples that are used to support the thesis can provide the highlights or an outline of the rest of the information that follows. Extended academic examples usually begin with a statement of fact.

> _Education is important for the economic survival of the poor._ For example, in the course of his or her working life, an average high school graduate can earn 1.4 million dollars. College graduates can earn 2.6 million dollars, and people with master's degrees, on average, can make 2.9 million. It seems clear that the more education workers have, the more money they can make. Educated adults have greater earning power and can have a higher standard of living.
>
> (From a student paper on the social causes of poverty)

What Academic Examples Should NOT Include:

- Narratives of personal experiences, as well as those of one's family members, classmates, roommates, or neighbors.
- Extensive explanations of personal opinions – if they are not based on demonstrable and verifiable facts.
- Stories or rumors that one has heard from other people.

Academic examples need to be selected carefully to include **clearly stated representative and factual information**. Occasionally (and only occasionally), an example of a dramatic situation or event can be used to illustrate how it relates to an extreme and untypical development.

Structures Not to Use or to Use Sparingly

Based on research in academic writing in English, two types of constructions occur frequently in L2 prose but rarely in formal text:

- Rhetorical questions.
- Presupposition words and phrases, such as **_obviously, as everyone knows, of course_**.

Rhetorical Questions

Many textbooks for writing usually recommend that writers ask "engaging" or "provocative" questions in introductions or use questions as an attention-getting device, similar to their uses in journalistic prose. For example, *Why do these young people get married? Who knows the truth? Why does the US government refuse to pay its U.N. debt?* or *The anti-terrorist bodies of government should know what they are doing, shouldn't they?*

However, in general, rhetorical questions are not typical of academic writing (Swales & Feak, 2012; Williams & Bizup, 2017). Corpus analyses demonstrate that questions are used at the rate of 0.05% of all words in formal written text, and in general direct questions are actively discouraged in academic prose in many disciplines (Biber, et al., 1999; Chang & Swales, 1999).

In various rhetorical traditions other than Anglo-American, rhetorical questions are often seen as a means of conveying suitable hesitation and/or uncertainty of facts, and their discourse function can be compared to that of hedging devices in English (see chapter 12). Studies of university writing demonstrate that rhetorical questions occur significantly more frequently in L2 than L1 academic texts (Gilquin & Paquot, 2008; Hinkel, 1997, 1999, 2002a).

> Rhetorical questions are highly infrequent in formal academic writing, and their use is not recommended.

Presupposition Words and Phrases

Presupposition markers, such as *obvious*, *obviously*, and *of course*, are used to refer to assumptions that the writer believes to be common knowledge, widely known facts, and universal truths (and in this sense, they are presuppositional), e.g.

— *?Of course, if children watch violent TV shows, they become violent.*
— *?Obviously, the oil company should pay for the cleanup because they were the ones who spilled the oil.*

According to Halliday and Hasan (1976), in formal writing, these markers imply a slightly adversative tone because they suggest that something is or should have been obvious, but may have been overlooked. Since at least the 1960s, a large body of linguistic work has been devoted to presupposition in pragmatics and conversational discourse because few interactional exchanges can be produced and understood without some sort of presupposed information. For instance, *How are you?* or *How's your day going?* are not actually real questions, but conversational and casual greetings.

In academic discourse, however, presupposition markers and similar references to "universal truths" make written texts particularly prone to misunderstandings and negative evaluations (Chafe, 1994; Moon, 1998).

> Presupposition words and phrases, such as *obvious*, *obviously*, and *of course* should be avoided in formal academic writing.

Punctuation of Cohesive Elements

In English academic writing, about a dozen punctuation rules make up the relatively rigid basics.

> An academic text written without the required – and basic – punctuation can appear ungrammatical, no matter how well it adheres to the rules of English sentence structure.

In all languages, punctuation rules are largely based on convention. For this reason, they may seem somewhat random and haphazard to L2 writers who were not exposed to them from the time when they began reading. One of the outcomes can be L2 writers' tendency to ignore punctuation rules altogether, with the exception of capitalization and periods, on which most writing teachers insist.

- In English, the fundamental purpose of punctuation marks is to divide sentences into their component parts.
- By and large, the rules of punctuation follow the rules of the sentence and phrase structure.

> In teaching, a useful technique is to present punctuation marks as visual sentence and phrase dividers or partitions to separate component parts.

The practical purpose of punctuation is to make the sentence and the text easier to divide and follow, but it is not always clear how sentences and phrases should be divided. For instance, a period marks the end of a sentence, but it may take serious guesswork to figure out when a sentence should end.

The basic punctuation rules outlined below represent the bare bones of the punctuation system in English. These rules must be learned and used in the production of academic writing.

The Basic and Most Important Punctuation Rules

Sentence Transitions and Prepositional Phrases

- All sentence transitions at the beginnings of sentences have to be "separated" by a comma, e.g.

  However, . . .   For this reason, . . .   In light of this information, . . .

  | Transition | |, | the rest of the sentence |.

- Sentence transitions in the middle of a sentence are separated by commas on both sides, e.g.

  - *Hill's research, **however**, emphasizes the importance of . . .*
  - *The American democracy, **on the other hand**, . . .*

  | The beginning of the sentence | |, | transition | |, | the rest of the sentence |.

- In compound sentences, two **short** simple sentences can be separated by a semicolon, e.g.

  - *The election is over; the country has a new president.*
  - *This is the first sentence; this is the second sentence.*

  | Sentence #1 | |; | sentence #2 |.

- If the short sentences in a compound construction are also conjoined by a transition, the transition has to be separated by a comma **in all cases**, e.g.

  - *Soil depletion is very costly; **however**, it can be prevented.*

- *Factories concentrate in cities; **additionally**, distribution networks center around major water ways.*

| Sentence #1 | ; | transition, | sentence #2 | .

Examples and Other Markers

- Example and other discourse markers have the function of connectives and transitions and follow the same punctuation rules.
  - o Example markers, e.g. **for example, for instance, namely**.
  - – **For example**, *glacier melt water can be pooled and stored during the summer.*
  - – **For instance**, *in German, all nouns are capitalized, but in English days of the week and names of the months . . .*
  - o Information sequencers and organizers, e.g. **in the first place, second, finally, also, to conclude**.
  - – **First of all**, *in Latin script and Roman documents, there were no lowercase letters.*
  - – **In sum**, *letter capitalization conventions differ in most European languages.*
  - o Adverbial emphasizers, e.g. **indeed, above all, most important**.
  - – **Above all**, *voters are in favor of the new funding for public education.*
  - – **Most important**ly, *water storage ponds benefit farming and irrigation.*

Prepositional Phrases and Sentence
Preliminary Information

- Sentence preliminaries at the beginnings of sentences serve as connectives and transitions and have to be separated by commas, e.g. prepositional phrases, adverb of all types (time, place, and evaluation), and infinitives.

In 2035, . . . In the state capital, . . . At the start of the 20th century, . . .
In the view of the author, . . . In light of the study findings, . . . In spite of
the rain, . . .
Usually, . . . Perhaps, . . . Fortunately, . . .

| Prepositional phrase/adverb | , | the rest of the sentence |.

- Prepositional phrases in the **middle** or at the **end** of sentences are not separated out, and **commas are not used**.

  - *The industrial revolution began in England **in the mid-1700s**.*
  - *Mass production techniques emerged **after World War I** and formed the basis of advanced industrial societies.*

Parallel Structure

In parallel structures, punctuation depends on the number of elements in the string.

- **Two** elements take **no commas**, e.g.
  - *rain or snow*
  - *advertising and marketing staff*
  - *bought and sold*

| xxx | and | yyy |

- **Three or more** elements: **comma after each element plus a required phrase conjunction (*and, but, or*) before the last element**. The conjunction marks the last element.

  - *soil, minerals, **and** water*
  - *production, trade, **and** distribution of goods*
  - *buy, sell, **or** trade commodities*

| xxx |,| yyy |,| **and** zzz | OR | aaa |,| bbb |,| ccc |,| **or** ddd |

Various punctuation marks have different "power," with the period (or question mark, or exclamation mark) being the most powerful sentence divider, followed by the semicolon, and the comma (see chapter 4). In some contexts, the semicolon and a conjunction + a comma can have the same power, e.g.

> *Inland water reservoirs often allow recreation, **but**/ ; special rules apply for the safety of the public and the quality of the water.*

- The comma, possibly because of its relatively small dividing power, has a large number of uses.
- It can set off prepositional phrases, sentence transitions, elements of parallel structures (words or phrases alike), subordinate clauses, or short simple sentences, when boosted by a conjunction.

It is in part due to the comma's flexibility that L2 writers find the punctuation rules dealing with commas confusing (and who can blame them!).

Chapter Summary

Cohesion refers to connections between sentences and paragraphs. Coherence can also refer to the organization of discourse with all elements present and fitting together logically. There are techniques that L2 writers can use to increase the cohesion and coherence of their writing.

- One effective way of teaching cohesion is to showing students how to provide known information, usually with repeated or substituted lexical items in the first part or a sentence with new information presented at the end.
- The new information from one sentence is presented as old or known information in the subsequent sentence. There can be multiple cohesive chains of old and new information in paragraphs.
- Enumerative nouns (e.g. **aspect, characteristic, issue**) are very frequent in academic writing. Learning and using them for lexical substitution can provide cohesion without excessive redundancy.
- In coherent papers, examples are commonly used in support of points, but constructing and using "academic" examples requires instruction and practice (just like everything else).
- For the most part, rhetorical questions and presupposition markers, such as **obvious, obviously**, and **of course** should be avoided.
- There are a few – around half a dozen – fundamental punctuation rules that are fairly straightforward. Applying these rules requires instruction, as well as consistent and persistent follow-up.

Strategies and Tactics for Teaching and Teaching Activities

> **Teaching Activities**
>
> A number of effective teaching techniques may be useful in instruction dealing specifically with text cohesion in academic writing. These can focus on the **judicious** usage of sentence transitions, lexical and semantic cohesive ties, lexical substitutions, parallel structure, and punctuation.
>
> To get started, the initial objective is to notice and identify how cohesion is established and maintained. Text excerpts from published sources can vary in length, from one or two paragraphs to several pages. The texts can be selected depending on students' proficiency levels and on topics of interest, e.g. sports, music, or fashion news reports, web posts, or introductory college textbooks.
>
> All these tasks can be assigned as homework, or for pair and group work, with follow-up discussions. Occasionally, these can be collected and graded to evaluate students' progress.

Identifying Cohesive Ties: Recognition Practice I

- The goal of this practice is to locate and identify cohesive ties and lexical substitutions.
- Using connecting lines or numbers works well to show specific connections.
- For high-intermediate and advanced learners, identifying known/old and new information in each sentence can add a level of complexity.
- Then in pairs or small groups, students can compare their findings.
- With short text excerpts at the beginning of the practice, the teacher should spot-check or guide the activity.

An illustration is provided below. The paragraph in (1) can be used as a stand-alone excerpt or used together with the paragraph in (2). Both have been completed, as an example.

(1)   Drying [1] or dehydrating technology is a method of preserving [2] food [3] by means of removing enough moisture [1] from the food [3] to prevent bacteria and mold from growing. Practically any food [3] can be preserved [2] by drying [1] including meat, fish [4], fruits [5], and vegetables. Historically, dried 1 meat and fish [4] have had a higher value [6] than fruit [5] and formed a major [6] source of protein in the remote regions.

(2)   Dried [1] fruit [5] consumption [3] is widespread because it is prized [6] for its sweet taste, nutritional value [6], and long shelf life [2]. Nearly half of the dried [1] fruits [5] sold are raisins, followed by plums, apricots, peaches, apples and pears. These [5] are referred to as traditional dried [1] fruits [5] that have been dried [1] in the sun or in heated wind dryers [1].

Note. At advanced levels, the work on academic vocabulary and cohesion can also include:

— *drying – dehydrating – removing moisture*
— *food – consumption*
— *preserving – shelf life*

Identifying Missing Cohesive Ties: Recognition Practice II

In addition to identifying cohesive ties and lexical substations that are established by the author of the text, it is also very helpful for students to work with text lacking in cohesion. This type of practice usually leads to excellent and very productive class discussions.

- For this practice, the teacher may choose a student text without sufficiently developed cohesion.
- For advanced levels, the task can also include adding cohesive elements to the text or re-writing phrases and sentences.
- It is important that the texts selected for correction contain a variety of cohesion problems / errors, including repetitive transitions, faulty parallel structures, and redundant lexis.
- In pairs or small groups, students can compare their additions and repairs.

An example of text with insufficiently developed cohesion is presented below. Some corrections are suggested in [square brackets].

Assignment Topic. *Choose one (or more) historical event, individual, or a group of individuals in American history that had an important influence on*

American education. Your paper needs to explain how this event or individual influenced or changed the currents in the norms of schooling widely accepted in their time.

Paragraph 1

Since puritans arrived in America, politics, economical [economics], *and other parts* [aspects of the United States] *have changed* [sentence 1 is not related to the rest of the text and should be deleted].

In the field of education, many things have occurred [possible introductory sentence: it requires a specific mention of what has occurred to lead to changes in education throughout American history].

Many American scholars have studied American history. They have tried to find out what made education change.

They state different causes about it [non-referential pronoun].

They [the third use of the pronoun <u>they</u> – too far away from the original noun] *view history from different sights* [perspectives/positions]. [The last four sentences are redundant, vague, and very broad – probably should be deleted.]

Paragraph 2

Some scholars argue that the political and economy situations and religion [politics, economy, and religion] *affect education.*

The content and method of political and education [political and educational] *change* [no main verb] *not due to the problems* [the first mention of <u>the problems</u> – to what noun phrase(s)/text do <u>the problems</u> tie?] *in education itself, but due to the political and economy situations and religion* [politics, economy, and religion] *at that time* [the first mention of <u>that time</u> – to what noun/noun phrase does the pronoun <u>that</u> point?].

They [non-referential pronoun: it is too far from <u>some scholars</u> in the first line] *stated that the reason for the change* [no specific <u>change</u> has been mentioned, but only <u>change</u> in general – to what noun or noun phrase does the change tie?] *are outside of* [delete <u>of</u>] *education.*

Paragraph 3

The texts and the essays of [<u>on</u>/<u>for</u>?] *education, which were written at that time* [to what specific time does the pronoun <u>that</u> point?], *supported this interpretation* [to what interpretation does the phrase <u>this interpretation</u> point?].

Noah Webster was a writer of texts, for example, Webster's spelling book [Noah Webster is mentioned for the first time – who was he, when, what was his profession? Noah Webster may be a good topic for the paper, but his historical role needs to be the focus].

Webster's Federal Catechism [Webster's work is mentioned for the first time – what was it? What was it about? What was it for?], *which were* [how many Catechisms?] *the most popular textbooks* [how many textbooks? Why were they popular?] *at that time* [at what time?] *in the late 18th and early 19th centuries.*

Webster believed that his texts would make good and patriotic Americans, develop American language, and unified nation spirit [and build/create a unified national spirit; faulty parallelism: the third verb is missing in make – develop – ??] [Why did Webster believe so strongly in his textbook? What did the textbook do, what did it include, and what was it for?]

Lexical Substitutions: Odd Man Out

- Sentences with words and a few near-synonyms are provided.
- Each set of near-synonyms includes one word that has a different meaning and does not belong in the set.
- The task is to write another sentence or two to follow the first and to make it cohesive with the first sentence.

Possible idea continuations are provided in [square brackets].

(1) *The exact causes of various natural disasters, such as torrential rains and hurricanes, cannot always be* (established – determined – separated – identified) *because a number of natural phenomena can combine to bring about a particular weather event.*

[A sentence or two about the work of scientists who work to predict – anticipate – foresee natural disasters or weather events.]

(2) *In the past several decades, it has become clear that individual physical* (features – characteristics – positions) *are hereditary and transferable from one generation to another.*

[A sentence about or a short discussion of the influence of heredity on physical appearance, e.g. height, or the color of hair or eyes.]

(3) *Biologists and medical scientists* (collaborate – work together – correlate) *in their research devoted to the* (role – influence – method) *of heredity on an individual's health, as well as psychological tendencies and habits.*

[A sentence about or a short description of possible connections between heredity and psychology or habits.]

(4) *The paintings of the 17th and 18th centuries often* (<u>focused</u> – <u>con-centrated</u> – <u>centered</u> – <u>leaned</u>) *on a historical or religious scenes that* (<u>depicted</u> – <u>portrayed</u> – <u>conveyed</u> – <u>proclaimed</u>) *a military victory or conquest.*

[A sentence about other types of paintings, drawings, or a work of visual art.]

(5) *In many cultures, paintings and drawing usually include several* (<u>main</u> – <u>prominent</u> – <u>crucial</u> – <u>essential</u>) (<u>elements</u> – <u>details</u> – <u>components</u> – <u>contributions</u>) *that attract the attention of the viewer.*

[A sentence about or a short description of a composition of a painting, a drawing, or a work of art.]

(6) *Cable TV broadcasts* (<u>rely</u> – <u>depend</u> – <u>hinge</u>) *on satellites to* (<u>transmit</u> – <u>relay</u> – <u>deliver</u> – <u>contain</u>) *the visual and audio signals to local stations that carry it further to their customers in the area.*

[A sentence about or a short description of how other similar instruments work, e.g. cell phones, radio, or computer networks.]

Functions and Limitations of Sentence Transitions

The goal of this exercise is to demonstrate that sentence transitions alone cannot make the text cohesive but can merely enhance textual cohesion that exists largely independently of transitional words and phrases.

- To highlight the function of sentence transitions as a relatively superficial cohesive device, students are asked to produce text without using transitions at all.
- Then the writers identify and mark meaning-based relationships between sentences or paragraphs in terms traditionally used to label the semantic groupings of transitions in many textbooks, e.g.

  o Additional information (*in addition, additionally, moreover*).
  o Result (*as a result, as a consequence*).
  o Concession (*although, even though*).

- This step can be combined with another for identifying a new idea in each sentence or a continuation of the same idea.
- After the meaning relationships are identified, a decision needs to be made about which sentences or paragraphs are easier to understand with the addition of a transition and which seem clear without one.

Punctuation/Sentence Combining

Any excerpt from student and/or authentic texts can be used for punctuation practice.

- All punctuation in the original should be eliminated before students work to insert punctuation marks (and/or to combine simple sentences whenever possible).
- For intermediate levels, the teacher may need to simplify authentic texts by replacing rare or advanced vocabulary items.

Endnotes

1 Superordinate words are called "general words" in Halliday & Hasan (1976, p. 279).
2 The uses of demonstratives and the pitfalls associated with their overuses in L2 text are discussed in detail in chapter 6. The mention of demonstratives here serves merely as a reminder of their important cohesive function.
3 Swales and Feak (2012) similarly report that the uses of the following sentence transitions may be useful: *however, thus, also, in addition, finally, therefore, on the other hand, then*, and *nevertheless*. These authors further point out, for example, that "conclusive" sentence transitions, such as *in conclusion*, are very rare indeed.
4 Other identical forms of prepositions and conjunctions include *but* and *but* (except, e.g. *all but one*) and *for* and *for* (*because*, e.g. *for he loved his country*), but the latter of the two in both these pairs is very rare.

Further Reading

Ferris, D. (2016). Promoting grammar and language development in the writing class: Why, what, how, and when. In E. Hinkel (Ed.), *Teaching English grammar to speakers of other languages* (pp. 222–239). New York, NY: Routledge.

A practical and teaching-oriented overview of how to implement successful language instruction to student writers. A discussion of the why of developing grammar knowledge within the context of writing instruction is followed by how a teacher can choose which of the many elements of English on which to focus. The crucial considerations of when and how a teacher might incorporate language-focused work could be applied to a wide variety of pedagogical contexts.

Halliday, M.A.K. & Hasan, R. (1976). *Cohesion in English*. London: Longman.

A major and highly influential work on cohesion within the English linguistic system, and its resources for constructing text and the range of meanings that relate what is being spoken or written to its context, genre, and semantic setting. A principal component of linguistic resources is cohesion that arises from semantic relations and connections between sentences. Cohesive ties can be grammatical and lexical, and the analysis of text ties provides a systemic account of its patterns that can be useful for English language learners.

Hinkel, E. (2019). *Teaching essential units of language: Beyond single-word vocabulary.* New York, NY: Routledge.

A textbook on practical and research foundations for teaching second language multiword phrases, also called collocations. Multiword units, such as *strong tea, beautiful weather,* or *would you mind,* cannot be readily understood or predicted by the meanings of their component parts. The chapters present a thorough and rounded overview of the principles and techniques for teaching L2 phrases in a variety of instructional settings around the world.

References

Biber, D., Johansson, S., Leech, G., Conrad, S., & Finegan, E. (1999). *Longman grammar of spoken and written English.* Harlow: Pearson.

Carrell, P. (1982). Cohesion is not coherence. *TESOL Quarterly, 16*(4), 479–488.

Chafe, W. (1985). Linguistic differences produced by differences between speaking and writing. In D.R. Olson, N. Torrance, & A. Hildyard (Eds.), *Literature, language, and learning: The nature and consequences of reading and writing* (pp. 105–123). Cambridge: Cambridge University Press.

Chafe, W. (1994). *Discourse, consciousness, and time.* Chicago: University of Chicago Press.

Chang, Y. & Swales, J. (1999). Informal elements in English academic writing: Threats or opportunities for advanced non-native speakers. In C. Candlin & K. Hyland (Eds.), *Writing texts, processes and practices* (pp. 145–167). London: Longman.

Cotterall, S. & Cohen, R. (2003). Scaffolding for second language writers: Producing an academic essay. *ELT Journal, 57,* 158–166.

Dong, Y. (1996). Learning how to use citations for knowledge transformation: Non-native doctoral students' dissertation writing in science. *Research in the Teaching of English, 30*(4), 428–457.

Dong, Y.R. (1998). From writing in their native language to writing in English: What ESL students bring to our writing classroom. *College English, 8*(2), 87–105.

Gilquin, G., Granger, S. & Paquot, M. (2007). Learner corpora: The missing link in EAP pedagogy. *Journal of English for Academic Purposes, 6*(4), 319–335.

Gilquin, G. & Paquot, M. (2008). Too chatty: Learner academic writing and register variation. *English Text Construction, 1*(1), 41–61.

Halliday, M.A.K. & Hasan, R. (1976). *Cohesion in English.* London: Longman.

Hamp-Lyons, L. (2011). English for academic purposes. In E. Hinkel (Ed.), *Handbook of research in second language teaching and learning* (pp. 89–105). New York, NY: Routledge.

Hinkel, E. (1997). Indirectness in L1 and L2 academic writing. *Journal of Pragmatics, 27*(3), 360–386.

Hinkel, E. (1999). Objectivity and credibility in L1 and L2 academic writing. In E. Hinkel (Ed.), *Culture in second language teaching and learning.* (pp. 90–108). Cambridge: Cambridge University Press.

Hinkel, E. (2001a). Matters of cohesion in L1 and L2 academic texts. *Applied Language Learning, 12*(2), 111–132.

Hinkel, E. (2001b). Giving examples and telling stories in academic essays. *Issues in Applied Linguistics, 12*(2), 149–170.

Hinkel, E. (2002a). *Second language writers' text.* New York, NY: Routledge.

Hinkel, E. (2002b). Teaching grammar in writing classes: Tenses and cohesion. In E. Hinkel & S. Fotos (Eds.), *New perspectives on grammar teaching in second language classrooms* (pp. 181–198). New York, NY: Routledge.

Hinkel, E. (2003). Adverbial markers and tone in L1 and L2 students' writing. *Journal of Pragmatics, 35*(2), 208–231.

Hinkel, E. (2005). Analyses of L2 text and what can be learned from them. In E. Hinkel (Ed.), *Handbook of research in second language teaching and learning* (pp. 615–628). New York, NY: Routledge.

Hinkel, E. (2011). What research on second language writing tells us and what it doesn't. In E. Hinkel (Ed.), *Handbook of research in second language teaching and learning, Volume 2* (pp. 523–538). New York, NY: Routledge.

Hinkel, E. (2015). *Effective curriculum for teaching L2 writing: Principles and techniques.* New York, NY: Routledge.

Hinkel, E. (2017). Prioritizing grammar to teach or not to teach: A research perspective. In E. Hinkel (Ed.), *Handbook of research in second language teaching and learning* (pp. 369–383). New York, NY: Routledge.

Hunston, S. & Francis, G. (2000). *Pattern grammar.* Amsterdam: John Benjamins.

Jordan, R. (1997). *English for academic purposes.* Cambridge: Cambridge University Press.

Laufer, B. & Nation, P. (1995). Vocabulary size and use: Lexical richness in L2 written production. *Applied Linguistics, 16*(2), 307–322.

Leech, G., Rayson, P., & Wilson, A. (2001). *Word frequencies in written and spoken English.* London: Longman.

Leki, I., Cumming, A., & Silva, T. (2008). *A synthesis of research on second language writing in English.* New York, NY: Routledge.

Mahlberg, M. (2005). *English general nouns: A corpus theoretical approach.* Amsterdam: John Benjamins.

Moon, R. (1998). *Fixed expressions and idioms in English.* Oxford: Oxford University Press.

Nesselhauf, N. (2004). *Collocations in a learner corpus.* Amsterdam: John Benjamins.

Paquot, M. (2008). Exemplification in learner writing: A cross-linguistic perspective. In S. Granger & F. Meunier (Eds.), *Phraseology in foreign language learning and teaching* (pp. 101–119). Amsterdam: John Benjamins.

Quirk, R., Greenbaum, S., Leech, G., & Svartvik, J. (1985). *A comprehensive grammar of the English language.* New York, NY: Longman.

Read, J. (2000). *Assessing vocabulary.* Cambridge: Cambridge University Press.

Scollon, R., Scollon, S., & Jones, R. (2012). *Intercultural communication* (3rd edn). Oxford: Wiley/Blackwell.

Shaw, P. (2009). Linking adverbials in student and professional writing in literary studies: What makes writing mature. In M. Charles, S. Hunston, & D. Pecorari (Eds.), *Academic writing: At the interface of corpus and discourse* (pp. 215–235). London: Bloomsbury.

Simpson-Vlach, R. & Ellis, N. (2010). An academic formulas list: New methods in phraseology research. *Applied Linguistics, 31*(4), 487–512.

Swales, J. (1990). *Genre analysis.* Cambridge: Cambridge University Press.

Swales, J. (2005). Attended and unattended "this" in academic writing: A long and unfinished story. *ESP Malaysia, 11*, 1–15.

Swales, J. & Feak, C. (2012). *Academic writing for graduate students* (3rd edn). Ann Arbor, MI: University of Michigan Press.

Tadros, A. (1994). Predictive categories in expository text. In M. Coulthard (Ed.), *Advances in written text analysis* (pp. 69–82). New York, NY: Routledge.

van Dijk, T. (2009). *Society and discourse: How social contexts control text and talk.* Cambridge: Cambridge University Press.

van Dijk, T. (2010). *Discourse and context.* Cambridge: Cambridge University Press.

Williams, J. & Bizup, J. (2017). *Style: Ten lessons in clarity and grace* (12th edn). New York, NY: Pearson.

Appendix to Chapter 11

The diagram **The Structure of an Academic Essay** is intended to illustrate the fundamental structure of the classical, traditional, and sometimes deprecated academic essay. The structure of written academic discourse and text has not changed during the past several decades, despite upheavals and revolutions in writing instruction (Scollon, Scollon, & Jones, 2012; Swales, 1990; Swales & Feak, 2012).

The advantage of a clear and not-too-complex diagram is that it is easy to draw or display in class. The academic essay structure is as follows:

- The **Introduction** that states and briefly describes the topic.
- The **Thesis Statement** that specifies how the topic will be approached and what supporting **Points** (1, 2, 3, or more) will be used to shore up the thesis. The thesis statement is **an outline** for the rest of the essay.
- The **Order of the Points** in the thesis statement that always determines the **Order of the Thesis Supports** (1, 2, 3, or more).

A useful analogy that can be made is that the Thesis Statement is the container that holds the entire essay together and in one place.

Thesis Support

Each **Point** made in the **Thesis** has to be **supported**. The information to support the Thesis should be divided into **Paragraphs**, one expanded and developed idea per paragraph (aka "one thought at a time"). Each paragraph should include a **Topic Sentence** that **supports the Thesis Statement** and is directly connected to a particular **Point in the Thesis Statement**, in the **Order of the Points**.

The Structure of an Academic Essay

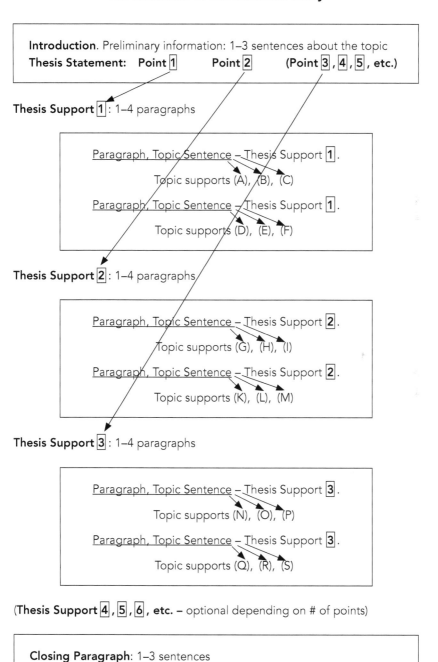

Introduction. Preliminary information: 1–3 sentences about the topic
Thesis Statement: Point $\boxed{1}$ Point $\boxed{2}$ (Point $\boxed{3}$, $\boxed{4}$, $\boxed{5}$, etc.)

Thesis Support $\boxed{1}$: 1–4 paragraphs

Paragraph, Topic Sentence – Thesis Support $\boxed{1}$.
Topic supports (A), (B), (C)
Paragraph, Topic Sentence – Thesis Support $\boxed{1}$.
Topic supports (D), (E), (F)

Thesis Support $\boxed{2}$: 1–4 paragraphs

Paragraph, Topic Sentence – Thesis Support $\boxed{2}$.
Topic supports (G), (H), (I)
Paragraph, Topic Sentence – Thesis Support $\boxed{2}$.
Topic supports (K), (L), (M)

Thesis Support $\boxed{3}$: 1–4 paragraphs

Paragraph, Topic Sentence – Thesis Support $\boxed{3}$.
Topic supports (N), (O), (P)
Paragraph, Topic Sentence – Thesis Support $\boxed{3}$.
Topic supports (Q), (R), (S)

(Thesis Support $\boxed{4}$, $\boxed{5}$, $\boxed{6}$, **etc.** – optional depending on # of points)

Closing Paragraph: 1–3 sentences

A practical exercise can be to ask students to underline the Thesis Statement in their assignment/essay, then to underline the Topic Sentence in each paragraph and connect it to a specific Thesis Point, one at a time.

Hedging in Academic Text in English   **12**

Overview

- The importance of hedges in academic text.
- Expanding the hedging repertoire.
- Various types of hedges and options.
- Developing stock vocabulary and hedges.
- Overstatements and learning to avoid them.

In the past several decades, much research has been devoted to hedging in academic prose, among other types of discourse. Analyses of large English-language corpora continue to underscore the importance and prevalence of various types of hedging devices in academic prose (Hinkel, 1997, 1999, 2003a, 2003b, 2005a; Hoye, 1997; Hyland, 1998, 2008, 2018; Hunston & Francis, 2000; Hyland & Milton, 1997). The lists of hedging devices differ among research findings, and only the most frequent are discussed in this chapter.

> Definition: **Hedges** and **hedging** are linguistic devices, e.g. words, phrases, clauses, and other constructions, that are used to limit or qualify a statement, reduce the degree of certainty and commitment, and project politeness.

Here are a few examples.

- *The rain in Spain stays **mainly** in the plain.*

— *When the dog bites, when the bee stings, when I'm feeling sad, I __simply__ remember my favorite things, and then I __don't__ feel __so__ bad.*
— *It's Supercalifragilisticexpialidocious! __Even though__ the sound of it is __something quite__ atrocious.*

In academic writing, hedging has numerous social and rhetorical purposes, and it can take many linguistic forms, including adverbs, adjectives, modal verbs, and conjunctions. In linguistics research, various definitions and classifications of hedging devices have been constructed to account for their complex and culturally bound, contextual uses (Hinkel, 2011, 2015; Leki, Cumming, & Silva, 2008; van Dijk, 2010).

The Functions of Hedging in Academic Writing

- In academic writing, the purpose of hedging is to reduce the writer's commitment to the truthfulness of a statement, e.g. **Many __types__ of fruit __can__ be pickled.**
- Hedging represents the uses of linguistic devices to show hesitation, politeness, and indirectness, e.g. **__Historical__ sources __claim__ that pickles have __long__ been __considered__ a beauty __aid__.**
- In Anglo-American formal written text, hedges are used extensively with the general goal of projecting "honesty, modesty, proper caution," and diplomacy (Swales, 1990, p. 174), e.g. **Archeologists __suspect__ that pickling and preserving food has been __around__ for thousands of years.**

> The uses of hedges are highly conventionalized in academic writing and practically requisite in expressions of personal positions or points of view.
>
> Corpus analyses of published academic prose demonstrate clearly that hedges are by far the most frequent features of presenting writers' perspectives because they serve to distinguish facts from opinions (Hyland, 1998).

In composition textbooks and writing guides for basic writers, hedging is not discussed in detail. Despite the prevalence and importance of hedges in written academic prose, textbooks for teaching academic and second language writing rarely focus on hedges of any kind, with the exception of modal verbs, e.g. ***can, may, might*** (Hinkel, 2003a, 2003b, 2005b, 2011).

Numerous other studies have found that L2 academic texts frequently contain overstatements, exaggerations, and authoritative assertions and that hedging is a critically important skill that needs to be taught (Hinkel, 2002, 2015; Hyland, 2008, 2018).

- In writing instruction, a key focus is to demonstrate how hedging assertions and claims reflects politeness and caution almost always requisite in English-language academic prose.
- In reading, insights into the functions of hedges in context can explain how politeness strategies are used in academic text and language.

In L2 writing, there may be a variety of reasons for the high frequency of overstatements and strong claims. But one important consideration is that rhetorical uncertainty and the uses of hedges are valued greatly in the Anglo-American but not necessarily in other rhetorical traditions (Dong, 1998; Hu & Cao, 2011; van Dijk, 2009, 2010). Furthermore, research has established that many L2 writers have a restricted lexical repertoire that

often leads to a "shortage" of hedging devices employed in academic prose (Hinkel, 2003a, 2003b, 2005b, 2015; Hyland, 2008, 2018; Jordan, 1997). Therefore, focused instruction in appropriate uses of varied hedging is urgently needed.

The discussion of various types of hedging devices presented in this chapter is organized to begin with the lexically and grammatically simple devices and then to move on to those of greater complexity. (For additional information about the hedging properties of conditional, concessive, and time (*if, although, though, when*) clauses, see chapter 10; the passive voice as hedging, see chapter 7; and indefinite pronouns as hedges, chapter 6).

Why Hedging Needs to Be Taught

In various non-Anglo-American rhetorical traditions, rhetorical persuasion does not necessarily call for hedging, and the desirability of hedging statements, generalizations, and claims is not an obvious consideration for many L2 writers (Dong, 1998; Hinkel, 2005a, 2015; Hu & Cao, 2011; Hyland, 2008; Taylor & Chen, 1991). In teaching, the need for hedging in academic prose has to be explicitly addressed. Noting the distinctions in uses of hedges in informal conversations (**basically, sort of**) and formal writing (**apparently, periodically**) is a good place to start.

In casual conversations, English speakers often say *I always forget to xxx!*, *You always do yyy!*, or *Everything is falling apart today*. Speakers of other languages say these things, too, in both English and their L1s. However, in all languages, informal conversations with friends require a different type of discourse and language features than, for instance, writing a petition to the dean. In fact, if someone talks to his or her friends and uses language similar to that in the petition, within a short time, this individual would not have many friends left.

> The language features employed in formal academic writing are almost always substantially and markedly different from those used in conversations.

In many discourse traditions, overstatements and exaggerations can be so common that practically no one notices them. Also, in English, some conversational exaggerations are not likely to get much attention, e.g. *I have a thousand things to do today* or *Every time I get in the shower, the phone rings*. On the other hand, in formal writing, these sentences may become *I am busy today* or *The phone often rings when I am in the shower*.

In casual interactions, exaggerations are usually assumed to be innocent hyperboles that are used to make a point, and both speakers and hearers are aware that the actual state of affairs is inflated. On the other hand, the information in formal written discourse is expected to be far more precise and cautiously hedged. In various types of formal prose, such as professional correspondence, memos, or reports, exaggerations and overstatements can be precarious and appear to be inflated.

- With conversational hyperboles, the speaker's and the hearer's shared and mutual assumptions apply to overstatements and exaggerations to allow them to understand the intended meaning.
- Apart from the shared and mutual assumptions that exist in the Anglo-American discourse tradition, there is little objective reason to believe that these assumptions should apply only to casual conversations, but not formal written prose.

It may not be very difficult to imagine that in non-Anglo-American rhetorical traditions, hyperboles can be perfectly acceptable in persuasion when both the writer and the reader assume that the actual value of the information in a statement is smaller than the stated. For example, in *Students always study hard*, the writer simply assumes that the reader knows that the intended meaning is **not** that *all (100%) students study hard at all times*.

The shared and mutual assumptions prevalent in various discourse types and traditions allow the reader to understand that the writer knows that 100% of students do not work hard 100% of the time. In this case, the reader does not necessarily think that the writer's text is overstated, and "reality" hedging is assumed by both the writer and the reader.

Talking Shop

The concept of **hedges** was originally proposed by George Lakoff in 1972 and defined as **"words whose job is to make things fuzzier or less fuzzy"** (p. 195). Lakoff's list of hedges was relatively short and included around 50 words and phrases, e.g.

more or less, one might say that, sort of, let us say that, kind of, might as well be, in a sense, to all intents and purposes, in one sense, for all practical purposes

Since then, the work on hedges has been taken up in pragmatics, discourse and text studies, corpus research, semantics, logic, and philosophy. In each of these areas, however, the definition of hedges differs to various extents, but these are largely immaterial in language teaching and learning.

The pragmatic – practical – functions of hedges are to qualify, limit, and soften statements, opinions, and claims, as well as to express a degree of vagueness, indirectness, and politeness.

The functions of hedges are relatively easy to notice when contrasting sentences are presented and discussed. Here are a few examples.

Example #1

- *Pickles are the best food, and everybody loves pickles.*
- ***In my opinion****, pickles are **delicious**, and **many** people **like** them.*

Example #2

- *Apple juice is the most widely consumed drink.* [A note: This is actually not true.]
- *Apple juice is **one** of the most widely consumed drinks **in North America**.*
- *Apple juice is a (very) **popular** drink **among children in North America**.*

[This is likely to be true in most cases – two hedges are included here, ***likely*** and ***in most cases***.]

The Snowball Effect to Expand Hedging Repertoire

In L2 instruction, the uses and functions of hedging often require persistent explanation and review because in many discourse traditions other than Anglo-American, hedging is not considered to be an important feature of academic prose. Teaching L2 writers to hedge their claims also has an attendant objective of helping them to expand their vocabulary base and advance their awareness of the important differences between academic writing and conversational language (Hinkel, 2015; Hyland, 2018; Jordan, 1997).

- In many cases, L2 writers have a restricted lexical range of accessible hedging devices.
- If a small number of hedges are used repeatedly, the L2 text may be appear to be repetitious.

Examples of Conversational and Academic Hedge Words and Phrases

Conversational Hedges	Formal Academic Hedges
anyway(s), anyhow, at any rate	possible(-ly), potential(-ly), somewhat
a bunch of (books, cars, money, people)	approximate(-ly), apparent(-ly), close to, rough(-ly), seeming(-ly)
pretty (good, bad)	reasonable(-ly), fair(-ly), general(-ly), acceptable
lots, tons, loads	relative(-ly) (high/good number/ quantity)
for sure, absolutely, completely, totally	likely, perhaps, probable(-ly), reliable(-ly)

- Instruction can begin with lexically and grammatically simple types of hedges, e.g. frequency adverbs (*usually*, *often*, *occasionally*) and quantifiers (*most, much, many, several*).
- Ubiquitous frequency adverbs and a few (this is a hedge) essential quantifiers can be used by L2 learners even at the low-intermediate level of proficiency.

> Building on this base, teaching the meanings and hedging functions of modal verbs, e.g. **can** and **may**, can further help students increase their lexical range at a relatively low cost in terms of work and time.

Adjective and adverb hedges are by far the most numerous in English, and they include a wide variety of lexically simple items, such as *possible* and *usual*, to more complex, e.g. *apparently* and *relative to*. However, because adjective and adverb hedges are very numerous, L2 writers certainly do not need to become fluent users of the entire group. In fact, in combination with frequency adverbs, quantifiers, and modal verbs covered earlier, a relatively good range of hedges can become accessible for use in essays and assignments if only a portion of adjective and adverb hedges are addressed in instruction.

> - An important ingredient in teaching L2 writers to construct academic text entails examining the constructions that **should be avoided**.
> - These include informal hedging that is rarely encountered in academic prose, e.g. *kind of, lots*, and *to be supposed to*.
> - A prevalence of informal hedges can make students' academic writing appear conversational and informal.

In addition, overstatements and exaggerations are identified not only by an absence of hedging, but also by explicit markers, as *absolutely, completely, extremely, strongly,* and *totally,* e.g. *I completely agree, The city was totally flooded,* or *My brother is extremely smart.* Conversational hedges and exaggeratives are also dealt with in this chapter.

Frequency Adverbs and Possibility Hedges

Frequency adverbs, such as *frequently, often, usually, occasionally,* represent one of the most common and simple hedging devices, with the exception of *always* and *never* at the extremes of the frequency continuum.

- Because frequency adverbs are lexically and syntactically simple, they can be accessible to most L2 learners with intermediate to advanced proficiency.
- Due to their ubiquity, frequency hedges can be used with verbs or whole sentences, and they are easier to apply in editing than other more complex types of hedges.

For instance, *sometimes, often, usually,* and *generally* are more common in academic prose than, for example, *ever* or *never,* which are particularly rare (Biber, et al., 1999; Leech, Rayson, & Wilson, 2001; Quirk, et al., 1985).

Although frequency adverbs can be definite (e.g. *hourly, daily, weekly, monthly*), the indefinite frequency adverbs have the function of hedges when used in appropriate contexts.

The Most Prevalent Frequency Adverbs as Hedges (in declining order)

- *frequently, often*
- *generally/in general, usually, ordinarily*
- *occasionally/on occasion, sometimes, at times, from time to time, every so often*
- *most of the time, on many/numerous occasions*
- *almost never, rarely, seldom, hardly ever* (negative meanings)
- *almost/nearly always, invariably*

Adverb phrases of frequency, such as ***on many occasions*** or ***at times***, can be placed at the beginnings of long sentences or at the ends of short sentences. For example, a student's sentence can be relatively easy to hedge by means of adverb phrases of frequency, depending on the intended meaning.

The Original Sentence without Hedging
Cracks propagate when loads are applied to structural components.

The Hedged Sentence
*[**In general/almost always/usually/on occasion/once in a while**], cracks propagate when loads are applied to structural components.*

Single-word Adverbs Follow the General Rules of Adverb Placement

- In front of the main verb, if the main sentence verb is **not _be_** (all examples are from student texts).

  - *Scientists [**generally/usually/often**] think that by conducting research on human cloning, they will make a better quality human kind in the future.*
  - *The definition of workplace competence has [**frequently/seldom/ occasionally**] included learning new knowledge and skills.*

- After **_be_**, if the main sentence verb is **_be_**.
  - *This definition is [frequently/usually/sometimes] too broad.*
  - *The reasons for the change are [generally/often] not outside educa-tion, but they are connected to it.*
- Most uses of frequency adverbs are accompanied by the present simple tense.

Possibility hedges can be used as adjectives with nouns (*a probable/ possible cause/reason*) and as adverbs in practically all other constructions, that is, with verbs, adjectives, whole sentences, and other adverbs. Adverb hedges such as *probably, perhaps, possibly*, and *in (this/that) case* are partic-ularly common in formal academic writing (Cutting, 2007; Hyland, 1998). Similar to frequency adverbs, they are lexically and syntactically easy to use. Their placement rules follow those for frequency adverbs.

Other types of possibility hedges are more characteristic of **conversa-tional** discourse (and clichés) than formal writing, e.g.

- *by (some/any) chance, hopefully, maybe*
- *if you know/understand what I mean (to say)*
- *if you catch/get my meaning/drift*
- *as everyone/the reader knows*

As with adverbs of frequency, possibility hedges are not particularly com-plicated to teach. For instance, formal possibility hedges can be added to a student's sentences, and conversational hedges and conversational overstate-ments deleted.

- *Statistics is [**perhaps**] the newest science of mathematics.*
- *In our society, it is [**probably**] used [~~everywhere~~] [**in many places/for many purposes**].*
- *[~~As everyone knows,~~] [Good/careful] judgment is [**possibly/probably**] the most important characteristic of a professional engineer.*

In the context of academic prose, instruction should explicitly address the extent of the writer's knowledge expressed in overstatements.

As the next step, the defensive stance and the power-reducing func-tion of possibility hedges can be demonstrated and emphasized.

Quantifiers as Hedges

Quantifiers refer to definite (*a half, a quarter*) and indefinite quantities and modify nouns. **Indefinite quantifiers** can function as hedges and include the following:

- *all, many/much*
- *some, a few/a little*
- *a number of* + noun/noun phrase
- *a good/great deal of* + noun/noun phrase
- *a bit (of)*

Clearly, the quantifier *all* would not make a very good hedging device, and its uses can make writers' claims appear somewhat overstated, e.g.

- *? **All** teachers worry about how their pupils learn.*
- *? Farmers collect **all** the rain water because they need it for irrigation.*
- *? The worst of **all** is when you lose your temperature records.*

On the other hand, an addition of, for instance, *many/a few* and *much/a little* with countable and uncountable nouns, respectively, can help reduce the effect of broad generalizations, as in these examples from an L2 essay about technological innovations.

- *[**Many/Most**] [P]eople have heard the concepts of facts, data, and knowledge.*
- *[**Many/Some/A few**] [S]cientists around the world seem to compete with each other for inventing new technology.*
- *[**Many/Most/A number of**] [P]eople believe that technology cannot be limited, and it will keep going forever.*

Negative quantifiers, such as *few/fewer* with countable nouns and *little/less* with uncountable nouns, can hedge the somewhat extreme position implicit in the uses of the indefinite pronouns *no one* and *nobody*, as in the following L2 excerpt on fossil fuel consumption and passenger cars.

- *[**Few consumers/drivers/car owners**] [No one] want[s] to return to the energy crisis and oil shortages.*
- *In the early days, low fuel prices allowed consumers to focus on vehicle prices, performance, and comfort, and [**few individuals/drivers/engineers**] [nobody] cared about the fuel economy in passenger cars.*

- [~~Totally,~~] [T]he cheap oil period can be divided into three small periods for analysis.

Investigations of student and university essays have shown that L2 texts include significantly greater frequencies of *every-* and *no-* words (*everybody, everything, nothing, no one*) than the prose of novice L1 writers (for additional discussion see chapter 6 on pronouns) (Cotterall & Cohen, 2003; Hinkel, 2002, 2005a; Hyland & Milton, 1997).

Research in formal academic prose shows that the quantifier **none** occurs at the rate of 0.01% and indefinite pronouns with **every-** 0.04%, as opposed to, for example, the quantifiers **many** and **some** with rates of 0.1% and 0.28%, respectively. **No-** words are rarer still (Biber, et al., 1999).

Modal Verbs as Hedges

In formal writing, the meanings and functions of modal verbs can be divided into three classes (Hoye, 1997; Quirk, et al., 1985; Palmer, 2001).

Meanings and Functions of Modal Verbs

(1)	Ability and possibility:	*can, may, might, could, be able to.*
(2)	Obligation and necessity:	*must, have to, should, ought, need to, to be to* (dated), *to be supposed to* (highly informal).
(3)	Prediction:	*will, would.*

Although most grammar textbooks state that the primary purposes of modal verbs are to express meanings of ability (*can, could*), possibility (*may, might*), and obligation (*have to, must*), in academic writing, the main function of modals is hedging.

Here are a few examples.

- *Mobile farmers markets **can be** effective in delivering vegetables to urban centers.*
- *Product promotions **may encourage** consumers to respond.*
- *The history of baseball in North America **can be** followed back to the 19th century.*
- *Packing a compact umbrella for travel **might provide** a flexible option.*

In addition to the meanings of obligation, ***must (not)*** can also express prohibition, and it is seldom employed in academic writing.

Will vs. *Can* and *May*

- The meaning differences among modals largely deal with **the degree** of certainty, probability, and / or possibility.

  For instance, ***will*** refers to the future with a high degree of certainty, and ***may*** indicates a possibility.
- The function of ***will*** is to predict the future. Unless the writer can assure the reader of the outcome certainty, the uses of the future tense in academic texts can appear to be somewhat overstated.

Studies have shown that the future tense occurs significantly more frequently in L2 academic prose than in L1 text (see also chapter 7, the Future Tense). Here's an example from a student assignment on the parental role in child development.

- *When parents take care of their children's social skills, their offspring **will** be far more successful than in families where children are ignored.*
- *Children from caring families **will** get along with their peer group and have a friendly environment.*

In this example, the uses of the future tense create an impression of definiteness and a direct relationship between the parental care and children's peer interactions. In such cases, the discourse appears to contain over-confident claims about definite outcomes. However, teaching appropriate structures in academic text in this case may be relatively simple when the future auxiliary *will* can be simply replaced with ***may***.

In academic prose, modal verbs of possibility can have the function of hedges, and necessity modals can refer to reasoning and making conclusions

(Chafe, 1994; Cotterall & Cohen, 2003; Hinkel, 1999, 2015). For example, the modal *may* expresses a possibility and *should* to a reasoned conclusion (from a student paper).

> *Ecological studies <u>may</u> give an answer to environmental problems in many countries. Our world <u>should</u> be healthier if pollution is controlled.*

> In teaching, the meanings of **may** and ***should*** can be contrasted with those of ***will***, which projects a great deal of certainty, and ***must***, which conveys a high degree of obligation or probability.

An example of definitive predictions of future events demonstrates somewhat ambitious uses of *will* in a student paper on medical experiments on animals.

> *For very sick patients with heart or lung diseases, doctors <u>will</u> use organs to help humans. The organs <u>will</u> be used as a "bridge" until doctors can find another human organ. However, animal rights activists <u>will</u> break into hospitals and laboratories where the operation takes place. The doctors and the surgeons <u>must</u> practice their skills on animals before they do any surgery on humans.*

> - The main distinction: **may** refers to a **possibility** and **can** to an **ability**.
> - In academic prose, both **may** and **can** are rarely used with the meaning of permission, as is indicated in many grammar textbooks.
> - Although **can** is very common in conversations, in formal writing **may** is typically more suitable, particularly so in humanities and social sciences.
> - In formal discourse, **can** rarely refers to abilities but rather to possibilities and implications.

The negative modal *cannot* occurs in academic texts that have to do with **denials, refutations, or counter-examples.** The weak meanings of possibility in *could* and *might* do not project great confidence in an outcome, action, or event.

Would

The predictive modal **would** in English may also have the function of a hedge in formal and informal academic writing when it reduces the writer's responsibility for the truth-value and accuracy of evidence (from the same assignment), e.g.

> This **would** really help saving human lives, but there are also people who disagree with this.

However, because **would** conveys hypothetical and presuppositional meanings, it is often difficult for learners to use in context.[1]

- In L2 academic writing, modal verbs can be used effectively to moderate claims and to avoid strong predictions and implications of certainty (Swales & Feak, 2012).
- Analyses of academic corpora have shown that **can** and **may** are by far the most common modals, while **must, should**, and **have to** are less frequent, as are **will** and **would** (Biber, et al., 1999; Collins, 2009).
- When teaching modal verbs as hedges, it is important to address the contextual meanings of some, but not necessarily all, modal verbs.

> Teach the uses of **may, can**, and **could**. Teaching the hedging uses of the other modal verbs is probably not worth the time and effort.

Adjective and Adverb Hedges

Adjective hedges modify nouns, and adverb hedges qualify verbs and whole sentences. In English, the number of adjective and adverb hedges is large.

- Adjective hedges work to limit noun meanings, e.g. **an approximate weight, a slight increase, a careful selection**.
- Adverb hedges have a similar effect on verb or sentence meanings, e.g. **according to the data, overall, generally, as above**.
- In academic prose, many adverb hedges function as markers of probability, e.g. **almost, nearly, practically**.

- Adjective and adverb hedges can be single-word adjectives or more complex constructions:

  - *apparent, approximate, essential, fair, slight*
  - *according to* + noun, *based on* + noun, *most* + adjective (*most advantageous*), *relative to* + noun

Adjective and adverb hedges differ in the degree of their formality, meaning complexity, and frequencies. Formal hedges are predominant in academic written discourse. In teaching, these can be contrasted with informal conversational hedges to bring writers' attention to distinctions between formal and academic writing and informal language uses.

> For L2 writers, it is important to note the crucial differences among various and varied levels of language formality, and focusing on hedges represents only one means of instructional practice.

It is not necessary, however, that L2 writers undertake to use a large number of hedges. Students simply need to have ready access to a stock of these words and phrases that can be used interchangeably throughout their essays and assignments, as discussed earlier.[2] For instance, with practice, **generally**, **nearly**, and **slightly** can be accessible to writers who know how to use **basically**, **almost**, and **a little bit**.

Formal Hedges for Academic Writing

about	according to (+noun)	actually	apparent(-ly)
approximate(-ly)	broad(-ly)	clear(-ly)	comparative(-ly)
essential(-ly)	fairly	likely	merely
most (+ adjective)	nearly	normal(-ly)	partially
partly	potential(-ly)	presumably	relative(-ly)
relative to	slightly	somehow	somewhat
sufficiently	theoretically	unlikely	

On the other hand, informal hedges are prevalent in conversational discourse, and their frequent uses in academic prose can mark the text as unacademically casual, colloquial, and less than carefully prepared (Carter & McCarthy, 2006).

Common Informal and Conversational Hedges

almost	at all	at least	basically	dead (+ adjective)
(a) few	enough	hardly	just	(a) little/bit
only	quite	pretty		

Conversational and Informal Hedges

Lexical hedges represent a simpler variety prevalent in conversational and informal exchanges that are often characterized by vagueness and not found in written academic corpora (Carter & McCarthy, 2006; Channell, 1994; Cutting, 2007).

Informal Lexical Hedges Not Found in Academic Prose

actually	anyway	in a way	kind of
like (that)	maybe	more	more or less
pretty	something like	sort of	whatever

Informal lexical hedges are often considered to be unsuitable in formal academic writing. Lexical hedges that include modifiers of nouns, verbs, and whole sentences are particularly vague and mark a shortage of factual information or knowledge. Here are a few examples from a student paper on the history of industrial production.

— *Before this turning point [in the history of industrial production], everything was **sort of** undefined and sporadic.*
— *They **just** ran production using their own intuitions with a **more or less** successful manufacturing.*
— *As a result, **lots** of creations could not be accomplished.*
— *This **kind of** working didn't hurt companies because there were not many competitors to share the market.*

The uses of such hedges as **sort of, kind of,** or **lots** in a formal academic assignment may actually create an impression of a vague familiarity with the subject matter without references to specific information to make the text credible. (See also Strategies and Tactics for Teaching at the end of the chapter.)

References to Assumed Common Knowledge

Vague references to common and popular knowledge (e.g. *as we know, as people say*) function as hedges in informal conversations, and partly for this reason they often find their way into L2 students' academic text (Hinkel, 2002; Shaw, 2009). This type of colloquial hedging has the goal of distancing the writer from the information by attributing it to an external source, such as assumed common knowledge. Their frequent uses in student academic writing, particularly when it comes to unsupported statements or claims, may create an impression of broad generalization-making and a high degree of certainty without a factual foundation.

Informal "Common Knowledge" Hedges

(as) we all know	as far as we/I know
as is (well) known	as you/everyone/the reader know(s)
as the saying goes	(as) everyone/people/they say(s)
from what I hear/know/see/understand	

For instance, references to assumed knowledge and sayings are not likely to warrant high praise in the context of academic assignments. A number of studies have shown, however, that these hedges are significantly more frequent in L2 than L1 academic prose (Hinkel, 2002; Shaw, 2009). The examples below are from student texts.

- *Technology, **as most people know**, is a very important thing in this decade.*
- ***As readers know**, studying history is necessary for us to understand our past.*
- *People always seek happiness, money, and excitement, **as of course everyone knows**.*
- ***As they say**, no pain, no gain. When deciding how to invest capital, investors have to be prepared to take risks.*

Usually, referring to common knowledge and general truths that "everyone knows" is considered to be unsuitable in practically any type of student academic prose, with the possible exception of personal journals.

In the case of references to common knowledge such as *as of course everyone knows*, informal and conversational hedges may simply not be acceptable in lieu of factual rhetorical support, according to the norms of the academic discourse community (Swales, 1990).

Action Point

In writing instruction, comparing two or three different types of written prose, such as blogs, editorials, letters, or opinion pieces, as well as published academic articles, can prove very fruitful. In addition to hedges, other differences between more formal or more informal types of language can be addressed and discussed.

Text #1

In this restaurant, the best hamburger ever! My family and I went to get some burgers for lunch, we were greeted by the nicest and friendliest employees ever. We sat down, and our food came out fast, hot, and amazingly delicious. We had one of the nicest servers without question. She was very attentive to all of our needs and great conversation. My young daughter loved the burgers so much she ate two which she never does, and their burgers are fantastic.

The fries are great – both the regular fries and the sweet potato fries. Their grilled onions are so, so good, and their salads are amazing and super-fresh. And really, for the quality of their food, it's priced right. My absolutely favorite burger is the barbeque bacon cheeseburger. This place is definitely the best for a delicious burger and fries, hands down. This is totally a must go to place.

Text #2

Possibly the best burger restaurant that I have been to in this area. The food is tasty and satisfying with homemade burgers and fries. They have many topping options including grilled onions and bacon. The cheeseburger is a nicely seasoned half-pound of meat with a good slice of cheese, and the fries are fresh-cut, sprinkled with sea salt, and delicious. Rotating burger specials change each day of the week. Flavorful patties pair well with house-made pickles, fresh lettuce, and locally-harvested tomatoes.

> *Adventurous burger creations include applewood-smoked barbeque, hot peppers, roasted green chilies, and honey-fried onions. Simple and direct, you won't find avocado or other strange ingredients on these burgers. Word of mouth has long drawn people from far and wide to try the burgers, and they are worth the trip. All burgers are served with thick fries, fresh salad greens, or spicy coleslaw made daily.*

Avoiding Overstatements, Exaggerations, and Emphatic Claims

A large class of adjectives and adverbs have the function of marking strong claims and overstatements by inflating the value or the importance of information:

- The adjectives usually modify nouns (*a major work, a huge achievement*).
- The adverbs intensify adjectives, other adverbs, and whole sentences (*I definitely/totally agree with this statement*).

For instance, in academic writing in English, extreme frequency adverbs such as *always* and *never* are often seen as inflated, and their inclusion in essays is not recommended, e.g. *Managers <u>always</u> think that if employees are paid well, they will do their best on the job.*

Intensifiers and emphatic adjectives and adverbs are prevalent in the conversational rather than formal written register and are often considered to be informal (Brazil, 1995; Chang & Swales, 1999). On the other hand, Hyland's (1998) corpus analysis of published academic articles shows that the use of emphatics is comparatively more frequent in such diverse disciplines as philosophy, sociology, marketing, applied linguistics, physics, or mechanical engineering than biology and electrical engineering.

Emphatics and overstatements often include numerous adjectives and adverbs, commonly found in L2 writers' texts (Hinkel, 2002, 2003a, 2003b; Shaw & Liu, 1998; Leki, Cumming, & Silva, 2008).

Conversational Intensifiers and Emphatics Frequent in L2 Academic Writing

absolute(-ly)	a lot/lots	always	amazing(-ly)
awful(-ly)	bad (-ly)	by all means	certain(-ly)
clear(-ly)	complete(-ly)	deep(-ly)	definite(-ly)

forever	enormous(-ly)	entirely	ever
exact(-ly)	extreme(-ly)	far (+ comparative adjective)	for sure
fully	great(-ly)	high(-ly)	huge(-ly)
in all ways/in every way	never	no way	perfect(-ly)
positive(-ly)	pure(-ly)	severe(-ly)	so
strong(-ly)	sure(-ly)	terrible(-ly)	too
total(-ly)	unbelievable (-ly)	very	

In many rhetorical traditions other than Anglo-American, strong statements and claims are often intended to convey the writer's degree of conviction or rhetorical emphasis (Dong, 1998; Hu & Cao, 2011; van Dijk, 2009, 2010). In academic prose in English, however, rhetorical persuasiveness can be conveyed by linguistic components other than strong assertions and emphatics. Here's an example from a student assignment on the necessary qualities of corporate managers.

- *Besides the skills leaders need to develop* **strongly***, corporate culture nurturing leadership* **every** *day is* **extremely** *important.*
- *Cultivating a leadership-centered organization is* **definitely** *the* **most** *important goal of leadership.*
- *Today, some large companies have tens of thousands of employees, and they produce an* **enormous** *number of products and have millions of customers.*
- *These changes in the business environment create* **great** *pressure and* **high** *uncertainty.*
- *In business textbooks, leadership and management are* **very** *well defined and the definitions are* **well** *accepted by* **everyone***.*

This example shows that a high degree of the writer's conviction can lead to increased frequencies of exaggeratives and emphatics in students' writing. The overstated tone of the text may not be difficult to correct by omitting or replacing several modifying adjectives and adverbs that combine to create rhetorically inflated prose.

> In L2 writing, developing vocabulary alternatives can help reduce the frequency of overstatements and strong claims.

Chapter Summary

In general, the purpose of hedging in academic text is to project hesitation, politeness, and caution. However, in L2 writing instruction, the uses of hedging devices are often not addressed in sufficient detail.

> In addition to the direct benefits of using hedging which are essential in academic text, focused instruction on hedges and their rhetorical functions can help learners identify distinctions between formal and informal discourse, be it spoken or written.
>
> Although overstatements and strong assertions are often acceptable in informal conversations in English, they are typically avoided in formal academic writing.

To provide L2 writers access to lexical and grammatical means of hedging, instruction can begin with simple hedging devices and advance to the more linguistically complex.

> A cumulative effect of learning to use various types of hedges can lead to a noticeable reduction in frequencies of overstatements and exaggerations in L2 academic prose.

- Frequency and possibility adverbs, as well as noun quantifiers, represent one of the simplest and most readily accessible hedges.
- Modal verbs as hedges can also increase the students' repertoire of essential and relatively simple hedging devices for use in L2 writing.
- Although a large number of advanced adjective and adverb hedges in English has been identified in research, L2 writers should not be expected to employ all of them in their text with equal degrees of fluency.
- Adding just a few accessible complex hedges to an established base of simpler ones can provide learners a sufficient range of hedges for uses in formal academic writing.
- Being familiar with conversational and informal hedges, as well as language elements in overstatements and strong assertions, allows L2 writers the option of avoiding them in formal writing.

Hedging statements, generalizations, and claims are not universal characteristics of formal written discourse, and in rhetorical traditions other than Anglo-American, hedging is not employed with the same functions as it is in English. Furthermore, because typically L2 learners are exposed to conversational and informal discourse to a far greater extent than they are to formal writing, instruction on the functions and uses of hedging in English requires persistence and focused attention. On the whole, learning to hedge academic prose appropriately is unlikely to take place in informal conversations or by means of fluency activities.

Strategies and Tactics for Teaching and Teaching Activities

Teaching Activities

As with much other work on vocabulary and grammar, a practical approach can begin with helping L2 writers notice that hedging is common in formal prose in English, but not in conversations. Then learning to distinguish between formal and informal hedges and other language elements is the next instructional objective. In addition to giving attention to academic hedges, it is also important to notice those that are not.

The teaching suggestions and activities are designed to progress from the simpler to the more complex.

- Noticing the functions and uses of hedges in written text.
- Distinguishing between the characteristics of formal and informal language.
- Developing editing skills to hedge academic writing and avoid overstatements.
- The cumulative effect of teaching and using hedging devices to increase vocabulary and grammar range.

"Growing" hedges represents one of the most effective and least work- and time-consuming strategies.

Diverse types of hedges are useful and usable in teaching because many hedges are actually lexically or grammatically uncomplicated.

Teaching activities can be based on written texts easily obtainable from students' own writing, textbooks, and other sources, such as science, business, and society reports.

For learning to notice the functions and uses of hedges, a good place to start can be simplified formal prose, usually found in teaching or school materials on the environment, geography, wildlife, plants, science, nutrition, sports, and other non-fiction.

Noticing Hedges in Academic or News Media Texts

Students can be asked to bring samples of written materials from their disciplines or the teacher can supply excerpts on health issues, science, or current news. Then a series of leading questions can focus on the analysis of the function and types of hedges in the text.

- *What hedging – softening, politeness, or limiting – devices can the students identify?*
- *Why did the author use these hedges?*
- *In general, what is the author's responsibility for the accuracy of his or her statements? In English? In students' L1s?*
- *Do writers in students' L1s also use various words and phrases to limit their responsibility for the accuracy or strength of their statements/ generalizations?*
- *Do broad statements need to be limited? What are some of the examples of such softening/limiting words and phrases?*
- *In this particular text or sentence, what is the extent of authors' responsibility for the accuracy of their text?*
- *Why did the author use this particular type of hedge in this particular sentence?*
- *What is the difference in the "power" of the statement/sentence with the hedge or without the hedge? If the sentence is used without the hedge, can its meaning be seen as "too strong" or "too certain"? What can be possible meanings for various individual readers if the sentence is used without a hedge?*
- *Can students think of other ways to hedge this particular sentence or several sentences in a paragraph?*

A few examples of sentences and text excerpts illustrate this activity.

(1) What are the differences in "strength" in the three sentences? Why are there differences in the meanings of these sentences? Can you identify the reasons for these differences?

- *People are totally against genetic engineering, but it provides benefits for humankind.*
- *Some people are totally against genetic engineering, but it can provide benefits for humankind.*
- *Some people are against genetic engineering, but it can provide many benefits for humankind.*

(2) In your opinion, which sentence is more "accurate" and can be applicable in more cases?

- *Genetic engineering improves the taste of food and the nutritional value of food products.*
- *Genetic engineering can improve the taste of some types of food and the nutritional value of many food products.*

(3) The excerpt below presents an author's opinion on a particular topic. Do you think the author accurately describes the situation? Why or why not?

What particular words and phrases make the author's opinion appear very strong? Can this excerpt be made to describe the situation more accurately and the author's opinion less strong?

- *We really need the information on the Internet to be free.*
- *We must not pay money for all the advertising companies put online.*
- *Information about smoking and alcohol leads to bad effects and will encourage people to become involved with them.*
- *It is also totally wrong to say that advertising is the main factor that causes these problems.*
- *People have to have all the information they need to make their decisions about their health.*
- *Therefore, advertisers have to reveal all the information about the products they sell.*

Hedges in Different Types of Writing

Non-academic, commercial prose, such as promotional fliers or company, product, and services advertisements, or beauty and fashion descriptions, can provide a useful venue for contrasting various types of written genres. That is, texts intended to inflate rather than hedge the virtues of their products. Promotional materials can be also analyzed, and their uses of intensifiers and emphatics can be effectively compared to those in academic prose.

- *What are the goals of the promotional materials?*
- *On the other hand, what is the purpose of academic texts?*
- *Why do promotions employ inflated language features, such as adjectives, adverbs, or nouns?*
- *Why are there fewer exaggeratives and overstatements in academic prose than in promotional materials?*

- In pairs or small groups, students can be assigned to write short texts, say, 100 to 200 words, for a promotional flier to advertise travel to their hometowns or their favorite travel destinations, e.g. cities, beaches, resorts, or hotels.

    o Advertisements and fliers can promote shopping in students' favorite stores or food and service in favorite restaurants.
    o Other popular advertisements can include beauty products, fashions and brand names, e.g. clothing, shoes, backpacks, handbags, athletic gear, as well as cars, phones, computer games, music, TV shows, movies, magazines, or celebrities, e.g. singers, movie stars, media personalities, or sports figures.
    o These "promotional materials" can be presented and described to other groups or the entire class in mock commercials or skits.

- In a follow-up exercise, to contrast inflated or hedged prose, students can also write up "academic" descriptions of similar or different places, items, or people. In "academic" texts, writers need to scrupulously stay away from exaggerations and provide real or invented facts to support their claims.

Formal and Informal Language in Speaking and Writing

In addition to written promotional materials, audio- and videotaped commercials, infomercials, and/or casual conversation clips from movies, soap operas, talk shows, or situational comedies can be used to help learners identify important and numerous differences between formal and informal language elements. Distinguishing features of informal conversational and formal written texts can also be highlighted, that is, academic essays cannot be written as if the writer is talking to his or her friends.

Editing and Adding Appropriate Hedges and Weeding Out Emphatics

> This is a very important exercise that can be used in stages through-out a course on learning to write academic prose.

The learning goal of this practice is to focus students' attention on various hedge types, e.g.

o   Quantifiers to limit the noun power.
o   Adverbs of frequency and modal verbs to limit the verb power.
o   Predicting the future and modal verbs.
o   Identifying and replacing conversational hedges.
o   Avoiding intensifiers and emphatics.

Students can work in pairs, small groups, or individually to edit their own text or texts supplied by the teacher. The practice can be varied between work on "stripped down" prose without any hedges or emphatics and text excerpts with added conversational hedges or emphatics that students need to find and correct.

(1)   Here's an example of a "stripped down" text where hedges need to be added (but not too many!).

   – *These days, students plagiarize their papers by using the Internet.*
   – *They do not write their own papers or do their own homework.*
   – *Students easily access the companies that sell various course papers online.*
   – *These students go to a website that sells papers and buy them.*
   – *Plagiarized papers get excellent grades.*
   – *In other cases, students get caught and expelled from the university.*
   – *Educators feel that students need to fulfill their responsibilities in studying, and they say that students cheat by buying their papers.*

Another version of the same text with a few hedges added. A few advanced-level hedges are underlined:

- *These days, [**some/many**] students [**occasionally**] plagiarize their papers by using the Internet.*
- *They do not write [**some of**] their own papers or do [**much of**] their own homework.*
- *Students [**can**] easily access the [**many/<u>numerous</u>**] companies that sell various course papers online.*
- *These students [**can**] [**usually/often**] go to a website that sells papers and buy them.*
- *[**Sometimes/<u>In some cases,</u>**] [**Some/Many/Most**] [<u>**Perhaps,**</u>] Plagiarized papers [**can/may**] get excellent grades.*
- *In other cases, students [**may**] get caught and [**possibly/<u>potentially</u>**] expelled from the university.*
- *[**Some/Many/Most**] [**Typically,**] Educators [**usually/may**] feel that students need to fulfill their responsibilities in studying, and they say that students [**may/possibly**] cheat by [<u>**evidently/apparently**</u>] buying [**some of/many of**] their papers.*

(2) Editing text with conversational hedges and emphatics (underlined) (from a student term paper in art history). Overstated examples, such as this text, can be easily edited by correcting and replacing some of the emphatic and conversational features. Other editing practice can come from shorter excerpts or sentence-level contexts.

- *There are <u>**lots**</u> of books written about the Four Great masters, and <u>**everyone really**</u> admires their paintings.*
- *The Four Great masters are well known <u>**all over**</u> China; <u>**all**</u> of them played a very important role in the history of Ming painting.*
- *Wen Cheng-ming came from a <u>**very**</u> rich and educated family.*
- *Therefore, he <u>**never**</u> had to worry about <u>**any**</u> financial problems and could <u>**definitely**</u> receive <u>**great**</u> education.*
- *He was one of Shen Choi's students; therefore, we can <u>**clearly**</u> recognize that his works were <u>**totally**</u> influenced by Shen Chou.*
- *But it was not Shen Chou but Wen Cheng-ming who was the <u>**most**</u> influential and the <u>**most**</u> widely copied among the local group of scholar-painters in the 16th century.*
- *In his early period, the structure of his painting is <u>**sort of**</u> similar to the style of Shen Chou, and both of them used the <u>**world**</u>-famous green-and-color style that presented <u>**kind of**</u> a tranquil feeling.*

(3) Sentence-level editing practice (all examples are from student texts).

- *Companies are really dealing with all kinds of businesses.*
- *Phones and tablets are the most popular equipment because they absolutely make our work easier and faster.*
- *A lot of students just stream videos instead of watching TV all day.*
- *Nobody wants any trouble in their life, and risk management is the best course of action for all investors.*
- *We have a lot of social media to give us a lot of information about everything, so that we know what's going on in the world every day.*

Endnotes

1 Palmer (1990) specifies that the predictive conditional **would** refers to future events that are contingent on a particular proposition that may be unreal or counter-factual. The predictive conditional with real or unreal meanings refers to the future in complex ways and depends on particular mixed time relations that preclude the use of the future tense maker **will**.
2 Teaching semantic differences between such hedges as **essentially** and **basically** is not worth the time it takes for both the teacher and the student, save for identifying their divergent levels of formality.

Further Reading

Hinkel, E. (2005). Hedging, inflating, and persuading in L2 academic writing. *Applied Language Learning, 15*(1), 529–532.

This empirical study analyzes the types and frequencies of hedges and intensifiers employed in L1 and L2 academic essays included in a corpus of student academic texts (745 essays / 220,747 words). A comparison of median frequency rates of hedges and intensifiers in student academic essays points to the fact that L2 writers employ a limited range of hedging devices, largely associated with conversational discourse and casual spoken interactions. These findings are further supported by a prevalence of conversational intensifiers and overstatements that are ubiquitous in informal speech but are rare in formal written prose.

Hinkel, E. (2011). What research on second language writing tells us and what it doesn't. In E. Hinkel (Ed.), *Handbook of research in second language teaching and learning, Volume 2* (pp. 523–538). New York, NY: Routledge.

An overview of a large number of studies highlights important and significant differences among the discourse and language properties of L1 and L2 text in similar or proximate written genres. Research on prominent patterns in L2 writing has led to a greater understanding of many issues that have and continue to confound L2 writing instruction. To make sense of the enormous number of studies, the chapter provides a brief overview of L2 writing research and its findings to point out what is known and what still requires further investigation, as well as a few prevailing trends in the curriculum design and teaching approaches in L2 writing pedagogy.

Hyland, K. & Milton, J. (1997). Qualification and certainty in L1 and L2 students' writing. *Journal of Second Language Writing, 6*(2), 183–205.

A data-based investigation of L2 academic essays with a focus on expressions of doubt and certainty. In a large corpus, this study compares the expression of doubt and certainty in the L2 written examinations of 900 Cantonese-speaking school graduates with the texts of 770 British students of similar age and educational level. Based on the findings, L2 prose differs significantly from that of L1 writers and relies on a more limited range of hedging devices with stronger commitments and greater problems in conveying a precise degree of certainty. The authors make a few pedagogical suggestions for developing L2 writers' competence in this important area.

References

Biber, D., Johansson, S., Leech, G., Conrad, S., & Finegan, E. (1999). *Longman grammar of spoken and written English*. Harlow: Pearson.

Brazil, D. (1995). *A grammar of speech*. Oxford: Oxford University Press.

Carter, R. & McCarthy, M. (2006). *Cambridge grammar of English: A comprehensive guide*. Cambridge: Cambridge University Press.

Chafe, W. (1994). *Discourse, consciousness, and time*. Chicago: University of Chicago Press.

Chang, Y. & Swales, J. (1999). Informal elements in English academic writing: Threats or opportunities for advanced non-native speakers. In C. Candlin & K. Hyland (Eds.), *Writing texts, processes and practices* (pp. 145–167). London: Longman.

Channell, J. (1994). *Vague language*. Oxford: Oxford University Press.

Collins, P. (2009). *Modals and quasi-modals in English*. Amsterdam: Rodopi.

Cotterall, S. & Cohen, R. (2003). Scaffolding for second language writers: Producing an academic essay. *ELT Journal, 57*(1), 158–166.

Cutting, J. (2007). *Vague language explored*. Basingstoke: Palgrave Macmillan.

Dong, Y.R. (1998). From writing in their native language to writing in English: What ESL students bring to our writing classroom. *College English, 8*(2), 87–105.

Hinkel, E. (1997). Indirectness in L1 and L2 academic writing. *Journal of Pragmatics, 27*(3), 360–386.

Hinkel, E. (1999). Objectivity and credibility in L1 and L2 academic writing. In E. Hinkel (Ed.), *Culture in second language teaching and learning* (pp. 90–108). Cambridge: Cambridge University Press.

Hinkel, E. (2002). *Second language writers' text*. New York, NY: Routledge.

Hinkel, E. (2003a). Adverbial markers and tone in L1 and L2 students' writing. *Journal of Pragmatics, 35*(2), 208–231.

Hinkel, E. (2003b). Simplicity without elegance: Features of sentences in L2 and L1 academic texts. *TESOL Quarterly, 37*, 275–301.

Hinkel, E. (2005a). Hedging, inflating, and persuading in L2 academic writing. *Applied Language Learning, 15*(1), 29–53.

Hinkel, E. (2005b). Analyses of L2 text and what can be learned from them. In E. Hinkel (Ed.), *Handbook of research in second language teaching and learning* (pp. 615–628). New York, NY: Routledge.

Hinkel, E. (2011). What research on second language writing tells us and what it doesn't. In E. Hinkel (Ed.), *Handbook of research in second language teaching and learning* (pp. 523–538). New York, NY: Routledge.

Hinkel, E. (2015). *Effective curriculum for teaching L2 writing: Principles and techniques.* New York, NY: Routledge.

Hoye, L. (1997). *Adverbs and modality in English.* London: Longman.

Hu, G. & Cao, F. (2011). Hedging and boosting in abstracts of applied linguistics articles: A comparative study of English- and Chinese-medium journals. *Journal of Pragmatics, 43*(2), 2795–2809.

Hunston, S. & Francis, G. (2000). *Pattern grammar.* Amsterdam: John Benjamins.

Hyland, K. (1998). *Hedging in scientific research articles.* Amsterdam: John Benjamins.

Hyland, K. (2008). Academic clusters: Text patterning in published and postgraduate writing. *International Journal of Applied Linguistics, 18*(1), 41–62.

Hyland, K. (2018). *Metadiscourse: Exploring interaction in writing.* London: Bloomsbury.

Hyland, K. & Milton, J. (1997). Qualification and certainty in L1 and L2 students' writing. *Journal of Second Language Writing, 6*(2), 183–205.

Jordan, R. (1997). *English for academic purposes.* Cambridge: Cambridge University Press.

Lakoff, G. (1972). Hedges: A study in meaning criteria and the logic of fuzzy concepts. *Chicago Linguistic Society, 8,* 183–228.

Leech, G., Rayson, P., & Wilson, A. (2001). *Word frequencies in written and spoken English.* London: Longman.

Leki, I., Cumming, A., & Silva, T. (2008). *A synthesis of research on second language writing in English.* New York, NY: Routledge.

Palmer, F.R. (1990). *Modality and the English modals* (2nd edn). London: Routledge.

Palmer, F.R. (2001). *Mood and modality* (2nd edn). Cambridge: Cambridge University Press.

Quirk, R., Greenbaum, S., Leech, G., & Svartvik, J. (1985). *A comprehensive grammar of the English language.* New York, NY: Longman.

Shaw, P. (2009). Linking adverbials in student and professional writing in literary studies: What makes writing mature. In M. Charles, S. Hunston, & D. Pecorari (Eds.), *Academic writing: At the interface of corpus and discourse* (pp. 215–235). London: Bloomsbury.

Shaw, P. & Liu, E. (1998). What develops in the development of second language writing? *Applied Linguistics, 19*(2), 225–254.

Swales, J. (1990). *Genre analysis.* Cambridge: Cambridge University Press.

Swales, J. & Feak, C. (2012). *Academic writing for graduate students* (3rd edn). Ann Arbor, MI: University of Michigan Press.

Taylor, G. & Chen, T. (1991). Linguistic, cultural, and subcultural issues in contrastive discourse analysis: Anglo-American and Chinese scientific texts. *Applied Linguistics, 12*(2), 319–336.

van Dijk, T. (2009). *Society and discourse: How social contexts control text and talk.* Cambridge: Cambridge University Press.

van Dijk, T. (2010). *Discourse and context.* Cambridge: Cambridge University Press.

Appendix A[1]

Formulaic Expressions, Sentence Stems, and Phrases for Speaking, Presenting, and Participating in Meetings

In spoken communications, in addition to grammar and vocabulary, each participant has a great deal to attend to. There are such matters as sound, word, and sentence parsing, timing, pacing, articulation, stress, intonation, volume, pitch, facial expressions, and body language. Conversations are highly structured, and they progress along predictable and routine patterns, with participants adapting, adjusting and readjusting, and tailoring what they are saying – or going to say – depending on the social setting and flow of discourse.

In the course of a conversation, participants have to take into account a range of key variables; here are a few examples:

o A reasonable degree of grammatical accuracy and fluency.
o Phonetic intelligibility.
o Cultural structuring and organization, e.g. turn-taking and turn length.
o Topic nominations, shifts, and cohesiveness.
o Timing and pacing, e.g. openings, pauses, and closings.
o Social and contextual pertinence, e.g. minding what's unsuitable to discuss.
o Appropriate wording, e.g. politeness.

For L2 learners and users, the cognitive load, that is, the combined amount of mental effort, including the working memory, required to perform a task, and the amount of attention that is needed simply to converse can be occasionally overwhelming. Having a stock of grammatically accurate and socially suitable constructions can greatly ease the task, project a degree of fluency, and simplify the job of discourse structuring.

> All sentence stems and formulaic expressions presented below can be used in teaching and learning a range of grammar constructions and vocabulary that frequently occur in spoken communication, formal and informal alike.

Getting Attention, Greetings, and Responses

Hey/Hi/Hello/Long time, no see.
Good morning/afternoon/evening.
How are you?/How are you doing?/What's going on/happening?/How's everything going?
Excuse me/Pardon me . . .

Responding to Attention Getters/Greetings

Hey/Hi/Hello, Good/Great/Fine (and you?)

Nominating and Shifting Topics

What's xxx/Where's xxx?
Do you know/remember yyy?/Have you heard about zzz?
. . . say . . .
By the way/As a matter of fact/OK, all right (so far) . . .
Not to change the topic/This is a bit off the subject/topic . . .
Oh, that reminds me of xxx/brings yyy to mind . . .
I'd like to suggest/mention/say something about xxx . . .
Speaking of . . .
This reminds me . . ./Oh, before I forget, . . .

Pre-closings

Well, that's about it/I guess that's all of it/That's about it.
I should go/I gotta go/run/do/fly.
(It's been) Nice/great talking to you/meeting you/chatting with you.

I shouldn't keep you / should let you go.
It's been fun / good to talk / catch up / to see you.
Thanks / Thank you (very much / a lot) (for xxx) / Much appreciated
I've enjoyed talking to you / seeing you (again).
OK, then / well / yeah / so far, so good.
Nice meeting you / talking to you / seeing you.
There you go / Here you are.

Closings and Partings

Bye / bye for now / goodbye / see yah / see you later / see you around / well, so
 long / 'till later / Stay well
So long / Toodle-oo
Have a nice day / rest of your day / afternoon / evening / time

Asking for an Opinion or Reaction

What's your opinion of . . .
What's your position on . . .
What do you think of . . .
I was wondering where you stood on . . .
Could I ask for / I'd like to hear your reaction to / your views on . . .

Giving Opinions

Strong Opinions

I really / honestly / strongly / firmly believe / feel / (think) that . . .
I'm completely / strongly / firmly / greatly convinced that . . .
There's no doubt / question (in my mind) that . . .
Without a doubt / question . . .
It's really / quite / very clear that . . .
I'm (absolutely) sure / certain / positive that . . .
It is my belief that . . .

Personal Opinions

I personally believe / think / feel that . . .
Not everyone will agree with me, but . . .

To my mind / In my personal experience . . .
From my point of view, . . .
Well, personally, . . . / In my case, . . .

Adding Reasons

And besides / also / in addition . . .
What's more / And another thing . . .
Not to mention that fact that / the situation with
Plus, the fact that / Not only that, but . . .

Neutral and Tentative Opinions

I think that / It is possible to think of it as . . .
In my opinion / As I see it / As far as I'm concerned . . .
From my point of view / perspective, / In my view, / From where I stand
It seems to me that . . . / I would say that . . .
As far as I am able to judge . . .
I think it would be fair to say that . . .

Agreements

Strong Agreements

I completely / totally / really / entirely agree that / with
I am of exactly / completely the same opinion

Neutral and Partial Agreements

I agree.
I think you're right.
I agree in principle, but . . .
I would tend to agree with you on that . . .
By and large, I would agree, but . . .
Although I agree on the whole / with most of what you say / have said . . .

Disagreements

Strong Disagreements

I completely/totally/entirely disagree with you.
I don't agree at all.
You are mistaken.
What you are saying/proposing/suggesting is not (possible/feasible/suitable) . . .

Softening Strong Disagreements

Frankly,/To be honest . . .
To put it bluntly,/be quite frank, . . .
I am afraid/sorry . . ./ don't see how . . .
I doubt (that) . . .
With respect, . . .
This raises the problem of . . .
Possibly, but . . .
What I am worried about is/bothers me is . . .

Neutral Disagreements

I don't completely agree with you on that . . ./I really can't agree with you on
*   that . . ./I can't say that I share your view . . .*
I can't help feeling/thinking that . . .
I'm not totally convinced by your argument/that . . ./what you said.
I can't help feeling that . . .

Softening Neutral Disagreements

I'm sorry, . . .
I'm afraid . . .
I agree up to a point/to a certain extent, but . . .
To a certain extent I agree with you, but . . .
You have a point there, but . . .
I can see/take your point of view, but (surely/have you considered) . . .

Interrupting

May/Could I interrupt you for a moment/second?
Sorry to interrupt, but . . .// Sorry, but . . .
Excuse me for interrupting, but . . .
I don't want to interrupt, but . . .
If I could just interrupt you for a moment, I'd like to . . .
Can I add here that . . .//Can I add something/ask a question?
May I ask something/a question?
I'd like to say something (if I may) . . .

Taking the Floor

May/Could I come in at this point?
But the (real) question is . . ./ I am sure you can see . . .
Could I (just) say something here (about) . . .?
If I could just come in here/say a word about . . .
If no one objects, I'd like to say a few words about . . .

Commenting

Excuse me, but I'd just like to point out that . . .
Excuse me, but I think/believe (that) it's relevant/important/useful to add that . . .
I wonder if I could comment on/say something about the last/earlier point.
I wonder if I could comment on/add something here (on/about) . . .
Before we go any further, may I point out/comment on/ note that . . .

Coming Back to a Point

As I was saying . . ./To return to . . .
To return/to come back/coming back to what I was saying . . .
I may just go back to the point I was making/what I was saying . . .

Preventing and Pre-empting an Interruption

If I might/could just finish . . .
Perhaps I could return to this point later (on).
With your permission, I'd like to/rather finish what I was saying . . .

If you'd allow me to continue/finish/say, . . .
If you'd be so kind as to let/permit me (to) finish, . . .
Very briefly, . . ./I'd just like to . . .
There are two/several points I would like to make.

Correcting Yourself and Conversational Repair

(The term "conversational repair" refers to dealing with problems in speaking, hearing, or understanding.)

Sorry, what's the word I'm looking for?
Let me rephrase/restate what I (just) said.
Let me put it in another way.
What I am saying is/trying to say is . . .
Sorry, I should just mention one thing.
Don't misunderstand me, . . .
Sorry, let me rephrase that.
If I said that, I didn't mean/intend to/have in mind that . . .
Sorry, what I meant is/was (this)/what I mean is . . .
So, just to give you the main points here.

Presenting and Making an Argument

Beginning an Argument

I would like to begin by . . ./to say a few words . . ./to comment on . . .
There are three points I'd like to make.
I would like to mention briefly that . . .
I would like to make a few remarks concerning . . .

Sequencing an Argument

To begin with . . ./First of all . . ./To get started . . .
Firstly, . . . Secondly, . . . Thirdly, . . . Finally, . . .
At the outset (beginning) . . .

Introducing a New Point

The next issue/question I would like to focus on is . . .
Turning to . . ./(Now) I'd like to turn (briefly) to/address/focus on . . .

I would like to introduce a new point/matter/consideration . . .
Another matter/topic . . .

Adding a Point

In addition, . . ./I might add that . . .
Not only . . ., but also . . .
Furthermore, . . ./Moreover, . . .
And another thing/point/factor/consideration . . .
Just a small point, . . .
Perhaps, I should mention/add/note/say . . .
Oh, I almost forgot . . .

Giving an Example

Let me give an example (of) . . .
As an/the example, . . .
For example, if/in /the xxx
An example of the xxx can be/is yyy
To illustrate this point, let us consider . . .
I'd like to mention/bring your attention to xxx, as an example
A case in point is . . .
By way of illustration . . ./To illustrate, simply (take a) look at . . .
An example/a few examples include(s) . . .

Balancing Points

On the one hand xxx, but on the other hand, yyy
In spite of zzz, I still think aaa/Despite (the fact that) bbb, I . . .
Although . . ., we/I should (also) think about/remember that . . .

Generalizing

On the whole, . . ./Overall, . . .
In general, . . ./Generally speaking, . . ./To generalize . . .
By and large, . . .
All in all, . . ./All things considered, . . .

Stating Preferences

I'd rather xxx than yyy
What I'd prefer . . . / My preference would be . . . / Preferably . . .
I prefer xxx to yyy
The main advantage of xxx is (that) . . .

Concluding

Let me conclude by saying . . .
I'd like to conclude by stating that . . .
In conclusion, I would like to reiterate that . . .
Allow me to conclude by stating/saying/reiterating that . . .

Asking Questions

Introductory Words and Phrases

Actually, . . . / Well, . . .
Frankly, . . . / To be honest, . . .
As a matter of fact, . . . / In fact, . . .
Okay (then) . . . / Alright . . .
As a point of departure, I'd like to . . .
To begin, . . . / As a start, . . . / At the start, . . . / To get started, . . .

Asking General Questions

Would you mind . . . ? / Would you mind if I asked . . . ?
I was wondering if you . . . ? / I wonder if you could . . . ?
May I ask . . . ?

Asking for Further Information

Could you be a little more precise?
I'm sorry, but could you explain in a little more detail / Could you give us some
*   details about . . . ?*

Could you expand on that? / Would you please elaborate on that?
I wonder if you could explain that / elaborate on that . . . / Would it be possible to . . .?

Stalling for Time

That's a very interesting question.
That's a difficult question to answer.
I'm glad you asked that question.
You've brought up / raised a good / important / excellent point here.
It is not hard to see / You will appreciate how important this point is.

Saying Nothing

Well, it's (rather / maybe) difficult to say . . .
I'm afraid I don't have enough information (right now) to answer that.
I'd need / will need to think about xxx / learn more about xxx / look into xxx further / in greater detail.

Further Questioning/Looking for Clarification

It depends / I'm not quite sure what you mean by . . .
I'm afraid I don't quite follow . . .
I don't think it's quite as simple as that . . .

Asking for Clarification

Clarifying When Communication Not Heard

Sorry, I missed that. Could you say that again, please?
Sorry, I didn't catch / get that. Could you repeat it / that, please?
Would you mind repeating xxx, please?
Sorry, I couldn't quite hear / hear well.

Clarifying When Communication Not Understood

Sorry, I don't quite follow you. Could you just run through that again, please?

Sorry, I don't quite see what you mean. Could you just explain that, please?

Clarifying After the Point Has Been Made

When you were saying/talking about/describing (to us)/dealing with/summing up/showing us/telling us . . .

You quoted/commented on/made the point that/(may have) said that/spoke on/about/referred to . . .

Could you tell us/say a bit more about/explain to us what you meant by that/be a little more specific/run us through that again.

Other Clarification Sequences

What exactly did you mean by . . .?

Could we go back to what you were saying about . . .?

How did you arrive at the figure of . . .?

I think I misunderstood you. Did you say . . .?

You spoke about . . . . Could you explain that in more detail?

Going back to the question of . . . . Can you be more specific?

You didn't mention . . . . Why not?

If I understood you correctly, ... Is that right?

I'm not sure I fully understood . . . . Can you run through/go back to that again, please?

There's one thing I'm not clear about: . . . . Could you go over that again, please?

Getting Information on the Phone

I am calling about/to ask/find out/hear about/in regard to/in connection with . . .

I'd like to ask (about)/find out . . .

Could you tell me . . .?
I wonder if you could tell me/help me . . .
I'd like to talk to somebody about . . ./if someone could help me with . . .

Endnotes

1 Earlier versions of Appendices A and B appeared in E. Hinkel (2016). Practical grammar teaching: Grammar constructions and their relatives. In E. Hinkel (Ed.), *Teaching English grammar to speakers of other languages* (pp. 171–191). New York, NY: Routledge.

Appendix B

Constructions, Formulaic Sequences, and Sentence Stems for Academic Writing

The teaching of grammar constructions and sentence stems can co-occur with supplemental instruction on grammar, vocabulary, and frequent academic collocations. Learning and using stock sentence stems in academic writing is probably one of the most efficient ways of expanding L2 writers' repertoire of form-meaning combinations and multiword units. Formulaic expressions can be particularly useful when they include variations on their discrete elements (as shown in Appendix A). Frequently occurring sentences, clauses, and phrases can be found in many languages, and these constructions dominate in formal writing.

> All sentence stems presented below can be used in teaching and learning a range of grammar constructions, vocabulary, and discourse patterns prevalent in academic and formal prose.

Openings/Introductions

The central issue in xxx is yyy . . .
The development of xxx is a typical/common problem in . . .
Xxx and yyy are of particular interest and complexity. . . .
For a long time xxx, it has been the case that yyy
Most accounts/reports/publications claim/state/maintain that xxx

According to Smith/recent (media) articles/reports/studies, xxx is/seems to be yyy.

One of the most controversial/important/interesting issues/problems/xxxS (recently/in recent literature/media reports) is yyy.

In recent discussions/debates/reports of xxx, a controversial/complex/intertwined issue has been whether yyy. On the one hand, some argue that aaa. On the other hand, however, others argue that bbb. (Modified from Graff, Birkenstein, & Durst, 2018.)

It is becoming increasingly difficult/challenging to ignore zzz.

Xxx plays an important/significant/prominent role in the maintenance/support/dissemination of zzz.

In the new global/changing/evolving aaa, bbb has become a central/most important/pivotal/persistent issue for ccc.

Xxx is an increasingly important area/field in ccc.

Xxx and yyy have been an object of research since the 1980s/1990s/2000s

Bbb is a major/vital/central area of interest within the field of zzz.

The issue of xxx has received notable/considerable critical/favorable attention.

Xxx is a classic problem in zzz.

Yyy has been studied by many researchers using/employing/utilizing vvv.

Negative Openings with Countable Nouns

few reports	*have discussed/examined zzz.*
few discussions	*have addressed/noted/examined . . .*
few articles	*have focused on/noted . . .*
few studies	*have investigated/dealt with . . .*

Thesis/Topic Statements

The purpose of this essay/paper/analysis/overview is to xxx
  e.g. take a look at/examine/discuss yyy.
The main emphasis/focus/goal/purpose of the/this essay/paper/project is to xxx
  e.g. is to analyze/provide an overview/discussion of xxx.

This paper describes and analyzes . . . xxx.
This paper discusses/examines/investigates xxx.
This paper claims/shows that xxx is/is not yyy.

This essay/paper addresses/examines/
 is designed to
  analyze/provide an overview of/take a look at xxx.

My aim in this paper is to . . .
In this paper, I/we report on/discuss . . .
I intend/will demonstrate/show/explain/illustrate that xxx
My (basic/main/most important) argument/claim is largely/essentially that xxx.
The idea/notion/concept/thought/proposition that xxx is yyy is a striking/ provocative/thoughtful/promising/thought-provoking one, and this is what I support/subscribe to/advocate.

Secondary purpose

The primary aim/purpose of this paper is xxx. In addition, it examines/ discusses . . . yyy.
Additionally, yyy is discussed/examined.
A secondary aim of this paper is to yyy.
Another reason/point/issue addressed/discussed in this paper is yyy.

Rhetorical Mode/Discourse Organization Statement

This paper (will) compare(s)/describe/illustrate xxx first
 by analyzing/comparing/demonstrating yyy (that yyy is zzz),
 then by yyying zzz, and finally by yyying aaa).
This paper first analyzes/discusses xxx.
 This is followed by an examination/illustration/overview of yyy and zzz.
The differences/similarities between xxx and yyy are important/pronounced/ striking/unmistakable,
  and they merit/warrant/deserve/call for a
   close/careful/thoughtful/thorough/rigorous examination/analysis/scrutiny.
While some differences between aaa and bbb are clear/evident/noticeable/ pronounced/unmistakable,
  the similarities are (also) evident/striking/prominent/noticeable/ relevant.
The main points/questions/issues addressed/discussed in this essay/paper are: aaa, bbb, and ccc.

This paper begins by ddd. It will then/later go on/move on to xxx.
The first/second/third section of this essay/paper will examine/take a look at/discuss vvv.

Introducing Review of Literature and Evidence from Readings

In recent discussions of xxx, . . .

The issue of zzz is important: (stated reasons).

In recent publications, the topic/issue of xxx has received considerable/ prominent attention.

Recently researchers/investigators/scholars have examined the effects of ccc on ddd.

In the past two/three/four decades/twenty/thirty years, a number of researchers/authors have sought/attempted to identify/determine . . .

Previous/Earlier studies/investigations have reported/noted/determined that . . .

A considerable/substantial/notable amount of literature has been published on vvv. These studies/reports/investigations have found that . . .

Surveys/studies/investigations such as that conducted by Smith (2025) showed/demonstrated that . . .

Recent evidence/findings suggest(s) that . . .

Several attempts have been made to . . .

A large body of literature on xxx has been published/made public on zzz.

A number of researchers/investigators have reported that . . .

Studies of ccc show/demonstrate/emphasize the importance of bbb in/for xxx.

Other Types of Sentence Stems for Essay Development

Assertion

It can be claimed/said/assumed that xxx
It seems certain/likely/doubtful that xxx
It is clear that xxx
It is possible to yyy
I/we maintain/claim that xxx

Agreement with the Author/Source

As XXX perceptively/insightfully states /
   correctly   notes /
   rightly   observes /
appropriately points out,   xxx is/seems to be yyy (adjective/noun).

I/we rather/somewhat/strongly agree with/support (the idea that) xxx.
XXX provides/lends support to YYY's argument/claim/conclusion that zzz.

Disagreement with the Author/Source

I/we rather/somewhat/strongly disagree with XXX/that yyy.
As XXX states (somewhat) unclearly/erroneously, . . .
XXX does not support YYY's argument/claim/conclusion about zzz/that zzz.
Although XXX contends that yyy, I/we believe that zzz.
However, it remains unclear whether . . .
It would (thus) be of interest to learn more about yyy/how . . .
Xxx is mistaken because he/she overlooks/neglects to account for aaa.
I disagree with XXX's view that aaa because, as recent research has shown
   that . . .

Comparison

Both xxx and yyy are (quite) similar in that zzz.
Xxx is like/resembles yyy.
Both xxx and yyy are/seem to be zzz (adjective/noun).
Xxx and yyy have/share some aspects of zzz.
Xxx is similar to/not unlike yyy (with respect to zzz).

Contrast

Xxx is (quite) different from yyy (in regard to zzz).
Xxx is not the case with yyy/the same as yyy.
Xxx does not resemble yyy (in regard to zzz).
Xxx contrasts with yyy (with regard to zzz).
Xxx is unlike yyy in that/with respect to zzz.

Recommendations

Let me recommend/suggest that xxx be/have/do yyy.
What I want/would like to recommend/suggest is that xxx.
One suggestion is/may be that xxx (do yyy).

Citing Sources/Supporting Arguments, Claims, Conclusions, and Generalizations

As proof/evidence/an example (for this), (let me cite/quote xxx) . . .
According to xxx, . . .
As XXX says/claims, . . .

XXX provides evidence/support for yyy/that yyy.
XXX demonstrates that yyy.
    shows evidence for yyy/that yyy.
Xxx is an illustration/example of yyy.

Citing Sources/Referring to External Sources of Knowledge

It is/has been (often) asserted/believed/noted that xxx   (YYY, 2033).
It is believed that xxx
                (YYY, 2029).
It is often asserted that xxx.
It has been noted that xxx.

Classification

Xxx can/may be divided/classified into yyy (and zzz).
Xxx and yyy are categories/divisions of zzz.
There are xxx categories/types/classes of yyy.

Result/Outcome

On the basis of the zzz . . .
Xxx is based on the aaa.

As can be seen, yyy.
As a result of the xxx / As a consequence of the xxx
For this reason, ccc.

Giving examples

As an / the example, . . .
For example, if / in / the xxx . . .
An example of the xxx can be / is yyy.
A well-known / prominent / notable / memorable / classic / useful / important
example of vvv is xxx / can be found in Smith (2025).

Generalization

Overall, / On the whole,
By and large,
In general, / In general, / In general terms,
On the whole,
Generally, / Generally speaking,
In most cases, / In much of the xxx,
One can generalize that xxx.
For the most part,

With the exception of xxx,
With one exception,

Summarizing

Reporting Verbs and Noun Clause Chunks for Summaries (author first)

The author goes on to say / state / show that xxx
The author further argues / explains / shows that
The article further states that
(Smith) also states / maintains / argues / asserts that
(Smith) also believes / concludes / feels that
In the second half of the article / report, (Johnson) presents xxx to show / explain that

Sentence Stems and Noun Clause Chunks
for Summaries (essay/paper first)

> *The article/report concludes that . . .*
> *This essay/paper has examined/reviews/given an account of vvv.*
>> *the reasons/causes for ccc.*
> *This essay/paper/project has argued/made it clear that vvv is the best/worst*
> *bbb to aaa.*
> *This assignment/essay/paper has explained the central/crucial/vital impor-*
> *tance of*
>> *ddd in aaa.*
> *This assignment has investigated . . .*
> *The present investigation has compared three different yyy in terms of zzz.*
> *This essay/paper has examined the role of ccc in/for ddd.*

Closing Statement

> *In sum/conclusion, / In short, / All in all,*
> *To sum up/conclude,*
> *To tie this (all) together, / To sum it all up,*
> *As a final comment/remark/note,*

Based on Biber, et al. (1999), Graff, Birkenstein, & Durst (2018), Hinkel (2015), Nattinger & DeCarrico (1992), Simpson-Vlach & Ellis (2010), and Swales & Feak (2012).

References

Biber, D., Johansson, S., Leech, G., Conrad, S., & Finegan, E. (1999). *Longman grammar of spoken and written English*. Harlow: Pearson.

Graff, G., Birkenstein, C., & Durst, R. (2018). *They say/I Say: The moves that matter in academic writing* (4th edn). New York, NY: Norton.

Hinkel, E. (2015). *Effective curriculum for teaching L2 writing: Principles and techniques*. New York, NY: Routledge.

Nattinger, J. & DeCarrico, J. (1992). *Lexical phrases and language teaching*. Oxford: Oxford University Press.

Simpson-Vlach, R. & Ellis, N. (2010). An academic formulas list: New methods in phraseology research. *Applied Linguistics, 31*(4), 487–512.

Swales, J. & Feak, C. (2012). *Academic writing for graduate students* (3rd edn). Ann Arbor, MI: University of Michigan Press.

Index

.